UNBELIEVABLE

"Live from Bedford-Stuyvesant, the livest one representing BK to the fullest"
—The Notorious B.I.G., "Unbelievable," 1994

LIEVABLE

The Life, Death, and Afterlife of The Notorious B.I.G.

A VIBE Book by Cheo Hodari Coker

THREE RIVERS PRESS

NEW YORK

Published by Three Rivers Press, New York, New York.
Member of the Crown Publishing Group, a division of Random House Inc.
www.randomhouse.com

THREE RIVERS PRESS and the tugboat design are registered trademarks of Random House, Inc.

Printed in United States of America

Editorial Director: Rob Kenner

Design by Mark Shaw

Library of Congress Cataloging-in-Publication Data

Coker, Cheo Hodari.
Unbelievable: the life, death, and afterlife of the Notorious B.I.G.
/ by Cheo Hodari Coker.—1st ed.
"A Vibe Book."
Includes index.
Discography: p. 301
Videography: p. 333
1. Notorious B.I.G. (Musician) 2. Rap musicians—United States—Biography. I. Title.
ML420.N76 C65 2003
782.421649'092—dc21   2003005009

ISBN 0-609-80835-4

10 9 8 7 6 5 4 3 2 1

First Edition

Dedicated to my unbelievable grandfather,
the notorious Lt. Col. Bertram W. Wilson, a Tuskegee airman
who flew with the 100th Fighter Squadron during World War II.
The finest man I have ever known.
I miss you, Granddaddy. Every day.

CONTENTS

FOREWORD	**THE THRILL IS GONE** by Bönz Malone	xiii
INTRODUCTION	**ALL ABOUT THE BENJAMINS?**	1
CHAPTER 1	**DOLLY MY BABY**	11
CHAPTER 2	**THINGS DONE CHANGED**	25
CHAPTER 3	**IT WAS ALL A DREAM**	45
CHAPTER 4	**GIMME THE LOOT (I'M A BAD BOY)**	73
CHAPTER 5	**WHAT'S BEEF?**	119
CHAPTER 6	**MO MONEY, MO PROBLEMS**	141
CHAPTER 7	**ONE MORE CHANCE (THE REMIX)**	199
CHAPTER 8	**YOU'RE NOBODY TILL SOMEBODY KILLS YOU**	219
CHAPTER 9	**THE LONG KISS GOODNIGHT**	247
CHAPTER 10	**WHO SHOT YA?**	267
EPILOGUE	**SKY'S THE LIMIT**	287
DISCOGRAPHY	**IF YOU DON'T KNOW...NOW YOU KNOW** by Chairman Mao	301
VIDEOGRAPHY	**BROOKLYN'S FINEST** by Ralph McDaniels	333
	AUTHOR'S NOTE	338
	SOURCES	340
	CREDITS	345
	ACKNOWLEDGMENTS	346
	INDEX	347

THE THRILL IS GONE

IS GONE

FOREWORD

by Bönz Malone

> **❝**Everyone has a talent. What is rare
> is the courage to follow that talent to
> the dark place where it leads.**❞**
> —Erica Jong

When Christopher "Biggie Smalls" Wallace was searching for a record deal in 1992, he came up to see me at Island Records, where I was working in A&R at the time. He rolled through with my man Matt-Life and offered me a brash challenge—from one Brooklynite to another. We would play Cee-Lo, the classic curbside Hustler's Convention dice game. And if he won? Well, I guess I would owe the brother a record deal.

Maaan, it was on! We rolled them bones from 5 P.M. till after 8. I was snappin' my fingers so hard they started bleeding. All of a sudden, the Notorious one started playin' hot. On the last roll, he threw a pound and told me I better "Go get a pen" so he could sign that contract.

Five years later—and forty-eight hours after the murder of my friend Christopher—I sat in my lonely studio apartment, thinking of how close we became, the meals we had together, and about how different both of our lives might have been if I hadn't rolled that game-winning head crack. One toss of the dice, in effect, delivered the Notorious B.I.G. straight to Bad Boy Entertainment.

Biggie was damn crafty; I'd never known any aspiring artist to get down for his crown with an A&R guy like that before. I'd never seen an MC standing in front of his building wearing a Bermuda shirt and shorts, draped with a .357 Magnum, either. When I asked him why he had the strap, he said, "Somebody called my crib and said they were comin' to get me . . . so I'm waiting for 'em."

Ultimately, this was a B.I.G. brother who believed that *real* people do *real* things. A grown-ass man who knew the difference between gun powder and divine power and trusted only the will of God, the luck of the draw, and the loyalty and respect of his fam—plus the whole Hip Hop Nation.

Biggie's voice is still on the air and his name is still in the air seven years after his family laid him to rest. Some people swear he's the greatest MC of all time. Others have portrayed him as a thug, a sex symbol, or a crime lord. Personally, I could live with the death of Biggie Smalls the image. But now, I'm forced to live without Christopher Wallace the person. And that's a difficult reality to face.

There are two sides to every one-way street and there's only one question that puts you on that yellow line in its center: Will you be an artist or a gangster? Both create images of hero worship. Both have plenty of underlings present to watch you destroy yourself at the height of your career. All young men are faced with this question once they get introduced to the street life. Although hip hop was created to defuse gang violence, it doesn't have the power to exempt you from making a choice. It can only help absolve you to yourself, in one way or another.

The title of this book may be *Unbelievable,* but for an only child raised by his mom, the story certainly is not. Christopher Wallace made his choice to be the Bad Boy of the block so that his kids and his crew could live off the lyrics he wrote for them and own property from their publishing. Because he believed it was all going to pay off for him one day, not pay him off some day. If Satan stepped to Christ himself and offered Him all the kingdoms of the earth, then jumping out on St. James Place with 24-inch dubz ain't nothing for the devil to do! It can happen to you too. And if you're like me, it already has.

Christopher Wallace and I were friends and I respected him, but so did those that hated him—because he had become both the artist and the gangster. Biggie absolved the two personas to himself with such command of presence that it became impossible to differentiate between them. Like many of our associates in the rap industry, he knew that the pen is mightier than the sword. He also knew that a pen *and* a sword make a king. The "nonchalance" of his delivery was labeled legendary from the moment he picked up the habit. It will live in infamy until the industry he conquered one day implodes. May the story of his life show both the blessing and the malediction of someone who did more for others than for himself, and who had the courage to make the wrong choice for the right reason.

The only way to serve God is to be a gangster of His will, in one way or another. Believe that.

ALL ABOUT THE BENJAMINS?

66 Stereotypes of a black male misunderstood
And it's still all good . . . 99

"Just relax, man. Kick back. It's all good."

The Notorious B.I.G. sat in the cabana area near the pool at the Four Seasons Hotel in Beverly Hills wearing his trademark Versace sunglasses, sipping from a glass of lemonade and puffing on a potent marijuana-filled cigar in clear defiance of a posted NO SMOKING sign. It was a sunny afternoon on February 14, 1997, and B.I.G. (born Christopher George Letore Wallace) was very much in character, acting like the hustler god he personified on his hit records. But the cane resting near his deck chair was not just a player accessory—he truly had trouble getting around since the car crash that had fractured his right leg five months earlier. He was taking his time, slowly re-learning how to walk on his own.

Not that B.I.G. ever had to exert much effort for anything he wanted. Old friends like Damien "D-Roc" Butler and James "Lil' Cease" Lloyd doted on him, intermittently popping in to see if he needed anything. His Arista Records publicist, Delana Walker, was on hand to make sure he adhered to his busy promotional schedule. Like the man said, it was all good. His pager buzzed incessantly with women sending Valentine's Day wishes. He ignored most of them because he'd already spoken with the first and most important love of his life: his mother, Voletta Wallace. Valentine's Day was also her birthday. He told her he was sorry he couldn't help her celebrate in person, but at the same time he was happy to be right where he was. New York was cold, and B.I.G. was way out west to make a music video, lace some tracks, smoke some sticky green chronic, and chase girls as well as a 300-pound man with a bum leg could.

I thought of the kid I met three years earlier, standing in unlaced Timberland boots on his block in Brooklyn. He'd recently returned from the Hamptons, a plush Long Island suburb where he and Sean "Puffy" Combs had filmed the video for B.I.G.'s first hit single, the rags-to-riches tale "Juicy." Combs would eventually

2

buy a $2.5 million house in the exclusive area. But Wallace remembered being unnerved by the quiet, wondering aloud how someone could make real rap records if they "woke up in the morning hearing birds and crickets."

"This is a long way from Brooklyn," I said to B.I.G., taking his "kick back" advice and loosening my Gap tie, but refusing a hit from the blunt.

"I know, right?" B.I.G. said with a laugh. "A few million miles."

I was fresh from my cubicle at the *Los Angeles Times,* where I worked as a staff writer. While I liked my job, and certainly appreciated the opportunity the *Times* had given a 24-year-old brother like myself, I was also frustrated. As one of a handful of young black reporters at the paper, I had a hard time convincing my superiors of the newsworthiness of some of the hip hop artists I wanted to profile. And since *Times* employees were not allowed to freelance for "competing" publications, I had to watch a lot of great stories pass me by. B.I.G. was the last straw. So far I'd been unsuccessful in my efforts to convince the editors that B.I.G. deserved a major feature, even though his next album, the follow-up to the double-platinum debut *Ready to Die,* was sure to be the biggest release of the spring. So when *ego trip*'s "Chairman" Jeff Mao and VIBE's Rob Kenner both called me asking if I wanted to interview B.I.G. while he was on the West Coast, I jumped at the chance. I was taking a major career risk by profiling B.I.G., since freelancing could have gotten me fired. I did not realize that he was taking an even greater risk by being in California.

Even those who were unaware of what made Wallace so "B.I.G." were quite familiar with his "Notorious" side—chronicled all too eagerly by the same mainstream press that ignored the artistry of his meticulously crafted records. Most infamous was Wallace's tragic falling out with Tupac Shakur, a close friend who became a bitter rival. After months of very public disputes with Wallace and Combs, Shakur was fatally shot on September 7, 1996, while sitting in the front seat of a car driven by Marion "Suge" Knight, CEO of Death Row Records. Even before Pac died—six days later, on Friday the 13th—there was widespread speculation about Wallace's supposed connection to the crime. He always avoided dissing his old friend on wax or in print, often sounding genuinely hurt and confused by the rift. Seven years later, the crime remains unsolved.

As he sat in the shade of his cabana that afternoon, Wallace seemed completely relaxed. But despite his laid-back demeanor, it's safe to say that there was a lot on his mind—and not just because he was in California so soon after Shakur's murder. B.I.G. was always the type to keep things running through his head. Unlike most other rappers, he never carried lyric notebooks into the studio. He would construct those intricately rhyming narratives inside his formidable brain, then step to the microphone and record them "off the dome."

B.I.G. sat watching kids splash around in the pool without a care in the world.

"This shit is beautiful," he said, taking a sip of lemonade. "You got palm trees and all type of stuff right here. I wouldn't want to lose it for nothing in the world."

Two young white kids, looking like they just stepped out of a Polo ad, approached the 6′3″ 300-pound rapper to get an autograph. Kenneth Story, a tall bald security guard posted just outside the cabana, tried to stop them. But B.I.G. nodded, allowing them past, requesting a pen.

"What's your name?" he asked, smiling. "Christie?"

Once feared, now revered, the Notorious B.I.G. was a star; no doubt about it.

B.I.G. believed that his forthcoming double album, *Life After Death . . . Till Death Do Us Part,* was going to take his career to the stratosphere. With the perfect mix of R&B grooves and hardcore hip hop, this was the record that could silence his critics, unite the coasts, and win over anybody still caught up in the overblown East Coast versus West Coast rap war. He would be the one to erase three years of heated tension, if not for love, then for money.

"I've noticed that change from when I first came out in '92 to now," B.I.G. said. "Everybody's trying to get paid." And getting paid seemed as good a reason to make peace as any other. "Why would you want to limit your money? Why would you want to be a rapper that could only get money on the East Coast, and have other rappers only get money on the West Coast? Why not blend all this shit together?"

The plan was simple: Spend some time out west, stop by the radio stations, let California know he not only had love for the West Coast but that he'd loved Pac as well. Earlier that week, Puffy Combs had appeared with Death Row artist Snoop Dogg on *The Steve Harvey Show* as a show of unity, to prove that successful black men could come together regardless of any geographic locations, affiliations, or bad blood between them.

"I thought it was something that had to be done," Wallace said. "It was a conversation that was held by Snoop, myself, and Puffy so long ago. I'm glad it took place, too. 'Cause that's all it would take is for Snoop to say, 'It ain't no beef,' for me to say, 'It ain't no beef,' Puff to say, 'It ain't no beef.' Then the fans would be like, 'It ain't no beef.' It's time for it to be over, man. Let's just get money, man."

But when I asked him "Is money really power?" he paused before answering.

"*You* answer that question," B.I.G. replied, a tinge of sarcasm in his deep voice. "Do you think money is power?"

"Yes," I said, keenly aware of how money had changed his life, for one.

"I think so," he said, nodding. "Money can't get you love, but it can get you respect."

There was no disputing the fact that people's attitudes toward him changed dramatically once he stopped hustling on street corners and started his music career. No longer was he "Considered a fool 'cause I dropped out of high school," as he rapped in "Juicy." But now he was besieged by people he called "playa haters." His fame had begun to alienate some of his hardcore fan base. Grimy rap heads wondered aloud why Biggie traded in his Timberland boots for alligator loafers. Instead of being happy for his success, many people simply resented it.

"I'm not that nigga on the streets no more," B.I.G. said, sounding a bit frustrated. "I can't be acting like it's something that I'm still going through. That would be unbelievable. No, B.I.G. is not selling no drugs, so why would you want to hear a song about that? I got other problems. These goddamn haters, man. They just can't say 'Damn, this nigga was from Brooklyn, he took a talent he had and just built that shit into something so strong. I'm proud of him.'" B.I.G. shook his head in disgust. "They can't even say that shit."

"Everyone knows you're big," I said. "But are you still hungry?"

"Starving," he replied. "I got a point to prove. That sophomore jinx . . . so many new artists who came up, their second album was trash. I know everybody want to know, 'Can he do it again?' I want everybody to know that I can. I want to *exceed* their expectations. Go to an even further length. I went all out on this one, man."

That was Biggie for you. When I asked about Tupac, the Notorious B.I.G. didn't answer my questions. Christopher Wallace did.

"Tupac, at one point, was my dawg," he said with a smile, his voice softening. "Funny muthafucka, too." You could hear affection and regret in his words: two emotions very much at odds with Wallace's public persona.

"There's a lot things people didn't know about him," Wallace continued. "That nigga could make a nigga laugh, man. And he liked to laugh . . . He liked to hang out and get drunk. He had such a serious outlook. In his interviews and everything, he just seemed so angry, but at the same time, so charming. It would fuck people's heads up. He liked that title as a 'troubled muthafucka.'"

Wallace's voice trailed off and he sat silently for a moment before continuing.

"I'm realizing that nothing protects you from the inevitable. If something is gonna happen, it's gonna happen, no matter what you do. Even if you clean your life up. What goes around comes around, because karma is a muthafucka."

More contemplative silence.

"When he died, that shit fucked me up," Wallace said, voice low. "I know so many niggas like him, too. So many rough, tough muthafuckas. When I heard he got shot, I was like, 'He'll be out in the morning, smoking some weed, drinking Hennessy or whatever.' You ain't thinking *him*. You ain't thinking he going to die."

Wallace sat up in his lounge chair, shifting his weight.

"You just keep thinking, a nigga making so much money, their lifestyle should be more protected. You know what I'm saying? Their lives should be more protected where things like a drive-by shooting ain't supposed to happen. That shouldn't have happened, man. He's supposed to have lots of security. He ain't even supposed to be sitting by no window."

We sat and talked for much longer than our allotted time. We talked about his childhood, his family, his career, his troubles, and his hopes for the future. We talked until dusk turned to darkness. Then it was time for him to go get a tattoo on Sunset Boulevard with some of his crew.

Playing back the interview tape during my long drive home, I heard Wallace say something that haunted me then, and still haunts me to this day.

"It's crazy for me to even think about saying this," he said, his voice reverberating through my Honda Civic hatchback. "Thinking that a rapper can't get killed, because he raps. That shit can happen, and I'm stupid to even think that it couldn't."

Twenty-five days later, shortly after midnight on Sunday, March 9, 1997, Christopher Wallace was the victim of a drive-by shooting, almost six months to the day after Shakur was shot. Wallace, too, sat by a window.

If you've picked up a copy of *Unbelievable* just to find out who killed The Notorious B.I.G., then you've come to the wrong place. Go get one of those other books, the ones written by people who never cared about Wallace until he was murdered. Enjoy.

While this book does deal with the facts of Wallace's murder, and examines the various theories about this unsolved crime, that's not really what the book is about. This is a book about the man in full. For what measure is a man's death if we know nothing of his life?

"It's like his life was art played out for everyone," observed Hubert Sams, one of Wallace's closest friends since childhood. "You might have heard the record where he says he was hustling to feed his daughter. But the struggle before, nobody really saw that. Nobody knew about the girls calling him 'Blackie.' Dark brothers, we go through it." Though young Wallace was sensitive about his dark complexion, his lazy eye, and his weight, through his lyrics he would later transform his so-called "ugliness" into something to be celebrated. "He didn't fold," Sams said. "He didn't just curl up at 226 St. James. He came out there, exposed himself to the 'hood. And further than that, he took himself to millions through his music. But people don't realize there was a lot of pain behind him."

"You never want anybody to know everything about you," Wallace once told me. Yet that's exactly what this book will attempt to do, to tell you just as much about Christopher Wallace as it does about the Notorious B.I.G. and the forces that shaped them both. If you want to find out how a sheltered Catholic school honors student was transformed into a hustler and then into the world's greatest rapper and unlikeliest playboy, then read on. If you want to know what brought Wallace and Shakur together and not just what divided them, read on. If you wonder why B.I.G.'s legend seems to loom ever larger with each passing year, what he represents in the evolution of the hip hop MC's art, or in the rise of rap as a billion-dollar industry, read on. If you want to understand how a man can survive the drug game only to get killed in the rap game, you've come to the right place.

If I've done my job, then after reading this book, May 21, 1972, should be just as important in your mind as March 9, 1997.

Wallace's astrological sign was Gemini, symbolized by the Janus twins. (Tupac, born June 16, 1971, was one, too.) Geminis are creative types, known for their mercurial nature: cool, calm, and reflective one moment, fiery and warlike the next. Extremely sensitive even when appearing tough.

"Is it better to be loved or to be feared," I once asked him.

"I would say feared," he replied. "Because once you give off a perception of just being a nice guy, a lot of people tend to take your sweetness for weakness. They're like 'Oh, B.I.G., he's cool. He's a great guy.' You know? Instead of somebody being like, *'Biggie's coming!'*" he said, widening his eyes in mock terror. "'How's he gonna act? We can't get over on him.' The fear keeps everybody on their toes."

So who was he? And how do you represent such a character with so many personalities and a name for every one? There was Chrissy-Pooh, the apple of his mother's eye. There was Cwest (pronounced "Quest"), the closet MC messing around with his grade-school friends on boom-box mix tapes. There was Big Chris, the cat with the black hooded sweatshirt hustling with his boys on the corner of Fulton and Washington near the check cashing spot. There was Biggie Smalls, the freestyle legend and Cee-Lo champion, unofficial mayor of St. James Place. And there was the Notorious B.I.G, the dapper don portrayed in videos, riding around in yachts and helicopters with Versace shades and Coogi sweaters. *Unbelievable* attempts to capture them all, along with many other people and circumstances that made Wallace's life and work so phenomenal.

The cornerstone of this book is the six hours of interviews I did with Wallace over the course of his life, from the first time, on his block in Brooklyn on September 27, 1994, to the final time, in his hotel room at the Westwood Marquis on March 7, 1997—just 36 hours before he was murdered. I've done many hours of additional reporting since then—talking with numerous friends, family members, artists, producers, and others who knew him. Some interviews come from my tape archives, which go back as far as 1992.

In trying to do justice to Wallace's story, I've also drawn on the work of fellow hip hop journalists as well as VIBE's archives. Nobody can take on a task of this magnitude entirely on their own. But I'm sick of reading other books that steal other people's hard work without giving them proper credit and respect. That's why I list every source at the back of the book. The only people not listed are those who spoke with me "not for attribution" or on "deep background."

Interviewing Wallace was always a joy because he never said "no comment." He was easy to find, not pretentious in the least, and funny as hell. He told the stories of his own life in vivid detail, much like his raps. The tales were often darkly comedic, in the same way that Quentin Tarantino's *Pulp Fiction* is essentially a comedy, despite its brutal violence. Whether talking about his childhood, his experiences as a drug dealer, or the challenges of his newfound fame, Wallace always had something interesting to say. This book attempts to tell Wallace's story in the same uncut manner that he related his story to me.

The rules of storytelling dictate that every hero needs a villain to define him. The Notorious B.I.G. may be the hero of this book, but that does *not* make Tupac Shakur the villain. This book explores how two friends with so much in common could become alienated by circumstances and people around them. It's a tragic tale, not unlike the split in the Black Panther Party between Minister of Defense Huey P. Newton and Information Minister Eldridge Cleaver. By telling it fully and truthfully, perhaps similar tragedies can be avoided in the future.

Once he had achieved all his goals—conquering the rap game, launching his own businesses, creating jobs for all his friends—what Christopher Wallace *really* dreamed about was a quiet family life. He said as much on *Born Again,* the posthumous tribute album released two years after his death: "Ten years from now where do I *wanna* be? I wanna be . . . just living, man. Just living comfortably with my niggas, man. A pool and shit, smokin' plenty Indo. You know what I'm sayin'? I got my wife, just loungin' with my wife. I got my [kids]. You know, just laid back, just chilling. Living. All my niggas is living."

Then he shifted from the hypothetical to the real. "Where I *think* I'll be? In ten years? I don't think I'm gonna see it, dog," he said, laughing. "For real, man. That shit ain't promised, man. And I don't think my luck's that good. I hope it is, but if it ain't . . . So be it. I'm ready."

Was Christopher Wallace really "Ready to Die?" Think of all the things he had to miss. He was a successful young black man who wanted to raise his family and live his life. To give his daughter T'Yanna away at her wedding and spoil her rotten. To teach his son Christopher things about being a man that his own absent father never taught him.

One day, when T'Yanna and Christopher Jordan Wallace are a little older, maybe they'll read this book. Like their father's music, this story is filled with candid moments, some of them funny, some bawdy, some violent, others downright vulgar, and a few that are just plain sad. Like Biggie's music, this book is not for kids—or even immature adults. But it's also balanced with Wallace's humor, sensitivity, and deep insights about himself and the world around him.

I just want T'Yanna and Christopher Jr. to know this: If you ever have any questions about whether your father loved you, know that, in his last hours—even before he knew they were his last hours—he was thinking only of you two. The Notorious B.I.G.'s music was filled with death, but Christopher George Letore Wallace wanted to be around to see both of you grow up. If you ever want to hear him say so in his own voice, I gave the tapes to your grandmother.

Christopher Wallace lives within you. And within all of us who loved him and his music. What else can I say about the guy? He was unbelievable.

CHEO HODARI COKER

Los Angeles, September 22, 2003

DOLLY
MY BABY

CHAPTER 1

"You I love and not another
You may change but I will never . . ."

The first time she saw the Manhattan skyline in all its splendor, Voletta Wallace gasped in awe. Miracles of glass and steel, the buildings reached upward to heights that seemed to taunt God. Nothing in Jamaica, not even the pictures she'd seen in magazines before she emigrated, could have prepared her for the sheer enormity of New York City.

"There must be a lot of religious people around here," Wallace remarked to a fellow expatriate, looking out on the Bronx from a subway car soon after her arrival. "Why do you say that?" he replied. The only brick buildings she remembered in the bucolic coastal town where she grew up were places of worship, so naturally she assumed that these towers must be chapels. Her recently Americanized friend laughed.

"Those aren't chapels," he told her. "Those are apartment buildings. People live in them."

The year was 1968. Wallace's island home of Jamaica had achieved independence from British rule six years earlier, and the economy was already dangerously anemic. There was a widening disparity between rich and poor, increasing strife between political parties, and problems with everything from road maintenance to the educational system. Many Jamaicans were leaving the island for better opportunities elsewhere. Thousands went to England and Canada. But a small minority moved to another land that had once suffered under Britain's heavy-handed absentee rule: America.

Her Majesty's dreary cobblestone streets never held much appeal for Voletta Wallace. "I never saw a happy England," she explained. Her aunt Ethel had left for London years before, and had always wanted her to come visit. But Voletta never had any desire to go. America was different. She'd seen photographs of its beautiful mountain vistas and wide-open prairies. She'd heard about the abundant opportunities, the rags-to-riches success stories, the political freedom, and the fine universities. All the little bits of legend that made up the American dream appealed to her imagination. The U.S.A. sounded like the Promised Land.

The fourth of ten children, Voletta Wallace was born into a solid landowning family in the rural parish of Trelawny on Jamaica's north coast. Her mother ran the household while her father worked as a butcher. Unlike so many others on the island, she never lacked for food, clothes, or shelter. Comfortable but by no means rich, the Wallace family taught Voletta that hard work, thrift, and religious piety were the cornerstones of a happy life. She attended church every Sunday, and spent most of her free time reading books and fashion magazines. "Good girls didn't do that," Wallace said with a laugh, when asked if she used to go to dancehalls. "I was a school girl, a home girl, a church girl."

While she was never one to rebel, Wallace realized that the last thing she wanted was to be married off as a teenager, exchanging her father's firm hand for that of a husband. She longed to see the world and to determine her own course in life.

At 17, she left Trelawny for Kingston, finding a job in Jamaica's bustling capital as a switchboard operator. But she still felt unfulfilled. The city was so crowded, and ofttimes dangerous, she couldn't see much of a future for herself there. By the time she was 19, Voletta Wallace decided it was time to make moves.

A postcard arrived in the mail one day from the Jules Jurgensen House of Fashion that sealed her fate. Her name was on the list because she had once purchased a watch through their mail order catalog. A friend saw the card and said it looked so official that she could probably convince the people at the American embassy she was a model traveling to New York for a fashion show. With her looks, why not? She was a beautiful young woman: 5-foot-3 and 98 pounds with long flowing hair and a slim, shapely figure. She put on her best American-made dress and went to the U.S. embassy in Kingston.

She told them she was a designer, and she needed a visa to go check out the fall collections in person.

"Most of my clothes come from the United States," Wallace told the interviewer, clipping her words with just the right amount of fashionista attitude. "I usually send for my clothes through a friend who goes to New York, but they always come back damaged, so I would like to go there and select my clothes myself."

"You want to make your complaints?" he asked.

"I made my complaints already," Wallace said curtly, cutting him short. "I just want to go up there to select my clothes."

The bluff worked. Voletta Wallace was granted a 14-day visa to do her shopping. She flew up to New York, applied for an extension, and never looked back.

And so began her adventure in New York, like countless other Caribbean people before her. She worked day and night, using whatever spare time she had to pursue her high school equivalency. "In Jamaica, you don't have the money to send your child for higher education," she said. "I put a great value on education when I came here." The first time she took the test she failed by one point, which only made her more determined. "What am I gonna do?" she asked herself. "Cry?" Instead, the future educator resolved to "just read, read, read." The second time around, she passed the test.

Despite her triumph, life in the big city soon lost its luster. Wallace took a job answering phones in a psychiatrist's office, and her surroundings were making her crazy. Though the city was beautiful by night, the morning light revealed a harsh reality. One day she looked out her window and said to herself "Is *this* the beauty I wanted to come here for?" Wallace hadn't fully appreciated the misty mountains and lush tropical climate of her birthplace until her first experience with soot-colored snow. "New York was filthy," she said. "The houses were ugly. And the people were rude." It was the general lack of respect that bothered her more than anything else. "My first shock was hearing a man use profanity toward a police officer," she recalled. "In Jamaica, that man would have been arrested and shot. But this man here was cursing out a police officer, and the officer just stepped back. I said, '*Huh?*'"

Voletta Wallace was distraught. Disappointed. "I felt like I was a swan amongst featherless fowls," she said.

She decided to try and make the best of her situation. She wasn't going to sit and sulk at home just because she didn't like her initial impression of the city. "I prayed and prayed and prayed for New York to grow on me," she said. She was determined to better herself, to achieve her dreams of self-reliance. She enrolled at Queens College where she studied nursing and worked as a home health aide. But she quickly realized that nursing wasn't for her. "I couldn't stand the sight of blood," she said. "I couldn't stand the pressure and the sickness and all that." She transferred to Queensborough Community College and began taking courses in early childhood development, moving closer to what would become her true calling.

And then in 1970, two years after arriving in the States, she met another expatriate "swan" who helped make her adjustment a little bit easier.

Tall, broad-shouldered, with kind eyes and an easy smile, George Letore had natural charisma. A welder by trade, he was also Jamaican, having emigrated to London years before relocating to New York. It didn't matter to Voletta Wallace that he was more than two decades her senior. She thought she was in love. She delighted in the man with the quick sense of humor who was twice her size and treated her like a little girl. "To be very honest, I can't say, 'Oh, my very first impression was love at first sight,'" Wallace said. "I like older men. For some reason, all my life, I have always dated older men."

George Letore and Voletta Wallace with their son Christopher on the day of his baptism in Brooklyn, 1972.

She soon became pregnant. It should have been joyous news, but there was only one problem—Letore had another family back in London and a son who was almost her age. Although she knew there was a good chance he wouldn't be around, Wallace made up her mind to be empowered instead of feeling abandoned. She had feelings for Letore, but they didn't compare to the love she felt for the new life that was kicking inside her belly. On May 21, 1972, at Cumberland Hospital in Brooklyn, New York, Christopher George Letore Wallace was born.

He was a big healthy baby—eight pounds—and labor was difficult for the petite mom-to-be. The child had to be delivered by cesarean section. The last thing she remembered before the anesthesia was a nurse saying, "Doctor, it's 10:21.'" Next thing she knew it was 5 A.M. and another nurse was telling her, "Mother, you have a baby boy.'"

Of course it was love at first sight. "After my son was born I found out that what I felt for George was not love, because I loved my son," she said. "*This* was love," she added, folding her arms as if she were holding the boy with the soft tuft of hair on top of his head again for the first time. "You know, this little thing right here, in my hands, that's love. Out there"—she said, dismissively waving her hand—"I don't love you. I was too focused on this little innocent right here in my hands. So I gave this person all my love, and I guess his father realized, like, 'Damn, can I get just a little bit of that?' But I couldn't give him any," Wallace said. "It was like, 'You go your way, and I'll stay with this little critter here.' And we just made life on our own." Eleven days after his birth, Ms. Wallace and Letore took their son to the place that he would call home for the next 20 years, apartment 3L in 226 St. James Place, between Fulton and Washington. Theirs was a spacious apartment, with a large living room, a dining area, a study, and three bedrooms. The one opposite the kitchen on the far end of the hall was Christopher's.

Wallace spent hours looking down at her son, just watching him sleep. She delighted in every coo, every sigh. He was so playful, and he looked up at her with such devotion. Each moment with him felt too short. She hated to leave him and go to work in the morning. "When I did," she said, "I was miserable."

Letore abandoned the family three months before Christopher's third birthday, but Voletta Wallace hardly missed him. "Knowing myself now, I don't think I ever loved him," she said. Her son was enough.

"From his birth until he was two years old, I made a secret prayer in my heart," Wallace recalled. "God, I wish he could stay like this forever. I never want him to grow up. Never never never never."

If he could just stay little, and under her protection, then he would never have to venture outside their apartment, and nothing bad could ever happen to him. She knew the world outside their door could be a very dangerous place.

Just the two of us: Voletta Wallace and one-year-old "Chrissy Pooh."

Just south of the Wallace apartment lay Fulton

Street, an east-west throughway that connected both sides of young Christopher's reality. At the western end was yuppified Clinton Hill, and to the east was rough and tumble Bedford-Stuyvesant. The border separating the two areas, Classon Avenue, was only five blocks to the east, but the perception gap between the two neighborhoods was immense. "If someone from the area did something good, the papers would describe him as hailing from Clinton Hill," one resident explained. "If they shot or robbed somebody, the papers said they were from Bed-Stuy."

In their late 19th-century heydays, both neighborhoods were among the wealthiest in New York City. The prominent people who built mansions along Clinton and Washington Avenues included pharmaceutical millionaires such as the Pfizers and the Bristols of Bristol-Myers as well as Charles Pratt, the oil executive who founded the prestigious art and design school, The Pratt Institute, at the north end of St. James Place. Those who couldn't afford mansions moved into beautiful brownstones. Victorian row houses and huge apartment buildings lined Gates, DeKalb, and Willoughby Avenues. Architects spared no detail, with sculpted gargoyles, roaring lions, wrought-iron gates, and Romanesque pillars on the exteriors, and high ceilings and intricate woodwork inside.

Emancipation, and the oppressive nature of life in the Jim Crow South, pushed many African-Americans north and west by the turn of the century. They came by train, bus, and foot, seeking a better way of life. The "Great Migration" saw huge numbers of African-Americans settle in industrial centers like Chicago, Detroit, and the mecca of the so-called "Promised Land": New York City.

As Bedford-Stuyvesant's population became darker over the decades, white citizens' groups like the Gates Avenue Association urged their membership in 1922 to limit "the widening spread of the black belt all over Brooklyn." But it was too late. The first West Indians had begun arriving. Cubans and Puerto Ricans and Dominicans were moving north to escape the sugar cane fields. And the year 1936 marked the expansion of the Independent Fulton Street subway line which stretched all the way to Harlem. Many Harlemites seeking to escape increasingly overcrowded tenements and rising rents uptown took the A train to Bedford-Stuyvesant, which became one of the largest concentrations of black people in America, second only to Chicago's South Side.

When the Japanese bombed Pearl Harbor on December 7, 1941, the U.S. Navy lost many of its mightiest warships, including the Brooklyn-built U.S.S. *Arizona*. The Navy needed new ships quick. Thousands of workers answered the call, including people who were previously locked out of the Brooklyn Navy Yard: African-Americans and women. The Yard became the area's largest employer.

When the war ended, many black people lost their jobs to returning soldiers. Having risked everything to move, they weren't about to go back down south. So they stayed put. And just like in Harlem, which was once a Dutch and Jewish neighborhood, Bedford-Stuyvesant experienced a major bout of white flight. The white folks took much of their money with them, but kept the apartments, slashing rents and turning some of them into flophouses. Formerly proud buildings suffered the neglect of basic repairs and upkeep.

After the neighborhood had been abandoned by both the white and black middle class, Bedford-Stuyvesant became the very picture of Langston Hughes's "Dream Deferred." In 1966, just two years before Voletta Wallace came to New York, the Brooklyn Navy Yard closed. Unemployment was on the rise. The prominent buildings in Clinton Hill and Bedford-Stuyvesant still stood, but the paint had faded. Politician's promises of more jobs, better schools, and clean, safe streets didn't materialize. Bedford-Stuyvesant increasingly led the city in violent crime, infant mortality, and unemployment. The Pfizers of Clinton Hill gave way to street pharmacists selling heroin and cocaine on the corner.

Strictly speaking, 226 St. James was in Clinton Hill, but in 1971, when Voletta Wallace moved in, it was far from cushy. "Two blocks over there was a methadone center," she observed. "There were a lot of addicts that would congregate around that block." And then at nighttime she would hear the sounds of the city. "Those weren't fireclappers out there," she recalled. "It was gunshots. All those police sirens couldn't have been false alarms. I was scared to death."

But she stayed. She had a beautiful apartment that she could afford, and she was close to where she worked and went to school. And on the bright side, Clinton Hill was a community filled with many young, working-class West Indians like herself, proud and frugal, who kept to themselves and closed ranks, keeping their old traditions alive. And then there was everyone else.

As long as Christopher stayed inside, came home on time, and minded his business, he'd be just fine.

"I was a sweet little boy," **Christopher Wallace** once said, looking back on his childhood. Then he laughed, rolling his eyes.

"I was a sneaky nigga, man," he admitted. "I was *real* bad, you know? And you know what made shit worse? Muthafuckas would tell Moms that I did something, but she just wouldn't believe them. She'd be like, 'Not *my* Christopher.'"

And why would she believe them? Polite, attentive, articulate, Christopher was considered a darling by family and friends alike. He never gave his mother any reason to suspect otherwise.

"He was adorable," said his mother, her eyes lighting up. "Just cuddly and kissable." He loved watching *Sesame Street* and reading Winnie the Pooh stories, thus earning the nickname "Chrissy Pooh."

After completing her studies at Queensborough, Voletta Wallace enrolled in a master's program at Brooklyn College. She became a teacher of young children, often practicing lesson plans on her son. He began nursery school at two years and five months, was writing his name in legible cursive at three, and displayed a vocabulary well beyond his age.

By the time he turned five, Wallace was bigger than many of the kids in his preschool class at Quincy-Lexington Open Door Day Care Center, but he never used his size advantage to push anyone around. If he wanted extra cookies, he'd find a student who would give him some. If he wanted to play with a certain toy, there was always someone willing to let him go first.

"He knew how to use his brain," said Melvin Blackman, his first teacher in preschool. "He had this charismatic quality. People wanted to go his way."

Among the first to go his way were Michael Bynum and Hubert Sams, his best friends at St. Peter Claver Elementary, a Catholic school located within walking distance from Wallace's apartment. Sams remembered Wallace as a student on the rise. "He had a knack for everything," Sams said. "He was on top of the class from day one. He had his ABCs down before everybody, and he was always on point, from reading to math." You name it, Chris had a gold star for it. "I don't think there's anything I could remember that he wasn't so good at," said Sams, "except for the streets." Chris, Mike, and Hubert endured their share of bumps and bruises, Sams recalled. "We weren't exposed to the raw deal until way late."

In their mothers' eyes, the St. Peter Claver uniform—yellow shirts and plaid ties—made Christopher, Michael, and Hubert look like well-groomed, successful young men on their way to learning important lessons. They learned important lessons, all right. Mike and Chris were only children, and Hubert had a little sister—none had an older brother to show them how to negotiate the rules as they moved among West Indian households, Catholic school, and the street. One thing they knew for sure: Their uniforms painted targets on their backs.

"We really stood out," Sams said. "The first thing you did when you left school was you snatched your tie off, right away."

From the second they hit the block, there was tension with the public-school kids. The trio could feel the eyes watching their every move, the unspoken challenge: *They think they better than us?* Even going to play video games at the arcade on Fulton Street became a border negotiation worthy of the Middle East. "If you wanted to stop at the game room you had to earn your stripes," said Sams. "We didn't have anybody to tell us, 'When you go to the arcade, don't jingle your quarters, because the big kids will take them away from you.' Back in that era, it was, Yo, if his sneakers are right, we can jump him. It was really, really raw."

Even something as simple as a bus pass could be a test of will. One had to adapt and overcome or perish. "After a while, you either got used to somebody taking your bus pass, or you fought for it," said Sams. "We chose the latter."

At that time, Wallace was the smallest of the trio, but had the most forceful personality. It was his idea to form The Hawks, a little protection crew that was,

Graduation day from St. Peter Claver Elementary, 1982. That's Captain Chris holding a paper in hand; best friends Heartbroken Hubert and Master Mike are at right.

in effect, the original Junior M.A.F.I.A. The three friends all bought hats with hawk insignias at a store around the corner. Wallace gave them nicknames and he even made up a theme song, which they all had to memorize. "Everybody's talking about the Hawks because we nice," went the rap. "Heartbroken Hubert, Captain Chris, and Master Mike . . . If you mess with the Hawks you're pressing your luck. Why's everybody always picking on us?"

Acting on his mother's advice, Chris preferred to use words to fight his battles. The Hawks could resort to other means if they had to, sometimes going as far as carrying around box cutters. But they were smart enough never to use them.

Doing well in school wasn't good enough for Christopher, because he found that easy. What he wanted was the neighborhood respect that was so elusive. It wasn't just about trying to make friends with the American kids. It was about becoming part of the *fabric* of the 'hood, to be out there wearing the right clothes, the right sneakers, doing exactly what they were doing.

Not that Christopher Wallace felt alienated from his Jamaican heritage—quite the contrary. His mother never wanted him to forget where he came from. "Christopher grew up in Jamaica," she says. Every summer until he was sixteen years old, they would go back down to Trelawny for a couple of months. Christopher loved island life, riding around on a donkey, soaking up the sunshine and fresh air. He loved the jerked pork, curried goat, roasted fish, and red-pea soup. He loved being around his Jamaican relatives, especially his grandparents and his uncle Dave, who worked as a disc jockey at local reggae clubs.

Voletta Wallace wanted him to remember that he came from a family that owned land, that he was somebody special. But when he got home, that knowledge didn't change his day-to-day reality. Christopher Wallace just wanted to be like the other kids he saw playing downstairs on St. James. His mother would barely allow him to wander past the front stoop of their building. Even when he did, she'd watch him from the window above like the eye in the sky at a casino.

"Put a label on me," Ms. Wallace said. "Overprotective? I don't care."

She tried to make up for not letting him out by giving him stuff that would keep him inside. The boom box he wanted ("Either the Sharp or the Sony," he specified), tapes by the Fat Boys and Run-D.M.C., and best of all, a slew of video games. Most kids at the time wanted either Atari, Intellivision, or Colecovision. Wallace had all three. Although it went against Ms. Wallace's old-school West Indian upbringing—the "spare the rod and spoil the child" approach—she thought it was a small price to pay to keep her deeply intelligent child off the streets.

When he played with his neighbor Arty B, whose West Indian mother shared Voletta Wallace's views on most of the kids in the neighborhood, it was all video games, blanket tents, and kung-fu movies on channel 5. "A typical Saturday for us would be hanging in the house all day," Arty recalled. "We'd get little bowls, and put in chips, Skittles, and cut-up fruits, like mangos, tangerines, cherries. We'd have a little picnic thing going on there . . . eating our snacks and talking about how we wanted to have all the things that Ricky Schroeder had in *Silver Spoons.*" It was as if Christopher was kept in a protected bubble, an oasis where, if Mom had it her way, he could stay forever.

But the longer the two of them stayed in Bedford-Stuyvesant, the more Ms. Wallace became aware that her son was at risk. She'd see the teenage boys hanging out on the corner every day while she waited to catch the bus. So angry. So sullen. So rude. So devoid of the sort of cultivation she'd grown up to expect and respect, men like her father and brothers. She'd seen the faces of mothers who had to bury their own children. She was determined to see that her son would never become another casualty.

Later on Christopher started inviting other kids from the neighborhood up to play his video games, charging them each a quarter. She didn't complain, as long as he stayed home. Her greatest fear was that her son would end up like the other kids she saw all over the neighborhood. The ones that ran the streets all hours of the day and night, stealing candy from the bodega, opening fire hydrants on scorching summer days, and in some cases, getting mixed up in violence. Christopher wanted to get out there too, but his mother wasn't having it.

"I don't want you out there because I see those other kids," she would tell her son. "First of all, they look dirty. And what mother would want their kids to be out there playing from morning until night without supervision?"

Everything that scared Voletta Wallace about living in Brooklyn enticed her son. It was all so close, and yet tantalizingly out of reach. And then one afternoon, when he was hanging out on the stoop, someone who was a part of that neighborhood fabric spotted him and walked over. They called him Chico Delvec.

"Why you never come off the stoop?" Chico asked.

"'Cause my mom won't let me do the things you do," Wallace replied.

Their friendship was sealed over video games upstairs in the apartment. Wallace started making friends with other kids in the neighborhood by charging them a quarter for each turn, just like at the arcade down the street. Each had something the other didn't have and the other wanted. For Chico, Wallace had video games, a full fridge, and just about every gadget you could imagine. And Chico had something Wallace valued above all else—freedom.

His mom didn't mind him inviting friends over. Going out was the problem.

And so his double life began. As long as he kept his grades up and kept up a respectful attitude at home, his mother would never suspect that he had a completely different personality when he was on Fulton Avenue.

"When she would go to work or to school, I'd be all over the place, you know what I'm saying?" Wallace recalled with a chuckle. "I'd be outside with niggas, smoking cigarettes and drinking Calvin Coolers. Just doing shit that I knew I wasn't supposed to do."

On weekends, however, when Ms. Wallace was home, it was a different story.

"Ma," he'd ask. "Can I go outside?"

"No," she'd say.

"Come on, let me go outside."

"I don't want you out there."

I'm out there all the time, he thought to himself. *You just don't know about it.*

"She just made me want to keep doing it," Wallace said years later. "Why does she not want me to play skellie, or 'run, catch and kiss,' and do shit that little boys are supposed to do? Keeping me in the crib—that shit ain't doing nothing but stifling me, man. Let me loose a little, give me some air. I ain't got no brothers and sisters or nothing. You gone all the time. What? You just want me to be a lonely bastard?"

When she did let her son outside, he had to be back in as soon as the streetlights came on, or as soon as he heard her yelling from down the block. It could be humiliating sometimes.

The stoop at 226 St. James Place, where Christopher Wallace would play while his mother watched from the third-floor window.

There was only so much that Voletta Wallace could do. A father might have been able to better understand the needs of a rambunctious boy, to provide the proper balance of freedom and swift discipline. But Christopher didn't have a father to turn to for a second opinion. He said he liked it that way.

"Don't know him and I don't want to know him," was Wallace's response when asked about his father. "I don't even remember that cat. For real. I've seen pictures. He looks like a lame. I don't need that cocksucker for nothing." He claimed he wasn't even envious of his friends who had fathers.

"I guess I knew he was a piece of shit for leaving my mom," Wallace said. "It just seemed natural for it to be just me and my mom."

The last time George Letore ever saw his son was in 1978, when Christopher was six years old. Voletta Wallace wasn't so much angry as she was confused about Letore's unexpected appearance. His son hardly knew him. The family reunion, such as it was, lasted for only a day.

After the energetic boy had gone to sleep, Letore and Wallace sat down to talk.

"I have something to give to you," Letore said

"What happened to you after all these years?" she asked. He didn't have a ready answer, and the look on her face let him know that the few hundred dollars in his hand could not begin to make up for his absence. Letore looked embarrassed. Wallace tried to explain that money was not the issue.

"Look," she said, "if you brought twenty dollars here for me to give your son, I would not turn it away. But he needs to see his father around," she said. "The least you could do is just come."

But he never came again. And as Chris grew taller, and every day a little more beyond Voletta's control, he would find other figures on the street who would fill the void that George had left.

Some nights, when his mother was home and there was no way he could sneak out, Christopher would just watch the block from his living room window. He could see the older hustlers hanging out on the corner of St. James and Fulton, drinking malt liquor and shooting dice, heads turning with every passing car, looking for the next challenge, victim, or enemy. He dreamed of the day when he'd be old enough to take his own place out there with them, doing his own thing, beyond anyone's control but his own.

It wouldn't be long now, he thought. Not too long at all.

THINGS DONE
CHANGED

CHAPTER 2

" If I wasn't in the rap game

I'd probably have a key knee deep in the crack game

Because the streets is a short stop

Either you slanging crack rock

or you got a wicked jump shot **"**

"You know what to get me, Mommy? Buy me the Timberlands."

Voletta Wallace looked at the price tag on the boots her son wanted. They were well over $100—enough to buy two or three pairs of normal shoes.

"What am I, crazy?" she said.

"Ma, if you buy me this one pair, then you won't have to buy me no more shoes for the rest of the year," Christopher pleaded. At last, she agreed. But it didn't matter how many trips she made to Mano a Mano, it was never enough.

"When I bought him the Timberlands, he'd go, 'Ma, get me a Tommy Hilfiger,'" she recalled with exasperation. "He didn't like it if his friends weren't wearing it," she said. No matter if they were the nicest quality, his clothes had to have the right label. She once made the mistake of buying him some Polo shirts before kids his age knew about Polo; the shirts went unworn at the bottom of his dresser.

Ms. Wallace could never fully understand why her son was so hard to satisfy. Growing up in Jamaica, nothing was taken for granted. She was grateful to have food on the table, a clean place to sleep, and a good education. She liked fashionable clothes too, but she didn't expect to dress like that all the time.

As the family's only breadwinner, Voletta Wallace sometimes worked two jobs in addition to studying for her master's degree at night. She made sure she maintained a perfect credit rating and tried to save some money so her son could go to the best schools. Education had been her passport to self-reliance, and she was convinced it would be the key to her son's future as well. He was growing into a sensitive, intelligent, extremely curious little boy with an artist's eye. He could look at a picture in a magazine and draw an exact replica freehand, without tracing. The streets weren't going to claim her son. Not her Christopher.

"I made sure my son had an education, a good mattress, clean sheets, good-quality clothes, and I gave him quality time," she said. "My son wasn't the pauperized kid he made himself out to be."

No matter how much jerk pork Christopher's mother served him, his attitude was American. Christopher was a boy growing up in America. And in America, just getting by meant you were poor. Having more than you needed was considered just breaking even. No matter how much you had, the important thing was to make it look like more than it was. Fresh wasn't just the cornerstone of an emerging hip hop culture. It was also a way of life.

"At an early age, you learn that everything gotta be fresh," Wallace's friend Hubert Sams explained. "You can't have scuffed up Adidas. You gotta get your toothbrush, keep them fresh. That's the thing, fresh. Personality is secondary. It's about what you have on. You walk around Brooklyn in certain circles, even to this day, people look at your feet first."

No longer the runt of the Hawks crew, Wallace had bulked up considerably since the fifth grade. He'd always been a somewhat husky kid, but at age ten he fell off a city bus and broke his right leg in three places. His mother was advised to sue the City of New York, which settled the matter for a five-figure sum. After paying legal fees, she put a nice little chunk in the bank to save for his college education. His leg was in a cast for six months. Laid up in the house with nothing better to do, he ate, putting on pounds that stuck around long after his leg healed.

By the time he turned 13, he was nearly six feet tall. Though he still had a baby face, with the extra weight he was beginning to look like a man. But Wallace didn't feel all that manly. A man wouldn't have to negotiate with his moms to stay fresh. A man went out and handled his biz. He was sick of being under his mother's thumb. He wanted to get out there and test the waters beyond the stoop.

Wallace had bagged groceries at Met Foods around the corner, but from his

Wallace fell off a city bus at age ten and broke his leg. He had to wear a cast for six months, during which time he did a lot of eating, watching TV, and getting bigger.

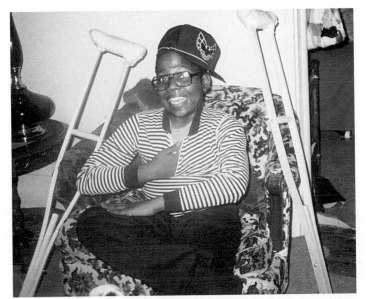

view, that was a dead end. Earning minimum wage, he'd have to save all his checks for a month or more to get the clothes he needed. And there was no point getting a $200 Adidas sweat suit without the proper shoes—if people saw you with the same kicks and gear all the time, they'd know you were broke. Forget about respect from the fellas—the girls really weren't gonna give a broke-ass nigga the time of day.

Wallace's childhood was behind him. He was about to start high school, and his mother kept reminding him how the next four years would affect the rest of his life.

His first act of rebellion was to tell her that he no longer wanted to go to Queen of All Saints School. No more uniforms, no special treatment—he just wanted to be a regular kid. When he transferred to Westinghouse High School he found the public school environment quite different from Catholic school. There was, essentially, no discipline. The student body—which included Trevor "Busta Rhymes" Smith and Shawn "Jay-Z" Carter—seemed to have the upper hand, while the teachers' chief goal was simply to maintain some semblance of order. For a kid as clever as Wallace, the curriculum just wasn't stimulating. Whenever he felt that one of the teachers had insulted his intelligence, he didn't hesitate to speak his mind.

"Christopher did very well in high school; it's just that he talked back a lot," his mother said. "He was a smart-ass."

"One day," she recalled, "he comes home and asks me, 'Mom, how much does a garbage collector make?'"

She just happened to know; she'd seen a magazine article that compared teachers' salaries with other professions.

"He did very well in school, it's just that he talked back a lot," his mother says. But when dressed for a junior high school event, Wallace was every bit the perfect gentleman.

The next day, Christopher went to school with the article in hand. After class, Ms. Wallace got a call from Christopher's guidance counselor.

"The guidance counselor told me how Christopher walked into class and said, 'Do you know how much a garbage collector makes, sir?'"

"No," the teacher replied.

"A teacher makes a starting salary of $22,500," Wallace informed him. "A garbage collector starts at $29,000."

"Do you have a point, Mr. Wallace?"

"Yes, sir. You said some of us inside here are gonna be garbage collectors. But we're gonna be making more money than you, so that's cool."

The longer Christopher attended Westinghouse, the more restless he became. At over 200 pounds, he had the build for football, but he didn't want to play. Career day came and went at school. Nothing really appealed to him.

Growing up in this section of Brooklyn, Wallace saw both sides of life, the legal and the illegal. Every day the men and women would walk to the C train on the corner of Fulton in search of their daily wage. And then there were the teenagers who stood outside the train station, shooting dice, holding 40-ounce bottles in brown bags, and turning their heads back and forth so they could check out the occupants of every passing car.

"Don't be a bum," his mother warned him, her regal Jamaican accent giving the words extra impact. "You're nothing if you don't have an education."

Yet it seemed to Wallace that the corner kids, the ones who had no place to be, had every advantage over those "respectable" people who looked so tired when they got on the train in the morning, and even more worn down when they emerged from the subway station at night. The guys on the corner did what they wanted. And they stayed forever fresh.

It didn't matter how much his mother browbeat him, there was no way for him not notice those kids. They were always out there, rain or shine, 24-7-365, selling a product that sold itself, a lethal substance that would transform the neighborhood, changing his life and that of everyone else it touched: crack.

Named for its rocklike texture, this smokable form of cocaine was cooked up on countless kitchen stoves with a little water and baking soda. The tiny gray chips could deliver a rush unlike anything anybody had ever experienced. The high was immediate, potent, and kept users coming back for more. It was the worst thing to happen to the black community since the first slave vessel pulled into Jamestown in 1619.

Cocaine had been around for centuries. The Incas were cultivating coca leaves for their magical properties as early as the 1400s. By the dawn of the 20th century, everyone from Sigmund Freud to Coca-Cola was singing its praises. The all-American soda contained traces of the drug until the recreational use of cocaine was outlawed in the U.S. by the Harrison Act of 1914. That law was championed by southern sheriffs who used a campaign of yellow journalism to claim that it caused black men to rape white women.

Nonetheless, cocaine became a fashionable drug among rich and famous people, many of whom believed it to be harmless. Until the early '70s, it was hard for most people to get cocaine if they weren't hanging out with rock stars or Hollywood actors. Movies like Gordon Parks Jr.'s *Superfly* glamorized it. Woody Allen made fun of it. In the most memorable scene of *Annie Hall,* Allen sneezed, sending thousands of dollars' worth of blow flying around the room. Sniffing cocaine said something about you—like having Cuban cigars, the smallest cell phones, black American Express cards, and Bentleys—only "true players" had access.

Cocaine had become so chic that Republican senator Tennyson Guyer con-

Tired of being teased for wearing his Catholic school uniform, Wallace transferred from Queen of All Saints to a public school. He dropped out altogether after his junior year.

vened a Congressional Cocaine Task Force in July 1979. To his surprise, most doctors called before the committee testified that the drug didn't pose nearly the same health risks to the American people as alcohol.

"Tell me the last alcoholic you saw with cirrhosis of the liver caused by Dom Pérignon," said Yale University's Dr. Robert Byck. So few people could even afford the drug, it was doubtful that sniffing cocaine would reach epidemic proportions. But a graduate student of Byck's had alerted the doctor to an alarming trend that was sweeping South America. Normally upstanding people were walking the streets like zombies from smoking something called *base* (pronounced "BAH-say").

"If this shit ever hits the United States," Byck's student warned, "we're in deep trouble."

Byck urged Guyer's committee to help counteract this menace. "We need our best minds to figure out how to do this without advertising the drug," Byck said. Unfortunately one of America's great comic minds was about to make it a household word.

Richard Pryor put "freebase" on the map in 1980 by setting himself on fire following a 72-hour smoking binge. But the high cost of making base kept that form of cocaine from being popular beyond the jet set—until Los Angeles street entrepreneurs like "Freeway" Ricky Ross started moving so much cocaine in the early '80s that the prices dropped.

"When I started getting involved in cocaine, no blacks were involved with it," Ross said. "It was still the white echelon drug. One of the things that I felt I did was I made it affordable for minorities—blacks, mostly—in my neighborhood."

The former Dorsey high school tennis star didn't invent "crack," just as

McDonald's founder Ray Kroc didn't invent the hamburger. But like Kroc, Ross quickly learned that if he could move his product fast and sell it cheaply, the sheer volume would make him rich.

Ross introduced "ready rock"—a precut, ready-to-smoke form of cocaine for fiends who didn't have the patience to prepare it themselves. And they came back so quick, again and again, it was worth the extra time spent processing the dope and rocking it up.

From the dealer's perspective, crack was a wonder drug. It was easy to make, and the drug's smokable form drove customers nuts, hitting the brain's dopamine and endorphin centers instantly. Best of all, a crack high lasted less than half an hour. Users kept coming back again and again until their money was gone. Two thousand dollars' worth of powder could make you as much as $20,000 worth of crack. If you were ruthless and ambitious, it could be a gold mine.

The rock epidemic that was taking over Los Angeles was largely ignored on the East Coast. But after Len Bias, the Maryland Terrapins basketball star and Boston Celtics number-one draft pick, died of a crack-induced heart attack, the drug officially entered the national consciousness. *Time* and *Newsweek* ran cover stories. President Bush held up a bag of crack during a televised address in which he announced a new war on drugs. Dan Rather did a two-hour program called *48 Hours on Crack Street* that was watched by 15 million people. The show was broadcast on September 2, 1986. Christopher Wallace was 13 years old.

"I heard about crack on the news and I was like, 'That's what niggas must be doing,'" Wallace recalled. "I knew they were fly as hell—they had $150 Ballys and bubblegoose jackets and sheepskins. I was like, 'Oh shit. These niggas are doing it.'"

Wallace didn't know any of the specifics, but he knew he wanted in.

Chico Delvec was the bridge. It was one thing seeing kids he didn't know blow up. But seeing Chico succeed convinced him to stop sitting on the fence.

"This nigga's coming through with the butter Fila velour shit, the big cables, four finger rings," Wallace recalled. "I'm like, 'Yo, we the same age. I'm sitting here fucked up, asking my moms to throw me down money for some ice cream. And this nigga is getting cash!'"

"Come on the Ave with me," Chico told him one day, in one of those simple conversations that can change one's life forever. "Just come see what it's like and meet some of my old-timers."

Wallace's heart was racing as he walked around the corner to Fulton Street. He met some of the hustlers like Cheese and Tony Rome—but the scene was too fast for him. Cars were zooming by, and you had to look in every one to make sure it wasn't a rival dealer or an undercover cop. Wallace had the added worry that his mother might find out what he was up to.

"I ain't with that man," he told Chico, all stressed out. "The police. My moms . . ."

"Just chill, Chris," Chico said. "You ain't got to do nothing. Just chill."

Wallace settled down, learning the game, and realized how much money he could make. Fear quickly turned into boldness.

"I feel like I was the bad influence," Chico said. "Because when I introduced him to the game, he just like got addicted to it."

He started off small, "hauling work" for others.

"They'd give me a little bit of paper," Wallace said. "The next thing I know, they was trying to make big moves. And they wanted me to be down. And I had my little cousin with me, my cousin Gutter. And we just got into it."

It was the speed that appealed to Wallace. The returns were quick, and the only limit seemed to be his own ambition.

"Within no time—*boom!*" Wallace recalled. "That's what made the shit so fascinating. It wasn't a situation where a nigga was struggling for four or five months like, 'Damn, when we gonna come up?' Within three weeks niggas was having six or seven hundred in they pocket. Niggas giving other niggas a hundred dollars to go get sneakers for them—'And get a pair for yourself.' Sweet shit like that."

Why even aspire to college? If the point was to get a job, he didn't need a degree for that. When he was a boy at St. Peter Claver, they would advise students to build on their talents and think about what they could do with it in the future. Wallace was a talented artist. There were times when he thought about becoming a commercial artist. The Pratt Institute was within walking distance of his apartment, and there were artists that lived in Clinton Hill. But a few afternoons standing on Fulton Street changed all that.

"After I got introduced to crack—commercial art? Nigga, please." Wallace explained with a chuckle. "I can go out here for twenty minutes and get some real paper. There's your art, man. I didn't want no job. I couldn't see myself getting on no train for shit. I didn't want to work in no barber shop, I didn't want to do no restaurant. I wanted to sell drugs! I wanted to chop up keys, bag up work, and get paid. That's the only thing I thought I was ever gonna do."

He wouldn't be the last kid with such notorious aspirations—and he was hardly the first.

The drug game, like the NBA, used to be a league for grown folks.

Street legends like Leroy "Nicky" Barnes and Frank Lucas spent years building their multimillion-dollar heroin organizations from the bottom up—and were well in their thirties before they began reaping their ill-gotten gains. The federal government estimated that in the late '60s and early '70s, over 50 percent of America's heroin users lived in New York, and 75 percent of those junkies lived in the Harlem neighborhoods where Lucas and Barnes sold their wares.

A disciple of Ellsworth "Bumpy" Johnson, Lucas ruled West 116th Street with an iron fist. His Blue Magic "package" outsold all other brands of heroin.

"My buyers, you could set a watch by them," Lucas said. "By four o'clock we had enough niggas in the street to make a Tarzan movie. By nine o'clock, I ain't got a fuckin' gram. Everything is gone, sold. And I got myself a million dollars."

Barnes and Lucas were Harlem royalty. They had flashy cars, chinchilla furs, tailored suits, Gucci frames, women and houses all over the country. They could be found uptown at the Lenox Lounge or Small's Paradise—the same club where a Detroit Red–era Malcolm X used to ball out with West Indian Archie and Sammy the Pimp.

Emboldened by beating so many cases, Barnes posed for a photo on the cover of the *New York Times* Sunday magazine, calling himself "Mr. Untouchable." The article got the attention of President Carter, and by the late '70s Lucas and Barnes were both in prison.

But during the years when they were running the street, the most a young teenager could do was aspire to be a driver or a lookout and, over years, work

When he started hustling, Wallace became a fixture in the neighborhood. Everybody knew the big kid on the corner. His wit and winning personality made him much more than a dealer. He was the "Mayor of St. James."

his way up the ranks. They didn't have Barnes and Lucas's overseas connections to import the stuff. You needed a Ph.D. in street sciences to make those kinds of moves.

Crack made it a G.E.D. game. Once the Medellín and Calí cartels started shipping cocaine to the United States by the ton, access was no longer the issue—distribution was. There was plenty of room for young, smart people with initiative to get into this deadly game. But the 18-to-20-year-old millionaire dealer in the 1980s didn't necessarily have the patience or sophistication as his older '70s counterpart.

As the game attracted more players, the league expanded. Each city had its own all-star players. Rich Porter, Alpo, and A.Z. were running things in Harlem. Queens had the Supreme Team, established near Jamaica's Baisley Park Houses by top guns Kenneth "Supreme" McGriff and Gerald "Prince" Miller. According to court papers, the organization made $200,000 a day at its apex, complete with bodyguards and rooftop lookouts with radios. Lorenzo "Fat Cat" Nichols and Brooklyn's Howard "Pappy" Mason also made major moves during this era. The exploits of Young Boys Inc. and the Chambers Brothers put Detroit on the map.

And one can't leave out Washington D.C.'s Rayful Edmonds, who drove to Las Vegas in 1987 for the Sugar Ray Leonard–Marvin Hagler title fight. While he was out west, he hooked up with an L.A. Crip named Melvin Butler, thus connecting the cocaine trade on the East and West Coasts. Butler's friend Brian "Waterhead Bo" Bennett had a direct connection to Colombia's Calí cartel. The resulting D.C.-to-L.A pipeline earned the Edmonds organization between $10 and $20 million a month.

As the popularity of crack spread, the dealers got younger, richer, and deadlier. Teenagers fronted in Porsches and Benzes, wearing thousands of dollars' worth of jewelry, making names for themselves.

With so much money, and the exuberance of youth, the competition got nasty. Young men who once had trouble affording a Saturday Night Special now had access to Uzis and AK-47s. Jamaican posses like the Spanglers and the Showers competed fiercely for U.S. drug profits. Crips and Bloods used crack to escalate their long-term vendettas against each other, each side taking up ever-deadlier arms.

Some kids didn't even care about the gang shit. They just loved the last 15 minutes of *Scarface*, and felt that killing their rivals bolstered their reputations. It was good for business. They didn't care who got hit. Drive-by shootings became routine, innocent kids dying right next to the street soldiers.

Pudgy and partial to track suits, Michael "Waterhead Bo" Bennett quickly became a legend in the game. By the time he was 24, more than 2,000 pounds of crack a week moved through his hands. By the time he was 25, Bennett, along with his Colombian sidekick Mario Ernesto Villabona, was sentenced to life without parole in late November 1990 after he was caught trying to smuggle and sell almost 1,500 kilos of cocaine.

Bennett's lawyer, David Kenner, felt the judge's sentence was grossly unfair, and that the federal government was persecuting his client—a young black man—for all the smugglers, money launderers, and politicians pulling the strings in the so-called "war on drugs" that they couldn't catch.

"They make kids like Brian scapegoats for their own inabilities," Kenner complained to the *Los Angeles Times*. "Busting a lot of people and confiscating a lot of kilos doesn't solve the problem. This is a demand-side problem, not a supply-side problem."

Kenner would know. The more drug dealers got caught, the more they demanded his high-priced services, and the richer he became. Born in Brooklyn in 1942, Kenner graduated from the U.S.C. law school and quickly made a name for himself as a tenacious, savvy defense attorney. He was part of a fraternity of lawyers who specialized in the defense of organized and drug-related crime. Some of the others included Anthony Brooklier (son of Los Angeles Mafia head Dominic Brooklier); Donald Re (who successfully defended John DeLorean's cocaine case); and Las Vegas law partners Oscar Goodman and David Chesnoff, who made entire careers out of defending clients with deep organized crime ties, including the likes of mob enforcer Tony "The Ant" Spilitoro, the model for Joe Pesci's character Nicky Santoro in *Casino*. (Goodman played himself in the film.)

One of Bennett's codefendants was a former Bounty Hunter Blood named Michael "Harry-O" Harris, a man who wasn't content just to be ghetto fabulous. "You didn't see dealers like Ricky Ross and Bo Bennett hanging out in Beverly Hills, going to movie premieres, eating at the Palm. But that was Harry-O's world," said one law enforcement source about the man whom L.A.'s CBS Channel 2 news once labeled a "Gang Godfather."

The smooth, articulate 29-year-old had a business acumen that far exceeded many of his drug-dealing peers. He owned a limo service, a Beverly Hills hair salon, an exotic car dealership, and a deli. But like a lot of people, what he really wanted to do was get in the only other "game" besides sports or drugs that made young black men like himself rich beyond their wildest dreams: show biz.

He made his first breakthrough in 1987, helping launch Denzel Washington's career on Broadway in the play *Checkmates*. But later that year, before Harris could parlay that success into anything else, he was arrested for the attempted murder of rival dealer James Lester. Harris was also one of 13—along with Bennett and Villabona—fingered in a massive drug-racketeering case.

Harris knew crime and he knew show business. And when he saw David Kenner, he felt the sharp-dressed attorney had the perfect mixture of streetwise swagger and conference-table savvy. In short, Kenner was "bad." In the middle of the trial, Harris fired his own lawyer and hired Kenner.

"I felt that if Kenner could do what he did with criminal cases in the entertainment business, he could be powerful," said Harris. "These other attorneys go home at five and it's over with. I saw a guy who's going to put his whole life into this. I said, 'David, you use that attitude over here and we'll get rich.'" Indeed, both men would help start a record company that would change hip hop forever.

The game was changing, and so was Voletta Wallace's boy. But she was the last to know.

"Prior to 13 years of age," she said years later, "he was just a son. A son any mother would like. At 13 he became notorious."

Ms. Wallace worked hard during the day and then took classes at night. By the time she came home, her son was usually sitting in front of the television, having left the block hours before.

The clues were subtle at first: a photo of Christopher with his friends from St. James, wearing jewelry or gold fronts on his teeth. But she never saw that stuff in person. He hid his secret identity in plain sight. Like Superman had his Clark Kent glasses and suit, Captain Chris had the benefit of his mother's doubt.

The only things he did bother to conceal from her were the fly clothes that influenced him to become a dealer in the first place.

"I used to hide all my shit on the roof," Christopher confessed. "I'd leave the house with all the busted shit my moms was giving me, act like I'm going to school, and change my whole outfit up on the roof, come down on the street, and then go to school. Every morning this was the task, I mean *every* morning."

When he got tired of the rooftop routine, he started telling his mother that he bought the stuff on the street for a discount.

If she got suspicious, he had an excuse ready. "I'd tell my mom some boosters were reselling it, and I bought it off the street for like forty dollars," he recalled. "She from Jamaica; she don't know how much that Tommy Hilfiger cost."

"I remember once I saw him with a jacket," Ms. Wallace said. "And I said, 'Where did you get that jacket?' He said, 'Oh, it's not mine. I borrowed it.' And I said, 'You're wearing other people's clothes? That's disgusting.' And then one day, someone asked to borrow one of his shirts. And I go, "'Is this what teenagers do?'"

"Everyone was scared of his mother," recalled Wallace's friend Damien "D-Roc" Butler. "Mrs. Wallace don't *play*. When I used to stay at Big's house, if we came in at, like, three in the morning, trying to tiptoe in the crib, she would be right there. She'd direct you into the living room and sit you down on the couch. And she wouldn't just be talking to Big. She'd treat everybody like her son. She'd say, 'Don't come in here this late. Y'all gotta be careful. You smell like reefer.' She'd just always be on us, but not in a bad way. I mean, you can't be mad at somebody who cares, you know?"

While Wallace maintained a positive front at home, he didn't bother to keep up the same level of deception at school. The former honor-roll student started missing classes days and weeks at a time. By the end of his sophomore year, the truancy letters began to pile up, and he was running out of excuses.

"I have a warrant for your arrest," his mother told him one day, waving the paper in his face. "You don't go to school, and the cops are out there looking for you. When they find you, they're going to arrest you and put you in a home." That got to him. "He was so scared," she said.

For a minute, anyway. But the money made things easier.

"We were making $1,200, $1,300 a day," Wallace remembered. He felt his mother's frustration, but at the same time, he couldn't see any reason for continuing with school. A high school degree seemed irrelevant; going to college was not even an issue.

"My mother was going to school for a long time," Wallace said. "It was hard. And I used to see her. School was hard. I was like, man, this ain't the shit for me. And I just started saying, Fuck it. I'm not doing this shit."

It broke his mother's heart. Even with him missing as many classes as he did, she felt that he still could have graduated with minimum effort.

But Christopher was adamant. He wasn't going back for his last year of high school, no matter how much she pleaded.

"How are you gonna live?" she would ask him, over and over. "I'm thinking about your future. What are you going to do out there? Walk about and be a bum? Have your mommy feed you and clothe you?"

The thought wasn't keeping Wallace up at night.

"All of us dropped out of school," he said. "We were sitting on six and seven grand a week, just living, y'know what I'm sayin'? And we had all the chicken-head bitches on our dicks and shit. We were just doing our thing."

Christopher Wallace was 16 years old, and he thought he had life all figured out. Of course, he didn't. The game was unpredictable, stressful, and sometimes scary. Life in the game wasn't all it was "cracked up" to be.

When West Coast and southern hustlers referred to crack dealing as "grinding," they weren't just talking about the texture of the product. They were also describing the lifestyle—the same thing brothers in Brooklyn meant when they spoke of "the struggle." Selling drugs was life on the swivel: constantly looking over your shoulder, always wondering if this was the day you were going to get busted.

Sometimes Wallace felt that he was working so many hours, he might as well get a real job. What looked like easy money turned out to be hard work.

"I'd wake up around nine o'clock to catch the check cashing place at 9:15," Christopher Wallace recalled. "The crack heads got checks from Social Security, and on Saturday they all get their welfare checks. And when they cash those in, they usually want to buy drugs. So we'd be up early—as soon as they got their money, we're gonna be the first person they see.

"Every day between 4:30 and 7:00 we'd come hustle right on the corner," Wallace said. "The train station would be flooded with business people from all over the area. And they'd see us every day. Every day they'd come out of the train and get hit with a cloud of marijuana smoke." Their radio was blasting rap music, their dice game was taking up the whole block. "They'd look at us like we the scum of the earth," Wallace said.

But you had to be out there, because that area of Fulton Street was an open market, and competition was cutthroat. You got lazy, you lost your customers. It was as simple as that. As on Wall Street, time was money.

"Everybody popped up with their own package," said one former dealer familiar with the Fulton Street drug scene. "You be at one bodega, and you looking across the street and somebody else there, and you're both hollering for the same customer. Whoever treated the customer better might have a chance."

The dealer's relationship with his client was close by necessity. From the crack-fiend's perspective, the quality of each "jack," or vial of crack, depended on the dealer, the quantity and texture—rocky or crumbly—how much they cut it, and what they cut it with. If a certain dealer sold a certain quality product, and you felt like you could trust him, that's who you dealt with.

From the dealer's perspective it was different. You had to know your clientele to avoid going to jail. Selling just one vial of crack to an undercover cop was guaranteed jail time. A pocketful of jacks could send you upstate for the rest of your natural life. And with the advent of TNT—the NYPD's Tactical Narcotics Task Force—street dealers knew they were public enemy number one.

"TNT sends you somebody new every day," said one former dealer. "They'd send you a decoy with marked money, and the van would come right after. You had to be selective. Had to do your homework. Some people didn't sell to anybody they didn't know—straight up. Or you had to come up with a good customer and stand there and vouch for them like, 'I know this guy, hook him up.' Sometimes you'd be paranoid, you'd get a twenty, and then run into the Arab store and break it real quick."

If it wasn't the cops busting the block, it was the crack heads shortchanging you. If you were charging ten bucks, they would try to give you eight. After a while it added up. If they kept shortchanging you, you had two choices—refusing to serve them, or beating their ass the next time they came up short.

"The drug game is so up and down," Wallace observed. "There's so much shit that can happen." When business was bad, it was very bad. During a drought or a police crackdown, it wasn't unusual to make $300 in a week (about minimum wage for all the hours put in on the corner). Or nothing at all.

And even when the money was good, he never saved it. Seven thousand a week might get split six or seven ways. He could easily blow his $1,500 on clothes, shoes, and weed. Next thing he knew, he'd be headed uptown to spend the last of his funds buying more weight so he could cook it up and start all over.

When he was on the block, "Big Chris" had no conscience—it was all about the dough. If someone wanted some shit, you sold it to them—no matter who that person was. You might have started out with scruples, but the longer one remained in the game, the looser those principles became.

"Once he got to the point where Fulton Street became his real stomping grounds, he wasn't even Chris no more," said Hubert Sams.

Sams was a student at Thomas Jefferson High School, where he played fullback on the football team. When he wasn't at practice, he'd sometimes visit his old friend Captain Chris, who was spending most of his time with his homeboy Suif Jackson, a.k.a. Gutter, and another friend everyone called O.

"You playing football?" Wallace asked, sounding impressed. Then the old humor came back. "Man, you gonna break something."

"I'm all right, yo," Sams said with a smile. "I'm all right."

"You gettin' big though," Wallace said.

"This nigga ain't big," Gutter said, wrestling Hubert to the ground and laughing.

The Christopher Wallace Sams knew at 16 was very different from the kid he knew at 6. He was still funny. He still had people following his lead. But the whole context had changed. Wallace's "scramblin'" days—when he'd buy just a little and sell when he got the chance—were over. "When I went to see him, we weren't chilling at his house anymore," Sams recalled. "He was on the block."

That's when the changes began to sink in. "Being sixteen, you think about hanging out with your friends as play time. But I realized Big wasn't out there playing. Yeah, there were some jokes being cracked, but it wasn't a game out there. I think that mighta helped me not to get in the game. 'Cause I saw what it was really about. And the motivation was money, man. The motivation was money."

"We used to have this rule that was, 'We ain't serving to no pregnant ladies,'"

That Brooklyn bullshit, we on it: Bigging up the Bed-Stuy crew, along with DJ 50 Grand and the Old Gold Brothers.

Wallace said. "And there was a pregnant lady who used to come see us every day from Jersey that used to want, like, ninety capsules. I'm like, Fuck it. I mean if I don't give it to her someone else will.

"It ain't like she gonna go home and be like 'Well, Biggie didn't give it to me, I'm going to sleep.' She's gonna get high. So I'm going to handle my business. And niggas was like 'Yo, you foul.'"

But Wallace remained unapologetic. "I didn't get in this game to feel sympathy for nobody. I got in this game because I can't do nothing else. This is what's going to help me eat. So I can't pass up no muthafucka. That's bread and butter, y'knowhatumsayin'? If I don't do that, I don't eat."

So he stayed out there, chasing the dollar and trying not to get caught.

Sams recalled visiting Wallace on Fulton late one evening when the police almost got his friend. They had gone into a bodega to get the hustler's staple—a turkey hero with cheese.

"We weren't on the Ave, so we didn't see them roll up," Sams said—"they" meaning the cops, of course. "Chris is a well-known figure. So when they hit the block, they know they're looking for the big guy. Usually he stashed his stuff. He didn't have it on him. And they'd talk to him like, 'You know you got it.'"

This time was different. "They walked in the store right behind us, and we at the counter," Sams recalled. "He had a few jacks in his hand. As soon as they came in, he threw them in his mouth. I saw him. They might have seen him. But it was kinda smooth. He was on point. You had to be."

The police officers patted both young men down.

"Open your mouth," one of the cops said to Wallace.

"What?" Wallace said, eyes wide.

That's when the cops grabbed him—and Wallace switched to plan B.

"Aggh! Aggh!"

"He just fell down and started screaming," Sams remembered. "So now they trying to wrestle with him." People in the store began crowding around to see the cause of the commotion, and the cops got distracted.

"They're looking up and away—one's got his knee in his back," Sams said. "So he looks up at me and he's whispering 'Take the jacks! take the jacks!' Like he wants me to bend down and take them out of his mouth. But the cops is standing right there."

The look on Sams's face told Wallace that idea wasn't going to work. "So he just keeps screaming," Sams said. "Yo, he could have won an Oscar. He was acting like they were killing him. And then he started crying."

At this point, the cops stood him up.

"Get out of here, man," they said. Frustrated, they turned and left.

"After they left and started getting in the car, he just turned around and started screamin'!" Sams said, laughing almost as loud as Wallace did.

"When he started laughing at 'em, I was like 'Yo, I wouldn't have did that.' 'Cause I wouldn't have wanted them to come back with a hard-on for me. But that was his attitude, man. He felt like he was almost untouchable. Almost."

Despite the money he was making, Wallace was still camped out at 226 St. James in his sweaty-ass "shack" in the back, across from the kitchen, with sneakers and takeout food containers stacked sky high. It was one of three rooms Wallace claimed as his own in the apartment—a far cry from the cramped conditions he would complain about on records. His digs were comfortable and he knew it. Despite all his talk of being a man, he wasn't ready to leave home. And though he knew he was doing wrong, he liked the idea that his mother thought he was a good guy. In some ways, both of their psyches depended on it.

"Shit, sneakiness was winning," Wallace recalled with a grin.

How deep was his mother's denial?

"I thought crack bottles were perfume bottles," Ms. Wallace said.

It's hard to believe that anyone could be so naïve—on the level of Lois Lane never suspecting that Clark Kent was Superman when his only disguise was a pair of wire-rimmed glasses and a tie.

Never underestimate the power of denial, particularly when it comes to single black mothers and their only sons.

There was the time that Wallace and his friend O left a batch of cocaine that they'd just cooked into a gooey white paste on a plate in Wallace's room. They had plenty of time to kill before they could crack it up and put it into vials, so they put the plate of wet paste under a fan and went downstairs to hang out.

"We go outside and get something to eat, and just happened to be in there with some broads, spending too long in there," Wallace recalled.

By the time they returned, they discovered that his mother had decided to come home early that day. When they went in his room, the plate was gone.

"Ma, you go up in my room?"

"Yeah."

"Did you see a plate on my bed?"

"The plate with the mashed potatoes?" she replied, sounding mildly annoyed. "They were so hard on the plate I had to flush 'em."

"WHAT?!"

"I threw some in the garbage."

"WHAT?!"

"I'm like taking crack out the garbage," he said, savoring the comedy of his story. "She got barbecue turkey wings all on the shit, and niggas are looking at me like 'You fucked up.'"

Eventually he did.

Standing out on the corner in early 1990, Wallace and some of his friends got arrested. Wallace had a loaded, unregistered gun on him—but no drugs. Because it was his first offense, and because he was only 17, the judge was lenient, and he was given five years' probation.

After the gun charge, it became impossible to hide what he was doing from his mother. It didn't help when the police came by the apartment to tell Ms. Wallace that her son was out on the corner selling drugs. They said one day they'd catch him with a few vials on his person and that would be all they needed to lock him up for a very long time.

"I think you have the wrong boy," she told them, even then. "Not my Christopher."

Her own son was the one who had to break it to her. "I really had to sit down and tell her that what they were saying was true."

Even if she suspected something was going on, it was hard to confront the truth. Her son had strayed from the path. He was no longer someone to be proud of.

"My moms was looking at me like I was crazy," Wallace recalled, his voice softening. Disappointing his mother was one of the few memories from Wallace's street life that caused him visible remorse.

"My moms was just flipping out," he says. "She'd be watching the news, seeing stuff about how crack is plaguing the city. She'd just lose her mind and go in my room and throw all my shit away. She'd be like, 'I don't want this shit in my house! If you're gonna do this shit under my roof you gotta leave.' You know me, Mister Bold and Beautiful. I'm like, 'All right. I'll go.'"

He came back within two weeks. Relieved but also reluctant, Ms. Wallace let him back in. He assured her that he had learned his lesson and was out of the game. Every morning she'd catch the bus to work, and every morning he'd be back on the corner near the check cashing place. It was a separate but equal existence, neither one trying to tread on the other's space.

His mother sealed their new arrangement by taking out a life insurance policy on her son. After he signed it, she looked him in the eye and said, "Do you know what you just signed? You signed away your *life.*"

But it was the life he had chosen for himself.

"I'd never say she accepted it," Wallace said about his mother's attitude about his dealing. "But I was basically uncontrollable. I wouldn't stop no matter what."

And so he was out there every day, gathering a crew around him that was down for whatever. Chico and Gutter were the guys that held him down. Veteran dealers like Cheese and Tony Rome looked on like coaches. To the untrained observer, they just looked like neighborhood kids who kept moving around. The crew was always changing positions to avoid being too conspicuous. But no matter where he went, you could always see the big guy.

James Lloyd, a.k.a. Lil' Cease, was a 13-year-old who saw him all the time.

"I used to come back and forth from school, doing my thing, and Big, he right there on that corner, hustling with the rest of the dudes. He'd be out there, shooting dice, breaking fools off while waiting for customers."

Trife and Larceny were some of the other youngsters who hung around. Money L lived nearby. D-Roc (short for Rockefeller) lived over on Bedford Ave., but Wallace would often visit him for a piece of his grandmother's pineapple upside-down cake. Butler remembered being impressed by Wallace's intellect. "He was so smart," said D-Roc, "you could ask him questions like, How many miles is Pluto from Earth? And he could break it down."

Wallace became a fixture on that corner. "This is where I made bread and butter," he would later say about this crossroads, "where we got stuck up, where we had shoot-outs, where stores got robbed, where niggas got beat down, people died . . . right

"That man had so much sex appeal," Jan Jackson said of Wallace. "I couldn't think of five men who had the charisma of his one body."

here." Everyone knew him, from little kids to old men, beat cops to bodega owners. Mothers on their way home from work. Often he'd be out there telling jokes, smoking trees, just holding court on the Ave like he was a politician meeting with his constituents. One of his friends said he was "like the mayor or some shit." The moniker stuck: Big was now the Mayor of St. James. He was in the bodegas so much that he even learned a little Arabic so he could joke around with the shopkeepers.

"He was a clown," remembered Jan Jackson, a sweet, heavyset girl who lived right around the corner from St. James. "That's the only way I can put it, a clown, but a charismatic clown. He would be standing out there all the time. He approached me one day when I was on the pay phone. And he just came up to me and started a conversation. And then every day after that, when I came home from work, he would be there and we would have a conversation. And it just started from there."

Jan progressed from fixing him a plate of rice and beans to becoming Wallace's first serious girlfriend. They were so close, some people assumed they were kin.

What started as a friendship would last the rest of Wallace's life. Some said they looked more like brother and sister than boyfriend and girlfriend. On the surface, both were the kind of people that white (and some black) society discriminate against. They were overweight, poor, and dark-skinned. It was them against the world. But they understood each other. Jan wasn't trying to change him. She could handle his mood swings. She could even understand the fact that he was hustling—and not be one of those people looking at him like he was "a piece of shit."

"That man had so much sex appeal," she recalled. "It's not even funny. I couldn't think of five men that I've met since then that have the charisma of his one body. 'Cause when you'd meet him, he was just like . . . he was my friend," she said. "We would just talk, and laugh, and you would feel so much at ease, and you wouldn't have a care in the world. It was like nothing or no one else was there."

The time they spent together would be simple but meaningful. He told her about the things he wanted to do if he had enough money.

"The cars. Always the cars," Jan said, laughing at the memory. "Always going to buy his mother a house in Florida. 'Oh, I'm gonna get a house in Florida. Oh, and I'm gonna have two houses, one for the boys, and one for me and you.'"

How all this was going to happen she didn't know. Nor did he. He always assumed that his future lay in the drug game. But fate had other plans for Wallace.

Christopher had this hobby, see. When he wasn't busy on the Ave, he spent most of his time rhyming, and he knew he was getting better. And as more people heard him, they would say he was the best in the neighborhood—possibly even better than that.

IT WAS ALL A DREAM

CHAPTER 3

" You never thought that hip hop would take it this far

Now I'm in the limelight 'cause I rhyme tight

Time to get paid, blow up like the World Trade **"**

Christopher Wallace came along at a pivotal moment in rap's evolution.

Born in 1972, he was a member of the last generation to remember what black music sounded like before hip hop was even a possibility. He was old enough to remember the soulful sounds of the Dramatics, Blue Magic, Teddy Pendergrass, Stevie Wonder, and Marvin Gaye. He was familiar with the explosive theatrics of Parliament-Funkadelic, Earth, Wind & Fire, and Kool & the Gang—and the father of funk, James Brown. He knew the isolated moments of disco genius—Chic, Diana Ross, and Donna Summer. Then there were those childhood trips to Jamaica, where jazz and mento, reggae and soul formed an ever-present sonic backdrop—sometimes seasoned with a bit of toasting, Jamaica's form of proto-rap. All of these influences, consciously or not, filtered through his ears, shaping his ideas and opinions about music.

Christopher was barely walking when some of the most groundbreaking events in the continuing evolution of black music were taking place. When DJ Kool Herc began setting up his massive sound system in the community center of 1520 Sedgwick Avenue in the South Bronx in 1973, it was more than an event—it was a musical education of earthshaking proportions. As a child, Herc experienced the power of a loud sound system in his native Kingston, Jamaica. Now, living in a section of the Bronx where gang violence was endemic, he wanted his sound to serve as a unifying force. Afrika Bambaataa had a similar philosophy, viewing the music as a way to transform his gang, the Black Spades, into a social, musical, cultural force: the Zulu Nation. But Bam played music a little differently than Herc did. He could slip any record into the mix and make it funky. The *Andy Griffith Show* whistling theme. Billy Squier. Thin Lizzy. The more obscure the better. Pop music garbage became hip hop symphony. In fact, that was the unspoken motto of the art form—taking other people's trash and turning it into gold.

A social movement began to evolve around these primal grooves, and the sounds and styles spread to youth in other boroughs. Names like DJ Hollywood and Pete Jones became famous. But it was a rail-thin kid from the Bronx, Joseph Sadler, a.k.a. Grandmaster Flash, who pulled it all together and became the prototype for the modern DJ. Flash was the matrix—the man who absorbed and integrated the boom-bap, the deep crates, the concept of timing and blending. An electronics whiz from Samuel Gompers Vocational School, Flash figured out how to preview one record while playing another. This allowed him to go beyond the blends heard in disco clubs. He could isolate and extend the break— that part of any old record that makes time stand still. Like the first few seconds of John Bonham's drums on Led Zeppelin's "When the Levee Breaks," or the Phelps "Catfish" Collins guitar solo on James Brown's "Get Up, Get Into It, Get Involved." Some dancers would wait for these special parts of the record to show off their moves. They became known as break boys, or B-boys for short.

While Herc, Bam, Flash, and other pioneers manipulated the dance floor like scientists in a laboratory, they needed someone to hold sway over the crowd— a Master of Ceremonies, Microphone Controller, or simply MC. Catchphrases that started off as spontaneous remarks became the cornerstones of style. "Throw your hands in the air, and wave 'em like you just don't care," said Cowboy. "Yes, yes, y'all," said Kid Creole. Along with Kid Creole's younger brother Melle Mel, these three formed the nucleus of Flash's eventual Furious Five.

Slowly but surely, people began to flock to jams to hear what the MCs were saying as much as what the DJs were playing, and rappers stepped to the forefront. Just as DJs once competed to see who had the best sound and style, MCs began competing with one another. Such was the birth of the battle.

"When you battlin' on the mike you could say some shit about a motherfucker and piss him off," said Harlem native Alonzo Brown. Along with his best friend Andre Harrell, they formed the old-school rap duo Dr. Jeckyll and Mr. Hyde. "You would rhyme about a nigga's moms," said Brown. "You would rhyme about a nigga being broke. You would rhyme about taking his bitch and his bitch be right there. But because you had the mike, you had all the power."

Tapes of those park jams and battles circulated throughout the five boroughs, but nobody was in a hurry to go to the studio and make a record. When the Sugarhill Gang scored a hit single in 1979 with "Rapper's Delight," it pissed a lot of people off. Most hip hop fans had never heard of Big Bank Hank, Wonder Mike, or Master Gee. Most of their rhymes were familiar, though, since they were lifted from MCs like Grandmaster Caz and Raheem. But the floodgates were opened, and soon records like Afrika Bambaataa's "Planet Rock" were preserving new sounds and states of mind. Not long after that, Grandmaster Flash and the Furious Five showed that hip hop could also carry "The Message."

And then in 1983, some kids from Hollis, Queens, changed the rules of the game all over again. Run-D.M.C. stripped rap down to its elements: two MCs and one DJ, minus all the fancy clothes and gimmicky routines. Run-D.M.C. were B-boys, not in practice, but in stance. Black Lee jeans and matching jackets, unlaced Adidas sneakers, and that "I don't give a fuck" body language. When they took the stage, you got the impression that they'd just stepped off Linden Boulevard, gotten into a car, and driven to the venue. "Sucker MCs" was not trying to cross over to the R&B charts. Run-D.M.C. showed the world what rap was supposed to sound like and marked a line in the sand. Anything that came before them was old school; anything that came after was new school.

Christopher Wallace listened intently to Run-D.M.C. and all the great MCs who came after them. LL Cool J brought similes and sex appeal to the MC's arsenal. Boogie Down Productions reflected the ravages of the crack trade through songs like "9mm" and "Criminal Minded." Ultramagnetic MCs dropped "Critical Beatdown" with Kool Keith's on-beat, off-beat style of rhyming and Ced Gee's mysterious samples and effects, zooming ahead while looking in the rearview mirror. In 1987 Eric B. & Rakim dropped *Paid in Full*, perhaps the most timeless rap album ever made. Rakim's voice made everything move in slow motion. He was the closest person to being holy in hip hop, as if what he was saying was as old as the Nile but futuristic at the same time. Slick Rick and EPMD kept the energy building, switching up styles and sounds and making some of the greatest records hip hop ever heard. Kool G. Rap was the progenitor of some of the rawest gangsta tales ever recorded, and his agile flow inspired thousands of MCs. But it was G Rap's Juice Crew rival who proved to be Wallace's greatest influence—Bedford-Stuyvesant's own Big Daddy Kane.

Kane began his career ghostwriting rhymes for Biz Markie, but ended up emerging as one of the fiercest MCs ever. His voice was so rich and smooth, he almost sounded melodic. His metaphors were simple but potent: "So full of action," he said on the underground classic "Raw," "my name should be a verb."

During those golden years between the end of 1987 and the middle of 1990, it seemed as if every single record that came out and every MC that came forward eradicated what came before it. And Christopher Wallace was there, absorbing it all. Hip hop never had a more devoted, attentive listener. The first time he heard "Rapper's Delight" and "Planet Rock" he wrote every word of the lyrics down in a notebook. Wallace and Hubert Sams collected as many "Uptown tapes" as they could get their hands on. They would listen over and over to those old-school sessions recorded live at places like Harlem World and T-Connection.

After school, when the three of them were able to get together, Sams and Wallace would go to Mike Bynum's house to mess around with his turntables and try to make songs in the three hours before Mike's parents came home.

Wallace came up with the MC name Cwest, and Sams and Bynum became his DJs, the Techniques. They messed around with crude boom-box tapes until Wallace met Donald Harrison, a New Orleans–born jazz saxophonist who had played with Art Blakey's Jazz Messengers.

Harrison, who lived at 218 St. James, on the same side of the street, would often see Wallace standing on the stoop.

"He was a little guy," Harrison recalled. "Always talkative, asking questions. He saw my saxophone case and said, 'You're a musician. What's going on. I can't leave the stoop 'cause my mom says I have to stay right here.'"

St. James itself, as Harrison remembered, wasn't that bad. There were doctors and lawyers and other professionals on the block, homeowners. But Fulton St. was a wasteland. Wasted talent. Wasted potential. Harrison wanted to show kids like Wallace that there was a world beyond the Ave. A world that had nothing to do with selling drugs. They didn't always have to be on the outside looking in.

"I always told them they could achieve anything. I told them, 'The sky's the limit.' I asked them what they liked and they all talked about rap music. So I was trying to teach them about jazz and they were teaching me about rap."

At every opportunity, Wallace, Bynum, and Sams would spend time at Harrison's playing around with his home recording equipment.

Who is Biggie Smalls? Calvin Lockhart played the gangster character that became Wallace's alter ego in the 1975 Sidney Poitier and Bill Cosby film *Let's Do It Again.*

"I used to fuck with Donald all the time," Wallace said. "He got my ears tuned into jazz music. He put me on to Herbie Hancock and Terence Blanchard." Many players, including Art Blakey, Blanchard, who recorded often with Harrison, and pianist Cyrus Chestnut stopped by Harrison's pad for impromptu jam sessions. Wallace and Chestnut shared a close resemblance, a fact they often joked about.

"Niggas don't even know I know Cyrus," Wallace said. "I knew Cyrus way before I ever thought about this rapping."

What Harrison liked about Wallace was his maturity and curiosity.

"We talked about everything," Harrison remembered. "Stocks and bonds. The world. If I was reading, like, *Time* magazine, some kids would be like, 'Man, I don't want to see that.' But Chris would check out what you were reading and get into it. He would investigate what you were talking about.

"I used to wear a lot of suits. Armani and Versace. We used to talk about these kinds of things. *GQ* magazine, all that stuff was around my crib. That's part of the jazz legacy, what you wear."

Wallace, Sams, and Bynum worked on their first songs together at Harrison's home studio.

Though they didn't rise to the level he would achieve later, those first songs showed elements of Wallace's distinctive rhyme style.

"He wrote really intelligent stuff using big words and rhyme schemes," Sams said. "He'd say some wild stuff. We always knew he had potential."

But as the trio grew older, their interests began to differ. Sams, whose mother died when he was 16, was busy with high school football. When he hung out with Wallace, they didn't work on music. Bynum, who went to Sarah J. Hale High School, also drifted away from music. And Wallace, who was knee deep in the street game, viewed rhyming as strictly a hobby.

Chico had turntables and a tape recorder, and Wallace would rap to make tapes for the Avenue. "They always ended the same, with Biggie talking about how he was going to make it big," remembered Jessie Lyons, Chico's sister. "Every rap ended with him having money and success and going away from here." Mabusha "Push" Cooper used to put on little shows on the block, and Wallace would routinely massacre the competition during the open mike segment. It wasn't anything he took seriously, though.

"I would play around with lyrics, do some parties," Wallace said. "I wasn't looking to get discovered. I was having fun."

By his late teens, Christopher Wallace was always on the Avenue, growing stockier and cockier. He and Harrison would still talk on occasion, but Wallace didn't want to come around and use his recording equipment anymore. The game of the streets was more enticing.

"He was highly intelligent, and he was highly talented. I feel like he could have played jazz if he wanted to," Harrison said. "But he made a choice about the way that he wanted to go. And he saw things. He needed certain things in his life. I think between me and his moms, we were trying to get him to go another way."

Sometimes Voletta Wallace would call and say, "Mister Harrison, would you go out there and get my son?" Harrison never said no. "I would go out there and get him, as long as I could," he remembered. "She wouldn't have to call me anymore. If I saw him out there, I would just be like, 'Let's go home, yo.'" But after a while even Harrison couldn't stop him.

"Initially I could go out there and walk him home," Harrison said. "We still could talk to each other. But he was in that, and that's what he wanted to do. He wanted some money."

Rhyming was his hobby. Selling drugs was his occupation. And now that he didn't have to worry about school, Wallace began going out of town on business trips. "What we were selling in Brooklyn you could sell for four times that in North or South Carolina," Wallace said. He caught the Greyhound bus down to Raleigh, North Carolina, where he hooked up with an older New York hustler by the name of Robert Cagle, a.k.a. Zauqael. They both recognized that they could get seriously paid down south by bringing in powdered cocaine from New York. They would rent a hotel room, give somebody a little weight to work off, then sit back and watch the profits roll in.

"Back when Big first came down I didn't know he could rap," Zauqael recalled by phone from Lakeview, a Brockton, New York, correctional facility. "Back then it was different. The drug game was kinda big at the time. And the rap game wasn't really that promising. But he was telling me that his name was Big, and he could rap. He didn't make a big deal out of it; he just said he could rap. And I figured everybody knows how to rap, you know?"

One evening they were chilling in a room at the Days Inn watching the Sidney Poitier and Bill Cosby movie *Let's Do It Again* on TV. "One of the characters was named Biggie Smalls," Zauqael recalls. "And I said, Listen, ain't you say your rap name is Biggie? He said yes and I told him, Listen—that's a better name for you right there. Biggie Smalls. And he said, Yeah, I like that. 'Cause it was gangster plus it was funny. But I told him, if you're gonna be named that, I hope your MC game is nice."

"Yo, I am nice," Wallace assured him. And then to remove all doubt, he started freestyling.

"I said, Son, is nice, but we drug dealers right now," Zauqael recalled with a laugh. "I was keeping it real." One night he took Biggie to a local club called the Zoo. Zauqael convinced the DJ to let him kick a few rhymes. Then he passed the cordless mike to Biggie. "When he started rhyming the place went crazy."

Between 1990 and 1992, Zauqael says he and Wallace were doing so well, they shared a three-bedroom house together at 2700 Alpha Drive in Raleigh. Biggie was a good roommate. He had a great sense of humor that Zauqael couldn't stay mad at him, even when he caught Wallace stealing his Häagen-Dazs and stuffing the container with bread to cover his ice-cream capers. Wallace mostly kept to himself, writing in a notebook of rhymes in his spare time. On one of their trips to the mall, Zauqael encouraged him to buy a rhyming dictionary. "I can't write like this," Wallace said. He looked up a couple of words, but preferred listening to the words in his own head.

On his trips back home to New York, Wallace watched as people he knew got played trying to get into the rap game. Nobody was going to catch *him* kissing some A&R man's ass.

"I would see niggas breaking their backs making demos," he recalled, "going to Funky Slice in Brooklyn, getting the crazy, crazy drum machine beats, bullshit breaks with the fucked-up mikes, sounding mad cheesy. I'm hustling on the block in the morning seeing niggas saying 'Yo, man, I'm about to shop my demo.

I got a meeting at Warner Bros.' I'm like 'Word, go do your thing, baby.' I knew I was nicer than them niggas. But I hate rejection, man."

He'd never have to worry about it.

When he wasn't selling drugs on Fulton Street, Wallace hung out with D-Roc and his peoples on Bedford Ave., across the Classon Avenue border in the heart of Bedford-Stuyvesant. Here he hooked up with a crew called the Old Gold Brothers and a DJ named 50 Grand, who lived closer to St. James, on Gates and Fulton. He wasn't trying to make music; it just kind of happened.

"I put all my time into hustling, 100 percent of my time," Wallace said. "But at the same time, we'd be on corners and niggas would go in the basement and bring eight or nine bags of weed with us, and just listen to music."

One day 50 invited Wallace, D-Roc, and a few other guys over to his crib. "We get to his basement, and he's got two turntables and a mixer," Wallace recalled. "I was like 'Oh word, you got equipment, kid?' He was like, 'Yeah.'"

"Word? You got a tape deck?"

"Yeah."

"I get busy, son," Wallace said.

"Word? Get the fuck out of here."

"No, for real, I get busy," Wallace emphasized.

50 Grand stepped behind his turntables and pulled out two copies of *Ultimate Breaks and Beats, Volume 24*. He pressed the square button on both his Technics 1200 turntables and placed the needle on track four: The Emotions' "Blind Alley," widely known as the backing track for Big Daddy Kane's "Ain't No Half-Steppin.'" The breakbeat hit the speakers, a luscious groove with a ticklish piano melody. Wallace grabbed the mike and started rhyming like a man possessed. Not a single person in the room could take their eyes off him. He flowed over the beat with such command it was shocking. This didn't sound like an amateur who rapped as a hobby—his freestyles were as good, if not better, than anything on the radio. When he finally paused, 50 Grand looked up from his turntables.

"Let's make a tape," 50 Grand suggested.

Wallace shrugged.

"Why not? Fuck it."

Hearing his voice played back on a tape, even if it was just for kicks, tickled Christopher. He might have told his friends he didn't want to be an MC. He might even have believed it sometimes. But he couldn't help himself. When he wasn't out on the corner, he'd be back in his bedroom blasting his cassette player, either stuff he taped off the radio, cassettes he bought at the Wiz, or now his own voice. He didn't sound bad, either. Not bad at all.

DJ Mister Cee shook his head.

Wallace and DJ 50 Grand linked up one afternoon in 50's basement. "I get busy, son," Big said. So they made a tape.

If only he had a nickel for every person who came up to him backstage or at the barbershop, talking about how they'd discovered the next big rap star. It was a cliché. Now here was his neighbor, DJ 50 Grand, saying the same thing.

"I'm telling you," 50 Grand said. "Biggie is nice. You need to check this kid."

"A'ight. A'ight," said Mister Cee, who was about to go on tour with Big Daddy Kane. "When we get back, I'll listen to it then," he said, blowing 50 Grand off.

The tour ended on September 23, 1991. Mister Cee was barely back in his house for an hour when he heard the knock on his door again. It was 50 Grand.

"I ain't even unpack yet!" Mister Cee protested. But 50 had the tape in his hand, and he was clearly on a mission.

"Just listen to it," said 50.

Cee popped it in the deck and turned up the volume. The beat came on. And five seconds later, Mister Cee couldn't breathe.

He wasn't even in his apartment anymore.

Just like that it was 1985 and he was a 17-year-old kid at Sarah J. Hale High School in Brooklyn, pounding his fist on a table to keep rhythm while his best friend, Antonio Hardy, captivated the crowd with his rhythmic gift of gab. Everyone knew Hardy was nice, but Cee saw something special. He witnessed the birth of Big Daddy Kane.

The voice coming out of his speakers was a little higher than Kane's baritone, but damn, if it didn't give Cee the same chills. And it had the nerve to ride Kane's beat as well as Kane did. Cee couldn't stop playing it. He rewound it over and over, and each time it got better.

"I always felt like it was just inevitable for me to have heard that tape," Mister Cee said later. "Because of all the things that was involved in it. Bed-Stuy Brooklyn. Rhymin' over the 'Blind Alley.' It was a message from God that I had to hear that tape. I just really believe that."

When Cee looked up at 50 Grand, he was damn near teary eyed.

"Yo, I gotta meet this dude," he said.

A few weeks later, 50 and Christopher Wallace showed up on Mister Cee's doorstep on Gates and Bedford. The future of hardcore hip hop wore a dirty white T-shirt, boots, and some grungy black jeans. Cee thought he looked "grimy, hungry." He didn't waste too much time with small talk.

"I'm gonna try to get you a deal," he said. "I said I can't make any promises to you, but I'm gonna try to make some things happen for you."

Wallace looked at Mister Cee skeptically, sizing him up.

"Yo, you know, man, you know, don't be promising me nuttin', Duke. You can't do nuttin' for me, just tell me straight up, man," he said. "Don't try to gas me."

"That was like the first thing he said to me," Mister Cee recalled. "Before even saying 'What up.' Those was his first words to me."

Unbeknownst to Mister Cee, Wallace had tried working on a demo with Daddy-O from the group Stetsasonic, who lived right around the corner. Wallace had respect for Daddy-O, but for whatever reason, things didn't work out. And Mister Cee was catching the brunt of it.

Big Daddy Kane's DJ Mister Cee was knocked out by Big's demo. "It was a message from God that I had to hear that tape," he says.

"Listen, man, don't be promising me nothing. If you can't do it, just say you can't do it," Wallace told Mister Cee. He could take getting shot at, but not shot down. Making a tape for his friends on the Avenue was one thing. Risking rejection and ridicule was something else.

"I wanna re-create the demo," Mister Cee said. "I have some equipment here. What I wanna do is re-create the demo. I wanna redo it. Record it in my house. Make it nice and clean. And try to present it to *The Source* for their 'Unsigned Hype' situation or whatever."

Wallace looked at Mister Cee and made a spot judgment. He decided that he was going to trust him. "Whatever, whatever you wanna do," Wallace said in his deep voice. "You know. Whatever." He knew there was a risk, but Cee's enthusiasm seemed genuine. And he wasn't asking him for anything.

Mister Cee sent the tape to Matteo Capoluongo, one of the editors at *The Source*. Writing under the name Matty C, he started a column called "Unsigned Hype," and he knew talent when he heard it. Artists who appeared in his column had a nasty habit of becoming superstars. An MC from Chicago by the name of Common Sense sent in his stuff and soon landed a deal with Relativity. Mobb Deep, DJ Shadow, and DMX were some of the up-and-comers whose eventual success came as no surprise to those who read Matty C's column.

As soon as he heard Biggie Smalls, he knew it was something special.

"Biggie was like Kane reincarnated to me," Capoluongo said. "It was like the essence of the classic hip hop feeling I got when I first heard Kane."

Capoluongo raved about the tape. He played it for anyone who came by his office. He couldn't stop talking about it.

Before he left his magazine job to become an A&R rep for Loud Records, other talent scouts would call him to see which aspiring rappers were ready for prime time. In those days, just knowing that a rapper was featured in "Unsigned Hype" was enough to generate a buzz that could get him signed. Some A&R reps learned the hard way that not calling Capoluongo to hear a tape featured in his column meant missing out on a potentially career-breaking artist.

The Washington, D.C., native had written about these two kids from Queens called Poetical Prophets, and he gave their demo to his friend Bönz Malone, a writer for *Spin* magazine who had just gotten an A&R job at Island Records. Malone loved the hardcore duo and signed them under the name Mobb Deep. There was only one problem—this other A&R kid liked the group, too. He was pissed that someone else had gotten to them first.

The A&R kid couldn't afford to make the same mistake twice. Rap stars were here today, gone this evening. You never knew who would be the next cat to heat up the street. So the second he heard about the demo featuring Biggie Smalls and his DJ 50 Grand, he picked up the phone and called *The Source*.

Reminding Matty about Mobb Deep, the A&R kid asked, "What else you got?"

"I got some other things," Capoluongo said.

"Why don't you come up here?" said the A&R kid. "We should meet."

So Capoluongo went to this kid's office. He was sitting behind a large desk with a television tuned to MTV. He nodded when Matty came in, but barely looked up from his sushi. He acted as if he wasn't the one who initiated the meeting.

After some quick but stiff pleasantries, Capoluongo played him the tape that Mister Cee gave him. The kid listened to it, nodding his head, but not revealing any emotion one way or the other.

Then the tape shut off. There was silence in the room for a moment. The A&R kid smiled. Suddenly he seemed more laid back.

"What does he look like?" was the first question out of his mouth.

"Well," Matty said after a brief pause, "he's fat. He's a big guy."

"How big?" the kid asked. "Heavy D big? Or Fat Boys big?"

"Call Mister Cee. You have to meet him."

The guy wasn't even signed yet, and already this A&R kid was thinking about how to market what he'd heard.

That would always be Sean "Puffy" Combs's special genius.

The revolution will not be televised—it will be marketed. And people close to Combs saw—from as far back as 1988, when he was a 19-year-old freshman at Howard University—that he was the Huey P. Newton of hip hop hustle.

That famous photograph, with Newton sitting in a wicker chair wearing a leather jacket and beret, a rifle in one hand and a spear in the other, was a more effective recruiting tool for the Black Panther Party than any rally, speech, or 10-point platform the organization could ever put out. Combs, too, would learn the power of using an image. His first lesson started with, of all things, a real revolutionary situation on Howard University's campus—a student takeover.

"They wanted to put David Duke on our board of directors," remembered Combs's college friend (and future employee) Deric "D-Dot" Angelettie. Actually, it was not the former Klansman, but Lee Atwater, a key Republican strategist for George Bush Senior's presidential campaign. Atwater may have had a soft spot

Biggie and his DJ's first exposure came in the March 1992 edition of *The Source*'s "Unsigned Hype" column. Sean "Puffy" Combs read the article and picked up the phone.

for the blues, but as the architect of the racially divisive Willie Horton ad, he was not thought of as an ally for black folks.

Founded in 1866, Howard was the largest, most prestigious historically black university in the nation. The concept of a right-wing politico being part of such an institution didn't go over well with the student body. Students had other grievances, too: Some wanted changes to the curriculum and complained about the facilities. They didn't want to wait for an institutional response. Compromise was not an option.

"So," remembered Angelettie, "we took over the school."

Led by Ras Baraka, son of the famed black revolutionary author (and Howard alumnus) Amiri Baraka, a group of students escorted people out of the administration building, padlocked the doors, and drew up a list of demands. They had seized the nerve center where all the school's academic and financial records were kept, effectively bringing Howard to a standstill. They could hear the security guards outside, preparing to take back the building, so they seized their moment.

"A group of us went on the roof, with our hands in the air," Angelettie recalled. "We got sticks, we got bats—some of us had chains around our necks. And some-one took a picture."

The whole thing was documented; there were dramatic photographs of police storming the building and hauling students out. Combs, who had not taken part in the protest, made a montage of all the images and printed up posters.

"He made hundreds of them, and sold them for ten and fifteen dollars apiece," Angelettie recalled, sucking his teeth. "That's the type of nigga I saw. All this protest shit is well and good, but who's getting paid off of it?" Angelettie laughed at the memory. "He was ready."

Combs was born ready. The sporting life was in his blood.

Few hustlers want their sons in the game. They want them to own the team one day, to have the money and the influence to trade pieces around the chessboard, like so many sacrificial pawns. Otherwise, why even play?

The goal is to have their family legacy and illicit money purified by the actions of sons with clean hands. It worked out that way for former bootlegger Joe Kennedy, as his sons John, Robert, and Edward made famous inroads in politics. And surely Melvin Combs wanted his son Sean Jean Combs, born November 4, 1969, to soar to heights he would never be able to achieve himself.

"Pretty Melvin" was known for his style and his laughter. He had a fur coat so long that it reached his ankles and he made sure his beautiful wife, Janice, a fashion catalog model, never lacked for stylish clothes or jewelry.

"He was a street man, a hustling man," Janice Combs said about her husband.

"We met at a party in the Bronx. He used to love to dance. We used to crack up on him because he thought he was the baddest thing."

Melvin had much greater ambitions than driving his cab—some of them admittedly dangerous. But he felt the inherent risks were worth it. Harlem's favorite son was out there making moves on Lenox Avenue so that his progeny would never have to.

So when Melvin Combs was discovered murdered on January 26, 1972, in Central Park, dead from a point-blank gunshot wound, Janice Combs made a decision. After identifying the body, she made up her mind that Sean, and the daughter kicking in her belly, Keisha, would never know how their father died.

If they asked, Sean and Keisha would be told that their father was a businessman who died in a tragic car accident.

She also decided that her two kids would never want for anything. Even though she only had a high-school degree, she'd work three jobs if she had to. No welfare or public housing. Sean would go to the best schools, and he'd never, ever end up anywhere close to the elements that killed her husband.

Sean, nicknamed Puffy by childhood friends because of the way he would huff and puff when he didn't get his way, was raised a charmed child. By the time he was eight, he was a model in print ads for Baskin-Robbins, and had appeared in *Essence* magazine, which was edited by one of Janice's lifelong friends from the neighborhood, Susan Taylor. He was the kind of happy kid who loved the spotlight—who danced harder than anyone else at family gatherings and house parties, who couldn't resist mugging for the camera when anyone wanted to take a picture—just like his father.

The family still lived in Harlem, but they moved in with Janice's mother to a middle-class apartment complex, Esplanade Gardens, filled with retirees and frugal professionals. Of course, the street was still out there, never far away, but Sean never saw much of it, as far as his mother knew. But Sean did hear the music coming out of clubs like the famous Harlem World near where he lived. He also heard his friends in grade school talking about what went on at the parties, relating tales told to them by their older brothers and sisters.

By the early '80s Janice had relocated the family to Mount Vernon, a Westchester County suburb about half an hour north of New York City. Congested streets, glass-littered concrete, and the sound of children splashing around in water from an open fire hydrant were replaced by wide-open vistas, manicured lawns, and the sound of children splashing around in backyard pools.

The house they moved into was nice enough, but it didn't have a pool. Sean wanted a pool more than anything in the world. The white kids across the street all had pools.

"They would never invite me over," Combs said. "I used to cry. My moms made sure that she got me a pool that was two times bigger than theirs. It took her like a year to save for it, and it was the only Christmas gift—no socks, nothing."

Soon water wasn't enough. Janice Combs always gave her son the best, but he always wanted more. He had this urge, this thirst, that he could never explain, to be in the mix, to stir things up, to earn his own money his own way.

During lunchtime at Mount St. Michael Academy in the Bronx, the Catholic school his mother sent him to, Sean made a habit of asking other students for fifty cents. By the end of the lunch period he'd have several dollars in his pocket—along with the lunch money his mother had given him. He worked in restaurants, amusement parks, anywhere to earn an extra buck. In Mount Vernon, even though he was too young to have a paper route, he figured out a way to falsify his birth date, and then he hired other kids to take on other routes and collected a percentage of their earnings, managing them so to speak.

"I could get anything I wanted on campus," Combs said of his years at Howard University. "If I needed an English paper, I knew where to go. If I needed some weed, I knew where to get it."

He had to mix it up.

And on those occasions when he'd go back to Harlem to visit his grandmother and to hang out with childhood friends who would eventually become his bodyguards—guys like Anthony "Wolf" Jones and Paul "Big Paul" Offord—he'd hear stories about "Pretty Melvin."

"As I got older, I knew about street life, so I knew who was hustlers," Combs said. "I would constantly hear how good everybody was living back in those days—furs, and how we was the only people in Harlem to have a Mercedes-Benz, and all that. And I also started hearing other stuff from other people. When I started putting two and two together, I was like 'Come on, man, my pops was hustling or something.'"

The *New York Times* laid out the details of his father's death in stark, terse terms. And Combs began asking more questions. His father, one of New York's biggest hustlers, shot in the head. Central Park West. Uptown.

"All the stories I heard about him—he was a good man and all that—he was hustling," Combs eventually realized. "He was running numbers or selling drugs or whatever. He wasn't known as a gangsta."

Combs suddenly had a newfound fascination with the street life he had always been sheltered from. It was a part of his legacy. And like a whole generation of "haves" before him, he suddenly had an interest in the "have-nots," especially now that he knew he was remotely connected to the street.

"The majority of kids in the suburbs was made, you know," Combs said. "Their parents made them a certain way. These kids from the ghetto had no choice. They didn't have shit, but they were real."

That was the thing he loved about hip hop: the realness. It was gritty, wild music, and it was getting wilder all of the time.

As Puff became a teenager, the music was beginning to come of age: Boogie Down Productions, Eric B. & Rakim, Big Daddy Kane. Street kids were becoming millionaires off crack, and uptown hustlers like Rich Porter, AZ, and Alpo ran the streets in this new crack/hip hop economy.

The music had also gone further underground. No longer was it important for artists to cross over like Run-D.M.C. and get a song played on the radio. Street and mix-tape respect meant everything. And the realest things were happening in New York City clubs like the Latin Quarter and the Red Parrot, and perhaps the most famous of all, the Rooftop in Harlem.

And Puff was right there, sneaking out of the house, getting in the mix, trying to be down. Fronting—and getting over.

"Parties at the Rooftop—that shit was one of the most incredible experiences ever," Combs recalled. "This was when crack first came out—niggas fourteen and fifteen riding around in jeeps with the tops off. If you wasn't hustling, you wasn't on the list. I wasn't hustling," he added, "but I had to make sure my gear was up to par."

Dances like the wop, that serpentine side-to-side move, originated at the Rooftop. "You'd have niggas wop like you've never seen niggas wop," Combs recalled. "We talking about some shit that looked like a fuckin' African dance."

He was beginning to realize his goal: to find the bridge between the Polo-and-Birkenstocks world of his private Catholic school and the Fila-and-Dapper-Dan realm of the Harlem streets he so much wanted to be a part of. One thing was certain—all the kids were listening to the same music. Even if they couldn't get into the same parties, their radios were tuned to DJ Red Alert, "Mr. Magic's Rap Attack," and the Awesome Two.

Music was the bridge. And if people couldn't cross between the worlds on that bridge yet, Combs was going to figure out the way to entice them across.

Handsome, fresh-dressed, and armed with a bright smile, Combs became popular on Howard's campus from the moment of his arrival in the fall of 1987. He had a special charm from the start, a way of doing things. He attracted people to him, and knew how to get them to do things for him.

"Puff would have *GQ* magazines, you know?" said Ron "Amen-Ra" Lawrence, another fellow Howard student from New York who was ahead of Combs.

"Even at his early stages, you could see his fashion," said Lawrence. "Every time I saw Puff he had on something slick. If it wasn't a shirt and tie, he had on a slick suit, and then he would flip and then he'd be rocking some hip hop shit. The way he's doing it now? He was doing it that way back then."

"I could get anything I wanted on campus," Sean Combs said about his years at Howard. "If I needed an English paper, I knew where to go. If I needed an exam or some weed, I knew where to get it."

Combs came to Howard to study business, but was quickly learning more outside the classroom than in it. He thought fast on his feet—especially on the dance floor—learning all sorts of valuable lessons in the club that he would later apply to the music business. He also began assembling the crew that would transform all of them into millionaires in a few years.

Ron Lawrence grew up with Salt-N-Pepa's producer Hurby "Luv Bug" Azor—and had his own aspirations for getting into the music business. Musically he was advanced—beyond his conservative looks.

"Ron was the bookworm producer guy, he wasn't the party-throwing guy," said Capoluongo, who would occasionally return from NYU to go home to Washington, D.C., for Howard University parties. "He was the first guy on Howard's campus to have an SP1200 drum machine."

"It wasn't an SP1200, it was an MPC-60," Lawrence said, laughing. He taught himself what he needed to know and soon he was building beats. "It was all trial and error," he admits. "When you read those manuals, it was Chinese."

Whatever he learned, he started teaching to Angelettie, who was a DJ back in Brooklyn. Howard was in need of a hipness injection, and Angelettie wanted to be the one to administer it.

"When I got down there, it was a lot of New York people, but it wasn't a lot of hip people there. Like, you know what I mean? Like, you have people from Detroit and California and Miami and the South and they all had their cliques," Angelettie said.

"Even within the New York clique, we had the hardcore characters—the characters who smoked chronic and wanted to hang out every night. Then you had the New York clique that was, like, half and half. Some of them rolled with us, but some of them were real book smart and you had the ones that didn't fuck with us at all. We hung with different people, you know?"

Although he should have been in class, Angelettie spent most of his freshman year trying to make a scene. He'd mess with girls, wake up late, and barely make it to class. But he did have his turntables. And slowly but surely, he was getting hired to DJ for the parties thrown by the black fraternities and sororities on campus.

It was at one of those parties during his sophomore year, that he first met the freshman Combs. Already Puffy was his trademark flamboyant self.

"You know you always had them guys that do all the dancing?" Angelettie said. "He was one of those dudes. Puffy's in the middle of the dance floor getting all the young big-booty chicks on his dick because he's dancing and doing flips. Him and his partner, they're doing all that dancing shit."

Angelettie and Combs kept running into each other. It became clear that they had similar attitudes about music, and both were extremely popular. They decided to join forces and promote parties together. They formed "A Black Man and a Puerto Rican Productions." Combs stacked the deck by inviting some of the biggest rap celebrities of the day to his parties, people like Heavy D, Guy, Slick Rick, and Doug E. Fresh. Other New York kids at Howard came around, too—future business partners like Chucky Thompson, Mark Pitts, and Don Pooh. And Puffy's syndicate was not content with just promoting parties. Angelettie and Harve Pierre used to rhyme against each other in the Blackburn Rec Center. Lawrence eventually formed a group with him called Two Kings and a Cipher.

Soon, the guys who used to run the party scene in D.C., Todd Johnson and Maynard Clark, were a thing of the past. It got to the point where if any major rap artist was coming through to Washington, Puff and his crew threw the hottest after-party. Sometimes the after-parties were liver than the concerts themselves.

Combs got up every Thursday by 5 A.M. to catch the morning train from Washington to New York City to be at his unpaid internship by 10 A.M. Things got so tight he'd hide in the bathroom for hours to avoid the conductors.

"We had our own club every Friday night," Angelettie remembered. "We rented a church basement and called it The Asylum." Their breakthrough came when the students asked them to throw Howard's biggest-ever homecoming party.

"We had over 8,000 kids come to this Masonic temple with a fence around it," Angelettie recalled. "We only had one entrance in. Kids were literally climbing up the fence, crawling in through the second-floor windows trying to come downstairs into the main room." That's when the fire marshal showed up.

Angelettie and Combs tried to reason with him. "We looked outside and there's a potential for us to make another $25,000, $30,000 easy. We're charging $30 or $40 a person because it's ridiculous in there. Some kids are paying $50 or $70 just to get into the joint. We both got on our knees and begged. The fire marshal was like, 'Nah, it's over.'"

But it was just getting started.

At the parties, Combs and crew studied what kids from different parts of the country were wearing, what kind of music they responded to. He learned how to approach them, how to make them react. The parties were just as important to their careers as the morning lectures they often slept through. Every gathering offered lessons about specialized marketing and promotion that would make them richer than they would have been had they become the doctors, lawyers, and accountants that their parents sent them to Howard to become.

Howard University would soon become to the hip hop business what Harvard was to Hollywood sitcom writers and Stanford to the burgeoning internet entrepreneurial class. Pierre, Lawrence, Angelettie, Thompson, Myrick, and Pooh not only became some of Combs's first employees when he launched his own record label, they also became, in their own right, some of the most influential producers, A&R executives, and artist managers in black music.

"We learned that if you touch one person, this person can reach at least a thousand others," Angelettie said. "We learned how to make fliers and our fliers went from real cheap to getting sexier. We learned a lot about marketing. That's why Puffy's parties are still the shit, because we learned what attracts. What do women want to hear? You know, how do the speakers sound? Should we have balloons? Should we have candles? All that shit came from just watching people."

And Combs always thought big.

"It was something he really wanted," remembered Ron Lawrence. "He was like, 'You know, one day I'm gonna have a record company.' And at the time you'd be, like, 'Yeah right.' It was hard to see the vision because everybody was either an MC or a DJ. Nobody was thinking about being president of a record company. For him to be thinking that far ahead . . ." Lawrence said, sounding awestruck. "Man."

The first thing Combs had to do was to learn, up close, exactly how a record company was run. It was through a fellow Mount Vernon resident, rapper Heavy D, that Combs first met Andre Harrell, the CEO and founder of Uptown Records—a Harlem man who would teach him everything he needed to know about making hit records.

Harrell—who started out as the first half of the old-school rap duo Dr. Jeckyll and Mr. Hyde—realized very early that he was never going to be a superstar. He decided that the real power was backstage. He took a job working as a $200-a-week assistant for Russell Simmons, the man who once managed him. At one point the two shared an apartment in Lefrak City Housing complex in Queens.

They had very different approaches to the music, in part because they came from different backgrounds—Harrell from the Bronxdale Projects and Simmons from a suburban home in Hollis, Queens. But their ongoing friendly argument gave each a better understanding of what motivated the other.

"My shit was the fly shit," Harrell explained. "His shit was more alternative."

When Simmons founded Def Jam Records with Rick Rubin in 1985, it became the first rap label to get national distribution from a major label. As a result, "alternative" was beginning to encroach on the mainstream—Def Jam was the first to truly break New York rap on a national level. LL Cool J, Slick Rick, the Beastie Boys, 3rd Bass, and Public Enemy were all Def Jam

Sean "Puffy" Combs as an eager young intern at Uptown Records, reporting to his mentor Andre Harrell (seated) in 1992. Even back then, Combs knew how to dress like a CEO.

artists. Run of Run-D.M.C. was Russell's little brother. Eric B. & Rakim, DJ Jazzy Jeff and the Fresh Prince, and most of the other hot rappers in the business were managed by Russell and his partner Lyor Cohen. Simmons had built a one-stop shop for hip hop.

Harrell says, "My shit is more Harlem, and his shit it way more Queens. Where Queens is 'Be like me! I'm the shit!' and 'We gonna shoot up the party.' And Harlem is more like 'We gonna scoop up the bitches and take care of this business.'"

When Harrell founded Uptown a year later, in 1986, the same Harlem-vs.-Queens style differences separated their visions.

Where Simmons's genius was pushing the raw, uncut funk to the masses, whether they were ready for it or not, Harrell's vision had nothing to do with capturing ghetto reality.

"When you're from the projects, you want to see the good life," Harrell explained. "You want style and you want glamour. You want champagne, caviar, fancy cars, and beautiful women. I wanted to make records that would get a pretty girl to dance with you at two A.M. even if you weren't great-looking. Girl-meets-boy, boy-meets-girl records."

The trouble was that by the mid-'80s, most kids with any taste were into rap; R&B was pretty much dead. Jimmy Jam and Terry Lewis had their Minneapolis sound but that was "adult" music for people in their mid- to-late twenties. Prince, another Minneapolis native, was considered by many young black folks to be a "rock and roll" artist because he played electric guitar and his singles didn't hit hard enough on the urban dance floor. Michael Jackson was becoming irrelevant, too. His increasingly ghoulish appearance alienated the millions of young black kids who were devoted to him during the *Off the Wall* and *Thriller* years. New York had Full Force, a family unit of artists and producers who could do both rap and R&B. They made fun, sexy hits with Lisa Lisa & Cult Jam, but they were already signed to exclusive deals elsewhere. Harrell was convinced that there had to be someone else.

That someone was Teddy Riley. A native of Harlem's St. Nicholas projects, Riley learned guitar by ear at the age of three. By ten he was holding concerts in the project courtyard with a Casio keyboard. As a teenager, he was producing records for Kool Moe Dee and Doug E. Fresh in his apartment studio. Riley's breakthrough was the invention of a sound called new jack swing: It had all the rhythmic grittiness of rap smoothed out with fat synthesized keyboards and simulated horn sounds. Like hip hop, it was electronic, futuristic, and hard-hitting, yet it was all syncopated to classic swing beats.

"I used to see artists a little differently from Russell," Harrell said. "He thought the sound that Teddy Riley was making was the commercial side of hip hop—or not authentic hip hop. I thought it was a Harlem glamorous slick side. It was hip hop that could also be R&B."

When Andre Harrell couldn't convince Russell Simmons to sign Dwight Myers, a.k.a. Heavy D—a fat but charismatic MC from Mount Vernon—Harrell quit his best friend's company and funded Heavy's first release by himself.

"Andre used to try to tell me he's a sex symbol," Simmons recalled. "I said, 'Nigga, there's no girl wanna give Heavy D no pussy.' "

Harrell founded Uptown Records, teamed Heavy D with Riley, and suddenly "The Overweight Lover" was in the house. Heavy D was Harrell's dream artist because he was suave and well spoken, the kind of guy who would rock your block party but at the same time you could introduce to your sister. He even made it seem cool to be fat. With the Fat Boys, obesity was something to be made fun of, but Heavy D let people see that large guys had style, too.

By the time Heavy D introduced Harrell to Puffy, Uptown was on the upswing. It was 1988, and Heavy D & The Boyz were riding high and Teddy Riley's vocal trio Guy was in the studio working on the follow-up to their multiplatinum debut. Uptown had also secured a rich manufacturing and distribution pact with MCA. Combs was eager to get in the mix any way he could.

"He called me Mr. Harrell, even though I asked him to call me Andre," said Harrell. "The first thing I asked him to do was get me a tape from the studio. He came back with it in five minutes. The studio was ten blocks away."

Combs got up every Thursday by 5 A.M. to catch the morning train from Washington to New York City to be at his unpaid internship by 10 A.M. Things got so tight that he'd even hide in the bathroom for hours at a time to avoid the conductors. No humiliation was too daunting for Combs. He'd wash cars, get sandwiches, and stand at attention in his button-up shirt and polka-dot ties.

"I didn't give a fuck," Combs said. "I was at Uptown."

At first he was Mr. Polite—the best intern Harrell had ever had. Attentive, quiet, and hardworking, Combs's "Puffy" persona had yet to raise its head in the corporate offices. He took the Michael Ovitz/David Geffen/Bernie Brillstein approach to being an intern—all of those multimillionaires had worked their way up from the William Morris Agency's mailroom to become titans in the business. They knew as did Puffy that delivering packages and other "menial" duties gave them access to everyone. They got an inside view of how companies worked—and where all the bodies were buried.

"I did everything," Combs said. "I drove Andre's car. If they needed something delivered, I would take a cab instead of a subway and pay for it out of my own pocket. I knew it was the place to be."

Combs soon realized that sneaking on trains to get back and forth from Howard's campus to promote parties wasn't where it was at. What was the point of going back to D.C. so he could pretend to pay attention during business administration classes? It was time to step in the arena and make real moves, which was what he'd been doing from day one at college anyway.

Like a fly on the wall, Combs would just watch, absorbing everything. He made lasting friendships with music producers and fellow Mount Vernon homeboys like Eddie F, Dave Hall, and Pete Rock. He moved into a room at Andre Harrell's plush house in New Jersey, giving him the opportunity to rub shoulders with celebrities and influential executives like Russell Simmons, Benny Medina, and "Fly Ty" Williams.

Privately, Combs would talk about his ability to spot hits, but in his humble position he had few opportunities to prove his ear. Only A&R people got to make those kinds of moves. So he waited—and good things came to him.

Four hungry, haggard kids staggered into Uptown Records' office one summer morning in 1990 with three cassette tapes full of songs in their hands. Their eyes were bloodshot and they smelled—symptoms of living in their car. They were two sets of brothers, Cedric "K-Ci" and Joel "Jo-Jo" Hailey and Donald "Devante" and Mr. Dalvin DeGrate from Charlotte, North Carolina. They didn't even have an appointment, and just happened to be lucky enough to have Heavy D hear them as they stood in the lobby harmonizing, practicing for their shot. Heavy rushed to Andre's office, Harrell heard them, and signed them on the spot.

Kurt Woodley, Uptown's A&R director, wasn't as blown away by the brothers, who were known as Jodeci. The group was quickly relegated to the state of limbo from which many signed artists never emerge, called "development."

All that began to change the moment Woodley resigned from his position to take a job at a rival label; Combs asked Harrell for the departing executive's job.

"I am your demographic," Combs told him.

The pitch worked, and Puff the A&R kid was born. He wasn't even old enough to legally buy a drink, and already Combs was a mover and a shaker. His success bred jealousy among others at Uptown—and marked the beginning of the "player hating" that Diddy still deals with more than a decade later. But more than anything, Combs was thankful for the opportunity, and he worked tirelessly to prove that there was an actual fire of talent behind all the Puffy smoke.

His first assignment was to shepherd Father MC's debut album through the pop music market. Father fit the Uptown mode of R&B-flavored nonconfrontational rap, but had only a fraction of Heavy D's talent. That didn't stop Combs from making decisions that led to a gold single and opened other doors.

For Father MC's hit single "Treat 'Em Like They Want to Be Treated," Puffy brought in Jodeci to sing on the chorus. On another song, "I'll Do 4 U," he enlisted the talents of another singer who'd been signed during the Woodley administration and was now languishing in the background—Mary J. Blige. Buoyed by a slamming Cheryl Lynn sample and Blige's sultry vocals, an otherwise forgettable song became a Top 20 hit.

As Combs began to amass power and authority, "Puff Daddy" was born. Making moves inside both the recording and styling studios, Puff produced a string of successful acts and gradually transformed Uptown's somewhat uptight image into something more urgent—and urban.

With Jodeci, the challenge was to transform four "countrified" young men who grew up singing in church down South into the hottest vocal quartet on the East Coast. Out went the Boone's Farm apple wine—in came the 40-ounce bottles of malt liquor. Since they had nowhere to stay, Puff had them put up in a Bronx housing project so they could absorb some flavor.

In terms of image, his assistant turned stylist extraordinaire Sybil Pennix suggested that he dress the guys in back-turned baseball caps, overalls, baggy jeans, and boots. Jodeci would do for R&B what Run-D.M.C. did for rap—they dressed like their audience. It wasn't about wearing clothes that fans couldn't afford—not yet at least. To get the teenage listeners, Puff wanted Jodeci to appear as if they'd just walked in off of 125th Street. They were speaking to the crowd as a part of the crowd—not from some lofty perch above them.

With the music, the approach was equally simple—and brilliant. When the time came to remix the group's first single, "Come and Talk to Me," Combs did something that seemed radical at the time but has now become commonplace. Instead of using the original backing track, he had one of his producers sample EPMD's underground smash "You're a Customer." The group's vocals didn't change a bit—just the beat. The result was instant street cred—an R&B record that slammed so hard even the staunchest hip hop head had to respect it.

Puff Daddy was the pioneer of hip hop soul—a simple but profound innovation that matched R&B vocals with unadulterated rap beats. The concept of blending R&B and rap was nothing new on the underground—DJs like Ron G and Kid Capri had been doing variations of it for years on mix tapes. But no one ever thought to record these hybrids in the studio, press them up, and turn them into hits.

Combs couldn't operate a mixing board or program a drum machine, but he spent so much time in the studio he learned exactly how to capture the exact sound he wanted.

"I'm more like an orchestrator," he explained. "You know those guys who don't actually play the violin? They just tell the violinist what they want to hear? Same with me. I say to my programmer, make the drums go ba-boom ba-boom and he sets the computer up to do it. I sing the chords I want to the piano player and hum a rhythm to the bass player. Pretty soon we got a song."

He was also an orchestrator of parties. His hits were climbing up the charts, so he needed a place to dance to them. He began holding weekly jams at a mid-town Manhattan nightclub called the Red Zone. (The DJ spot was held down by a DJ named Funkmaster Flex.) The party became so popular it was almost a second job for Puffy. And with fights breaking out on the dance floor, the whole thing started to become too hectic.

"I didn't want party promotion to become the main thing in my life," Combs said. Especially not when things were going so well at Uptown. His relationship with Harrell grew into almost a father/son bond, with Harrell filling that void in Combs's life.

"My moms was driving me crazy," Combs said. "Andre let me live at his house. Right before he moved out, I put a hole in the wall, which cost 30 grand to fix. Then he let me live at his house in Alpine, New Jersey. I mean I was 20 years old, living in a mansion with a bad-ass pool."

Combs sometimes got wild, threw temper tantrums, and acted like a spoiled child. "The whole company hated me," Combs admitted. "People were like, 'Dre created a monster.' I was aggressive. I would trash the office. I'd call Andre a wimp and a house nigga." But Puffy's bad-boy behavior was indulged as long as the hits kept coming. Andre always seemed to understand where Combs was coming from, no matter what he did.

Magic Johnson shocked the world in October 1991 when he announced that he was retiring from basketball because he'd tested HIV-positive. In December of that year, Combs and Heavy D decided to organize a celebrity basketball game to benefit AIDS charities. The goal was to raise money and HIV awareness while promoting Uptown artists. It was a good idea, but things got way out of hand.

A teenage Wallace rocking the mike at a street-corner jam in Brooklyn. Though he called rap a "hobby," Big slaughtered all competition.

Heavily promoted on radio and by word of mouth, the game turned into a bigger event than anyone ever imagined. There were too many people and not enough police at the Nat Holman Gym at City College in Harlem. Organizers closed the doors in an attempt to sort out paying customers from those who still needed tickets, but it quickly became a bum rush.

"People started jumping down the staircase," said Combs. "People started piling on top of each other and glass started breaking in the doors. People started getting scared and running. Pushing and pushing. It was more pressure. And we started seeing some scary shit."

By the time it was all over, nine people were dead. Combs had blood on his hands—literally—from trying to save people who had been trampled, as well as attempting to revive some victims with mouth-to-mouth resuscitation. "I'm seeing my girlfriend bugging out because her best friend is there not breathing and I'm trying to give her mouth to mouth," Combs recalled. "And I start to feel this feeling in the breath I'm getting back that people were dead. I can feel the death going into me. Later I went home and I kept saying to myself that it was all a bad dream. That I was going to wake up. But I never woke up."

As Combs panicked, Harrell flew back from his vacation in Barbados, hired famed attorney William Kunstler, and helped his young apprentice regroup. While no criminal charges were filed against the organizers, Combs was haunted by the incident. "I started to lose it," he said. "I felt like I didn't wanna even live no more. I was so fuckin' sad. The lawyer's advice was not to go anywhere, not to talk to anybody. But I wanted to go to the wakes and the funerals and try to provide some comfort, even though I knew my presence probably wouldn't have given comfort. But what I was going through with the blame and stuff was nothing compared to what the families were going through."

Combs was sustained by the knowledge that others had it worse than he did. "If they had the strength to go on," he said, "I had the strength to go on and handle people looking at me, thinking whatever they gonna think."

He poured his pain into his work. On the surface, it might have looked like denial. But Puffy had made himself two promises: to do a better job of building his own empire, and to remember that life had to be lived to its fullest because nothing was promised. But before he could think about his own empire, there were still Uptown artists who needed his attention and expertise.

Mary J. Blige, a beautiful but tortured soul from the same rough-and-tumble section of Yonkers that spawned rappers like DMX and the Lox, had all the vocal chops in the world but no control, musically or otherwise. She sang beautifully, with a fierce attitude that was part church, part house party. Her voice spoke of a tough childhood and perhaps a broken heart along the way. When photographers asked her to be more open, more sexual, Blige toughened up like a tomboy. She wore boots and pulled her bent-brim baseball cap low over her eyes—masking shyness and vulnerability with an air of brooding toughness.

Instead of trying to dilute that attitude, Puff embraced it and turned it into Mary's trademark. Combs helped Blige become the patron saint of ghetto girls. She sang for all the 16-year-olds pushing baby strollers and the girls stuck doing nails and braids when they should have been finishing high school.

Her first song was "You Remind Me," a cut from a soundtrack album that was the only memorable thing about the movie *Strictly Business*. The single shot to No. 1 on *Billboard*'s R&B chart, and cracked the Top 40 on the pop singles chart while she was still living in the projects.

Her first single, the one that pumped all summer long during the summer of 1992, "Real Love," had a familiar backing track: the drums from Audio Two's seminal 1988 rap classic "Top Billin'." The sample was a line in the sand. This was hip hop soul—not R&B with a little hip hop "flavor." Instead of rapping over a breakbeat, Mary would sing over it. She had the sneer of a hardcore MC but the voice of an angel.

Puffy's genius was in melding the two in such a way that one genre did not subvert the integrity of the other. Her subsequent album, *What's the 411?*, featured cameos from Busta Rhymes—who was just beginning to emerge from his group, Leaders of the New School—and a title track with Grand Puba from Brand Nubian, on which Mary actually rapped. The hip hop beats on Mary's album felt organic, not like a sales gimmick. Perhaps that's why they did sell—moving two million copies at a brisk pace.

Both the Jodeci and Mary J. Blige albums were complete departures from the spit-and-polish "new money Negro" image that Andre Harrell had crafted for his company. They were also massive smashes, making Uptown a major force to be reckoned with, the jewel in MCA Records' crown. By the time Combs was 21 years old, he was named the vice president of A&R—the youngest boss in the industry. He had money, ghetto fame, and a white BMW to match.

But Combs was nowhere near satisfied. The problem with Uptown was that, even with all those R&B hits, none of the records Puffy was responsible for truly reflected the reality of what was going on in the clubs and the streets. He felt left out—and rightly so. Hip hop was in the midst of one of its most exciting periods ever, with the emergence since 1990 of Leaders of the New School such as Main Source, Nas, the Geto Boys, Brand Nubian, Cypress Hill, the Wu Tang Clan, and Snoop Doggy Dogg to name a few. Dope MCs were popping up like dandelions, and Puffy wanted to start weeding them out. He didn't yet have the juice, but he had an idea: Bad Boy Records. Bad Boy would be a satellite of Uptown, a sub-imprint where all the grimy niggas that didn't fit into Andre Harrell's idea of what an artist should be would find a home.

"I don't like no goody two-shoes shit," Puffy said when he was forming his company. "I like the sense of being in trouble. It's almost like a girl, y'know-hatumsayin'? Girls don't like no good niggas. Girls like bad boys."

Puffy wanted to make real street music, with real hardcore MCs, but stuff that would have a universal appeal—a mixture of thugs and hugs. It wasn't just about making compelling gangsta rap records—lots of people could do that. It was about an MC that represented the full package. It was about finding the next Big Daddy Kane or Rakim. Someone who had undeniable skills and true street appeal, but at the same time who could be marketed to the masses. Someone who sounded hard even when he was rhyming on a pop radio record. Combs had the vision thing all worked out. All he needed now was that mystery voice, that person who could set things off and put his fledgling company on the map.

Then Matty Capoluongo walked into his office one day with the tape that would change his future, and that of hip hop.

Puff didn't waste any time with small talk.

"Listen to this kid Biggie Smalls," Capoluongo said.

Before the end of the first verse, Combs knew he'd have to close the deal fast.

"He sounded like no other human being I ever heard in my life."

GIMME THE LOOT
(I'M A BAD BOY)

CHAPTER 4

66 Goodness gracious the papers!
Where the cash at? Where the stash at?
Nigga pass that . . . **99**

Mister Cee walked the three blocks from his apartment on Gates to the corner of Fulton with the frenzied enthusiasm of a man who has to pee and suddenly spots a restroom. He couldn't get there quick enough.

Wallace was standing on the corner as usual, in the middle of a Cee-Lo game, an L hanging from the corner of his mouth. D-Roc lamped against the wall, arms folded, watching everything and everybody. Wallace looked up from his dice-rolling crouch and smiled.

"Puffy liked the tape," Cee said.

"Puffy who?" Wallace asked.

Cee reminded Wallace of the March 1992 issue of *The Source*—the one that contained his "Unsigned Hype" write-up. In that same issue Heavy D had written a guest editorial expressing remorse over the deaths that occurred at the celebrity basketball benefit he and Puffy had organized. More important—for Wallace's purposes—Puffy was the man who could get him a deal with Uptown Records.

"Uptown?" Wallace said, shaking his head. "Heavy D and the Boyz? Guy? Jodeci?" He took a hit from the L and exhaled a thick cloud. "They ain't gonna know what to do with a nigga like me."

"Puff says he wants to try something new," Mister Cee insisted. "He wants to do hardcore shit. He was diggin' you, man."

Wallace stared at Cee for a second and then shrugged.

"Well, you know, I ain't gonna be doing no talkin' in the meeting," he said in a low voice. "You gon' do all the talkin'. I don't really know Duke and I ain't talking to him. *You* talk. You make everything happen."

True to his word, Wallace barely opened his mouth at the meeting.

Puffy Combs sat behind the desk in his smallish office with a few plaques on the walls while Mister Cee did most of the talking. In the other chair, dressed in standard Brooklyn guerrilla gear—army jacket and Timberland boots—sat Wallace, looking toward the window, toward the corner, everywhere but at Combs.

Combs, meanwhile, couldn't take his eyes off Wallace. He'd wondered what this Biggie dude would look like and now he knew. He was tall and a bit heavier than husky, with sullen but expressive eyes and rounded features. It wasn't a pretty face, but, as they say, beauty fades. This was the kind of guy whose silent presence would make people nervous coming out of the subway at night. But then again, Wallace had this mysterious charisma about him. What made him scary also made him appealing. He did not, at first glance, possess the "fuckability" Andre Harrell preferred his artists to have, but this cat had something else. Combs couldn't put his finger on it, but maybe Biggie could help him figure it out.

"Yo, man, could you kick a rhyme for me right now?" Combs asked.

"Yeah, man, you want me to kick a rhyme?" Wallace said nonchalantly.

Combs assured him that he did, then got up from his desk and closed the office door. Rocking a demo was one thing, but an MC's voice, flow, and presence would have to translate live and direct if he had any chance to become a real star.

And then Wallace started rhyming.

As soon as he opened his mouth, Christopher Wallace *became* Biggie. Sitting there silently, he seemed almost shy. But when he rhymed in that thick commanding voice, his shoulders lost their hunch, and the eyes that once looked at your shoes now pierced your soul. The transformation was instantaneous and breathtaking.

"I didn't want him to stop," Puff recalled afterward. "It just sounded so good and so refreshing."

But Wallace did stop, and Combs gulped. He tried his best to maintain a poker face. It was the only leverage he really had in this negotiation.

"I could have a record out on you by the summer," Combs said, sounding calm. "Would you be cool with that?"

Mister Cee smiled and Wallace just sat there, as cool as Combs wished he could be. This part of the game was like dating—the more you played hard to get, the more money would get spent in the long run.

"Well, you know, you know," said Wallace, mumbling offhandedly, "just talk to Cee, know what I'm sayin'? Whatever he wants to do, I'm down with."

It wasn't a resounding vote of confidence Combs might have hoped for, but it would have to do.

"I was thinking, Now how am I gonna market *him?*" Combs recalled. "My man looked like a liquor store robber. But damn he could *spit.*"

There was only one more hurdle before Wallace could join the Uptown Records family: a meeting with the Big Man himself, Andre Harrell.

A few weeks later, there they all were—Harrell, Combs, Mister Cee, and Wallace—

at Sylvia's on 125th Street. "I figure a big man likes to eat, let me give him some soul food," Combs recalled. Over a plate of short ribs and collard greens, Mister Cee talked about how Biggie was the future of hip hop. Harrell liked the demo, but he was still on the fence. And the artist was not helping matters at all. "He didn't eat," Combs recalled. "He didn't talk. He just sat there real quiet."

Lunch ended on an undecided note and then they all piled into a black Lincoln Town Car. While riding the 50 blocks back down to Uptown, Harrell decided to put Wallace to the test.

"Yo, Money, I want you to rhyme right now, in the car," said the CEO.

This time around, Mister Cee was prepared. "Can I put a beat in?" he asked.

Puff's T-shirt shows appreciation for Dre and Snoop's West Coast funk as Big kicks his '93 lyrics ruff, rugged, and raw.

"Sure," said Harrell. Cee passed him the cassette; he put it into the car stereo, and then Biggie started rhyming. The sullen Wallace persona was replaced with raw MC power. Harrell witnessed the transformation firsthand, and he was unable to keep his composure for more than a minute.

"Okay, Puffy will draw up the paperwork, and we'll get everything going," Harrell said. The business at hand was suddenly urgent.

Combs wasted no time hooking Biggie up to rhyme on the remix to Mary J. Blige's smash hit "Real Love." When Puff got hired to remix "Dolly My Baby" by the Jamaican dancehall don Super Cat, he had "Big Poppa" close the song with 16 bars of uncut Brooklyn funk. Wallace's friends on the block couldn't believe it—their boy was on the radio! It was all good, except for one thing: He wasn't making any ends. He wasn't so sure about the music game.

"It seemed like everything took forever," Wallace complained. "I was doing whatever I had to do, paying my dues with all the stuff they wanted me to do." When it came time to do his album, they'd have to do it his way. But even for these one-off jobs, the money was incredibly slow to come. And the real money, the money he expected to receive when he finalized his album deal with Uptown— that would take much longer. Meanwhile he was expected to wait by the phone, hoping that Puffy could work it all out so he could sign up and get that paper. Summer came and went, and Wallace still didn't have a record deal. He kept calling Puffy, keeping the pressure on. But he needed to figure something out, because he was about to get hit with a whole new set of pressures.

Voletta Wallace was sitting back on her bed, trying to relax after a long day at work when Christopher came into her room. It didn't matter how big her son grew; his large, expressive eyes always made him appear childlike to her.

"Yo, Ma."

She looked up at him. He looked like he wanted to say something but couldn't find the words.

"What," she said. "*What*, Christopher?"

"Jan's pregnant."

"I beg your pardon?" She sat up, blinking her eyes.

"She's pregnant."

Jesus Christ, she thought. "I thought you broke up," she said.

"We did."

He sat on the edge of the bed, saying nothing more. After a lingering silence, he turned to look at his mother.

"Is that your baby?"

"She say it's mine," he said. "It's mine."

She exhaled. "Christopher, can you afford a baby emotionally?"

"Of course I can," he said. His eyes glimmered with a sudden pride. Then, childlike again, he added: "If I can't take care of it emotionally, you can."

She stood up, her temper flaring.

"Christopher," she began, "what the hell are you going to do?"

"What you mean, what the hell am I gonna do?"

"When I was about to have you, I don't think I was ready to be a mother. But at least I had a job. I started planning for your future. What do you have?"

Wallace bristled. "I got a deal."

"Where is this deal? For weeks, you've talked about this deal. It's not cemented yet. You have to do something. Do you know what you're going to do?"

Wallace knew what he had to do—although he wasn't going to tell his mother. He would go get his hustle on for real. He didn't want to do it, but he just wasn't cut out for a "May I take your order, please?" type of existence. Yes, he was a high-school dropout, but he didn't want to live like one—and he wasn't about to let his child want for the things that were needed. From his perspective, the street was the only place where he could hope to take care of all those issues.

Jan was happy about the record deal. But she also knew he was thinking about making moves—the kind of moves that might have been okay for a boyfriend, but were risky for a father.

"We've gotta prepare for this baby's future," Jan said one afternoon.

"You think I don't know that?" Wallace said. "She's gonna be okay. She's my girl."

"So what are you doing?"

"You don't know what I'm doing to prepare for this child's future," he snapped. "Stop beating me in the head with that."

"So what are you doing?"

"I don't have to tell you everything I'm doing. Just trust in me to know that I'm making sure she's gonna be okay. I'm doing everything I'm supposed to do."

Although he had been arrested for drug possession during a trip down South the previous year, the opportunity for fast money was just too good to pass up. On the streets of Brooklyn, where crack was readily available, it was a buyer's market. If you didn't like the price on one corner, you went to cop somewhere else. Wallace had spent many a day in the rain or in the cold, lucky if he earned a few hundred dollars on the corner. It was hard for any street-level dealer to make big money—you had to move up the food chain for that.

In North Carolina he was a much bigger cheese. And it was a seller's market. Crack was still somewhat exotic down there, and the fiends bought in bulk—like they were never gonna see those rocks again. There wasn't a central strip. It was all word of mouth. Some fiends traveled 30 miles to score. Plus getting out of town was the only way he could provide for himself and his family while preventing Combs from knowing too much about his business.

He wasted no time heading back to Raleigh and the money was coming fast. Wallace and Zauqael, by the latter's estimation, were making $30,000 every two weeks. But Wallace kept getting pages from up in New York. Somehow Combs had found out where he was.

It wasn't hard for Combs to figure out what Wallace was up to.

"What the fuck are you doing!" Combs yelled into the phone. "I thought I told you about that shit!"

"What?" Wallace said, playing dumb.

"I know why you down there, nigga. You know that is only gonna lead to jail or death. But you don't need to be down there. I just got a call from your lawyer. Deal's closed, man. You can come by the office Tuesday morning. I got a check waiting for you, ready to cash, right here."

"Word?"

"Word."

"I'ma come back, but if we don't hit off big, I'ma be mad," Wallace told him. "'Cause we getting ready to do our thing down here."

The more he thought about it, the more he wanted to get to New York as soon as possible. What if something happened with the train and he got there late? He didn't want anything fucking up his payday.

"Something told me, Yo, let me just leave Monday," Wallace later explained. And that's what he did. Good decision.

"Don't you know Monday night, police ran up in the house that we were staying in and locked those niggas up?" Wallace said.

"Big left that morning and we got arrested that afternoon," Zauqael confirmed.

Wallace took his miraculous good luck as a sign he was on the right path. When he got to New York, there was no looking back. He appreciated the opportunity he had been given. Wallace left the hustling life behind and decided to give this music business thing a shot.

"He was one hundred and fifty percent focused on rap," said D-Roc.

The $125,000 budget Uptown gave him wasn't a lot of money—recording costs and many other expenses would have to come out of that.

"The original deal was a standard, very cheap deal," said Mister Cee, who had his lawyer broker the contract through Cee's production company. All the same, Wallace was happy. He had a little cash in his pocket and some legitimacy. Now the only thing he had to do was write some dope rhymes and record them.

His creative process really evolved from hanging out. Wallace would sit in his room and watch music videos, studying Ralph McDaniels's *Video Music Box* and *Yo! MTV Raps*. He'd always been a fan, but now he was listening to every rap record he could get his hands on.

Lil' Cease, who was 15 at the time, had dropped out of school and was getting caught up in the Fulton Street scene. Wallace, who always admired his character, pulled him off the Avenue and into his new rap world.

"I'd go to the pay phone and call him," Cease recalled. "He'd tell me to come to the front window." Wallace would open the window and drop the money downstairs. "Get me a dime, two Phillies, and two Pepsis," Wallace would tell Cease. It got to the point where Wallace didn't even have to say it. He'd just drop the money down and Cease came back with the order. Then Wallace got busy. "We'd go in the crib and we'd kick it. And he'd just work on his music."

The "One Room Shack" that Biggie would later refer to in the song "Juicy" was Wallace's bedroom—funky yellow walls, a bed and a chair, clothes and assorted junk all over the place, a TV with a VCR, and two big party-size speakers. It was in that room that Biggie Smalls the rapper worked out his rhymes.

"That was the shack," Cease recalled fondly. "Ten, twenty niggas in there, and it was yay small. Small as a motherfucker, where it was some niggas hangin' in the closet. Just to be in there. That's how it was back in the day in the 'hood. That was all a nigga needed."

No matter how rowdy it got, there were rules. This was Ms. Wallace's apartment, and some of the toughest roughnecks on Fulton Street cowered in her presence.

"I wasn't an ogre," she said. "But there's just certain principles I maintain in my home. You cannot wear a hat inside my house. It's a form of respect. Take your hat off. Tie your sneakers. Do not walk into my house with some laces flying all over, your shirt open, your hood on like you're a bum. You come into my house with your shirt into your pants and your sneakers tied, and take your hat off. And yes, you can sit in my living room, but you do not put your feet on my coffee table. You know, rules are rules, principles are principles, and manners is manners. You come into my home, you respect my home."

Wallace and his friends played the music loud, kept the windows open, and were quick with the Lysol spray if he sensed his mother was coming.

"Turn down that noise!" she'd say.

"One of these days," he said with a smile, "that noise is gonna make you rich."

When he finally got a chance to record a song of his own for Uptown Records—rather than just appearing on somebody else's remix—he tried to re-create the energy of those bedroom sessions. His first opportunity came in 1993 when Combs was putting together a soundtrack for the hip hop comedy *Who's the Man?* The song was "Party and Bullshit," produced by Brooklyn's own Easy Mo Bee.

Easy Mo Bee was the last producer to ever work with Miles Davis and the first to work with Christopher Wallace. Being a lifelong friend of Mister Cee, he heard about Big before everyone else in the industry did.

"Mister Cee was like, 'There's this cat I want you to hear,'" Mo Bee remembered. "And I was like, you know, I think the cat is nice. But I never knew that we would hook up."

Once Big got signed, they seemed to gravitate toward each other. After hours of auditioning beats, Wallace heard some of Mo's tracks and liked them. Mo never forgot the voice. The match between them was organic.

"I used to come over there and pick him up and we'd ride around, you know," Mo Bee said. "The guy used to lean my car over on one side, man. I didn't care, I just liked riding around with him."

The idea for "Party and Bullshit" grew out of just listening to music. Mo Bee had a cassette copy of the Last Poets' self-titled debut that he'd scored off a Nostrand Avenue street-table tape vendor. If he was educating the young MC to the origins of hip hop, the Last Poets were a good place to start.

The Poets emerged from Harlem's Black Arts Movement, a radical cultural groundswell that took place during the late '60s and early '70s. The goal was to channel the progressive spirit of the Black Panthers through the arts, in hopes of reaching people who wouldn't dig the speeches. Revolutionary playwrights included Amiri Baraka, Ed Bullins, and Richard Wesley; the musical component featured Gil Scott-Heron and the Last Poets.

With its insistent bongos and its chorus addressing "Niggas . . . all niggas," the Last Poets' "Niggers Are Scared of Revolution" used sarcasm, frustration, and humor to make the point that not enough young black people were taking the struggle for equality seriously.

"Niggas will party and bullshit, and party and bullshit," complained Poet Umar Bin Hassan. "Some will even die, when the revolution comes."

The deeper implications of the song passed through one of Wallace's ears and out the other. He gravitated toward the line "party and bullshit."

"Yo, Mo, we gotta use that," Wallace said. "You gotta put that in something."

Much as he would later steer New York hip hop away from revolutionary themes and toward the gangsta party, Wallace flipped the revolutionary anthem into a punch line that people could dance to. In the process he totally subverted the song's message, transforming a line from "Niggas Are Scared of Revolution" into its very antithesis—a party record.

"I was a terror since the public school era," Biggie rapped. "Bathroom passes, cuttin' classes, squeezing asses. / Smoking blunts was a daily routine / Since thirteen. / A chubby nigga on the scene."

The song was brilliant on many levels: the flow, the casual way that Wallace showed what a detail-specific MC he could be. On first listen, the song was supposed to be about how he was just another buck-wild kid who loved to bring guns to parties and start trouble. But on further reflection, the lyrics contained their own powerful post-crack social commentary. All the rhetoric of Public Enemy, Brand Nubian, and X Clan had not truly altered the reality of the streets. There was a whole new generation of cats raised in the drug game whose only love was that paper—and Wallace would be their spokesperson.

As Mo Bee remembered, the recording session for that song was almost as wild as the song itself. That was the day he discovered that "keep it real" wasn't just a catchphrase when it came to Wallace's art.

At the end of the third verse, you could hear the sound of a fight breaking out at the party Biggie has been describing, just as he's about to leave with a young lady. ("Can't we just all get along," he says afterward, with a sly reference to Rodney King's post–L.A. riots lament, "so I can put hickies on her chest like Lil' Shawn?") That fight wasn't in the original plan. While rhyming off the top of his head, Wallace just came up with the idea for a sonic transition—and had the spontaneous creative energy to make something new.

"I remember after he did the second verse he stopped all the music," Mo Bee said. "He called all of us—me, Chico, Cee. We all go in the booth."

"Yo, we gonna do this little interlude," Wallace told them. "This what I want y'all to do. We gonna take the chairs, the mike stand, everything; we just gonna throw mad shit around in the booth." It was an unorthodox idea, but Mo Bee went with it, recording all the frenzied pushing and shoving as they mashed up the booth. The final result sounded exactly like one of those fights that break out at hip hop parties. As interludes go, this one was unusually effective, giving the song a sense of realism and immediacy.

"If you listen to the background in the song, you can hear me real low, like, Yo, what happened to the music?" Mo Bee said with a chuckle. "I had never seen nobody do that before. Never. Then he came back, 'Can't we just all get along?' Dude is creative, man. I was just trying to get the hang of him, right there. I was like, 'Okay, he got something up his sleeve.'"

Biggie Smalls throws up an M to represent Junior M.A.F.I.A. while the Blastmaster KRS-One and ace producer Easy Mo Bee show love.

In the final mix, Combs took time on the closing overdubs to announce "Bad Boy" and "Junior M.A.F.I.A." as future concepts. Neither entity actually existed yet—but they soon would.

"Who's Junior M.A.F.I.A.?" Lil' Cease asked when he heard the song.

"That's y'all," Wallace said, as if he should have known.

"Everything with him was all about 'my niggas,'" Mo Bee said with admiration. Wallace was that rare individual whose dreams about making a better life extended beyond himself. "He used to always talk about Junior M.A.F.I.A., Junior M.A.F.I.A., Junior M.A.F.I.A."

The crew was thick, and every record that he appeared on—"Dolly My Baby," "Real Love," and "Party and Bullshit"—was a hit. His name was getting out there, and he was beginning to earn fans beyond the streets of Brooklyn.

"You heard this shit yet?" asked Tupac Shakur, punching the rewind button on the car's tape player. It was the first time director John Singleton had heard "Party and Bullshit," but he would hear Biggie's song many more times while on location in Los Angeles for his 1993 film, *Poetic Justice*. Shakur was the film's romantic lead, starring opposite Janet Jackson. When he wasn't on camera, he kept playing the song over and over again, laughing every time.

"Tupac loved that song," said Singleton. Even though some people warned him that Tupac was trouble, the Academy Award–nominated filmmaker chose Shakur for his follow-up to *Boyz N the Hood*, one of the first films to cast a rapper (Ice Cube) alongside professional actors (Laurence Fishburne, Cuba Gooding Jr.). Although Singleton and Shakur had some spirited disagreements, the director was enjoying the experience of working with him. One of his fondest memories was the weekend he and Shakur spent in Atlanta during the black spring break celebration known as Freaknik, chasing girls and promoting the film. They rented a limo and cruised up and down Peachtree Street, blasting the song by this guy Biggie all the while.

Neighborhoods all over the country were pumping Biggie's voice, but Christopher Wallace's real life was no party. Trouble seemed to follow him like a cold wind.

He and D-Roc were walking down Gates Avenue one night, having just left D-Roc's grandmother. "We was talking about how we would buy 4Runners if Big went gold," D-Roc recalled. "All of a sudden the police rolled up on us." They took off down the block, and as they ran Wallace threw away the gun he was carrying. The cops caught up with them, and after a brief search, the unregistered gun was found. The two men sat in an interrogation room at the 79th precinct.

"There's two of you, but only one gun," the arresting officer said. "Take some time and figure it out." He left the room.

The two friends looked at each other. They both knew it was Wallace's gun, but he was already on probation for gun possession and an old drug case. Another violation would mean serious time in jail—at least a few years. He had a baby on the way, and he'd lose his record deal if he took the rap.

D-Roc took responsibility for the gun charge. Wallace accepted his friend's display of loyalty and promised to look out for him when he got out of jail. It was a sacrifice he would never forget.

D-Roc was sentenced to four years. Wallace had his freedom, and his future. He was wanted in the studio and to make promotional appearances. He shot a video for the "Dolly My Baby" remix with Super Cat. He was invited to appear on Heavy D's upcoming album, *Blue Funk,* on the posse track "A Buncha Niggas." Money was finally starting to flow.

Wallace had his freedom. But the wind kept blowing.

One night while Jan was still pregnant, she and Christopher had an argument in his room. She hadn't seen him for a while, and she assumed it was because he was off enjoying his new life as a budding rap star. He had other reasons.

"You don't have any idea what I'm going through," he said heatedly.

"What *you're* going through?" she responded.

Jan was met with silence. She was surprised to look up and find him crying. "What's wrong?"

Wallace collapsed in sobs, revealing his secret: His mother had cancer.

"I saw a different side of him I had never seen," Jan said, still moved by the memory. "And to see him like that made me cry. He felt so helpless."

"She just came home from the hospital," Wallace told her. "She's so weak, she can't even lift a tissue off the night table," he said.

"Why didn't you tell me?"

"She didn't want me to tell anybody," he said. "She just doesn't want anybody to know."

In the end, Voletta Wallace had 20 lymph nodes removed. She didn't have to undergo any chemotherapy. Christopher was overjoyed as he watched her slowly regaining her strength. His mind was clear enough to get back into the studio and begin the first tracks of what would eventually become his debut album.

His mother soon had enough energy to take her annual vacation back home to visit her family in Jamaica. Before she returned, T'yanna Dream Wallace was born on August 8, 1993. Voletta Wallace was a grandmother—albeit a reluctant one.

"Ma, the baby's here," Wallace told his mother on her return. "You should see her. She's beautiful."

Voletta shook her head. She was still mad at her son for becoming a father in the first place.

"I don't want to see that baby," she said.

"Why not?"

"I just don't," she said severely. "You made the baby. You've been planning for the baby. You're a grown daddy. Go be a father. Take care of your family."

She could be just as stubborn as her son—but rather than being put off by his mother's harsh words, he persevered.

"When you see her, you're gonna fall in love with her," he said. Every time he saw her, he'd say the same thing, slowly working her.

"Fine," she said one day. "I'll go see her. Just to get you off my back."

"I fell so in love with that little girl," Ms. Wallace recalled, smiling with a grand-motherly glow. "The tears were rolling down my eyes. It wasn't because I was happy. I was crying because there was such innocence, she was such a gift, and we didn't know what was in store for this kid."

Look at you, she thought as she watched her son play with the little girl, rubbing his nose against hers. *You're a bum. You don't even have a job. You're not a lawyer. You're not a teacher. You have nothing. No profession. And you bring this innocence into this world . . .*

She said a silent prayer that her son would be able to take care of the new life that had been entrusted to him.

But Wallace was having enough trouble taking care of his career. In July 1993, just weeks before Wallace's daughter was born, Combs was fired from the job at Uptown by his mentor Andre Harrell. It was the story of Wallace's life: one step forward and two steps back.

It wasn't that Combs was doing a bad job—he was fired because he was too good. His success with Jodeci and Mary J. Blige had made him arrogant. It didn't matter that he had the track record to back up his attitude—he was just beginning to get on people's nerves.

His days of wearing polka-dot ties and saying, "Yes, Mr. Harrell," were long gone. Now he had millions of sales under his belt. Kids all over the country were dressing like Jodeci, because Jodeci was dressing like him. Anytime he went to a club, he was sure to hear one of his remixes. He sensed that he was standing on the verge of something really big.

"At first I was shy," Combs said, "then one day I realized that shy shit ain't gonna get me nowhere in this world."

So he started making himself known. Strutting around with his silver briefcase, showing off his company logo, talking to anyone who would listen about Bad Boy. He had his "street team" hit the pavement with fliers of a photo of his godson, in a diaper, one hand grabbing his tiny nuts, with a caption announcing "THE NEXT GENERATION OF BAD MUTHAFUCKAS."

But all the bravado began to backfire. The beginning of the end for Combs was Mark Siegel, the white general manager Harrell hired while Combs took a brief leave of absence following the City College tragedy. It was a classic showdown of the bean counter and the boy wonder. The boy wonder, of course, didn't like being told that he was spending too much money on studio time, on street promotions, on all of the things that made Puffy Puffy.

"I felt like I was busting my ass for four years to be behind a black company," Combs said, "so I told Andre that I wasn't gonna be respectin' the man he brought in because I didn't feel he knew the music and respected it."

Maybe it was Puffy's appearance in a Karl Kani advertisement. Maybe it was his penchant for saying his name on all the remixes. Maybe it was the way he played his stereo louder than anyone else in the office, stated his opinions with more disdain than anyone else, showed open disrespect toward Harrell and Siegel—or anyone else who got in his way. Maybe it was a perception that he took credit for more than he really deserved. Or maybe it was just his spending habits. For whatever combination of reasons, Puffy was pissing off the corporate brass at MCA, which had acquired a 50 percent stake in Uptown.

"He was a disruptive force in the system that was just too much of a headache," said Harrell's old partner Alonzo Brown. "Grabbing for power, grabbing for power, and Andre was like, 'Let me get you the fuck up out of here.' "

"There can only be one lion in the jungle," Harrell told Combs. He explained that making hit records was not the whole picture. Harrell was trying to expand Uptown into television. "Besides," he said to his young protégé, "you're ready. Go make it happen. You're ready to fly."

Combs was escorted from Uptown's offices the same day he was told to pack.

"Dre can be like that," Combs said later. "Real cold. He doesn't cry at anybody's funeral, but I told him he was gonna cry at mine." Combs shed a few tears himself that day. "It was like leaving home," he said. "I wish that I'd never left."

But Harrell didn't shut Combs out completely. He agreed to extend his payroll and those of his staff for a limited time. Still, there was a lot at stake. Combs had signed his artists to Uptown, and had financed their recording sessions with the label's money. A number of tracks had been recorded for Biggie's debut album, and now it was quite possible that they would never see the light of day. There was another artist, too—this kid from Long Island named Craig Mack. Both projects were now in jeopardy.

When Combs was fired from Uptown, he worked hard to convince Wallace that his future was in good hands. "I'm a visionary," Combs said. "You have to trust me."

The songs that the executives did hear they didn't like. "They didn't know what to think," said one MCA insider. "Biggie's songs were violent." Somehow the secretary of MCA's president had gotten a copy of the lyrics to "Dreams." Also known as "Dreams of Fuckin' an R&B Bitch," the tune was a wickedly ribald freestyle over an old James Brown loop on which Big fantasizes about sexing every female singer in the business: "Sade— Ooh, I know that pussy's tight / Smack Tina Turner give her flashbacks of Ike." That tune alone may have ensured that Uptown would never have anything to do with the unruly rapper's project. "A lot of people were really offended," said the MCA employee. "Some of the artists he mentioned were on the label."

Wallace was depressed about the fact that his album might never come out. If he had never released a single, he would have been okay with it. But to get so close to his dream only to see it taken away bothered him to no end.

The job of keeping Wallace encouraged and on the straight and narrow path fell to Howard alum Mark "Gucci Don" Pitts.

"I was with him 24-7, always by his side," said Pitts, ever the businessman. "We lived in Brooklyn, I came and picked him up. I made sure he got up, I was just there with him every day. We just got tight."

It was Pitts who made sure that Wallace didn't fall back into the drug game during this period of hiatus. Pitts was the one with the relationship with Wallace's parole officer, the one who made sure that he was doing the things he needed to do. When Wallace got impatient, Pitts knew how to calm him down.

"I was the pain-in-the-ass big brother, you know what I mean?" Pitts said. "I would threaten him sometimes. It was tough love at times. I had to do what I had to do. Because he had a promising career ahead of him and I ain't want to see him mess it up."

Whether he admitted it or not, Wallace appreciated the attention and the care.

"Mark used to come to my crib and I'd be like 'Fuck you, I ain't doing shit.' But he would take a hot rag, wipe my face and help me up," Wallace said with a smile. "I can ask him for anything, at any time. That's why I call him the manager extraordinaire."

While Combs spent the summer of '93 trying to get a new situation together, he also made a trip out to Brooklyn that fall to reassure his impatient young star that their luck was going to change. Wallace's close friend dream hampton remembered a dinner the three of them had at Junior's, a Brooklyn institution famous for its cheesecake. Combs tried to assuage Wallace's concerns, doing his best to assure him that his future was in good hands.

"I'm a visionary," Combs said. "You have to trust me."

Combs's ego might not have been affected by being fired, but he was running out of time. All he had was his Beemer, his chutzpah, and big plans for remaking the whole rap world in his image.

"Andre taught me that music could be a movement or a lifestyle," he said. He hadn't fit into the Uptown lifestyle, so Combs decided to build his own empire, the sort of place a Bad Boy could call home.

He gathered his troops—Howard University–era cronies like Harve Pierre, Mark Pitts, Nashiem Myrick, and a few others—and began running his own thing from an extra bedroom in his mother's Mount Vernon house, as well as a home studio in Scarsdale, New York.

"I don't think I ever worked that hard in my life," said Pierre. "Every day, all day." Combs had everyone in the crib up at eight in the morning, filling out daily reports. Eight A.M. may not seem that early for most folks, but in hip hop terms, those are the 4 A.M. milk-the-cows, feed-the-chickens hours of a farmer.

"That was the inception," said Pierre. "One computer, four or five people working every day, going back and forth to the city." Biggie, Craig Mack, and the female vocal trio Total would travel to Scarsdale every other day and record in the studio that Myrick had built there. "That's where we started Bad Boy—just recording in the house, having the artists writing, the same way we have these studios now, we were doing them in a house in the beginning."

Combs's lawyer, Kenny Meiselas, began brokering meetings, trying to find Combs some overhead money and a distribution deal. Combs, meanwhile, had to figure out what the Bad Boy "movement" was going to be.

It started off as a logo, and a cool thing to say on a remix. Now he had to convince a major white conglomerate to invest in his vision—and at the same time prevent them from interfering with his creative process —and wreaking havoc on what was so cool about his vision in the first place.

"I was scared to death," said Combs. "I knew I wanted to get to a point of Berry Gordy and Quincy Jones, but I wasn't thinking of how they got to that point. I was forced to handle a situation, and then I had to grow up real quick." He was fortunate to be understood by an old white man whose ears had always been attuned to young black artists: Clive Davis, the head of Arista Records.

A Harvard Law graduate and former CBS attorney, the man behind Santana and Janis Joplin rose through the record-industry ranks in the late '60s. He was smart and charismatic enough to sign some of the most talented artists of his generation—the Grateful Dead, Chicago, Bruce Springsteen, Billy Joel, and Aerosmith, to name a few—while they were still young, hungry, and relatively cheap.

Producer Deric "D-Dot" Angelettie and A&R exec Harve Pierre, two of Combs's most reliable associates who helped build the Bad Boy empire.

Like Combs, he was also fired by his parent company—Columbia Records—for spending too much. He was let go in 1976 after being audited for submitting exorbitant expense account fees—and was later cleared of any wrongdoing. By then Davis had moved to a failing label—Arista Records—negotiated a 20 percent personal stake, and signed the likes of Barry Manilow, Neil Diamond, and a resurrected Aretha Franklin. When Aretha's former backup singer Cissy Houston revealed that her daughter Whitney had talent, Davis was in the right place at the right time once again.

And like Combs, Davis had a healthy ego. Some in the industry joked that he thought the CD was named after him. Others pointed to the fact that A&R man Gerry Griffith was actually the one who signed Houston. He quit after Davis had him cropped out of a magazine photo.

"I'm a noteworthy figure," Davis had explained. "The picture would be somewhat diminished by an unknown A&R man."

With Whitney, Arista became an R&B powerhouse. Davis signed label deals with some of the hottest names in R&B: L.A. Reid and Kenny "Babyface" Edmonds, and Dallas Austin. But he could see that the company's one weakness was that there was no pipeline into the emerging hardcore hip hop scene.

"Arista was really young in the rap game," said one insider. "They had a couple of hits but nothing major. There was a lot of apprehension like, 'What the hell is this shit?' It wasn't just the white people. You'd see the R&B promotions cats, with their Sunday shoes on on a Tuesday. They're like, 'How the fuck am I gonna get this shit played on the radio?'" But Davis wasn't as straight-laced as his employees. Rap was hot and he wanted in.

"Clive was old school, but he knew a hit when he heard it," said the Arista insider who remembered Davis playing the video for Naughty By Nature's "O.P.P." during a weekly meeting when the song was still quite new.

"This is what I'm talking about," Davis said. "This is what I want to see. This has all the elements of a hit. The song is hot. The lyrics are great. There's a catchy hook. This guy Treach is a star."

Clive wasn't stupid. Rap may not have been his personal taste in music but he understood that a hit was a hit. Would it sell records?—that was the question.

That's where Combs came in.

When the two men met in the Arista offices, they were mutually impressed: Combs with Davis's stature and smarts, and Davis with Combs's ambition and perspective. A deal was struck: Davis gave Combs a $1.5 million advance and complete creative control. Combs immediately used the money to buy back from Harrell the tracks that had already been recorded for Wallace's album, plus negotiated the release of Total, Faith Evans, Craig Mack, and a few other artists.

With the distribution plan in place, Christopher Wallace could focus on what he did best—creating an album that would rock the whole hip hop nation. His vision was simple but powerful: "It's gonna be some real ghetto shit," he declared. "It ain't Brooklyn shit. It's the shit that niggas in Houston can get with. Shit that niggas in Idaho can get with. It's just reality laid out on the table."

The blueprint for what would become *Ready to Die* was laid out, inadvertently, at Matty C's apartment during the fall of 1992. Capoluongo, who lived around the corner from Wallace, often saw the rapper after the "Unsigned Hype" column appeared in *The Source,* and the two became friends. Both men were connoisseurs of good weed and potent beats. And as an editor at *The Source,* Matty C had access to records months before they came out. One of the records that he had, before anyone else, was Dr. Dre's masterpiece, *The Chronic.* Its influence on Biggie was immediate and long-lasting.

"The first time he heard *The Chronic,*" Matty C recalled, "he listened to the whole thing, then he was like, 'I gotta go home and write!' "

The Chronic not only changed the kinds of records being made, it also altered hip hop's business landscape. All of a sudden the only records that sold on a national level were gangsta rap records. It wasn't all Dr. Dre's fault—equal blame goes to the man who made the record possible in the first place.

Marion "Suge" Knight Jr. had always dreamed about things no one else around him dared to even think about.

"When I was a kid in Compton the other kids would say, 'When I grow up, I want a Chevy,'" Knight once recalled. "I would say, 'I want a Porsche or a Rolls-Royce.' I wanted something other than what I saw in the ghetto."

Born in Los Angeles on April 19, 1966, Knight was raised in Compton, a middle-class area that, like Bedford-Stuyvesant, fell on hard times when the white folks left and black folks' jobs disappeared. On the surface there were plenty of neatly mowed lawns and working families, but there were also gangs like the Tree Top Pirus and the Southside Crips fighting over different segments of a small area. Sunny, cloudless days were often riddled with the sound of gunshots.

Knight compared the neighborhood to the ocean. "It's real pretty but anytime something can happen."

Knight was lucky enough to be raised by two doting parents, Marion Knight Sr. and his mother, Maxine, who gave him his nickname—short for Sugar Bear. Knight was a big kid who played football just like his father before him. His skills as a defensive tackle allowed him to bypass gang membership without anyone calling him a punk.

"He was always involved in sports," said Manuel Johnson, an ex-Crip turned football coach for Compton High School. "As long as you're in sports, no one will mess with you."

Knight excelled at Lynwood High School and then El Camino College, transferring to UNLV in 1985. The quiet soft-spoken guy off the field was a monster on it. Number 54 would punch, kick, scream, and do anything he had to to break through the line and get the quarterback.

Knight was named a defensive captain. He had dreams about playing for the NFL, but he was cut from the L.A. Rams after the 1987 season. He was arrested in Las Vegas later that year for attempted murder, grand larceny with an auto, and the use of a deadly weapon—charges that were later dropped.

"Ain't nobody perfect in this world except God," Knight said about the incident. "We all make mistakes."

While Knight was trying to make moves with the L.A. Rams, another Compton native was making serious moves in the rap game. Former drug dealer turned record entrepreneur Eric "Eazy-E" Wright founded Ruthless Records in 1986 with a $7,000 investment of his "retirement" earnings.

Wright recruited hot local DJ Andre "Dr. Dre" Young, and his "World Class Wreckin' Cru" partner Antoine "DJ Yella" Carraby to produce for Ruthless. Dre in turn recruited a friend of his cousin Sir Jinx named O'Shea "Ice Cube" Jackson. Wright picked local rappers Lorenzo "MC Ren" Patterson and Tracy "D.O.C." Curry to round out the group, who would be Compton's answer to Run-D.M.C.

The idea was to make raw, violent records that would never be heard on radio airwaves. Records that would combine the bawdy humor of Richard Pryor's comedy routines with true stories of the violence taking place on the gang-infested streets of South Central L.A. Ice Cube handled most of the lyrics, all set to Dre's high-octane beats. It was a new sound, a new style of speak. On the seminal song "Boyz N the Hood," Eazy's cold nasal tone recounted Cube's harsh story that included everything from domestic violence to a courtroom shoot-out. The song had an eerie presence unlike anything else. The lyrics seemed so "real" that for the audience the separation between fantasy and reality felt thinner than ever.

Needless to say, "Boyz N the Hood" sold like hotcakes. Eazy E's small investment paid off tenfold. All he did was go to Macola Records, press up his vinyl for a flat fee, and he controlled his own master recordings free and clear. Eazy was collecting every penny of the profits from Ruthless Records. At the pressing plant, he met former Creedence Clearwater Revival manager Jerry Heller, who said he thought Eazy's song "Boyz N the Hood," was "the most important music I had ever heard." Heller became Eazy's partner at Ruthless, helping him secure distribution through Priority Records, a fledgling company owned by former K-Tel executive Bryan Turner. While Wright and his partners focused on the dough, Dre came up with the concept for what would become the biggest Ruthless release.

"One day Dre and Eazy picked me up in the van and they was like, 'You know what we gonna call the group? Niggaz With Attitude,'" Cube remembered.

"Niggaz With Attitude," he replied. "Nobody gonna put that out."

"We'll break it down to N.W.A and wait till people ask," Dre told him.

It sounded like a plan.

The album, *Straight Outta Compton*, was released in 1988. It cost only $8,000 to make and took just six weeks to complete. The FBI was so concerned about N.W.A's song "Fuck Tha Police" that a federal agent wrote to Priority Records to express disapproval. The notoriety only served to make N.W.A hotter. They hit the road in 1989 and sold out venues across the country. The tour netted over $650,000 in gross receipts.

The money changed everything. Ice Cube, who had written the lion's share of the lyrics, asked why he had no royalties or publishing. He refused the $75,000 flat fee that everyone else in the group accepted. Cube soon went solo, and D.O.C. came off the bench as the group's chief lyricist. As formidable a presence on the mike as he was with a pen, the D.O.C. was every bit Ice Cube's equal. *Rolling Stone*'s Jonathan Gold likened his voice to a finely tuned Stradivarius. His record "No One Could Do It Better" wasn't as much conjecture as it was a statement of fact: He was the man.

When D.O.C. started doing shows in the L.A. area, Suge Knight went with him, having transformed himself from a football player into a bodyguard. Knight found that being a bodyguard was a lot like being invisible: half the time people didn't even acknowledge his presence. Plus you got to go everywhere—lunches, dinners, attorney meetings. Knight's size worked to his advantage for two reasons—no one would ever mess with him, and people didn't mind talking around him because they assumed he wasn't smart enough to know what was really going on. He didn't smoke. He didn't drink. He didn't do anything but watch.

"I was out there, looking and learning," he said. "I'm hearing it all."

Knight was part of Bobby Brown's entourage but he also became close with Dick Griffey, the owner of S.O.L.A.R. (Sound Of Los Angeles) Records, the former label of Shalamar and of The Deele, L.A Reid and Babyface's R&B group. Knight learned about how people got paid in this business, about getting "points" on record sales, and about publishing. He learned that the real power was behind the scenes, not in the spotlight.

From bodyguard, Knight progressed to manager. He began managing D.O.C. as well as D.O.C.'s friend from Dallas, rapper/producer Mario "Chocolate" Johnson. Suge founded a publishing company, management firm, and record label Funky Enough Records.

"In the beginning they thought, 'He must be a dummy,'" Knight said. "They were arrogant toward me. They didn't respect me as a man. But they underestimated me. They didn't know I had a briefcase full of tricks."

Had the D.O.C. not fallen asleep at the wheel of his jeep on August 20, 1989, it's doubtful that Knight would have delved into that briefcase, or that N.W.A would have broken up, or that Death Row Records would have been founded.

The fateful accident cost D.O.C. his rap career when he was thrown from the car and his larynx was crushed. Knight was one of the first people at the hospital after D.O.C. was brought in. He was shocked to learn that D.O.C. couldn't pay his medical expenses. Despite having a million-selling album, he was broke. Suge got a copy of D.O.C.'s contract and soon understood why.

"If they fuckin' with mine," D.O.C. said, "you know they fuckin' with Dre too."

Meanwhile, Chocolate, the producer Knight managed with D.O.C., had written a number of songs for a white kid named Robert Van Winkle from the suburbs of Dallas. Chocolate—who used to dis Van Winkle when they were both rappers in Dallas—wrote and produced "Stop That Train," "Life Is a Fantasy," and most important, "Ice, Ice, Baby."

"They paid me $1,500 for the two songs that I was supposed to do," Chocolate said. "And when I got there I ended up doing five more songs. I did ['Ice, Ice, Baby'] for free, and ended up leaving from Dallas coming to California. Next thing you know, a year later, the song blew up. That's when I called Suge and told him, Look, man, that's a song that I did."

As Chocolate's manager, Suge was entitled to a percentage of Chocolate's earnings. Anybody messing with Chocolate's money was also messing with Suge's.

Knight and the people close to him say that he used only legal means to get what was owed to his client. Vanilla Ice, in an infamous TV interview, implied that Knight came to his hotel room and coerced him into signing over his rights by threats of violence. No matter who you believe, the bottom line was that Chocolate got half a million dollars.

"To be straight with you, Suge was the only brother that I ever knew who liked to see black men get paid," Chocolate said. "He never used to player hate nobody about making money. If I didn't have Suge on the real, I wouldn't have got all my money. He made it happen. He was on it every day. I respect that about him."

"Suge Knight was the only brother that I ever knew who loved to see black men get paid," said a former associate. "He never used to player hate nobody about making money. He made it happen."

With his percentages of Chocolate's $500,000 production and publishing deal with Sony, Knight had the seed money for his next venture.

Knight had Dick Griffey look into Dr. Dre and D.O.C.'s Ruthless contracts. "They had had the worst contracts I had ever seen in the history of the record business," Griffey said. "If I said 'draconian,' that would be a kind word."

Dr. Dre, who felt he was not being paid fairly by Ruthless Records after producing records that sold over eight million copies in a six-year period, wanted a change. He went from ridiculing Ice Cube on N.W.A records like *Efil4Zaggin* to privately sympathizing with him. He considered Eazy-E to be his partner and closest friend, but didn't realize how much the deal he had brokered on the strength of trust favored Eazy.

"Suge brought it to my attention that I was being cheated," Dre said. "I'm not no egotistical person. I just want what I'm supposed to get. Not a penny more, not a penny less. There was some sheisty shit, so I had to get ghost."

Knight got Dre, D.O.C., and some other artists released from their Ruthless contracts. Eazy-E contended that he negotiated under threat of a beating with metal pipes. Not only did he file a claim in Los Angeles Superior Court in August of 1991, he followed it up with a civil suit.

People who knew Knight wouldn't comment on the allegations, on or off the record. But everybody agreed that he was the wrong man to piss off.

"Suge is cool. He's just temperamental," said one friend. "He's the type of brother who can't take no. He just feel like he gotta always have that last word." But sometimes words were not enough. "Don't get me wrong—Suge'll smack the shit out of you. In a heartbeat. I done seen niggas get the shit beat out of them. Believe me. I seen a hallway of niggas at the Palladium get cleared out by that nigga. I done seen him make two niggas slap each other. He ain't no coward. I'll tell you that. That nigga'll demonstrate in a second."

Once Knight had Dr. Dre, and Dre's younger half brother, Warren G, hooked up with Snoop Doggy Dogg and Nate Dogg, Suge had the nucleus of talent that would become Death Row Records. The single "Deep Cover" was the first salvo, a story of killing undercover cops set to a beat so seductive it rocked the East and West Coasts simultaneously. Folks fell in love with Snoop's voice. The Long Beach rapper possessed a flow that was countrified yet as intricate as anything a New York freestyle champ could have come up with at the time.

Bolstered by the positive reception, Suge and Dre's next move was to record an entire album that was calculated to cement their position in the rap game. But they didn't want to get into another situation where they would have to fight for their sovereignty. As much as he would criticize him in later years, Knight learned a valuable lesson from Eazy-E: full ownership meant everything. The secret was to do like the white boys did—own your masters, stay independent, and plug into a major distribution network that could pump your records nationwide.

"I knew the difference between having a record company and having an organization," Knight said. "First goal was to own our masters. Without your master tapes, you ain't got shit. Period."

The album they wanted to make would cost about $250,000 to record. For years, they would claim that that money came personally from Suge's bank account, from his share of Chocolate's perpetual Vanilla Ice publishing settlement deal. But a lot of that money was tied up. The lawsuit that Eazy-E filed was draining Knight's resources—court dates and motions were expensive.

But there was talk of a silent partner. When famed defense lawyer David Kenner started showing up at S.O.L.A.R. Records for some of Dre's recording sessions, people in the know took notice.

Among other big-time drug dealers, Kenner represented cocaine kingpin Michael "Harry-O" Harris, a Bounty Hunter Blood who shared a mutual acquaintance with Suge Knight. He had heard about Knight, the young ambitious man who was going places fast. Knight, of course, had heard many tales of the street legend who was as smart with his legitimate earnings as he was with his illegal money. Kenner had the juice to set up a meeting between the two men at the Metropolitan Detention Center in downtown Los Angeles. Harris had some money to invest, and he was looking for a partner on the outside who could make it grow.

Dr. Dre and company stayed in the studio. The bills got paid. Kenner remained a consistent presence, eventually becoming Dr. Dre's own criminal attorney. And the album that would become *The Chronic* got finished. And after months of being turned down by major labels that neither believed in the music, nor in granting Knight and Dre's demand that they own their own master tapes, Death Row Records finally signed a $10 million deal with Jimmy Iovine and Ted Fields at Interscope Records that met all their demands. Everything was in place.

"I know you've heard all the stories," Knight said. "But you have to realize one thing: results." He sounded like a coach who applied the can-do attitude of a winning football team to the rap game. And the smashmouth tactics.

"People don't always like it, but one thing about me, I'm 12 o'clock. That's a street saying. It means that I'm straight up and down. If I promise you I'm going to do something, you can believe it's going to happen. Mark my words, Death Row is going to be the record company of the decade."

The Chronic hit the rap world like a 10-megaton bomb on December 15, 1992. It wasn't just Dre's production, so heavily influenced by Parliament-Funkadelic, but Snoop Doggy Dogg's nimble vocals. It was the casual way they painted their violent pictures and the morbid, tongue-in-cheek attitude with which death was depicted: "Rat tat tat tat / tat-ta-tat like that," Snoop rhymed. "And I never hesitate to put a nigga on his back."

The records were so hard that Snoop and Dre didn't even have to curse and they still sounded gangsta—yet at the same time, songs like "Nuthin' But a G Thang" and "Let Me Ride" were so smooth, the mainstream pop audience had to pay attention. Not only did the album go multiplatinum in a matter of months, the videos crossed over into regular rotation, the first time a non-corny rapper had ever accomplished that feat.

There was just something about that Cali style that Wallace loved, a new musical attitude. East Coast rap at that time was very much on the positive tip. A Tribe Called Quest, De La Soul, Brand Nubian, Public Enemy, and Pete Rock & C.L. Smooth were the biggest stars. Philosopher thugs like Nas and the Wu Tang Clan had yet to fully emerge. Meanwhile, the hardcore lyrics propagated by the Kool G Raps and the Pretty Tone Capones of the world were too far underground to make much of an impact outside the Tri-State Area.

Christopher Wallace wanted to make the kind of ribald, violent, darkly humorous hit records that Snoop was making out West or Scarface was making down South—but he wanted to do it with East Coast flavor. From his perspective as a former dealer, he knew he could bring a new level of realism to his rhymes about the game.

Previous gangsta rap records talked about drug dealing, of course, but always from the fictional standpoint of the "Don." The lifestyle epitomized by Ice-T was one of flash and big dollars—boats, planes, and all types of crazy player shit. Wallace wanted to break the game down to a more realistic perspective. He would depict the stress of a street level dealer standing out on the corner, to show how treacherous the game could be—from stickup kids and undercover cops to betrayal by friends. He would even address the self-loathing that comes from making a living as a merchant of death—whether the death of the users or the murderous competition among traffickers and sellers. "When I die, fuck it, I want to go to hell," he would rhyme on "Suicidal Thoughts," the rawest track on what would be a thoroughly hard-boiled album. "I'm a piece of shit it ain't hard to fuckin' tell . . ."

The album's rather morbid title, *Ready to Die,* was Puff's idea. Biggie wanted to call it *The Teflon Don,* evoking John Gotti, whose ability to escape scrapes with the law was dominating the New York news media at the time. Puff thought the reference was too regional. "We can't do that," he insisted. "We gonna hit 'em hard, but we gonna do it in a way where we're gonna represent for the masses." After a long discussion, Big agreed to do it Puff's way.

But before he could get started telling stories, the beats had to be tight. That's where Mo Bee came in. Since he was a Bed-Stuy neighbor, Wallace would often come over to Mo's place and listen to instrumentals—not only the ones that Mo Bee came up with, but demos by other producers as well. Wallace was meticulous—before he could write it, he had to feel it.

"We'd load up beat after beat," Mo Bee said. "He'd be like, 'No, no, no.' He was real picky. We'd go through a hundred beats and he didn't like any of them."

One beat that Wallace did like was actually meant for another "Big" rapper—Big Daddy Kane. Based on an Isaac Hayes sample, it was slow, brooding, and rippled with menace. Mo Bee nicknamed the beat "Raising Kane," but when Kane passed on it, Biggie grabbed it. The song became one of the first that he recorded for his new album, a paranoid narrative of greed and betrayal called "Warning."

After a beat passed Wallace's screening process, it was off to the studio. The sessions, Mo Bee remembered, were all pretty much the same. He would play the track through the giant studio monitors, and Wallace would sit there in the room, smoking weed and nodding along with the pounding drums, seemingly lost in his own world. And then, just when you thought that all these hours of listening had been wasted, Wallace would stand up, walk into the booth, and perform an entire song off the top of his head.

"He ain't take no long time to do no song," Mo Bee said. "When Big went in the booth, he usually knew what he was going to do. All the other times he's sitting over there in the chair looking big and fat. He just be cutting his eyes left and right, looking at everybody, sitting there mumbling to himself. Breathing hard, just mumbling. Then he'd say, 'Mo, I'm ready.' And he'd just go in there and knock it out."

And the things that Wallace would "knock out" were sometimes surprising to Mo Bee. It wasn't just his talent for visual detail, or his genius at evoking a menacing aura—it was the fact that he was scared of nothing. He would say anything in a rap song, the more outrageous the better.

His first encounter with this side of Wallace came when they recorded the very first song for the album—the title track, "Ready to Die."

"Fuck the world, fuck my Moms and my girl / My life is played out like a Jheri curl," he said right before the chorus. "I'm ready to die."

Mo Bee looked up from the mixing board.

"You know what you just said?" he asked, sounding upset.

"Yeah, man," Wallace said, stepping out of the booth.

"Fuck your *Moms?*"

Wallace's working method in the studio involved long hours of smoking weed and listening to a beat. Then he'd stand up, walk into the booth, and do an entire song off the top of his head.

"I'm just trying to say that I'm ready to die for this shit," he explained. "This is urgent. You got to be willing to do whatever you got to do to make this paper."

Mo Bee just kind of nodded. He knew he was in for a hell of a ride.

The producer didn't speak up again until they were recording another song, "Gimme the Loot," a song that would later be considered a hip hop classic.

The track was a lyrical tour de force with Wallace rapping from the perspective of two different stickup kids arguing about who to rob next. Rapping in different voices was nothing new—Slick Rick, rap's master storyteller, had done it all over his 1988 album, *The Adventures of Slick Rick.* But Wallace took the tech-

nique one step further. Not only did he rap in two different voices—each voice had a completely different rhyme style and personality.

"Slick Rick played different characters, but the characters sounded the same," Wallace explained. "And with 'Redman Meets Reggie Noble,' he played two different people, but both the characters sound the same. I wanted to make them two completely different dudes, to the point where someone could wonder, who was that rapper with Big on 'Gimme the Loot'?"

The deeper voice Wallace used on the track—the more reasonable of the two—tries to coach his eager young partner on how to rob. "You ain't got to explain shit," the higher-pitched voice replies. "I've been robbing muthafuckas since the slave ships, with the same clip, and the same .45 / Two point-blank a muthafucka's sure to die."

The verse was a brilliant display of all of Wallace's gifts—crisp visual detail, dark humor, and subtle culture-specific references. "Since the slave ships," linked Wallace's stickup kid to Stagolee, the original "bad nigga" who had been immortalized in song and fable since the days of slavery. Later in the song, he describes a victim's mother singing "It's so hard . . ." This was a coy reference to Boyz II Men's remake of the tearjerker "It's So Hard to Say Goodbye to Yesterday," the death theme for the character Cochise in the film *Cooley High.* Boyz II Men's revival of the tune had become a popular request at funerals for black men and women who died before their time.

Wallace's "calm" character, to prove his worth, tries to outdo the younger character, proving how hard he is, too. "Then I'm dipping up the block, and I'm robbing bitches too / Up to herringbones and bamboos / I wouldn't give a fuck if you're pregnant / Give me the baby rings, and the #1 Mom pendant."

The lyric gave Mo Bee pause, but he kept his cool. (Puffy would later have the line edited out on the final mix of the album.) It wasn't until Wallace recorded another song with blasphemous overtones, "If I Should Die Before I Wake," that Mo Bee had to step back.

"Hail Mary / fuck her, I never knew her / I'd probably screw her / Left her body in the sewer."

Wallace came out of the recording booth to high fives and catcalls. As offensive as the lyrics were, the power of his performance made them sound hot. That was the whole point of the song, to come up with lyrics that were so outrageous, even the most jaded listener would be shocked.

Like Wallace's mother, Mo Bee was a devout Christian. For him the line about the Virgin Mary was over the top. He was nobody's father, but he felt he had to say something. Combs stood behind the mixing board next to the engineer. Wallace sat in the back of the control room, listening to the playback, swigging from a 40-ounce with Lil' Cease. Mo Bee looked at Combs.

"You sure you want to release that?" Mo Bee asked him.

Combs raised his eyebrows. "What?"

"The women's rights organizations, the churches, all that shit, they gonna come after you after this shit comes out."

Mo Bee turned his head when he heard a huge chorus of laughs from the other side of the room. It was Wallace, flanked by Lil' Cease and other members of what would soon become Junior M.A.F.I.A. Cease was laughing the hardest.

"Mo, you sensitive, man," Cease said. "Mo Bee's too sensitive."

The whole room was laughing at the producer. Wallace walked over to Mo Bee, letting him know that even though they were cracking on him, there was still love.

"I'm serious, man," Mo Bee said.

"Nah, nah," Wallace said. "We just having fun, man."

"Big ain't stress it," explained Lil' Cease. "Big was like, It's just a rhyme. I guess he was testing his waters, like, Let me go write some outlandish shit. 'Cause when you got that type of mind where you intelligent like that and you really got that pen sharp? You can talk about anything. He was just experimenting."

And so it went, beat for beat, and blunt for blunt, until they had enough tracks to choose from. As choosy as Wallace was about beats, Combs was about which tracks would make the album, and which wouldn't. Some songs, like "Dead Wrong" and "Come On, Muthafuckas," a duet with Brand Nubian's Sadat X, didn't make the final cut. Combs had other concerns besides street-level appeal. With almost two years of recording going into the album, and the huge sums that he spent buying back Wallace's tracks from Uptown, Combs knew that Wallace's album had to have a few commercial hits.

The Chronic had laid out the blueprint for video and radio breakthrough. You had to come with something slower and funkier—but maintain enough of a gangsta edge that the song would still be considered "real."

The songs that he and Wallace had completed up until this point would wrap up New York City—no doubt. But Combs knew he needed something that could rock anywhere. Imagine *Thriller* with "PYT" but no "Billie Jean" or "Beat It." Following the Quincy Jones–Michael Jackson model, Combs needed a lead-off single that would knock everybody out of the box.

Wallace and Mo Bee wanted the first single to be "Machine Gun Funk." It was funky, upbeat, and attitude to spare. But Combs wanted something smoother.

Wallace wanted to fight Puffy's decision, but he knew Combs had an uncanny feel for the crossover. If he wanted to get paid, that was the man to listen to. He was sure Combs wouldn't let him do anything to play himself.

"Puffy tells me, Yo, do your thing," Wallace said of their collaboration. "I'm gonna get busy. You can give my little limitations, but when I get a track, I ask him, 'What do you want from this, you let me know.' And he might be like,

'You need to be partying on this joint—you don't need to be killing nobody's mother on this one. Take it easy.'"

This time Combs wanted a party joint. The kind of song that would make women shake their hips so fiercely that it sent men to the bar to buy fancy drinks.

Such was the evolution of songs like "Juicy" and "Big Poppa." When Combs couldn't entice Mo Bee into something as simplistic as looping Mtume's "Juicy Fruit" or the Isley Brothers' "Between the Sheets," he found other people to make the hits that he heard in his head.

Puff, as Wallace had seen, was less a knob- and drum-programming producer than he was someone who tried to re-create a lifestyle. It's about being in the mix, and from Combs's perspective, the sound of the mix. "We may be all in a club one night," Wallace explained. "Me, him, and a couple producers. And he'll see people dancing to Diana Ross's 'Upside Down.' He'll see that come on in the club and he'll see how everybody just jumps up on the dance floor. And he'll be like, 'Yo, I want to hook that up.'"

"He'll tell one of the producers, they'll track it, and I'll rap to it. Then we'll give it to Puffy and Puffy will give it that gloss. It's the way he EQs it and the way the snares hit. People look at him like he's not a producer; to me he's a producer because he takes a hundred percent record and takes it to two hundred percent."

Despite putting his heart into songs like "Machine Gun Funk" and "Everyday Struggle," Wallace slowly came around to the fact that he had to entice a new audience with his album. If he didn't have a radio joint, he might not be able to expose that audience to his "gutter" joints.

"That's when he started learning how to make records, toward the end," said Mark Pitts about Wallace's musical evolution. "He started making records for a hit, and hooks for the radio."

If Wallace lost the battle for the A-sides of his singles, so be it—as long as he got to do whatever he wanted on the B-side. If he lost the street, he lost everything, and having a "gutter" joint that would keep the Ron Gs, Kid Capris, and other underground mix-tape kings happy was the only way to go.

There was only one person to call.

DJ Premier sat in a corner of D&D Studios, his head bowed down, nodding over his MPC60 drum machine.

The beat reverberated throughout Studio B—a smoldering complexity underneath a sparse, spare rhythm, like a shark swimming underneath the surface of a calm sea. Wallace wanted a hot underground joint, so he visited the master.

"I just need that gutter shit," Premier remembered Wallace asking him. He was almost done with his album, he finally had a September release date, but Wallace felt as if he just needed one more thing, one more final touch that would

DJ Premier was one of hip hop's most sought-after producers, and the songs he made with Biggie were always classics.

send the album over the edge. And he needed it quick.

"You talking about having it done in, like, two days," Premier said.

"I know you can do it," Wallace said. "I don't give a fuck. Just loop 'Impeach the President.'"

"For real?"

"Flip that and just do some shit to it," he said.

"All right," Premier said. "Meet me at the studio."

And a day later, he did. Instead of sampling the Honeydrippers' classic Nixon-era breakbeat, Premier programmed a variation of the beat—making the drums a little more synthetic, a little more spaced out. Flipping it, so to speak.

Premier had gotten into his favorite workshop, D&D Studios' "B" room, and had been working the whole thing out since 5:30 in the afternoon. Wallace showed up a few hours later, entourage in tow.

"It's a smash," Wallace said when he first heard it. He offered Premier a suggestion about using another rhythm to counter the main rhythm, to give the track a jittery feel. Primo nodded and got back to work.

Wallace mostly sat in the back of the room, saying nothing, writing nothing down, just nodding his head and mumbling to himself, over and over again.

Then he disappeared into the lounge.

Premier felt a tap on his shoulder. It was Dave Lotwin, one of the two D's who co-owned the studio.

"Do you know what he's doing back there?" Lotwin asked, his eyebrow raised. "What?"

Lotwin leaned close and whispered in his ear, "Go check it out."

Primo got up and opened the door in the middle of Studio B. He walked down a short corridor. The vocal booth was just off to his right, and a little bit farther back was the Studio B private lounge, a little place that at one time was probably a storage room.

He opened the door.

Wallace was there, leaning back on the couch. His pants were open. Two attractive women had their heads between his legs.

"Yo, Preme," Wallace said. "You want some of this?"

"Nah, I'm good," he said. Primo closed the door and chuckled.

Wallace eventually came out and sat in the room. It was getting late and they still hadn't even tracked his vocals. He sat around listening to the track over and over again, saying nothing.

"We had been in the studio for the longest time doing nothing but listening to the track," Premier said. "I was getting worried. We still smoking and drinking, and he ain't writing nothing."

Wallace looked up. "I'm ready."

No notepad, no notes, nothing. Premier watched him step into the booth, the same booth where he had watched Nas a few months earlier do the exact same thing for "New York State of Mind." Just step up to the mike and do it.

Premier hit the button on the board. And Wallace closed his eyes, nodding his head for a few seconds, letting the rhythm play for a few beats. Then he started rapping: "Live from Bedford-Stuyvesant, the livest one / Representing BK to the fullest, gats I pull it / Bastards duckin' when Big be buckin' / Chickenheads be cluckin' in my back room fuckin' . . ."

Premier sat there amazed. Even what just happened in the back room of the studio had made its way into his lyrics. It was like he picked the rhyme out of thin air and assembled the pieces in real time, at will. Within less than an hour, the whole song was recorded, three perfect verses.

They didn't have a song title, but Wallace had an idea for the chorus, based on the last line of each verse, where Wallace says, "unbelievable." They could scratch in the vocal hook from R. Kelly's single, "Your Body's Calling."

"You sure that's gonna fit?" Premier asked.

"Yeah, it's gonna sound just right. Don't worry about it."

Premier picked up a copy of the R. Kelly 12-inch at Rock & Soul Records a few blocks from the studio. Much to his surprise, when he scratched it and looped it, the hook did fit perfectly. The bigger surprise came a few days after the final mix-down: Premier and his brother were driving back to Brooklyn late after a recording session when they heard another car booming the track. Premier caught up with the car at a stoplight, irate that the song had already been bootlegged.

"How'd you get a copy of that!?" he yelled, rolling down his window.

"It's on the radio," said the driver, who rolled up his window and sped off.

Premier idled at the curb, shocked. The song wasn't even a week old, and it was already getting radio play. That had never happened to him before.

Within a year, he'd also have the first gold single RIAA plaque of his career.

Somehow "gutter" became "butter," and Wallace was the cause.

He was getting Big, now. Notoriously so.

Just as "Juicy" hit regular rotation on BET and MTV, "Unbelievable" was becoming the hottest track in clubs. The only thing critics and fans in New York City could talk about was the Notorious B.I.G. Though his earliest releases used the name Biggie Smalls, he was forced to adopt the Notorious B.I.G. (He sometimes said the acronym stood for "Business Instead of Game," though Cease said the crew would sometimes flip it to mean "Bullet in the Gut").

"I changed the name because there was a little white boy on Atlantic Records named Biggie Smalls," he explained. "His lawyers stepped to me, and were like, I can't use the name or I'll be sued. But I still say Biggie Smalls in my rhymes. I just have 'The Notorious B.I.G.' as a stamp on the front of the record. Everybody knows who the real Smalls is."

If the Wu-Tang Clan was the new super group, Nas was New York's savior, and Black Moon the darlings of the underground, the Notorious B.I.G. was poised to become, as he put it, "the black Frank White," Christopher Walken's starring role in the movie *King of New York.* And *Ready to Die* would remove all doubt.

From beginning to end, the album was a revelation. Not so much in content as in function. People have asked what happened to the black protest novelists, people like Chester Himes and Donald Goines and Richard Wright, who used to tell stories that exposed the reality of what was happening in the ghetto. That art form didn't die as much as transform itself. Rapping rather than writing became the most effective medium for getting the word out about anything. The history of popular music, of any race, has always been shorter, flashier, faster. Why spend 300 pages to make your point when, with the right beat and the perfect lyrics, a comparable emotional impact could be delivered to a larger audience in three minutes?

In the introduction to *Native Son,* Richard Wright described the real-life men who shaped his fictional protagonist, Bigger Thomas—the tough guys and "bad niggers" who would never bow down to anyone, black or white. "His rebellious spirit made him violate all the taboos and consequently he always oscillated between moods of intense elation and depression," Wright wrote. "He was never happier than when he had outwitted some foolish custom, and he was never more melancholy than when brooding over the impossibility of his ever being free."

It's not clear if Wallace ever read *Native Son,* but *Ready to Die* was the musical personification of everything Wright communicated in that novel. The character Wallace portrayed as Biggie Smalls walked the razor's edge, gat in hand, a self-described menace to society (and sexual dynamo). But the man of action also has a conscience, and he is haunted by his own propensity for heartless violence and self-destruction. The album was a pitch-perfect depiction of the desperation of life in the Brooklyn ghetto—*Manchild in the Promised Land* as street opera.

The album's introduction neatly summarized the evolution of a street thug, from delivery room to domestic violence to doing dirt. Then the music kicked off with "Things Done Changed," one of the most powerful depictions of modern-day life in the 'hood ever recorded. The song recalls the innocent games of youth and describes in dramatic fashion how they were transformed when crack cocaine was introduced to the neighborhood. Jump ropes were replaced with yellow crime-scene tape, plastic bottles of juice with 40-ounce bottles of malt liquor, skelly games with gun battles.

"Back in the days, our parents used to take care of us," he rapped. "Look at 'em now. They're even fuckin' scared of us. / Calling the city for help because they can't maintain. / Damn, shit done changed."

Rather than being a distant narrator, Wallace peppered the song with details from his own life: "Shit, my mama got cancer in her breast. / Don't ask me why I'm muthafuckin' stressed. / Things done changed."

The album's next three songs served as a showcase for his lyrical gifts. The stories depicted on "Gimme the Loot," "Machine Gun Funk," and "Warning" were bloody yet sarcastic. Like the filmmaker Quentin Tarantino, Wallace managed to make profound statements about the nature of violence by depicting it as random, brutal, and terrifying. In "Everyday Struggle," death lurked around every darkened corner, either at the hands of a corrupt cop, or another stickup kid like himself, itchy to write his name on the wall with someone else's blood. Nobody could accuse Wallace of glamorizing a life of crime. If you listened to his album from start to finish, all the gangsta trappings of money and fame ring as hollow as the sound of a bullet casing bouncing off the pavement.

Despite the funkiness of "The What," the disarming poignancy of "Me and My Bitch," and the freestyle master class that was "Unbelievable," the album's most memorable moment was "Suicidal Thoughts." Nothing could prepare listeners for a song in which Biggie apologizes for the wrong turn his life has taken, then blows his brains out. The sound of the crisp gunshot and the phone receiver dropping to the ground is chilling, reckless, and yet compelling.

The most important thing about *Ready to Die* was that it displayed Wallace's talent as more than just being a potent freestyler. He could drop message rap if he wanted to, yet he didn't want to be boxed into any category. Biggie reveled in the good life in a way that was compelling no matter how one felt about the sex or violence. And yet it was now impossible to listen to others rapping about the excitement and riches to be had in the drug game without recalling the stress of "Everyday Struggle" or the self-loathing apathy of "Suicidal Thoughts."

There was no way Uptown Records would ever have put out this album, because there was no way to predict the audience's reaction. But "Puff Daddy" anticipated that the public was looking for something new, something raw. And he provided them with an album that would make some people party, make some people mad, and that just might make some people think.

Christopher Wallace stood near the stoop of the apartment building he grew up in, a lit blunt in his mouth, his eyes looking toward Fulton Street. On the surface, if someone from the neighborhood had been watching him, it would have seemed like nothing had changed.

Yet everything had changed. Every single car that passed was blasting a different song from *Ready to Die*. These days, the outsiders who came to the neighborhood with notepads in hand weren't detectives but journalists. And instead of serving up crack, Wallace stood on the very same corner as before serving up quotes about his perspective on life.

Meeting him for the first time on a blistering Tuesday afternoon in late September, it was easy to see why folks called him the Mayor.

"I run this, dog," he explained. "I mean, I've been doing this for the longest. Everybody know Biggie. There ain't a nigga out here that don't know me. From down in that area they call Park Slope to all the way up in East New York, you know what I'm saying? And they all go through me. If they don't know me, they know of me. And they give me my respect—a lot."

He just stood there and people found their way to him, some to say hello or

Wallace in the foyer of the apartment building where he grew up. "I wasn't trying to get discovered," he said. "I put all my time into hustling."

to give him a pound. Some would stand just within earshot, just to hear him talk. Some had other ideas.

Two short kids, eyes red from an afternoon of smoking blunts, walked up to Wallace in the middle of our interview. The rapper had been telling stories about growing up in the neighborhood, selling crack, dodging bullets, and some of the other things that directly influenced the content of his album.

Wallace acknowledged the kids with a nod. They were Trife and Larceny, part of a crew of youngsters Wallace called "The Snakes."

"You got that deuce-deuce?" Trife asked him.

"Why, what's up?" said Wallace, curious what use his friend could have for a .22 caliber pistol.

"We gonna throw this nigga down for his VCR, kid," said Larceny. "That shit is butter."

"Take it!" Wallace said. "I don't know where my shit is, though. Fuckin' Moose has an M-1, though."

"Nah, that shit is too big," Trife said, shaking his head.

"What about that Eight?" Wallace said, referring to a .38-caliber pistol someone had.

"Never mind," Trife said. He nodded his head and Larceny followed him down the street.

"I know exactly where that gun is," Wallace said with a mischievous glint as soon as the two were out of earshot, "but I'm not gonna be a part of that shit there. Fuck that!"

He wasn't concerned with concealing what had happened from the journalist standing next to him. Yet as he watched the two young men walk away, he expressed his need to help things change, even if it was only one step at a time.

"You've got to understand," he said, "you got a group of niggas over here who are fifteen and sixteen years old, and ain't doing nothing out here. Their parents look at them like they're doomed, but I can't let them do that, because I didn't do that. Either get some kind of hustle, or roll with me, but don't be sitting there just smoking lah and giving your life over to the weed."

"Even if niggas don't go to school, you're going to be doing something," he insisted. "You ain't just going to be sitting there disappointing your parents. You're going to get some kind of paper. Try to play some ball. You're going to do *something*, man. You can't just sit there because that's what really hurts parents the most, to just watch their son give up and not do nothing to fix it."

Those who focused on the negativity of *Ready to Die*—from the bleak-sounding title to the album's closing track, "Suicidal Thoughts"—missed the fact that it was fundamentally an album about survival, as summed up in the line "Another day another struggle." Wallace used this very line as he talked about his young friends in the grind, and I asked him to explain what it meant to him: "A struggle in my eyes is living," he said with a meaningful pause. "*Living.* Waking up is a struggle for some of these niggas, man. For a lot of these niggas—eighty-five percent. They between the ages of fourteen and eighteen and they got single parents. That's the struggle right there. Just waking up dead-assed broke."

One of the by-products of Wallace's newfound success was to realize his dream of having a group of his own put a record out, his Junior M.A.F.I.A. "He steps in the door, get his feet wet, and he go spread it," Cease said. "That's how Big did." The goal was to give the kids in his crew something to do—even if some of them couldn't rhyme. Blake and Banger were already rapping a little. And Cease's sister had a friend named Lil' Kim who could kick serious rhymes. (She'd soon be kicking it with Biggie as well.) Big Poppa wanted to put everybody on: Chico, Lil' Cease, Klept, Nino, Trife, Larceny, and Gutter. They would have an opportunity because he had an opportunity—and he would use another brother from the neighborhood to form his own record label and make that dream a reality.

Lance "Understanding" Rivera was that brother, a heavy-set dude with impeccable street credentials. Rivera's younger brother Justice was one of the first people to recognize Wallace's talent, circulating some of the tapes he made with 50 Grand to people he knew in the industry like Kedar Massenberg, who would one day rise to be the president of Motown, working with the likes of Erykah Badu, India.Arie, and D'Angelo. (Massenberg later admitted to Rivera that the worst decision he ever made in his career was having a young Christopher Wallace on his couch and not signing him.)

"My brother had wanted to be in the music business since he was little," Un said. "But I ain't never really paid any attention to it."

Justice, of course, brought Wallace to Un, and Un was impressed with Wallace's style, but not enough to take the plunge.

"I used to sell drugs and shit and I was getting some money," Un said.

Un "understood" the game and was smart enough to recognize opportunity. Because of his brother, he was in the right place in the right time, right before Wallace blew up with the success of *Ready to Die.* He was always there to loan money to Wallace when he came up short, to make sure that everyone in the crew had pocket money.

But it wasn't until he met Sean "Puffy" Combs for the first time that he realized exactly how he wanted to be involved. Wallace invited Un to a Jodeci video shoot and Un sensed that Combs was intimidated by his massive presence.

"Puff pulled up across the street and he called Big over," Un remembered. "I seen him talkin'. Then I seen Big put his head down. Something told me they was over there talkin' about me. So when Big came back across the street he just looked at me, and he ain't want to say nothin'. I was like, 'You ain't got to explain.'"

Un was insulted. Combs hadn't even tried to find out who he was. He just took one look at him and decided that he was trouble. As he left the video shoot, he vowed to make Combs pay for this slight. And he would not get his revenge on the streets, but in the boardroom.

"I got on the phone and called my brother," Un said. "I told him, 'I want to be in the music business because I want to become a thorn in Puff's side.'"

"I knew the nigga Big was dope," Rivera reasoned. "And I knew the nigga Puff needed Big. So I would get in the middle of they shit, not to really be disruptive, but to manipulate certain situations."

Wallace liked having Un around because he put money in his pocket when he didn't have any. More important, he was "real"—he had a credibility in the streets that Wallace respected and looked up to. As much as Wallace wanted to lead a bigger, better life outside of Brooklyn, he was just as afraid to change his lifestyle.

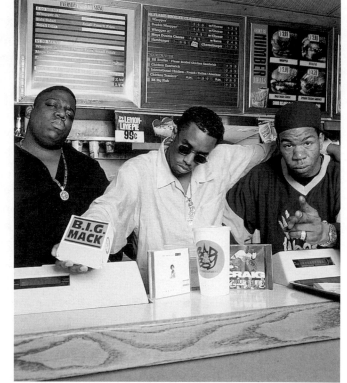

Wallace, Combs, and Craig Mack in a Bad Boy promotional shot. Combs helped Wallace understand that he was selling a product with his music.

"Ain't no real Brooklyn niggas blew up to the point where they could be considered a superstar, and stayed," Wallace said wistfully. "Everybody moved. I'm gonna get me a spot one day, but I have to be surrounded by my niggas. I'm afraid of how my shit's gonna sound if I don't fuck with my niggas. That's the reason Chubb Rock fell off. He live in the Hamptons. There's no 'hood out there."

Wallace took in his surroundings for a moment. "How real can your music be if you waking up in the morning hearing birds and crickets?"

And what would he rather hear instead?

"A lot of construction work, the smell of Chinese takeout, and someone banging a different track from my album," he said. "Brooklyn is the love borough."

His love for Brooklyn, however, didn't prevent Wallace from being paranoid. Quite the contrary. He knew the mindset of people who lived by taking things away from those who had much. Now he was on the other side. On one hand he enjoyed his success. On the other, he realized he had something to lose.

When Touré went to Wallace's house to profile him for the *New York Times,* he peeped the security protocol. "Every time the door opened, somebody would look down to see who it was," he said. "Even little girls just coming back with milk were interrogated, like, Who are you? That street sense that they had to watch out for everything and everybody never went away." Toward the end of the interview he watched as Lil' Cease went to Wallace's bedroom. "He just calmly reached under the mattress and pulled out a pistol and put it under his fuckin' pants like it was nothing," Touré recalled. "I was like, Wow, these niggas are still mobilized for street warfare."

Throughout all his interviews, Wallace always seemed to have a hard time envisioning himself living to a ripe old age. "I'm scared to death," he once said, "scared of getting my brains blown out."

"I ain't gonna lie to you," he told Louis "Atco" Romaine from *Rap Pages*. "I really never pictured even being like 35, I guess 'cause I was always living day to day, and there's always so many things that coulda just snuffed me out. The way niggas be trippin' out here, I can't really plan that far ahead. And when you plan, shit be going wrong anyway. We just living day by day."

That didn't stop him from making permanent moves. By the time I met Wallace on September 27, 1994, barely two weeks after the release of *Ready to Die,* he was already married to a backup singer and songwriter, who up until that point no one had ever heard of, named Faith Evans. Just the mention of her name made Wallace smile sheepishly.

"When you start hustling, you get introduced to shit real fast," he said. "You be getting pussy real quick, because you be fuckin' the users sometimes. I done had every kind of bitch. Young bitch, old bitch, users, mothers, grandmothers, dumb bitches, every kind of bitch I done fucked and I *never* ever met no girl like my wife," he said with pride.

"She talks to me like nobody else on earth talked to me before. The conversations be striking me like no other honey I ever fucked with," Wallace said.

"So where is she?" I asked.

Wallace smiled.

"She ain't speaking to me right now, but it's all good."

That's how the whole thing started between the two of them. Just a little harmless conversation followed by a whole lot of drama.

He first saw Faith at a Bad Boy promotional photo shoot in June 1994. "She was killing me with those eyes," Wallace recalled. "I rolled up to her and said, 'You're the kind of girl I would marry.' And she said, 'Why don't you?' So I was like, 'Fuck it then—it's on!'" Faith remembered being introduced to Wallace by the female rapper Hurricane Gloria, who was close with Redman, another mutual friend. "During the lunch break or whatever, he asked to see some pictures I had," Faith said. "And obviously he was really slick 'cause he got my phone number off the envelope."

Born in Lakeland, Florida, to a black mother and an Italian father she never met, Evans moved to Newark, New Jersey, as a child and was raised by her grandparents. They made sure she was in church, which is where she honed a voice that was deep, powerful, and poetic. Faith was a hybrid of influences: Mahalia Jackson's power, Aretha's soul, and Sarah Vaughn's nimble touch when it came to phrasing. She won talent pageants, sang at weddings and funerals, and after graduating from Newark's University High, she went to Fordham University.

She dropped out a few months later and ended up in the New York music scene. Her boyfriend, Kiyamma Griffin, produced tracks for Christopher Williams, an Uptown artist who was working with Combs at the time.

Combs and future Bad Boy executive Kirk Burrowes met Evans through her boyfriend. "He was working on Usher's album and we were pursuing him to be a Bad Boy producer," said Burrowes. "He brought along his pregnant girlfriend, and we didn't have anyone to do a background vocal. He said, 'My girlfriend can sing.' And she did. Puffy said her voice sounded like rain."

Faith signed to Bad Boy as an artist and composer. She had to support herself and her daughter Chyna, so she did background vocals on Mary J. Blige's *My Life* album, writing songs for Blige and Color Me Badd as well as composing tracks for herself. Combs believed that she would be a big star and wanted her introduction to be perfect.

"Faith is very complex," Combs said. "She's a true diva. A lot of people that be kicking that shit aren't divas. True divas don't act like divas. They don't say they're divas. They're just interesting and they're fly."

Evans was intrigued by the heavyset dude with the suave demeanor. "He was pretty quiet then," she recalled, "but he had a certain charm about him. I was talking so much I don't know really what attracted him to me. I was kind of familiar with the name Biggie Smalls, but I really wasn't that much into hip hop at the time, so I didn't know that was him." Biggie didn't even know Faith was an artist signed to Bad Boy. "He thought I was a background singer or something," she said with a smile.

"I gave him a ride to Brooklyn from the photo shoot and we just ended up"— she paused and smiled—"you know . . . He said he was gonna call me. He did, and of course it was a very short courtship." They were only apart for a few hours before Wallace asked her out to a movie. Evans doesn't remember what they went to see at the Newport Center Mall in Jersey City, only that Wallace kept making her laugh. They walked around the mall talking and holding hands.

"We just kind of hung out doing all fun stuff," she said. "We went to a couple of parties, then after like a week or so he told me he was gonna marry me, and I said okay."

The whole thing wasn't as crazy as it might have seemed. Faith and Biggie had a lot in common. Both were artists on Puffy's hot new label, and both had been through the frustration of working on projects for years only to see them languish as Bad Boy Records made the transition from Uptown to Arista. Both were studio rats—perfectionists willing to spend hours upon hours in the lab to get a song exactly right. Both were close to their mothers and haunted by fathers they never knew. Both were Geminis—needy free spirits who hated to be held down, yet at the same time extremely jealous and codependent. Both adored their daughters—Wallace had T'Yanna, and Faith had Chyna, her little girl from a previous relationship. She loved to cook. He loved to eat.

Faith found herself attracted to Biggie not because of his money—he was flat broke at the time, and, ironically, she was the one with more financial stability, having already written songs that were recorded by people like Mary J. Blige. Faith also liked the fact that Wallace had so much game—his whole approach, from the way he got her phone number, down to the way that he called her that night for a date that never really ended.

"Let's get married," he said one night. They were in Faith's car, which is where they spent a lot of their time. Like Quincy Jones and Spike Lee before him, Wallace never learned how to drive and was famous for convincing people not only to pick him up but take him anywhere he wanted to go. This time they were on the way to pick up some Chinese food near Wallace's apartment on St. James.

"Are you serious?" Faith said.

"I'm dead ass," he said.

"All right, okay," she said. She smiled warmly at the memory. And the funny thing was she had no doubts about it.

"Absolutely nothing occurred to me like, *Hello, you don't really know him. You just met him,*" she said. "It was a different feeling. I felt the same way that he did. I had never met anybody like him."

Wallace told everybody who would listen that he was getting married. And like the boy who cried wolf, nobody believed him.

"I'm getting married, Ma," Wallace told his mother one evening. She laughed at him. He pouted.

"Mark ain't believe me. Puffy ain't believe me. Ma, I'm getting married on Monday." This conversation was taking place on a Friday night.

"Congratulations," she said, her voice brimming with sarcasm. "Who's the lucky one?"

"Ma, I'm serious. I'm getting married. I found this honey, Mom. This is the one. This is the one."

Ms. Wallace began to lose her temper.

"Christopher, cut it out!" she scolded him. "Every second you come in you found one. Please, no, you found one hundred. Get a life!"

Wallace called Jan. The two of them had been separated for several months, but they still had feelings for each other. Jan even thought there was a small possibility they would get back together, based on the fact that he was just as flirtatious as ever. Those hopes ended when he told her he was getting married.

"For real?" she said, her voice suddenly small.

"Yeah, for real."

"I only have one question," Jan said, collecting her thoughts. "If you had the chance to let me go, why didn't you let me go? You brought me back for this?"

"If I let you go, I thought I'd lose my baby," he said. "I was being selfish."

Jan promised him that she would never keep T'Yanna from him. She said she just wanted him to be happy.

"Damn, that was too easy," he said. "I was expecting you to trip, and you didn't."

"I'm not gonna trip," Jan said, though the news hurt bad. "If you're happy and that's what you want to do," she said, "then I'm happy for you."

Kim was another story. Her lovers' quarrels with Big were growing more frequent and more heated.

Knowing that he wasn't going to lose T'Yanna was all Wallace needed. He left with Faith for Rosslyn, New York, a small town in upstate New York. One of his boys from the 'hood, Gutter, stood as his witness. On August 4, 1994, the bride and groom got dressed up to stand in front of the justice of the peace.

"*Kind of* dressed up," Faith corrected. The groom wore jeans and a button-down shirt. The bride wore a simple dress. There was no cake, and no time for a honeymoon. In ten minutes they were married, and within hours she dropped him back in Brooklyn so he could go to the studio and she could pick up her daughter.

He came home later that night, tired from the drive and the session. His mom was still up. "Guess what," he told her as soon as he arrived home. "I did it."

"Did what?" Ms. Wallace said, suspecting nothing.

"I got married today."

Ms. Wallace stared at her son for a minute, with no expression. "It was like hearing a ten-year-old telling you he was getting married," she would say later.

"Does she have a name?" Ms. Wallace asked.

"Faith," he replied.

"Faith? Lord have mercy. We both need faith."

Wallace still pouted. His mother didn't believe him; neither did Combs or Pitts.

Ms. Wallace still didn't believe him until she got a phone call at work from her sister Melva a day later.

"Are you listening to the radio?" she asked. "Christopher got married. He was just on the news saying hello to his 'wifey.'"

That's when Voletta came home and confronted her son. "Christopher," she asked, "are you really married?"

He rolled his eyes.

"You don't believe me when I talk to you, do you? Puffy don't believe me. Mark don't believe me. Nobody believe me. I'm married."

"I wanted to slap him," Ms. Wallace remembered.

"What is she like?" she asked, horrified. He went into his room and came back with one of her promotional photos.

"Is she white!?" Ms. Wallace asked. No, he explained to his mother, she just had a very light complexion.

It was weeks before Faith got up the nerve to go meet Ms. Wallace. Or maybe it was Biggie who had to work up his courage. He told his wife to avoid his mother. Meanwhile, Ms. Wallace just got angrier.

A few days later, Ms. Wallace called Mark Pitts, whom she trusted to give her the straight story. "She's a very nice girl," he told her. "She looks like she's very decent. She's somebody that I think you'd like."

It was weeks before Faith got up the nerve to go meet Ms. Wallace. Or maybe it was Biggie who had to work up his courage. He told Faith to avoid his mother, and Ms. Wallace got angrier and angrier at the daughter-in-law she never met. "What kind of a woman would marry a man knowing that he has a mother," she asked herself, "and not even want to meet her?"

One night, a few weeks after their wedding, Faith called 226 St. James, and Ms. Wallace picked up the phone. "May I speak to Christopher?" the voice on the phone asked tentatively. "It's Faith."

There was a long pause. Ms. Wallace exhaled, trying her best to keep cool.

"Do you have a mother?" she asked.

"Of course," Faith said.

"How would your mother feel if you ran off and got married?" she asked.

Faith was apologetic, almost to the point of tears. "Ms. Wallace, I'm so sorry, but Christopher told me to stay away from you. I know you're very upset right now, and I know exactly how you feel, because my mother would feel the same way you do, and that's how I would feel."

The two began their conversation as adversaries and ended it as friends. The door opened. Christopher came home.

"Ooh, I wanted to kill him," Ms. Wallace said. "I had fire coming out of my ears."

"How dare you tell that little girl to stay away from me!" she said.

Her son looked at her.

"Ma, you are furious. Aren't you?"

"*Christopher!*"

"Ma, look. I love you and I love her and I know you're mad. I just didn't want you to say anything because, Ma, you're a little bit opinionated. You know what I mean? And you might say something to hurt her feelings. So, I just told her to stay away from you right now."

She shook her head. What could she say? He was right.

When she and Faith finally did meet, they liked each other right away. Christopher was going on one of his promotional tours, and Faith came by their home and picked up the rest of his furniture to put it into the duplex that they had rented in Brooklyn's Fort Greene.

"It was a beautiful apartment," Ms. Wallace said. "I went over, but I just let them live their life, you know. I said, 'God, at least somebody's going to take care of him.'"

But the newlyweds hardly had a chance to enjoy the apartment or each other.

"I wouldn't even give it two weeks, a week maybe of him and I both being there at the same time," Faith said. "We got new furniture, and then he started going on his promo tour with Craig Mack." He was on the road and she was in the studio and even when she went to visit him, there was never any real time to be together. There was always pressure from one career or the other.

"It was really crazy," Faith said, looking back. "I even think about the times when I did go and visit him on the road. I would have to leave the next morning or I'm getting a call from somebody as if I'm doing something wrong. Like, 'What are you doing?' What am I *doing*? I'm with my husband."

Her husband was blowing up. It was what they both wanted. And they would have to adjust their marriage accordingly. "It wasn't like it took a long time," she said. "He just blew up. Like boom."

Ready to Die sold 500,000 copies in its first week alone. Suddenly the video for "Juicy" was all over MTV, the radio was playing his song three times an hour, and it seemed like everywhere he went, people knew who the Notorious B.I.G. was.

By November, not only was Wallace a success, but Bad Boy Records was no longer considered a fledgling label. People were beginning to know who Sean "Puffy" Combs was, and what he was capable of. Craig Mack's "Flava in Ya Ear" was No. 1 on the *Billboard* rap charts for three straight weeks. "Juicy" backed by "Unbelievable" entered at No. 5.

And there was Puffy, in the middle of it all. Racing from the set of Biggie's video shoot for "Big Poppa" at Nell's nightclub in New York, then down to a party in Philadelphia on Saturday, back up to New York for another video shoot for "Warning" on Sunday, then catching an hour's worth of sleep before going to a Mary J. Blige video shoot on Monday.

"Sleep is forbidden," Combs said. "When most are sleeping, we are working."

Puff still consulted with Harrell on some of the biggest acts at Uptown, Jodeci and Mary J. Blige. Combs reveled in the fact that he was scaring the competition. Within a year, he went from being fired to being in a position to knock both Def Jam's Russell Simmons and his best friend Harrell off the map. He had a penchant for making young men look like old men, and by embracing the street, made his rough-and-tumble artists the East Coast's platinum standard.

But Harrell was too busy to worry about Combs making him look bad. Suge Knight had been hanging around Uptown artists like Mary J. Blige and Jodeci of late, insinuating himself into their contract negotiations.

"I saw that Jodeci weren't being paid right, and I did something that's never been done before: I went to MCA, their label, and renegotiated a contract on a record that was already out. MCA gave the group a $2 million advance and doubled their point spread. Then I went to Uptown, their production company, and told Andre Harrell to give the group $75,000 a week. It didn't matter how he felt about it," Knight said. "It needed to be done. Same thing with Mary J. Blige. I told Mary to speak her mind, that she didn't have nothin' to worry about. Then I told them they was letting her out of that fucked-up deal. And they did."

There were persistent rumors that Knight had physically intimidated Harrell in the Uptown Records offices. Both Knight and Harrell denied the talk, but Harrell did hire the Fruit of Islam to guard his offices soon after the renegotiation. Both Blige and Jodeci denied any threats, instead basking in the attention Knight lavished on them.

"I know Suge's got this reputation for being a guy who goes around strong-arming," said Jodeci's Devante Swing, "but I think those rumors just come from jealous people. The thing is he won't let anybody walk over him or any of his artists—and a lot of people really resent that."

"I have had so many people take advantage of me that it's nice to finally have someone on my side," Blige said. "Suge's like that guy in the movies who goes around getting the bad people—Charles Bronson, right?"

According to a source, Knight even turned up at one of Wallace's recording sessions to see Combs and proved a quiet but powerfully menacing presence. Cease said that Knight and Combs were friendly, even posing for a picture with Wallace at a movie premier. Combs wasn't sure what Knight's intentions were, but he couldn't worry about that right now. He was focused on his own vision, and it was a beautiful thing.

"My artists are bad boys, bad boys for life, and they basically depict that type of image," Combs said. "It's the confidence they have about themselves. We just got a little bit more flavor. That's what the kids want: the realism, the lingo, the attitude, the bounce.

"That's what separates me from Russell and Andre," Combs added, feeling himself. "I live for the music. I think they live for the money. I stay up longer than either one of them; I can be out in the street a lot longer."

Combs was still close with his former mentor—after all, Harrell was the godfather to Combs's youngest son, Justin—but the two couldn't help exchanging digs in print.

"He's not a competitor yet, but he's got a great start," Harrell told a reporter from the *New York Times*. "It's not enough to have a hit record, you have to have a hit career."

Yet Combs was well on his way. *Ready to Die* was climbing the charts, and Craig Mack's "Flava in Ya Ear"

was also doing damage. It was just like after City College. When they thought he was down, he came back stronger than ever.

He threw himself a party at Roseland on the night of September 11, 1994—it was large in a style that could only be described as "Puffyesque," a term that folks would be hearing a lot more in the years ahead. It was also the first major party he had thrown since the tragedy that was City College. Video monitors featured Combs dancing in the background of videos. Many of the songs that played were hits that he cultivated for Uptown and Bad Boy, everything from Fine Young Cannibals and Doug E. Fresh to Mary J., and now Biggie and Craig Mack.

The party, more than anything else, was an announcement: We're here—and we ain't going nowhere.

Wallace was in the VIP lounge, of course. And there he held court with one of his closest friends in the rap game, an established star who identified with Big since the first moment he heard "Party and Bullshit": Tupac Shakur.

The two of them had been tight for just over a year. Every time Tupac was in town, Wallace and his friends brought the weed and they would all hang out.

Though the money was slow to come at first, by late 1994 Wallace was starting to enjoy the first fruits of Biggie's fame. The butter leather coat, the Land Cruiser. Still he wanted security for his family.

The two were both kindred spirits and physical opposites. Each saw in the other something he lacked. In Shakur, Wallace not only saw an elder in the rap game, but also someone who had survived the tumultuous childhood and abject poverty that Biggie rapped about but never actually lived. And in Biggie, Tupac recognized an artistic genius as well as someone who rolled with real thugs—gun-toting outlaws with two feet in the street life.

Shakur was at Combs's party taking a break from a highly publicized rape trial, and he was shocked to see some of the very people he held responsible for his predicament hanging close to Wallace. Wallace, who understood the New York streets, did his best to warn his friend about the shady figures he had offended, telling him, ever so subtly, to watch who he was rolling with. But it was a party, there were blunts to be smoked, champagne bottles to be popped, and even in this slightly tense environment, a good time to be had by all. For Bad Boy it was the birth of a nation, for Wallace, a first taste of superstardom, and for Shakur, the last fun night he would ever have in New York City.

WHAT'S BEEF?

CHAPTER 5

" Beef is when I see you.
Guaranteed to be in I.C.U. **"**

The first time Christopher Wallace met Tupac Shakur they clicked right away. The year was 1993. "Tupac really respected Biggie as a lyricist," said Sybil Pennix, who was Combs's assistant at the time. After they connected, she said, "They were, like, immediate friends."

Lil' Cease remembers Wallace talking about meeting Shakur after coming back from a show in Maryland with Puff to support his first single, "Party and Bullshit," in early 1993.

"Big went out there to perform that song," Cease recalled. "He said Pac was loving that shit. He stepped to Big like, 'What up, Big? I like your shit.' " Big respected his work, too, and they hit it off.

The morning after the party, at around 8 A.M., there was a knock on Wallace's hotel room door. He opened it and there was Shakur, smiling, with a bottle of Hennessy cognac in his hand.

"What up! Nigga, let's kick it." And so they did, as often as they could, sometimes speaking on the phone on a daily basis.

They might have made for an unlikely pair—so different in size and appearance—but these young men had more in common than met the eye. "Pac and Big, they really connected," Lil' Cease said. "They both was Geminis, so they both had the same personality, the same persona. They kind of looked at shit the same way." They were both book smart—and both went to great extremes to downplay the fact with their homeboys. Both men loved weed and Hennessy, and both had a spontaneous, powerful gift for storytelling. Moreover, each of them represented something that the other—in his own perverse way—envied.

The son of black activist Afeni Shakur, Tupac really did come from the kind of impoverished background that Wallace would later fabricate on the introduction to *Ready to Die*. Between being blacklisted for her revolutionary past, periods of homelessness, and sporadic drug use, Shakur's mother had seen the

WHAT'S BEEF? | 121

worst that life had to offer—and wasn't always able to shield her children from those horrors. While she was in jail during the New York Panther 21 case—accused of plotting to blow up various buildings throughout New York—she had to fight for eggs and milk to care for her unborn son.

Shakur recalled many times when his family had nothing to eat and no money. He would get picked on and teased because of his raggedy second-hand clothes. To Big, this represented a realness that he had never experienced. Shakur grew up without Colecovision, designer clothes, or expensive stereo equipment. Every day really was a struggle.

Shakur, on the other hand, respected Wallace's street pedigree. Although he had known hustlers in New York and Baltimore, he wasn't really a street guy. Shakur was a student at Baltimore School for the Arts, where he studied with Jada Pinkett. He also suffered from the same problem that the Black Panther Huey P. Newton once had—he was so handsome, he had to fight that much harder to make people fear and respect him on a street level. Wallace, with his huge girth and lazy eye, didn't have that problem—some people would cross the street when they saw him coming. And despite his middle-class upbringing in a cultural sense, Wallace had a certain authentic wildness hardened by his years as a hustler on the Fulton Street strip. Wallace was the real deal and Shakur knew it. And Wallace sensed the same thing about Shakur, who had the advantage of being a veteran of the rap game, and could warn Wallace of the ups and downs he had yet to experience. In some strange way they completed each other, almost like a hip hop yin and yang.

Wallace came back from Maryland and told Cease all about Tupac, who was a big star to them. "Dawg is real," Wallace said. "I gave him my number, and told him when he come up here we'll kick it, or when I go out there we'll kick it. We're gonna keep in touch. He's supposed to come up here and do a movie." Cease said they used to talk every other day. "That was Big's homie."

During one trip to California Wallace stayed with Tupac and slept on his couch. Another time Shakur visited Fulton and Washington with much fanfare. "He came through the 'hood, and I was respecting that shit," said Lil' Cease. "That's gangster. He was big to us." Shakur arrived in a stretch limousine to pick up Wallace for a show he was doing at the Ritz that night. "A white limo pulls up on the block," Cease recalled. "Pac jumps out. The 'hood's going crazy."

Wallace, Cease, and the rest of the crew took Shakur downstairs underneath a pizzeria on Fulton that doubled as an underground gambling spot. Cease was surprised that a rap superstar who wasn't from the neighborhood had no problem rolling up his sleeves and shooting Cee-Lo with the rest of them.

"Tupac was down there and everything," Lil' Cease said, "keeping it gully."

Later that night, Wallace and Shakur performed onstage together at the Ritz. Cease watched them rock the crowd side by side, East meets West–style.

"They'd just feed off each other," said Cease. "You couldn't really take them apart. Them niggas was together every day. He had to prove something to Big and Big had to prove something to him. Pac was that thug nigga in the industry. And Big was the next thing to come from the 'hood that was gonna fuck niggas' heads up. And they were building, together. That shit was looking strong. They was really looking out for each other, and they did records together."

In September 1993, Pac was doing a show at the Ritz and invited Big to come open for him. "Big's out there doing his song and everybody was giving him love," Cease recalled. "Big got so hyper that he fell and bust his ass right on stage! The whole crowd saw, but he kept on goin'. It amazed me 'cause nothing stopped his flow. He was on his back still rhyming. The crowd thought it was part of the show and they went crazy."

Their most memorable show together was the legendary performance at the Budweiser Superfest in October 1993. Biggie and Pac shared the Madison Square Garden stage with Big Daddy Kane, Kane's dancers Scoob and Scrap Lover, and Shyheim the Rugged Child, alongside DJ Mister Cee. Big electrified the crowd by demanding "Where Brooklyn at?" before ripping a rhyme about his "seven Mac-11s, about eight .38s, nine 9s, ten Mac-10s / The shits never end . . ." Pac cheered his friend's masterful verse and then took over microphone duties. "No matter how you try / Niggas never die," Pac proclaimed. "We just retaliate with hate until we multiply." It was a seminal event in rap history, a session that solidified Shakur's East Coast fan base while introducing Wallace as the hottest new MC of the moment.

Backstage at that show Wallace introduced Shakur to his neighbor Easy Mo Bee, who would later produce most of the tracks on Shakur's *Me Against the World*. Mo Bee also produced the first duet between Wallace and Shakur, "Runnin'," which was meant to appear on Shakur's first Thug Life album. When it was shelved at the last minute, "Let's Get It On," a song Big and Pac did for Eddie F & The Untouchables with Mount Vernonites Heavy D and Grand Puba, became their first official joint release in 1994.

Shakur and Wallace also recorded a song for *Ready to Die* along with Randy "Stretch" Walker of the Live Squad, a New York–based gangsta rap trio. But Combs thought the song was too raw for the direction he wanted to take Biggie, and the song was never released.

In some interviews, Tupac said that the plan was for Wallace to be an unofficial member of Thug Life. Their cliques began politicking at the "Runnin'" session—Wallace, Shakur, members of the Outlawz and Junior M.A.F.I.A. all hung out together smoking trees. "It was a cool vibe—he was a real nigga," Lil' Cease said. "It was our team and they team, but we were all together as one. That shit used to be fun."

Just about any time Shakur was in New York, he and Wallace would hang out. If Pac needed weed, protection, anything, Biggie was there for him. "We used to make sure he was good," Cease recalled. "What you need? Whatever it is. You got it. Big can't make it, he'll send lil' niggas up there. Yo, go take him these two nines. Put 'em in a bag, get on the train, go drop 'em off. We used to do that type of shit for the nigga up here. We taking our chance to do it for another nigga. But that's 'cause we was thorough niggas. He was cool and we was fuckin' with him. Big about to get out there, he out there poppin'. Shit was lookin' right. So a nigga was doin' it for him out of love."

Shakur spent his time traveling between New York, the Bay Area, Atlanta, and California. Wallace stayed with him once on a trip to California. The two communicated daily. But when Shakur came to New York in late 1993 for the filming of *Above the Rim,* he started making new friends.

Jacques Agnant, a.k.a. "Haitian Jack," was a music promoter and all-around player

Gemini brothers Wallace and Shakur blowing up the Palladium, New York City, 1993. "They'd just feed off each other," said Lil' Cease. "You couldn't really take them apart."

with all the respect, admiration, and fear that comes from being a "real street nigga." Shakur met him while researching his role Birdie in the movie *Above the Rim*.

It might seem contradictory for a gangsta rapper to have to research a role on how to play a street thug if he was truly "keeping it real," as he said on his records. But to question Shakur would be to misunderstand his seriousness as an actor. Tupac Shakur had more in common with a young Dustin Hoffman than with other rappers who made the transition from recording studio to movie screen. A star pupil in the Baltimore School for the Arts' prestigious acting program, Shakur was taught that acting is telling the truth under imaginary circumstances. He was familiar with the Method—a way of making a character real by going beyond the script so as to understand not only what a character was doing and saying but why. The only way Shakur felt he could do that was to walk around the world in the character's shoes—to get close enough that one could understand his soul.

One School for the Arts teacher who was particularly close to Shakur throughout his life, Donald Hicken, had long discussions with his former pupil about the separation between Tupac the person and 2Pac the artist. Hicken believed that authenticity of performance was different from authenticity of life, that what made an actor credible was his ability to make the journey between those two worlds. If you lived the life you portrayed, he felt, there was no journey.

"[Tupac] had a completely different take on it," Hicken said. "His point of view was that he didn't want to be a phony. He needed to be authentic. He needed to be real. And in order to do that, he needed to live what he said. What he wrote was what he lived."

"I know how to play a West Coast bad boy," Shakur explained. "But I don't know how to do that whole East Coast thing. I was hanging around the real thing—that's how I do it: that's how I did it with *Juice,* that's how I do it with everything. So I'm hanging around these dudes—and I'm picking up their game. I didn't have to dress with a hoodie to be a thug. So I was dressing like they were dressing. They took me shopping, and that's when I bought my Rolex and my jewels. They made me mature. They introduced me to all these gangsters in Brooklyn. They was showing me all these guys who I needed to know to be safe in New York."

Shakur was seeing a whole new world—big-time dealers, the kind of guys with money-counting machines, not "shoebox" money. Agnant and his friends chided Shakur for hanging out with the young rap crowd. They were going to be his introduction to a whole new world—the "upper echelon." Shakur said Agnant promised him, "We're not gonna let you get into no trouble."

Agnant took him to Nell's, where he first met 19-year-old Ayana Jackson. And it was there on the club's dance floor that Shakur said Jackson had oral sex with him before leaving with him to have sex. Then, on the night of November 18,

1993, Ayana Jackson came to the rapper's $750-a-night suite at the Parker Meridien Hotel. Shakur said Agnant fixed drinks for everyone after she arrived. Wallace was reportedly there, too, chilling with Shakur and planning to go with him to a show at a New Jersey club. But Wallace decided to leave soon after Jackson showed up.

Jackson and Shakur retired to the bedroom, where they got comfortable.

"That's all I'm thinking about—getting another blow job," Shakur said. But before anything could go down, Agnant and Pac's road manager Charles "Man" Fuller entered the room. Shakur said nothing. The unspoken gangster code about women—especially those who were considered groupies—was that unless you claimed one as your "girl," they were to be shared with the whole crew. Holding out would be considered a sign of weakness. And Shakur, always aware of his street rep, made a decision he would later regret.

"How do I look saying 'Hold on'?" Shakur reasoned in his interview with Powell. "That would be making her my girl. I'm not making her close like that." Shakur said he left the room, sat down on the couch, and fell asleep.

His next memory, he said, was of being woken up by Agnant. He felt groggy. The lights had been turned up.

"The whole mood had changed," Shakur recalled. "When I woke up, it felt like I had been drugged. I didn't know how much time had passed."

Jackson was screaming and crying. "Why did you let them do this to me?" she demanded of Shakur. "I came to see you! You let them do this to me! This is not the last time you're going to hear from me," he recalled her saying.

Moments later, Shakur received a call from his publicist to come down to the hotel lobby. As soon as he stepped out of the elevator, police pounced on him.

Shakur, Agnant, and Fuller were arrested on the spot. They would be bailed out that same night, but Shakur refused to use Agnant's lawyer, who was affiliated with the PBA, a police union.

Shakur's lawyer, Michael Warren, had lots of questions about Agnant but Shakur refused to tell him anything. "I wouldn't give up no information about these guys," he said. "I thought they were criminals; I needed to protect them from the world."

Shakur's lawyer now believes that Agnant was a confidential informant working with police. Warren said that he had a long rap sheet in different states, but never seemed to do any time. Agnant was able to have his case separated from that of Shakur and Fuller, and he pleaded guilty to sexual misconduct, receiving probation. As Pac's case moved closer to trial, communication between the men dwindled. Shakur and Agnant would never speak again.

Shakur spent the morning of Tuesday, November 29, 1994, at 100 Centre Street in courtroom 677, where the Honorable Judge Daniel P. Fitzgerald was presiding over his

trial for sodomy, sexual abuse, and weapons possession. Shakur sat next to his codefendant Charles "Man" Fuller with an impassive expression as he listened to Assistant District Attorney Melissa Mourges argue why both men deserved the maximum, 25 years. Today was judgment day: after closing arguments by both sides, the jury would convene and then deliver their verdict. Though he was usually restrained in court, Shakur saved his bold statements for

the horde of press waiting outside the courtroom for a juicy quote. As witty and verbose as Muhammad Ali in his prime, Tupac seldom disappointed. "No matter what happens," he told reporters that afternoon, "innocent or guilty, my life is ruined."

Even before the verdict was read, Shakur's reputation suffered as a result of the rape charge. His close friend, director John Singleton, who had cast him opposite Janet Jackson in *Poetic Justice,* was forced to drop him from the movie *Higher Learning* at the urging of Columbia Pictures execs. Shakur was furious, and the two former friends fell out over it. Pac's biggest crossover hit was "Keep Your Head Up," a heartfelt tribute to black women, which took brothers to task for disrespecting them—asking, at one point, "Why do we rape our women?" Now, in the press and on the street, black women were taking him to task.

"This trial is all about my image. It has nothing to do with me," said Shakur. "This is what I do for a living. I'm selling records. Don't get it twisted. This is not my life." Shakur steadfastly maintained his innocence from the start. He made no apologies for connecting with many of the women who threw themselves at

Nobody who knew Tupac before he became 2Pac believed he was guilty of rape. But they worried about his judgment when it came to choosing his friends.

him from coast to coast. But why would he need to force himself on anyone when there were so many women willing to do whatever he asked? Almost nobody who knew Tupac before he became 2Pac believed he was guilty of rape. But they worried about his judgment when it came to his friends—friends who didn't always have his best interests at heart. But Shakur could be stubborn.

"I had already got a call from Mike Tyson saying, 'Pac, don't hang with Jack, he's bad news,'" Shakur said. "But I thought Tyson was being paranoid, so I was like, 'I'm not going to leave Jack until I see it for myself.'" But when Agnant had his court case separated, Shakur had a change of heart. "I was angry," he said. "I put it in the newspapers."

A "hanger-on" is what Shakur called Agnant in an item that appeared in A. J. Benza's popular gossip page in New York's *Daily News*. At the time the celebrity grapevine was buzzing about Shakur dating Madonna and hanging out with Mickey Rourke. But those in the know read the quote about Agnant and anticipated trouble. Word was out on the street—they had beef. "This was the first time I had ever said anything against him," Shakur said. "So I was nervous, waiting for him to attack."

At this point Big and Pac were still cool. Pac had understood when the song they recorded together did not make *Ready to Die*. But he was disappointed that he wasn't even thanked in the album's liner notes. "I heard a lot of Pac in that album," said Money B of Digital Underground, the Oakland crew that gave Shakur his start in the rap game. "He was not even mentioned, no shout-out, nothing. I was like, Pac's gonna be mad."

Mad or not, that didn't stop them from hanging out. "We'd get on the train and go meet him at whatever hotel he was staying in," remembered D-Roc. On April 4, 1994, journalist and filmmaker dream hampton captured one such session on a video camera purchased by Shakur. The men smoked blunts and drank Hennessy in Shakur's hotel room at the Royalton in midtown Manhattan.

"I'm staying right here in this little-ass room," Shakur said. "Nigga got to stay out of trouble."

Shakur pulled out a tiny wireless microphone he had just picked up from a spy store. "From now on, bitch wanna fuck with me, I'm getting it all on tape," he told Big, laughing. "Whatchusay? You wanna give me some pussy . . . repeat that? What's that? You want to engage in consensual sex in my hotel room?"

He pondered aloud whether he should use the device to record his so-called friends, to see if they would plot against him while he was out of the room. He imagined coming back into the room Chow Yun Fat–style, guns blazing, *"Blaow! Blaow! Blaow!"*

All jokes aside, Shakur showed visible concern for his safety. Before leaving the room, he changed shirts, and then slid into a bulletproof vest.

"Good luck catching a cab," Wallace said, giving Shakur a quick embrace.

"That's all I got is good luck," Shakur said.

But Shakur's luck was running out. He and Fuller were still the only ones on trial for raping Jackson.

Months later, Shakur ran into Agnant at Puffy's party at Roseland. He was shocked to see him among Christopher Wallace's entourage. " I was hurt," Shakur fumed. "I was like, I'm going to trial, I'm probably going to get convicted, and this nigga's showing up at a party with champagne, hanging with Biggie. I was like, Damn, he's just bouncing from rapper to rapper."

Wallace greeted Shakur warmly at the party, introducing him to Faith. As soon as they had a few moments alone, Wallace pulled Shakur aside.

"You still kicking it with Jack?" Shakur recalled Wallace asking him.

"No."

"Don't," Wallace told him. "Be careful." Shakur was struck by the fact that two different people with strong Brooklyn roots—Biggie and Iron Mike—had warned him about the same man.

"We knew of them, but we didn't know them like that," said Lil' Cease

Inside the studio Junior M.A.F.I.A. was recording "Player's Anthem." The mood in the room was celebratory. Wallace was nodding his head to the beat when Cease said, "Yo, Big, I just seen Pac outside."

of Agnant. "That was Pac's friend. Those were his people. We did our own separate thing with Pac."

At the party Shakur simply ignored Agnant, never acknowledging his presence. This was a serious no-no. Even bitter rivals, when caught in public but neutral territory, were supposed to recognize each other with eye contact and the briefest of nods. But Shakur kept on talking to Wallace, never looking in Agnant's direction.

"Even though I didn't like them, I used to pretend," Shakur said. "But now I couldn't pretend no more, because I knew they were snakes. When I saw them with Biggie, that's what let me know they were snakes. I was like, 'Damn, they just bounce to the next nigga.' They weren't sending me any money. They weren't trying to help me through my charges, even though it was them that set me up. I was through with these niggas."

As Shakur's trial dragged on, he became desperate for cash. Because of the trial, he couldn't leave the city to do any performances. Even if he could, few people would book him due to the perceived security risks. Despite his skills as an actor, no completion bond company would insure a studio for his contract, which virtually blacklisted him from feature film work. He had talked with Andre Harrell, executive producer of *New York Undercover,* about appearing on the TV show, but Harrell knew that it would take a lot of convincing to get Dick Wolf and the Fox network to approve an appearance. "They don't want to get involved with too many people that have controversial issues going on," Harrell said, "like open rape cases."

One of the few outlets left for Shakur to express himself and make some money was the recording studio. Most of the earnings from his shows, and royalties from his last album, the multiplatinum *Strictly 4 My N.I.G.G.A.Z.*, went to cover various legal fees as well as supporting members of his family. When he wasn't in court, Shakur spent much of his time in the recording studio, pouring his frustration into his next album, *Me Against the World*. Shakur did not specialize in the nimble cadences and intricate internal rhymes that were Biggie's forte. But what he lacked in technique, Tupac made up for in raw emotion and naked emotional truth. Songs like "Dear Mama" and "If I Die Tonight" were masterpieces of pain and frustration.

"Pac was going to court by day most of the time," remembered Mo Bee. "When he'd come out of court, it'd be six or seven o'clock by the time he got to Unique Studios. Then BOOM! Tupac would bust through the door and be like, 'Mo Bee, throw me some weed!' He used to be stressed out, so when he came in the studio, he was ready to spit. He would do everything in one take. When we did 'If I Die Tonight,' all of that anger and everything—I just seen it, man."

Shakur was so quick on the microphone—and was having such trouble getting film parts, due to legal troubles and bad publicity—that whenever he needed money, he'd go to the recording studio. His system was cash on delivery. As long as the producer had his money ready, he'd come record a freestyle.

November 29—the evening of his jury deliberations—was one such night. Shakur needed cash. He needed an escape. And he also felt the need to drop a hot tune since he knew it might be a while before folks heard from him again. His first stop was to visit the uptown apartment of mix-tape king Ron G. For another DJ, a Tupac session would run several thousand dollars, but Shakur did his verse for Ron G on the strength. A hot cameo on a Ron G tape could be worth its weight in gold, waking up New York's rap underground and helping Pac reconnect with his East Coast roots.

While he finished up with Ron G, Shakur's pager went off—Lil' Shawn's manager was calling. Again. The rapper, who had become well known for a novelty record called "Hickies on Your Chest," had asked Shakur to appear on a song with him and Biggie. Despite his reservations about working with anyone he did not know very well, Shakur needed the money.

Pac called back and set his price. "You get me seven G's and I'll do the song."

"All right," the manager told him. "I got your money."

Shakur took his time after finishing the song with Ron G. They picked up some food and hooked up with a couple more friends and stopped at a weed spot. After an hour or so, the studio paged him again.

"Where you at? Why you ain't coming?"

"I'm on my way," Shakur said. They got in a car and drove down to the studio.

While they were in the car, Shawn's manager called again to say he didn't have the money.

"If you don't have the money," Shakur replied, "I'm not coming."

The manager called back within minutes. "I'll give you the money out of my pocket," he said. "I'm gonna call Andre and make sure you get the money."

They parked the car near Times Square, and all four men—Shakur, Walker, his friend Freddie Moore, and Zane, the boyfriend of Pac's younger sister—walked to Quad Studios. As they drew near the building, they heard a voice from above.

"Yo, Pac!"

Shakur looked up and saw Lil' Cease high on a balcony at Quad Studios, a blunt burning between his lips. He waved at Shakur. Shakur waved back. Behind his bloodshot eyes, the 24-year-old rapper was fatigued, stressed, and paranoid. But he seemed happy to see a friendly face.

"Yo, Cease, what up?" he hollered. "What the fuck you doing?"

"We up in the studio," Cease replied. "I'ma come down and get you and bring you upstairs." Seeing one of Wallace's closest friends put Cease at ease, too. But it was the last pleasant exchange the two men would ever have.

Cease came off the terrace and went back inside the studio where "Player's Anthem," the first big hit from the Junior M.A.F.I.A. album, was being recorded. Wallace was running the session, nodding his head as the chorus blasted: "Grab your dicks if you love hip hop." The mood of the room was celebratory and the Junior M.A.F.I.A. posse was excited. This was the first song they had ever recorded, and for some was their first time in a big time studio. They had finally arrived.

Lil' Cease walked toward Wallace.

"Hey, Big, I just seen Pac," said Cease.

"Pac's outside?" Wallace asked.

"I'm gonna go downstairs and get him," Cease said.

"Bring him up here," Wallace said.

A few floors down from the Junior M.A.F.I.A. session, Mark Pitts and Sean Combs sat in the lounge, talking to Andre Harrell.

Combs had just finished shooting his portion of the Hype Williams video for "Warning," a shot of him driving down Seventh Avenue, the lights of Times Square reflecting off the car. He saw a member of his Bad Boy Records staff heading toward Quad Studios. He knew Wallace was working with Junior M.A.F.I.A. that night, but didn't realize the session was so close by.

Combs had originally decided to stop by the studio to check on Big, but when he got off the elevator, he saw his old boss, Andre Harrell.

Harrell saw Combs and smiled. Even though they'd had their differences, he was happy to see his young protégé doing well for himself. In fact, everything going on at Quad Studios was the realization of a dream Harrell had had since he was a young boy growing up in the Bronx. There were four sessions going on in separate studios, each representing the future of black music: SWV was on one floor, Deborah Cox on another, along with the harder sounds of Mobb Deep, Junior M.A.F.I.A., and Lil' Shawn. So many people were dropping in on each other's sessions that the whole studio complex felt like one big party. For a while.

"Puffy just came up the elevator and everyone was happy to see him," said Harrell. "We was just sitting there, and everybody was just kind of reminiscing. From my era going all the way back to the current era with the new generation of young producers and music executives. Hope was in the air and success was all around. So everybody was excited about Pac comin' in. We were starting to get antsy, like, 'Where's Pac?' It was just excited energy for him to arrive and see how this was getting ready to set off."

Shakur turned to tell Stretch something didn't feel right—but by then it was too late. The strangers in camouflage pulled out two identical 9-millimeter pistols. "Everybody on the floor! You know what time it is."

Shakur was not feeling the party vibe. As soon as he and his crew entered the studio lobby, he felt something was amiss.

"There was a dude out there with army fatigues with a hat low on his face," Shakur said. "And when we walked to the door, he didn't look up. I've never seen a black man not acknowledge me one way or the other, either with jealousy or respect. I get either one, always. But it didn't click to me yet, because I had just finished smoking chronic."

Shakur, Stretch, Moore, and Zane entered the lobby and looked around.

"While we're waiting by the door to get buzzed in, I saw a dude sitting at a table reading a newspaper. Both these guys were in their thirties. At first I'm like, these dudes must be security for Biggie. I could tell they were from Brooklyn from the army fatigues. But then when they didn't look up I said, 'Wait a minute. Biggie's homeboys love me.'"

Stretch also thought the guy at the door might have been a part of Wallace's extended Brooklyn family. He sensed nothing unusual when the man in fatigues walked into the lobby behind them. "He looked like somebody who was with Big, or somebody from Brooklyn," said Stretch. "I had just seen Cease and them upstairs, so I figured that it's probably crowded upstairs."

As he pressed the elevator button, Shakur turned around to tell Stretch that something didn't feel right—but by then it was too late. The strangers in camouflage pulled out two identical 9-millimeter semiautomatic pistols.

"Don't nobody move!" one of them yelled. "Everybody on the floor! You know what time it is. Run your shit. Run your shit!" Tupac just stood there.

"All my homeboys dropped to the floor," Shakur said, "but I wasn't going to get on the floor. I'm thinking Stretch is going to fight because Stretch is so big he was towering over these niggas. And from what I know about the criminal element, if niggas come to rob you and they see the big nigga, they always hit the big nigga first. But they didn't touch Stretch. They came straight to me. Everybody dropped to the floor like potatoes. I'm the only nigga who didn't go to the floor."

From his vantage point on the ground, Stretch couldn't figure out why Shakur was still standing. He figured that it might have something to do with the fact that Shakur was the only one of the four men holding a gun.

"I'm the nigga that goes for mines," Stretch said later, "always forever. But I ain't no dumb nigga. Niggas run up to me with guns, and I ain't got no gun? What the fuck am I supposed to do? I ain't fighting no niggas with no guns. I can be towering over niggas, but I'm not towering over no slugs."

Shakur kept on standing. Less than thirty seconds had passed, but it felt like a whole hour.

"Take off your jewels," one of the gunmen said. But then the other seemed to be losing patience.

"Shoot that muthafucka!" he roared. "Fuck it!"

"Then I got scared," said Shakur, "because the dude had the gun to my stom-

After being beaten, shot, and robbed in the lobby of a New York recording studio, Shakur was sure he had been set up. He became mistrustful of everyone, even old friends like Wallace.

ach. All I could think about was piss bags and shit bags and all that shit. I drew my arm around him to try to move the gun to my side. He shot, and the gun twisted, and that's when I got shot the first time. I felt it in my leg. I didn't know I got shot in my balls. Everything in my mind said, Pac, pretend you're dead. Do not move no more so they don't shoot you

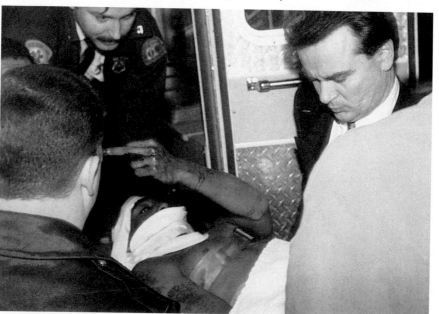

no more.' It didn't matter. They started kicking me, hitting me. They wasn't touching nobody else. They were snatching my shit off me while I was laying on the floor." That's when he felt a blow to the back of his head. "I thought they stomped me or pistol-whipped me, and they were stomping my head against the concrete. I just saw white, just white, and I didn't hear nothing . . . And then they hit me again, and I could hear things and I could see things, and I knew I was conscious again."

Cease and Nino Brown of JM rode the elevator downstairs to meet Pac. Cease was excited; he admired Shakur and enjoyed his music. It still tripped Cease out to be in a recording studio working on his own Junior M.A.F.I.A. record. If Wallace hadn't blown up, he might still be on the corner selling drugs.

But those pleasant thoughts were interrupted as soon as the elevator door opened. They saw Shakur and Walker lying down on the floor. At first Cease thought they were playing around, drunk. But as soon as they stepped a foot closer, Cease and Nino saw two men in fatigues, one standing over Shakur and taking off his $40,000 pieces of jewelry.

"Get the fuck back on the elevator," one of the men in fatigues said. They did.

The assailants promptly ran out into Times Square. There was momentary silence in the room as everybody tried to figure out what had just happened. Walker saw blood running from a wound in Shakur's head. They needed help. Shakur, Stretch, Zane, and Fred stumbled outside. A stripper who worked at the club next door was standing outside.

"Pac starts screaming for the police," Stretch remembered. "We asked this bitch, 'What did you see? Did you see something? Where'd the niggas go?' And the bitch was like, 'I don't know nothing. I didn't see nothing.'" They went back inside the studio building.

While one elevator took Shakur and Walker upstairs, Cease and Nino had already jumped on the other to alert the Junior M.A.F.I.A. session about what was going on.

"Yo, Big!" Cease said. "Pac downstairs getting robbed right now."

"You fuckin' lying," Wallace said.

"I'm serious. Homeboy's getting banged down right now and shit."

"Y'all niggas don't move," Wallace said, rushing to the elevator.

Fifteen minutes passed. No Big. Cease went down to see what was taking him so long. When the elevator door opened, a police officer stood there, his gun drawn and pointed at Big and Chico.

"Police was hemming us up," Lil' Cease said. "Taking down our information. They was saying he was dead. So that's what happened. But he was coming to the studio anyway. You know what I'm saying? He wasn't coming there to see us."

Just then the elevator door opened on the floor where the Lil' Shawn session was taking place. Shakur stumbled out. Bloody. Wounded. Pissed. Mistrustful of everything and everyone.

Stretch and Zane followed him out. Andre Harrell was there. Puffy was there. All in various degrees of shock. "You were the only one who knew I was coming," Pac said.

During the wait for the police to show up, the studio began to thin out. "They immediately knew the rules," Harrell recalled. "They knew the type of police that was coming and what was involved. Everybody started whispering, 'Yo, Homicide is coming.' Everybody united on one front," said Harrell. "The inner-city young black male Public Enemy Number One front.

"The main thing all of them were concerned about was the frisk," Harrell continued. "Because people evidently had guns. I didn't see guns, but I realized niggas was starting to talk about stashing they joint. And Puff was standing in front of me and I looked in Puff's eyes, and Puff's eyes opened when he heard about the detectives coming. And I remember thinking, You mean *you* got a gun!? I didn't say that, but he was looking at me like, I don't want you to know I got a gun, Dre. And I was looking at him like, What you got a gun for?"

As Wallace said in the song, "Things done changed." Could this really be the same eager intern whom Harrell had taken under his wing three years ago? The same one who addressed him as Mr. Harrell and wore bow ties to work was now rolling with thugs and acting like a real "bad boy."

"It made me realize that the element of energy being young and black right now in the inner city is so violent that young people just feel the need to have that level just in case," Harrell said sadly. "If it goes there, they got the potential at least to make them back off, because they're prepared to have the final say. And you know, gun play is the final say."

Down in the lobby there was blood on the floor, police were everywhere, and yellow crime scene tape was going up. The police wouldn't let Wallace back upstairs to where Tupac was. Then the elevator door opened and Shakur was carried out on a flat stretcher by two paramedics. They had cut off his clothes, and he was wearing a neck brace. As he was being loaded in the ambulance, a photographer emerged from the shadows. Even in his weakened condition, Shakur managed to give him the finger.

Fading in and out of consciousness as the ambulance made its way to Bellevue Hospital, Shakur kept asking himself, Who did this? He was sure it wasn't a random robbery. "They were mad at me," Shakur continued. "I felt them kicking and stomping me; they didn't hit nobody else . . . First I was thinking that it was the girl and her people, because we had an argument in court one day." But he kept thinking. The attack was coming on the day before the verdict, and soon after he'd dissed his former codefendant in the *Daily News*. He said that the assailants reminded him of "the type of niggas Jack was introducing me to."

Inside the trauma unit, doctors surrounded him, marveling that he was still alive, let alone conscious. "The doctors were going, Oh my God! Oh my God! They were scaring me," Shakur said. "I didn't feel no pain, really . . . They started cleaning and sewing me up. The whole time I'm talking and joking with people."

"You don't know how lucky you are," one doctor told him.

"What are you talking about?" Shakur replied.

"You got shot five times."

The next afternoon Shakur was rushed into surgery to repair a damaged blood vessel on his right leg. He was out of surgery by 4 P.M. and—against the will of his doctors—checked himself out by 6:45. He had been in the hospital less than 15 hours. "I haven't seen anybody in my twenty-five-year professional career leave the hospital like this," said his surgeon, Dr. Leon Patcher.

Shakur said the unfamiliar faces of doctors poking around him were too upsetting. And he didn't like that people knew where he had been taken. "My life was in danger," Shakur said. "I knew what type of niggas I was dealing with."

According to Cease, Tupac had a gun on him when he was attacked. It was stashed in a piano at the studio before the police arrived.

"Big went back to the studio, got [Pac's] burner, and took it to him at the hospital," said Cease. But Tupac had already checked out.

After Pac was admitted to the hospital, Big tried to visit him, but he had already checked out, fearing for his safety. Wallace and Shakur would never exchange a friendly word again.

On Thursday, December 1, two days after the shooting, Shakur surprised everyone by appearing in Judge Fitzgerald's courtroom to hear his verdict. His entrance was characteristically dramatic, as he was rolled in with a wheelchair, his head swathed in bandages and covered with a wool Yankees ski cap. He sat there for four hours, until 2 P.M., leaving for Metropolitian Hospital Center on East 97th street, due to the numbness he felt in his leg.

"I knew I had to show up

no matter what," he said. "I swear to God, the furthest thing on my mind was sympathy. I just thought, I want to show them that I'm standing up for my responsibilities. All I could think of was—stand up and fight for your life, like you fought for your life in the hospital. So I came to court."

The newspapers, however, read his appearance as a naked plea for sympathy and near jury manipulation. The timing of the incident made some skeptics believe that Shakur himself might have set it up. "What thug would want to shoot Tupac?" went the thinking. "Tupac is a thug hero."

No matter. Within hours of his departure, the jury found Shakur guilty of fondling the plaintiff against her will—but innocent of the much more serious weapons and sodomy charges. A few jurors had even argued for a full acquittal due to lack of evidence, but were outvoted.

Because of his medical condition Shakur remained free on $25,000 bond. He checked into Metropolitan Hospital under the name Bob Day. They told him nobody knew he was there, but he kept getting strange phone calls. "The phone was ringing and I answered it and a man would say, *'You ain't dead yet?'*"

Still, Shakur couldn't bring himself to cooperate with the police.

"When the police said, 'Who shot you?' I was like, 'I don't know,'" Shakur said. "And I knew the dudes' faces as clear as hell. They'll never leave my head. But I didn't want to tell the police. I don't know why, but I couldn't even tell them about Jack and them."

Shakur checked out of Metropolitan and stayed at the apartment of actress Jasmine Guy, a longtime friend of his, under the care of a private doctor, as well as a security force made up of the Nation of Islam's Fruit of Islam security detail and his mother's friends in the Black Panther Party, revolutionaries who had known him his entire life.

While there, he had recurring dreams about being shot, hearing voices screaming, "Shoot that muthafucka." Waking up with sweats. Two weeks later, Shakur read a piece in the *Village Voice* called "The Professional: Tupac Shakur Gives the Performance of His Life." Touré's brilliant but scathing piece compared Shakur's life to an open-ended work of conceptual art. His lifetime practice of intermingling his life and his art had raised the question of whether he was truly in pain or just an actor giving the most brilliant portrayal of his life.

Touré called Shakur "a master performance artist whose canvas is his body, and whose stage is the world. If Tupac escapes jail time, he's the Teflon don, able to leap multiple convictions in a single bound. If he's locked down, he's the realest of the real, going back to his roots (remember, he was in jail as a fetus). Either eventuality carries the bonus of keeping him onstage, which for all its surface political insubstantiality gets at the heart of a very black male necessity: Through all the contradictions and posturing and bullshit, it's really about nothing more than never for a single moment being invisible."

After he read the article, Shakur said he closed the paper and cried "like a bitch. It just tore me apart. That's what helped me see that I had to be for myself."

In January of 1995, Shakur did exactly that. He went for self.

When Shakur agreed to meet with VIBE correspondent Kevin Powell, in the visiting room at Rikers Island during the weeks while he awaited sentencing, in his mind his image, his integrity, and his life were on the line. He was alone, behind bars, unable to promote his upcoming album, and feeling as if he might be forced to spend his best years locked up, with the people around him powerless to do anything. Whether or not it was true, he felt certain that people in prison wanted to kill him—and might succeed. The bad press, the shooting, and all the frustration of the past two years had reached a boiling point. So he did what he'd done his entire life, for better or for worse.

He spoke his mind.

In one of the most controversial interviews in modern music journalism, Shakur let it all hang out. He talked about who he thought set him up. He also suggested that Andre Harrell, "Puffy" Combs, Lil' Cease, and Christopher Wallace were somehow complicit because they were all present that night. He even implied that his road dog Stretch Walker might have been in on the setup. He went on to compare himself to Marvin Gaye and Vincent Van Gogh. Like them, he felt that his genius would not be appreciated until after he was dead. He also declared that Thug Life, the movement he had once championed (the name was an acronym for "The Hate U Give Little Infants Fucks Everybody"), was now dead.

"This Thug Life stuff, it was just ignorance," Shakur told Powell. "My intentions was always in the right place. I never killed anybody, I never raped anybody, I never committed no crimes that weren't honorable—that weren't to defend myself. So that's what I'm going to show them. I'm going to show people my true intentions, and my true heart. I'm going to show them the man that my mom raised. I'm gonna make them all proud."

Harrell, Combs, Wallace, and Walker, and others mentioned in the article were asked to comment before the Q&A was published, but they declined.

During a break in a studio session, Combs read an advance of the Shakur-Powell cover story that was circulating around the music industry like wildfire.

"We say nothing," Combs told Wallace. "Niggas come up to you, start asking questions, reporters start asking you shit . . . Nothing. Complete silence."

Wallace nodded.

Combs himself was heated, but his former mentor urged calm. Harrell focused on Shakur's statements toward the end of the article that reflected his growing maturity, not the rants and raves of a firebrand who had just been shot and was confused and frustrated about his fate.

"This was a major issue for Puff, that he was being portrayed as a sucker," Harrell said later. "I looked at him and said, 'Nigga, you've said worse things about me. And me and you got an ongoing love affair. I don't give a fuck about all that. It will pass, nigga.'"

But it didn't pass. Instead, the accusations were about to become an all-out war. A few weeks after the piece ran, they all went on the record with Fab 5 Freddy to deny Shakur's allegations.

At the time, Christopher Wallace had other things to think about: his career. His record label. His marriage. His family. He didn't have time to stop and ponder why a close friend, who should have known he was innocent, thought he helped set him up.

"Why would Big do something like that?" Lil' Cease said. "[Tupac] knows where Big's mom lives. He know where Big stay at. I called you upstairs. You my nigga. Hell no, I didn't know about it. Why would I come downstairs if it was a setup? I wouldn't want it to be known I was there if that's what it was. Nigga, I saw you. I was calling you upstairs. I'm telling you to come to me. I ain't know you was coming to work. I just so happened to see you then told niggas you was gonna be downstairs. He wasn't telling the real story. Big got a record deal just like he got one. Big is promised the same career this nigga got. Why would Big want to set him up?"

Shakur repeated his accusations in other interviews, and they seemed to get more virulent with each retelling. "I used to share my experiences in the game and my lessons, and my rules, and my knowledge on the game with [Wallace]," Shakur said. "He owed me more than to turn his head and act like he didn't know niggas was about to blow my fuckin' head off. He knew."

"That's when I lost respect for him," Cease said. "He went against the grain on some real niggas that was holding him down. Big used to have us taking risks for that nigga, because that was the love that Big had for him." Lil' Cease searched for an explanation. "He was kinda paranoid and I think Big was just his target to take his frustrations out on.

"But damn, you supposed to be our nigga," Cease continued. "Why would you think a nigga would really do that to you? And then to really go with it and try to make you look like the foulest, punkest muthafucka out there. I thought that was foul. Nigga, we kept it to the utmost realness with you . . . And you really trying to destroy a nigga."

Wallace reacted to Shakur's scathing comments not with anger, but with confusion—and concern. He acted as if Pac was still his boy, and the whole thing was all a misunderstanding.

"You get shot and then you go to jail for something you ain't even do—that could twist a nigga's mind up," Wallace told Fab 5 Freddy. "But I want an apology."

"He knows that I was at the hospital with his mother when he got shot in that studio," Wallace would say two years later. "He knows me and Stretch was there.

He knows after he left the hospital and went to his girl house uptown, me and Stretch went up in some weed spots to get this nigga a half ounce of weed, and bring him some weed to his girl crib. He know this."

"There was a whole bunch of shit that went down, man," Wallace continued. "Shit that I really can't talk about, that I was there for that nigga. That shit hurt me, man. It hurt me."

Wallace always figured that, over time, the paranoia and confusion of those tumultuous days would work themselves out. He figured that he would run into Shakur sooner or later, sit down, and iron everything out. The situation was hot, but he was sure it would eventually cool off.

Wallace was wrong. Dead wrong.

MO MONEY, MO PROBLEMS

CHAPTER 6

"I be that cat you see at all events bent
Gats in holsters girls on shoulders
Playboy, I told ya . . ."

By the summer of 1995, Christopher Wallace was no longer the same kid standing near the corner of St. James and Fulton wondering if he was going to rely on rap or crack to keep little T'Yanna in OshKosh B'Gosh. No longer did he have to try to convince his mother that yes, people did think he had talent as a composer and performer even though he couldn't sing. No longer was he merely "a chubby nigga on the scene"—as he'd put it on his first record, released just two years earlier.

Now he was a star.

Wallace had single-handedly dismantled the notion that the East Coast's rock-solid fan base would rather listen to a mix tape than purchase a full album by an artist they loved. "My album dropped on Friday the thirteenth, when I was on the road and niggas was betting on how much I was selling per week!" he bragged to his friend Bönz Malone in his first *Source* cover story. "I sold damn near a quarter of a million records in New York, dog! That's damn near impossible! Nothing gonna stop me from lettin' me or my family eat." The cover image featured a larger-than-life Wallace standing between the Twin Towers and a tagline that would stick with him throughout his career: King of New York.

Ready to Die had gone double platinum and was still rocking the clubs. The million-selling remix to "One More Chance" would eventually knock Michael Jackson's "You Are Not Alone" out of the top spot on *Billboard*'s pop singles chart. By the end of the year, Michael Jackson would invite Wallace to record a rhyme on Jackson's song "This Time Around."

The makers of the rap documentary *Rhyme & Reason* captured the moment when Wallace unwrapped his RIAA-certified platinum plaque for *Ready to Die*. Dressed in a butter leather jacket, Kangol, and Versace shades, Big Poppa was characteristically laid-back, but at the same time visibly happy about his success.

"I'll have to prop these up," he said. "First Brooklyn nigga to go platinum, you know. It's all good. Got my gold joint from 'Juicy.' Straight out the 'hood, a nigga did good."

Videos like "One More Chance" and "Big Poppa" seemed to be on television constantly. Ever since Dr. Dre's *The Chronic* had so much success, MTV had begun to loosen its stance on playing rap videos outside the confines of *Yo! MTV Raps*. Snoop could now appear in heavy rotation next to the Metallicas and Pearl Jams of the world. White middle-class kids weaned on Vanilla Ice now wanted the real deal Holyfield. *The Chronic* became to gangsta rap what Bob Marley's *Legend* was to reggae—the record that started a mainstream fan on the true path. Dr. Dre perfected the Gangsta Pop formula with Snoop Doggy Dogg's *Doggystyle*—pop songs with the hardcore aura intact, rendered broadcast-ready by radio edits that, somehow, didn't castrate the groove.

DJ Enuff, who played the beats for Biggie when he went on tour, said Big openly admired these West Coast stars. "I remember Big always saying, 'I wanna be like Snoop, I wanna be like Dre and them. Like, I wanna get it the way they're getting it.' It was very important to him. That was the same kind of level he wanted." While it seemed that Snoop and Dre, Ice Cube, and Cypress Hill had the video and sales charts in a lock, Wallace was the first MC to bring mainstream acclaim back to the East Coast. And it was one of those Puffy songs that Big didn't want to record—the G-funk player rhyme "Big Poppa"—that was responsible for that paradigm shift.

The creative tension started back when they were selecting the first single from *Ready to Die*. Wallace wanted "Machine Gun Funk" to be his introduction to the world—a great song, but definitely aimed directly at New York's hoodies-and-boots hip hop audience; it might not have moved folks in Milwaukee. Combs tried to push the music in an R&B direction, knowing that Wallace's lyrical delivery would always have hardcore appeal. He urged Biggie to look beyond the borough of Brooklyn and take the chance of crossing over with "Juicy," a reworking of Mtume's 1983 electrofunk hit "Juicy Fruit."

"Puffy was on some, 'Yo, let's get rich' shit," remembered Wallace. "He said, 'If you put out "Juicy" you'll have a gold single.' I wasn't even with 'Juicy,' but he's saying, 'Let's go get the money,' so I'm like, fuck it."

DJ Enuff witnessed the impact of Puffy's strategies firsthand on the road. "The early records, like 'Gimme the Loot' and 'Warning' and 'Unbelievable,' were all good records," he said. "But it wasn't until 'Big Poppa' and 'One More Chance,' the remix, that the rest of the country was, like, Wow! This guy is dope. He's not just an East Coast MC." Still Biggie wasn't always comfortable in the crossover role. He knew how quickly rap's core audience could turn on a star who got too gassed up. "I remember Big huffing and puffing, like, I gotta do this 'cause Puff says so," Enuff recalled. "He wasn't really too happy about it. Even though Biggie might say, 'Fuck what Puffy says,' when Puffy came around, he'd do exactly what Puffy told him to do, you know what I mean? 'Cause he knew it was right."

The compromise was the B-side. Wallace agreed to "Juicy" as long as it was backed by his "gutter" joint "Unbelievable"—the best rap B-side since Public Enemy's "Rebel Without a Pause." The single went gold and Wallace got major airplay, yet he lost no credibility. "My niggas weren't mad at me," Wallace said, relieved, "so I was straight."

But the creative tension returned when Puff announced that he wanted to follow up with "Big Poppa." The last song that Wallace recorded for *Ready to Die* was also the last song that Wallace ever wanted to release as a single. But Combs prevailed again, and it was becoming clear that Daddy knew best. The smooth Moog sound and the Isley Brothers' "Between the Sheets" loop gave the song a West Coast feel, as if it was something off *The Chronic*, but Wallace's lyrics, even without the profanity, gave the song an East Coast underground feel. The single (backed by the chilling crime narrative "Warning") sold a million copies.

"It's a straight commercial joint," Wallace said. "But at the same time I'm talking about getting girls pregnant, I'm telling niggas I got infrared on my heat. I still spit that shit that makes niggas be like 'All right, he be kickin' some shit!' I think the mistake other niggas make is they say, 'Fuck it, we gonna come out with a radio joint too.' They get their little loop, but they just be so clean, it's corny. Put it like this: I coulda did the same song to a hard beat and you wouldn't have ever known. It was just the beat that made it commercial."

The video also expanded the song's commercial prospects. Hype Williams, with his slow-motion tracking shots, beautiful lighting, and ingenious use of color filters, greatly expanded the look and feel of rap music video, helping the genre keep up with rock videos. The video for "Big Poppa" was no different. Not only did the clip change the way that the Notorious B.I.G. was portrayed, it altered the entire landscape of what was considered hip hop by offering a glimpse of a new lifestyle: ghetto fabulous.

"The power of images is like the power of the word—it conveys a thought," said

Combs and Hype Williams direct Wallace on the set of the "Big Poppa" video at Nell's nightclub, NYC, 1994.

Williams. "Whatever that thought is transcends having to take the time to elaborate. People can draw any particular conclusion they want from what they see."

What the director gave them to see was young black men enjoying the good life: Wallace and his friends dressed to the nines, popping bottles of expensive champagne, rapping to gorgeous ladies in a chic nightclub. Combs spent the whole video soaking in a hot tub with his blond pony-tailed girlfriend Misa Hylton—the stylist who had first convinced him that Big was not too ugly to be a star. Nobody was aware of it yet, but a change was coming.

Hip hop fashion had gone through many phases—from track suits, Kangol hats, sneakers, and gold chains to jeans, work boots, and oversized hoodies. Before that video, no self-respecting hardcore rapper would be caught dead in a designer suit. But "Big Poppa" changed all that. "There was no Versace, none of that shit, before 'Big Poppa,' " Williams said. "Before he did that, Biggie was wearing camouflage. Nobody knew it was going to turn into an era of everybody wearing all this fuckin' jewelry and shit."

Sean Combs wasn't the only influence on Wallace's choice of clothes. Voletta Wallace could just as easily be blamed for the birth of ghetto fabulous.

"No rappers out there look good," Voletta Wallace would often tell her son. "I'm sure their clothes cost a million dollars, and their shoes are expensive, but they look like bums. Do not embarrass me on television. I don't want you going up there looking like a bum."

Her fashion standards may have been high, but Ms. Wallace was pragmatic. She saved her money and invested in things. Her credit was impeccable. Remembering her son's quick-money past, she worried about how he was handling his finances. "I'm reading things," Ms. Wallace said, keeping up with the rap press. "Okay, he's got a house. He got himself a car. He got two cars. Okay, he's fine. So Christopher, please, do you have any money?"

"Ma, I'll never be poor again," he told her. "Trust me, Ma. If I have a question about my money at five o'clock in the morning, I'm calling my accountant, How much money I got?"

"Okay, but if you read about Hammer, who was up there doing very well, he went bankrupt," she warned him. "Christopher, please, keep your money."

Even though they kept the apartment on St. James, Wallace worked on getting his mother a place in Florida. It was the closest thing to Jamaica. But she wanted to be closer to home, so he looked into real estate in parts of New Jersey. She finally settled on Pennsylvania and he began making plans to build her a house out in the Poconos.

As for himself, while Brooklyn was in his heart, Wallace realized that being on his old street with his newfound wealth made him a target for stickup kids even more than when he was in the crack game. "Call the crib," he had rhymed on his album, "Same number, same 'hood, it's all good." But he understood the hustler's mentality well enough to know that he wouldn't be safe there forever. Just a few years ago if he had seen someone like himself slipping, showing off the cash, he'd have been tempted to make a jack move. So first he and Faith moved into a Fort Greene duplex, and then, subsequently, into a gated community in Teaneck, New Jersey.

"To me, if you stay in the same spot as you were in when you were doing nothing and now you're doing something, that's not progression," Wallace told a *New York Times* reporter who asked whether rappers had to live in their old neighborhoods. Wallace had always thought so, but he was beginning to change his mind about what "keeping it real" was all about. "Being real is taking care of your family, your mother, your children, and doing things with your money," he said. "When you think of doing well, you think of mansions. Ain't no mansions in Brooklyn. You don't want to deal with subways and gunshots. You want to be comfortable and safe."

Although he was out of the drug hustle, Wallace felt safest with a lot of firepower. Visitors to his crib were impressed by the elevator, the oversized Jacuzzi, the bedroom decorated with framed posters of Al Pacino in *Scarface* and Marlon Brando in *The Godfather*. But most of all, they noticed the guns. "He had two joints with infrared scopes," remembers a visitor, "couple joints on the wall. He kept pulling out all these guns. It was kinda hot seeing that. I was like, Wow! But I was also kind of scared. He was kinda like the Godfather in his world."

Lil' Cease said the guns weren't for committing crime but for deterring it. "When we started getting known it was like better safe than sorry," he said. "That's just a 'hood thing. Just in case something should go down."

Financing the new lifestyle took money. And money, which had always been a major focus for Wallace, became an even bigger concern. For the first time in his life, he had something to lose. His albums were selling like hotcakes, but it still wasn't always enough.

"I still haven't gotten money from [*Ready to Die*] itself yet," Wallace told VIBE in October 1995. This was after the album had already been certified double platinum. Two million times $15 per CD meant Wallace's debut had generated some $30 million in gross revenue—and Wallace still hadn't seen a dime. And it wasn't that Bad Boy and Arista were going out of their way to jerk Wallace. This was standard operating practice in the music industry.

Artists typically do not make any money from royalties until after the record company has "recouped" all the dollars it has spent. Everything from photo shoots and music videos down to every last caterer's tray, airplane ticket, and hour of studio time—all of it gets charged to the artist. If any money starts coming in from album and single sales, the person whose talent made the whole thing possible in the first place is the last to get paid. After managers, lawyers, accountants, and Uncle Sam took their piece, there was hardly enough left to clear the samples on the next record—let alone pay the bills that go along with being Big Poppa.

In Wallace's case, he did spend a lot of money, especially on the recording itself. He voiced many of the songs at the Hit Factory, one of the most expensive studios in Manhattan, which cost up to $3,000 a day. Instead of writing his songs before getting there, Wallace would spend hours smoking weed and vibing on the beat before spitting his lyrics. He was capable of recording songs in a single take, but he had a tendency to ruthlessly critique his own performances. The whole process could take anywhere from six to twelve hours. Even if every session resulted in a classic song, time was money, and the time added up. Added to this, of course, was the close to one million dollars Combs had had to pay Uptown to release tracks that had been previously recorded for Wallace's album, in addition to the costs of the new songs under the Bad Boy deal.

"I spent a lot and the record company had to recoup first," Wallace said. "That's why I sold half my publishing to Puffy." Publishing is where the money is made in the music business. Companies like ASCAP and BMI track the sales and radio play of every single song in their catalog—and there's a fee that goes along with virtually every use of a song. Michael Jackson purchased the rights to much of the Beatles' song catalog for $47.5 million in 1985, a catalog that is now worth almost $1 billion. Every time a Beatles' song gets played in public, John, Paul, Ringo, and George got checks—but Jackson, now the "fifth" Beatle, gets his check first. When Biggie sold 50 percent of his publishing rights, he collected $250,000 for a few minutes of signing. "I was broke, and if a nigga could make a quick quarter of a million just from signing a few papers, you gotta let it go." It was a lot of money—just not enough for someone who spent money like Wallace.

And it was nothing compared to what he could have earned in the future.

At the time, there were few venues for rap songs to make money—the advertisers on Madison Avenue hadn't, in 1994, fully tapped the earning and selling power of hip hop music. But that was starting to change. Those publishing rights could net millions. "If I would step to niggas now," Wallace joked, "they'd be like, I'll buy your publishing and give you some head."

But meanwhile, to earn his "champagne wishes and caviar dreams" money, Wallace had to hit the road on the out-of-town hustle. Things had changed since the old days when he'd troop down south to move drugs. Now he'd show up in

Podunk with his crew, rock a show, and get at least $20,000 cash for maybe half an hour's work—legal work.

Wallace also realized his dream of forming a record company when he set up Undeas Entertainment with Lance "Un" Rivera—a fellow hustler from Brooklyn. He helped get Junior M.A.F.I.A. a deal through Big Beat/Atlantic. Not only was Wallace able to keep his promise to give his best friends a legal living, he also made money off their hits—as a label owner, writer, and producer. He was watching Puffy and learning that it paid to be the man behind the scenes.

Once the Junior M.A.F.I.A. deal was in place, Wallace could try his hand at being a record exec while making good on a promise to his friends.

Opportunity was everywhere, but there were drawbacks to all the work. He and Faith had been married only a short time, and they were constantly apart from each other. She had just finished her own first solo album and had to go out and promote it. Wallace had paid performances, television appearances, and promotional gigs to help build the type of loyal following that can sustain a long career, not just a novelty single. And with Junior M.A.F.I.A., his responsibilities were doubled. "You won't be around next year," warned Craig Mack on the first Bad Boy release "Flava in Ya Ear," and now Mack's own words were coming back to haunt him. He'd released more singles, but hadn't scored a significant hit. Wallace made up his mind that he wasn't going out like that. As much as his wife missed him, she'd have to understand that he had a job to do.

"Big understands what he has to do, and being on the road is a part of that," said "Hawk" Burns, one of Wallace's Brooklyn homeboys who became his road manager. So there he was, in the back of a broken-down tour bus with JM, Total, and other Bad Boy acts, smoking cheap weed and living off McDonald's.

Years in the drug game taught Wallace a lot about marketing. Holding down an audience wasn't that much different from holding down a corner. "I look at y'all as my customers," Wallace explained. "I gotta sell my product. They both exactly the same to me." Every day was another concert or radio promo show, and always more hands to shake like he was a presidential candidate meeting the voters that could put him in office.

Being the Playa President was a career in itself.

Meanwhile, at Clinton Correctional Center, the Dannemora, New York, prison that was once home to Charles "Lucky" Luciano, Tupac Shakur sat for hours in his cell, watching his career go nowhere.

His album *Me Against the World* hit stores on February 27, 1995, and shot to No. 1 on the strength of the heart-rending million-selling single "Dear Mama." But Shakur also spent his share of money while recording the album, he hadn't recouped, and almost all of the money he did have went straight to his legal fees and his impending appeal. He couldn't book shows; he was in jail. He was the sole support of his mother and other members of his extended family.

All eyes were on him. And their hands were out.

For $1.4 million, he could be bailed out and back on the streets. Only problem was the same problem he'd had since he was a boy—he didn't have any money. He didn't save. Hell, he didn't think he was going to live past 25 anyway.

Shakur remembered the time when Shock G from Digital Underground, concerned about all the legal troubles he was having in 1993, offered him keys to his condo in Los Angeles. "This is for my condo," Shock told him. "If you ever want to be someplace where nobody knows where you're at, you got a place. There are threats out there."

"All I wanted to do," Shakur replied, "was have my voice on a record and be in a movie, and I've done that. All the rest of this shit, I don't give a fuck, so don't worry about me."

But he was wrong. What good did all of that do him in a place like this? A place where inmates could threaten his life. Where the guards went out of their way to humiliate him. What good was having a No. 1 record if he couldn't dance, travel, or do anything else he wanted to do? Write? He'd even have to ask them for a pencil. A cage was a place for an animal—not a man. And coming to jail showed him just how wrong he was.

It didn't matter to him that people whispered about him getting raped in jail. That wasn't going to happen. There were enough people in the Black Power movement, people with ties to his stepfather, Mutulu Shakur, and Geronimo Pratt and his mother, who could prevent something like that from happening. It was the stuff that he couldn't control that messed with his head.

He could be messed with even when he met with his lawyers. Once, before he met with one of his attorneys, Stewart Levy, the guards gave him a rectal search. He conversed with Levy for six hours, in a locked room, under complete supervision, with no chance that anything but papers, could be passed between them.

But when he left he heard the voices, taunting him.

"Tupac! Tupac! It's time! It's time!" The guards were smiling, putting on plastic gloves, with mocking falsetto voices. They gave him a second prolonged rectal search.

The longer he stewed in jail, the more paranoid he became. Things he had once dismissed began to seem plausible. So what if Biggie had warned him about Agnant. What if that was just a smoke screen? Where were his friends now? Could he trust anyone?

Shakur was so angry about being shot that he never questioned the motives of those in prison telling him that people connected to Wallace had set him up at Quad Studios.

Shakur overlooked the fact that this kind of disinformation was used to weaken and eventually split the Black Panther Party, of which his mother was a member. Through a secret campaign known as COINTELPRO, FBI director J. Edgar Hoover sought to neutralize any groups he considered a threat to the United States. The stated goals of the program, according to a March 4, 1968, FBI memo, were "to prevent the rise of a messiah who could unify and electrify the militant black nationalist movement today." As the son of a Black Panther leader, Tupac Shakur was raised to be "the Black Prince of the revolution," as he put it. "I'm the future of black America," he said. "I represent five million fucking sales and no politician is even checking for us. But by the next election I promise I'll be sitting across from all the candidates. I guarantee we will have our own political party. It won't just be for blacks—it's gon' be for Mexicans, for Armenians, all you lost tribe muthafuckas. We built this nation and we get none of the benefits."

It wasn't far-fetched that Shakur, because of his rebellious spirit and his influence over young people, could be considered a target. Politicians from Dan Quayle to Bill Clinton had spoken out against his music. The Los Angeles rebellion that broke out after police were cleared of criminal charges in the beating of Rodney King on April 29, 1992, freaked out a lot of white people in power. Crips and Bloods ended years of violence against one another and joined together in unity. Members of the Los Angeles Police Department feared that the gangs might unite and take on the cops—and there were reports of some cops actually trying to heighten tensions between the sets to prevent that kind of unity from happening.

A handful of rappers had more sway over this element of the youth culture than any politician—Shakur especially. Not only did he specialize in so-called thug records, he had also called for black youth to rise up against the cops. "Fuck Tha Police" got N.W.A on the FBI's map—but some considered Shakur even more dangerous because he didn't just talk the talk, he walked the walk.

Tupac was charged with shooting at off-duty Atlanta police officers Mark and Scott Whitewell on Halloween Night 1993. Though the charges were later dropped, Tupac's stepfather, Mutulu—an incarcerated former

Panther who had considerable firsthand experience when it came to these matters—worried that Pac would become a prime target for police reprisal.

"When Tupac stands up to a white cop, shoots it out, wins the battle, gets cut free, and continues to say the things he's been saying—the decision to destroy his credibility is clear," Mutulu said.

With so many family members in jail or dead,

"I couldn't believe that everybody was treating Biggie like the biggest star in the world," said Shakur. "Biggie is not a player."

it made sense for Tupac Shakur to be paranoid and distrustful. But his imprisonment made him bitter—and made him suspect that somebody at Quad Studios that night must have known something was going to go down and didn't tell him because they weren't true friends—no matter what they said.

People were talking a lot of shit—even saying that the B-side of the single "Big Poppa," a track called "Who Shot Ya," was a direct taunt at him. The track was not intended to be a comment about Shakur's shooting. "He knew that song wasn't about him," Lil' Cease insisted. "He was around at that time. He knew the shit was an intro for Mary's second album. But the shit was too hard, so Big kept it and said, 'I'm gonna put it out.' That song was done before he even got shot. It's just a conincidence. Timing is a muthafucka." It didn't even matter to Shakur that the song was recorded in September of 1994, months before the shooting—he thought it was disrespectful that the song would even be released for people to speculate that it *might* be about him.

He saw the video for "Big Poppa" with Wallace, dressed in leather, hanging out at the club that Jack introduced him to, Nell's. Big was around when he got that first Rolex and now he was living Shakur's dream while he was stuck in here, rotting. "I couldn't believe that everybody was treating Biggie like the biggest fucking star in the world," Shakur said. "I couldn't believe that people was buying into the player image. Biggie is not a player."

No visits. No phone calls. No letters. It all began to build in his mind.

Doing all the push-ups and sit-ups in the world and reading until he needed glasses couldn't get rid of the time.

He read VIBE, with the responses from those he held responsible for the Quad Studios shooting. Something that Combs said stuck in his head.

"If you gonna be a muthafuckin' thug," Combs said, "you gots to live and die a thug, y'knowhatumsayin'? There ain't no jumping in and out of thugism. If that's what you chose to do, you gots to go out like that."

Being a revolutionary, and dealing with movement lawyers, was only going to keep him in one place—jail. He appreciated the letters from friends like Jada and Jasmine, even strangers like Tony Danza, but none of that was action.

He was haunted by nightmares about the shooting. Maybe he was in hell.

"Hell is when you sleep, and the last thing you see is all the fucked-up things you did in your life," said Shakur. "And you just see it over and over again, 'cause you don't burn." Maybe hell was jail.

He needed to get out of here.

Only one person he knew had $1.4 million. It was the same guy who asked him to jump to his label while recording the *Above the Rim* soundtrack. The

By 1995, Death Row Records CEO Marion "Suge" Knight was the most feared man in the music industry. "The rumors are useful," he said, "but not true."

same man who gave him $200,000 for one song, one goddamn song on the soundtrack—"Pour Out a Little Liquor"—as if it was nothing. The one man who could move like he moved, ride like he liked to ride, and have his back so that even his worst enemies would have to think twice about stepping to him.

Marion "Suge" Knight, the CEO of Death Row Records, was that man. Other people sent him flowers. Suge sent a bullet-proof vest with a Death Row logo on it. "I was saying 'I care about you,'" Knight later explained. "I'm gonna treat you like a man. I ain't gonna treat you like no baby."

By the time the August 1995 Source Awards rolled around, there were two superpowers in hip hop: first Death Row, and now, Bad Boy.

While people loved Sean Combs, they feared Knight. His reputation preceded him. The 6'4", 315-pound former defensive end rolled like a freight

train, the kind of man you loved to have behind you and would never want to cross. Stories circulated about Suge beating people down for everything from cheating him out of money to unauthorized use of a telephone. He openly flaunted his ties to the Bloods street gang, wearing red suits in every photo shoot and even stipulating that rap magazines use red type when he appeared on their cover. It was said that even Dr. Dre, the musical mastermind behind Death Row's success, faced punishment if deadlines were not met. There was also, of course, the story of how he improved the royalty rates for Puffy's Uptown artists Jodeci and Mary J. Blige by hanging Andre Harrell out of a window (or, depending on who was telling the story, parading him around the Uptown Records office at gunpoint, naked). Andre and Puffy never commented about the stories except to deny them.

But there were other stories. About how his artists had some of the highest royalty rates in the business. How he bought them Ferraris and Range Rovers, expensive jewelry, condos, and houses. How he worked 24-7-365. And how he showed tremendous loyalty to those people who were down with his team. When Snoop Doggy Dogg was charged with murder when his bodyguard McKinley Lee shot and killed Phillip Woldemariam in a park on August 25, 1993, just before the release of Snoop's solo debut album, *Doggystyle,* Knight not only guaranteed the rapper's million-dollar bail, he also made sure that his legal defense was the best that money could buy. In November 1993 Snoop's album would debut at No. 1 on the pop charts, the first gangsta rap album to achieve this level of success.

"Did you see what Snoop was wearing?" Knight pointed out to a reporter, referring to an expensive diamond-encrusted dog-bone pendant. "I bought it for him. Anyone who's my artist, they say, 'I want,' I say, 'You got it.' The people who started with me, they end up with me."

Knight, it seemed, didn't care what anybody said one way or the other. "I leave my judgment to God," he said. "The rumors are helpful, but not true. They get me additional respect, and this business is about getting the respect you deserve so you can get what you want. I don't worry about all of the talk."

And whatever you thought about the man, you couldn't question the results. Getting Dr. Dre out of his contract with Eazy-E's Ruthless Records—no matter how he did it—paved the way for Death Row, clearly the most successful rap label the music world had seen since the rise of Def Jam. In less than three years, the label had sold over 10 million records and made over $100 million—numbers that took Def Jam nearly a decade to reach. With Dr. Dre and Snoop Doggy Dogg, Daz and Kurupt, and the Lady of Rage, he had an arsenal of talent that the East Coast had to respect—and the multiplatinum sales of Snoop and Dre's records proved that many did have respect for "the Row." There was only one label that came close to matching its success—Bad Boy.

On February 9, 1995, Suge Knight stood in a downtown Los Angeles Superior courtroom. On the opposite side of the courtroom stood deputy district attorney Lawrence M. Longo. Longo had been handling Knight's case for two and a half years, vowing to the *Los Angeles Times* that he would put this "dangerous" man behind bars.

But now as they stood in front of Superior Court Judge John Ouderkirk, the D.A. completely reversed his opposition with a plea bargain hammered out by Longo and David Kenner: a nine-year suspended sentence, thirty days in a halfway house, and five years of probation.

To cap things off, the Stanley brothers, in 1994, dropped a pending lawsuit against Knight in exchange for a $1 million recording deal. As part of the bargain, the duo testified in court to Knight's sterling character.

Calling the plea bargain "rather unusual," Judge Ouderkirk approved the measure. A month later, Longo gushed to a reporter about the same man he once labeled a societal menace: "Marion Knight is one of the few guys I have ever prosecuted who I actually believe can turn his life around and really change the community from where he came," Longo said. "I have never seen a guy transform as much as this guy has since he was first booked. It's remarkable."

It was funny what selling 15 million records could do for your reputation. Death Row Records had changed the game as Knight had always promised. Not only did the company that no one wanted to touch gain mainstream respectability, Dr. Dre's song "Let Me Ride" won a Grammy.

It would later emerge that Longo had rented his Malibu beach house to Knight, and Knight had signed his daughter Gina to a recording contract. There was nothing exactly illegal about the arrangement, but the apparent conflict of interest was embarrassing.

Now that Knight's legal problems were behind him, he could focus on other challenges ahead. The most serious was Snoop Doggy Dogg's murder trial.

Meanwhile, Time-Warner, which distributed Interscope Records, was facing scrutiny from shareholders after C. Delores Tucker of the National Political Congress of Black Women joined with right-wing pundit William Bennett to call for a boycott of Time-Warner because of its dealings with "foul-mouthed criminals."

Knight, who had his artists working around the clock, didn't seemed fazed either way. "There's a billion dollars on top of a hill," he said. "And we're running. We're not getting distracted. We're going to get our prize. It's important to keep your eyes on the prize."

Sweaty and spent, Uptown Records president Andre Harrell, Def Jam Records chairman Russell Simmons, and Uptown Television president Alonzo Brown sat down on the blacktop under the basketball court of the huge house Simmons

Biggie virtually swept the 1995 Source Awards, but his victory was obscured by bicoastal bickering.

was renting in Southampton. It was a hot August afternoon in 1995.

The three friends laughed about the old days, before there was any real money in hip hop, back when Andre and Alonzo were Dr. Jeckyll and Mr. Hyde, rapping in school gymnasiums.

They had gone from being broke to making real money.

Power lawyer Allen Grubman stopped by. Grubman was the man who negotiated Def Jam's landmark distribution deal with Columbia Records. Today Grubman wanted to talk with Harrell, who was about to become the newest president of Motown Records. Harrell was truly a man at the crossroads. He had grown up in the projects, and now he was poised to take over the label founded by his idol, Berry Gordy.

That night Simmons and Harrell were supposed to go see Michelle Pfeiffer in *Dangerous Minds*. But they never made it inside the theater, because their conversation turned into an argument that lasted long into the night. The argument came down to this question: Did the music that had made them millionaires doom an entire generation of black youth? Was rap money as bloody as drug money?

It was a fascinating, passionate debate. And I was there on assignment for VIBE, getting it all on tape.

"It's one thing for someone to shoot somebody in the streets of Chicago," said Harrell. "But when there's a video like that and the record becomes number one and starts to play a hundred times on the Box for a number of weeks, then it becomes a way of life for many people."

Simmons, as usual, played the rebel. And he insinuated that Andre was playing Uncle Tom. "Even Latifah would smack you for talking the shit you're saying!" he replied. "Your opinion is so ridiculous!"

"Now the murder fashion is the whole fashion," said Harrell, raising his voice. "When you see a kid walking down the street in fatigues, you don't know for sure if this nigga is going to school, or if this nigga is a murderer?"

"Andre, the world is changing," said Simmons. "The reality is that it's a different time and there are more guns. The music didn't make them all have guns."

"You're not listening! Harrell said. "We're not scared of each other, we're scared of our children. We should accept that we're glorifying these people," he continued. "They're part of a reality that we're putting on television at three o'clock with no parents home, and these kids are walking around singing these songs, and feeling like life is really like this all the time. They exaggerate so much they make it the reality, and Tupac is living proof of that. Middle-class kids are the main culprits—fantasizing, taking it all the way until they are tough."

Simmons shook his head.

"None of them advocate living the life they living. None."

Driving back to the city in his drop-top Benz, Brown broke down the passion behind their discussion.

"When you come from the shootouts at Mitchell Gym, when you come from the stampedes at the concerts, all of that shit all of your life, all you want to do now at this point in your life is go up as high as you can," Brown said. "That's why I can't understand muthafuckas that got everything and still want to live on that level," he said, pounding the black leather steering wheel. "Talking about 'Keep it real.' Once you get a hit record—at that point everyone is upper class. You get the hit record, you get the Mercedes-Benz, and you get the house, and you got the baby, and you taking care of mama or whatever, you do whatever you can not to jeopardize that shit and keep your level right there.

"What you want to do, be king of the ghetto all your life? That ain't what it's about. Not for me. I've been in the ghetto all my life. I've been shot at. I don't want to be shot at. What's wrong with that? What's wrong with wanting a better life? Russell's out in the Hamptons. So fuckin' what he's out in the Hamptons? You had thirty million dollars, where would you be? In the projects?

"Niggas don't be thinkin'," he said, turning onto an exit ramp. "They usually on their own dick to understand what real power is all about. In any of the interviews that Puffy had, did he ever give Andre any props? No. Not really. He's too busy taking the credit. That's what bothers me."

Sean "Puffy" Combs had no interest in being in Andre Harrell's world anymore. His father's world was a lot more interesting, and with his newfound street credibility he no longer felt the need to kiss any more corporate ass.

"Dre doesn't undertand the street anymore," said Combs. "He's too busy hanging out with white people, smoking cigars, being a mogul. And they don't even want to see my ass in the Hamptons. I embarrass them."

But Puffy could be embarrassed, too.

When Knight and the rest of his Death Row posse came to New York for the 1995 Source Awards, there was electricity in the air. Collecting a trophy would be nice, but what they really wanted was respect. Of course, you had to respect their dough, but New York MCs were always reminding cats from the rest of the country that N.Y.C. was the birthplace of hip hop. It was as if they looked down at rappers from the rest of the country. Now that they had their own hometown champions in Wallace and in Combs, they wouldn't bow down the way Death Row thought they should.

Knight and Combs knew each other well. In 1992 and 1993 they would hang out with each other whenever one was visiting the other's hometown. Combs respected Knight's balls and business savvy—the way he made the mainstream respect his music, and his determination to maintain control of his lucrative master recordings. Knight might be loath to admit it, but he respected Combs's knowledge of his fan base, his hustle, and his genius for self-promotion. Nonetheless, Knight would belittle Combs every chance he could.

But these Source Awards were different. The stakes were high and getting higher. The rap business was worth more money than ever before, and now the factions were aligning along coastal lines. Knight wanted the world to know there could only be one king, so he threw down the gauntlet.

On the evening of August 3, 1995, Knight confidently took the stage at Madison Square Garden. It was the first time that many in the audience had ever seen the man who had been whispered about so much. Holding the mike with a diamond bracelet sparkling on his right wrist, he gave the audience something to remember.

"Any artist out there that want to be an artist and want to stay a star and don't want to worry about the executive producer all up in the videos, all on the records— dancing, come to Death Row!" His sarcastic remarks were clearly a broadside directed at Puffy.

The audience gasped in shock and there were a few scattered boos. People couldn't believe Knight had the gall to disrespect Combs that way, openly trying to scoop his talent in his own backyard. In truth, some on the East Coast felt the same as Knight did about Combs's attention-grabbing ways. But it was bigger than that now. By virtue of the fact that they were in New York City, they had to stand by Combs—and they did.

By the time Snoop Dogg came onstage, the audience rained down a chorus of boos. Snoop—who had paid tribute to Slick Rick on his debut album—had always gotten nothing but love from the East Coast. But now he reverted to his Long Beach Crip roots, the timbre of his voice changed and his eyes were blazing.

"The East Coast ain't got no love for Dr. Dre and Snoop Doggy Dogg? And Death Row? *Y'all don't love us!?*" He wore a blue kerchief around his neck and brandished a machete in his right hand, swiping the air next to his leg for emphasis. "Then let it be known that we got no love for the East Coast then!"

It was on.

When Sean Combs came to the stage with Faith and Chris Webber to present an award, he tried his best to calm the crowd, but it was already too late. "I'm the executive producer that a comment was made about a little bit earlier," said Combs sheepishly, his face low and close to the podium, and his hat turned backward.

"Contrary to what other people may feel, I'm proud of Dr. Dre and Death Row and Suge Knight for their accomplishments. I'm a positive black man, and I want to bring us together, not separate us. All this East and West, that need to stop. One love!" Combs even presented Snoop with the award for Best Solo Artist.

But Wallace had won awards for Best New Artist, Best Live Performer, Best Lyricist, and Album of the Year—a virtual sweep. But the scent of beef hung over the ceremony like a dark cloud. It got even darker after the Dogg Pound got on the stage to perform, and Dat Nigga Daz, surly as ever, looked out at the crowd and said, "Yo, from the bottom of my heart, y'all can eat this dick!"

By the time the news hit the ghetto grapevine, and the mix-show DJs and magazines started discussing it, the friction played out at the awards show took on a life of its own. A few weeks later Quincy Jones organized a summit meeting at a New York hotel to help ease the tension and discuss the future of hip hop. Though Shakur did not attend—he was still in a jail cell—Knight and Dr. Dre were there, as were Combs and Wallace along with the likes of Colin Powell and Minister Conrad Muhammad. "Speaker after speaker talked about power as a form of responsibility," Jones wrote in his memoirs, "about being guided by the inner conscience, even if anger is the initial motivator for your actions." But it was no use—rumors of war were in the air.

On September 24, 1995, they went from rumor to reality. Knight and Combs both were invited to a birthday party for Jermaine Dupri, founder of So So Def Records in Atlanta. Atlanta police allege that during an after-party thrown at the Platinum City Club, members of the Bad Boy crew got into some friction, woofing about what Knight said at the Source Awards. The cops suspected that one of Combs's bodyguards, Anthony "Wolf" Jones, shot Jai-Hassan Jamal, a.k.a. Jake Robles, a Death Row executive who happened to be one of Suge Knight's closest friends. According to Chris Howard, an off-duty Atlanta police officer who worked for the club, the tension got so thick that he had to separate Robles and Jones. Eventually both posses had to be ejected from the club. Howard asked the Bad Boy camp to leave first. Then, as he was escorting the Death Row crew to their limo, they were ambushed. "All of a sudden Puffy's guys came from around the corner," Howard said, "and one of them had a gun.

"We wild, we young, and we tight like how a Mafia would be trained," said B.I.G. of his Junior M.A.F.I.A. crew. "These niggas are getting paid now. They're like sex symbols. I love it."

I chased the guy with the gun around the corner. He handed the gun off to another guy. It was a .45. By the time I got back out front, that's when the guy took a shot at Suge's partner. He shot him two or three times." Howard said the assailant jumped into a car along with "all the guys who were with Puffy." Robles died within weeks of the shooting. A year later, an informant told New York authorities that the shooter "is a guy named Anthony Jones, street name Wolf."

Even though Combs clearly wasn't the shooter, Knight maintained that he was responsible. Combs denied having anything to do with the incident. "At the time there wasn't really no drama. I didn't even have bodyguards," Combs said. "I left the club, and I'm waiting for my limo, talking to girls. I didn't see Suge go into the club; we didn't make any contacts or anything like that. All I heard is that he took beef at the bar. I see people coming out. I see a lot of people that I know, I see [Suge], and I see everybody yelling and screaming and shit. I get out the limo and I go to [Suge], like, 'What's up, you all right?' I'm trying to see if I can help. Then I hear shots ringing out, and we turn around and [Robles]—God bless the dead—gets shot, and he's on the floor. My back was turned; I could have gotten shot and he could have gotten shot. But right then [Knight] was like, 'I think you had something to do with this.' I'm like, 'What are you talking about? I was standing right here with you!' I really felt sorry for him, in a sense . . . he was showing me his insecurity." A snowball of hatred was rolling downhill, gaining mass and momentum. And nobody was doing anything to stop it.

Meanwhile Wallace stayed on the paper chase, traveling from city to city, appearance to appearance, trying to keep getting money. And after each show, he had an opportunity to meet interesting people from different parts of the country, like in Sacramento, California.

Months earlier Big had given an interview to a free magazine called *Peace!* in which he was asked to rate different rappers on a scale of one to ten. He had been smoking before the interview took place, so he was extra candid in his ratings. When asked about the Sacramento rap mogul E-40, Big said, "No rating! Zero! I don't fuck with duke at all."

After rocking the crowd in Sacramento, Big and his six-man crew were returning to the hotel when they noticed they were being followed by several cars. At first they assumed the cars were full of groupies looking forward to an after-party. But when they reached the hotel, they realized that the cars were tricked-out low-riders. People in New York didn't have rides like that. They'd never seen such vehicles outside of a Snoop video. "And it wasn't one car," said DJ Enuff. "It was five, six, seven cars—and four dudes in every car. So the cars do this big circle thing, circling the entire parking lot, then everybody gets out of their car and we see they're all gangbangers."

Twenty or thirty riders closed in around the seven out-of-towners. Only one

"Throw ya hands in the air if you're a true playa." B.I.G. worked hard, but he played even harder. And he could dance, too.

of them spoke. "What's up, Big?" he said. "You in Sacramento now." Then he handed Wallace a cell phone. E-40 was on the line, wanting to discuss Big's magazine interview. "You know what's the craziest part?" Enuff recalled, "Big didn't even look fazed. They're all flashing their guns and shit and Big is talking slick to E-40 on the phone. None of us were suckers, but there were seven of us with no guns, no knives, no mace, no sticks, nothing."

"My people is here," E-40 told him.

"Yeah, I see them," said Big.

He went on to explain that his comments in the interview referred to E-40's music only—after all, they'd never met, and for all Big knew, E-40 might be a wonderful fellow. And so a potentially nasty situation was avoided.

"As soon as that's done," Enuff said, "the same motherfucker who stepped to us was like, 'Can I have your autograph?'" The DJ was a bit shaken by the whole experience, but eventually found the whole thing funny. "Hip hop is so much like high school," he observed. "Everybody wants to test."

Despite the occasional run-in with unfriendly locals, Big was having the time of his life on the road. But Faith, who stayed home working on her own album, was missing her husband. And he missed her, too—sometimes.

"Not seeing him at all was terrible," Faith said. "A few months after our anniversary, it seemed like he was getting caught up in all that 'Big Poppa' stuff." One line from that song goes "Money, clothes, and hoes, all a nigga knows..." And at the moment, that's how Wallace was living.

"That star shit didn't really hit me until like a couple of months ago," Wallace told VIBE's Mimi Valdés, who joined him on the road during the summer of 1995. In Raleigh, North Carolina, as he performed "Player's Anthem" with the rest of Junior M.A.F.I.A., women in the audience rubbed their breasts on beat as he got to the chorus, "Rub your titties if you love Big Pop." A riot damn near ensued after Biggie's hype man Money L threw two hundred one-dollar bills into the crowd during the song "Get Money." The money throwing was Biggie's idea. He used to do it himself until he tossed a $5,000 ring into the audience by mistake.

Despite the attention, life on the road was a grind. Ride on the bus for twelve hours between cities, barely have time to shower and change, and then back on stage to perform. Between the McDonald's food, the blunts, and the constant travel, it was hard to know whether you were coming or going. The bus could break down, and an eight-hour drive could suddenly take fifteen.

Not that anyone was watching the clock. Wallace passed the time playing spades or Cee-Lo with Hawk Burns, Don Pooh, his onstage hype man Money L, DJ Enuff, or Lil' Cease and D-Roc, sometimes for as much as $1,000 at a time. Lil' Kim was either right next to the boys in the middle of the action, or sleeping.

Some of the shows on that first tour were busts. "I did five venues where there were like thirteen people in 'em," said Wallace. "My boys were telling me it was the promoters not doing their jobs, but I was slowly but surely thinking it was over. Then we came to Chicago, and my muthafuckin' ego was back on point."

Big enjoyed the bigger cities because, if he was there for a couple of days, he could relax. He could do laundry or shop, and he and the crew could always find a decent steakhouse and not have to subsist on McDonald's hamburgers.

"I'm still trying to lose weight from being out on the road with Big," said DJ Enuff with a laugh. "He'd always eat steak, shrimp, the best of everything on the menu. If it cost fifty dollars he'd get it. I'd go in his room sometimes and see, like, a buffet. And he'd be like, 'Eat. Come here, man. Eat.'"

When he wasn't actually performing, he kept busy with the Junior M.A.F.I.A. project. The record was released in 1995 and "Player's Anthem" and "Get Money" became instant hits. Even though they were not on Bad Boy, Cease and Lil' Kim, the stand-out stars from the crew, were treated like family, and Kim even turned up on Puffy productions. Wallace was proud of them, happy he could look out for his people. "It's great, man," he said. "It feels great to know that when I was saying 'Junior M.A.F.I.A.' at the end of my records there was no Junior M.A.F.I.A. And I just felt that would be a tight name for the niggas to roll with. We wild, we young, and we tight like how a Mafia would be trained. These niggas is actually getting $10,000 a show right now. They're getting paid. They're like fuckin' sex symbols. They're in magazines. Yo, this is great, man. I love it."

Another thing that made him proud was the success of Lil' Kim. Not only did people like her style and her rhymes, but the 4'11" around-the-way girl now had a deal of her own through the label Wallace started with his heavyset homeboy Un.

"To take Kim, this little raunchy broad from the 'hood, man . . ." Wallace said, shaking his head in disbelief. "Kim was crazy, man. She was a female Big, going all out for her ones, whether it be fucking a nigga to get some paper, whether it be robbing a nigga to get some paper, or whether it be anything she had to do to get some ones, she was doing it. To see her come up and be the fuckin' Queen Bitch of this game right now? It's dope." Whatever Kim meant to him, she clearly saw Big Poppa as much more than a boss.

Kimberly Jones remembered the day they met with crystal clarity. He was sitting on a trash can outside the Fulton Mall. "We were just there talking. He was not the kinda guy I was used to talking to," she said. "I would deal with niggas with money. But he had this confidence about him. This was around the time he did that Mary J. remix. He was the biggest manipulator in the world. Later he got me to rhyme for him. After I rhymed he said, 'I'm fucking with you, Ma. We gonna make some money.'" They also made time to get together, though Big kept their relationship on the low.

That was his life: shows, studio sessions, and steering the careers of Junior M.A.F.I.A. 2 Live Crew's Luther Campbell, one of the first rap artists to build his own successful company, was always impressed with Wallace's business acumen. "A lot of other people take a lot of credit for the business aspect of that whole crew," says Luke. "It may have been Un running the label, but Biggie was really the brains behind it all. Puffy takes credit for a lot of things with Faith and Kim, but a lot of that was Biggie. This cat did it without receiving the glory. Nobody talks about that."

"There's a reason for his incredible respect as one of the most brilliant lyrical craftsman known," said Atlantic Records co-president Craig Kallman. "He really had an incredible mind. He just struck me instantly as someone who had so many creative ideas that just needed a platform and a stage on which to unfold."

Wallace built up the Junior M.A.F.I.A, and spun off Lil' Kim as a solo artist. It wasn't enough for him to make the transition from 'hood nigga to "it's all good" nigga if he couldn't bring his boys.

"Everybody was eating," Lil' Cease said. "Before you knew it, you're fifty niggas strong on a tour bus, rolling town to town. That's fifty muthafuckas from the street. And everybody advances and takes other people. That's how it ran."

Wallace felt more comfortable making his moves low-profile style. It wasn't always easy clearing these side projects with Puffy and his boss, Clive Davis. Sometimes there was drama, but Wallace usually got his way in the end. He had to make that paper, and there was no time to waste worrying about who got the credit. Plus he had to make time for his fans.

"Big Poppa, Big Poppa," the women would scream before he got onstage. "Please, please, please come over here so I can feel on you." One constant that never changed in his life were the girls. They were everywhere. In Raleigh, they waited in the hotel lobby at all hours. In Cleveland, right before the concert, they spotted Wallace backstage right before he went on to perform. Part of being "Big Poppa" meant showing love to all the ladies. Even the heavier ones or the ones who might not be considered so attractive—although he did not necessarily pursue them romantically, Poppa would be there with a kind word for his fans. Homely women might have gotten a little love on the microphone to boost their self-esteem, but backstage was a different matter. Only the dime pieces—the hot girls—got up close to Big Poppa.

"It was really amazing the kinds of chicks that Biggie would pull," DJ Enuff said, "He was the Don, he was the leader. We just had to respect that." Everyone else got whoever was left. Not that they complained much.

"Orgies—anything you wanted," said Lil' Cease. "The power of Big Poppa was like, 'Ain't no questions.' It's just, 'What you want?' 'I want some head right now.' 'Just go upstairs and take care of that.' It's like, Big got three upstairs. I got one over there. Roc got one over there . . . In the car, the dressing room, backstage, you know. They was happy to have fun. This when the M.A.F.I.A. was out. And we wasn't no ugly niggas either. No, we were sharp. We was flashing. We was with the hottest nigga running the game right there. Every bitch wanted a piece of that shit. Every bitch. We was getting paid so everybody had the jewelry, the suits, we had the cars. Extra rooms. Suites. And mad bitches."

Christopher Wallace had no illusions that he wasn't the classic sex symbol. "Black and ugly as ever" was how he put it in "Big Poppa." But his charisma—and stardom—got him over. "I'm a realist. I know, I see pretty niggers. And I see ugly niggers. And I know I ain't no pretty nigger. But I got a little, a little style to me. I don't know, I don't know what it is. I just think that I'm cool to be with."

It was more than that.

"Big knew how to break them down," Lil' Cease said. And even though he thought of himself as a great MC, he never considered himself a star. He was always approachable.

The sexual attention took its toll on his relationship with Faith. Wallace never really had a chance to settle down with Faith, who had an album of her own to promote. The responsibilities of the road took a toll on their marriage.

"Temptation is a muthafucka," Wallace said with a weary expression. "You're in the industry. Girls sucking your dick for nothing. Suck your man's dick just to get to suck your dick. That's the way it goes. It's crazy, but it's real.

"Now you got me. I'm going from state to state. It's possible for me to fuck ten bitches a day if I wanted to. It's crazy, but it's true. Now, if you're in a relationship for how long? Let's just say two or three years. And in that time I fuck four bitches, you gonna flip over that? I mean, shit, I could have fucked four thousand bitches. And you gonna scream on me like, *You cheating muthafucka!* You in Louisville, Kentucky, somewhere, and the shit come over you. Everybody makes mistakes. Shit happens, y'knowhatumsayin'? As long as it ain't no keeping-in-contact-type shit, like the girl from Louisville is trying to move to New York and be a part of your life and shit. Just take a fuck for what it is. A fuck. Y'knowhatumsayin'?

"You're my only girl. You're the one that I love, the one that I'm with. If I happen to fuck up and make a mistake, I apologize, man. Just don't lose it. 'Cause it could have been a lot worse. Give me an E for effort, at least. Goddamn. I couldn't get an A, so I got a B-plus. Don't be mad at me. My feelings for you ain't changed."

Wallace shook his head. "I know that sounds crazy, and girls definitely don't want to hear that shit."

Faith certainly wasn't having it. She wasn't the Rita Marley or Jackie O type who would look the other way. If she sniffed anything, there was drama.

"Part of me wanted to be like, well, what did you expect? He is out there on the damn road," Faith said. "I mean you're not there. But then again, it's not at all like that's at all acceptable."

And she didn't take disrespect lightly.

"He called me one night from this phone in his hotel room after a show he had," Faith said, recalling a show that Wallace did in Virginia. "He's telling me, well, I'm letting such and such use my room tonight, 'cause one of the guys, he gotta share a room with Cease and he got a girl with him," Faith said.

"It just didn't sound right. First of all, you ain't giving up your room for nobody. I know you *way* better than that." She laughed. "Secondly, why would you call me and tell me that, when if you're going in their room, you could very well call me from their room anyway. So don't block me from calling you. I know he definitely didn't think that one out all the way."

So Faith called her best friend and had her come to the duplex in Brooklyn to watch her daughter, Chyna. She caught the earliest flight she could, and took a cab to the hotel, knowing that Wallace wasn't an early riser. When she got to the lobby, she saw Hawk Burns at the reception desk taking care of the bill, and sneaked past him so he wouldn't see her.

"I went straight to his door and knocked," Faith said. Nobody answered, but she kept knocking. She knocked to the point where it got annoying.

"Who is it," a female voice asked.

"Housekeeping," said Faith.

The girl on the other end opened the door just a crack, and Faith kicked her way in the room. "Faith beat the shit out of her," Big told Mimi Valdés in his first VIBE cover story. "Punched homegirl in the face like thirty times."

"I just grabbed the girl and went bananas," Faith said. "I looked over at him, and he was sitting in the bed, looking at me like 'Oh my God.'" Both Biggie and the girl were fully clothed, but it didn't matter to Faith.

"She was still in his room," Faith said heatedly. "I don't give a fuck! She don't got no damn business being in there. I was cursing him out and hitting her the entire time."

"I ain't fuck her! I ain't fuck her!" Wallace kept saying.

"If you didn't fuck her, you should have, stupid, 'cause she just got her ass beat!" replied Faith.

"He was over there looking at me all pitiful like, 'Why are you doing that to that girl, Faye?' I didn't care. I ain't say nothing else. I got right back in the cab and was back at the airport within a half hour. And I got on the next flight back to Brooklyn."

Her point was made. "That's the illest, right there," Wallace said. He and D-Roc caught the next plane back to New York.

"I was so nervous, I jetted to New York, 'cause I wasn't going to leave her buck-wildin' like that. The girl was mad cool, and I felt horrible, but fuck that," Wallace said. "I got on that plane."

"He was all over Brooklyn, asking, 'Have you seen my wife,'" Faith said, chuckling at the memory. "He finally caught up with me and wanted to plead his case and all, and I was like, you know, 'There's just really nothing you can say right now, buddy.' I was so mad."

Not that that lasted for long.

"That's the awkward thing about love," Faith explained. "He always knew the right things to say. Always. Always. That's probably how he got over so well. He always knew the right thing to say, no matter what."

Faith laughed again. Sometimes he could just look at her and make her melt.

"You mad at me, Ma? You know I love you." That's all he had to say, with the right look in his eye, and the right voice, and much was forgiven.

"I was definitely weak," said Faith, smiling. "Weak for him. Definitely so."

Just when things were taking off for Wallace, he was arrested and charged with assaulting a New Jersey concert promoter.

If things were tumultuous in Wallace's love life, there was plenty of drama in his professional life as well. It seemed that as soon as he escaped the streets, some street shit would happen, pulling Wallace back in.

A perfect example was what happened on May 6, 1995, after a show that was supposed to happen in Camden, New Jersey, at Club Xscape. Brook Herdell, the promoter of the show—and the second half of his $20,000 fee—were missing. Wallace reportedly demanded that the driver for the promoter, Nathaniel Banks Jr., take him to the promoter. Some patrons, also pissed for being out their money, followed the caravan.

When the promoter refused to come outside, Banks said Wallace got agitated. "If I don't get my money, I'm going to start punching muthafuckas . . ." is what Banks remembered Wallace saying. Before he knew it, Banks was on the ground getting stomped. He was also robbed of a necklace, bracelet, watch, cell phone, and $300 in cash.

"I look up and see this three-hundred-pound mutha kicking me in the head, making grunting noises, and wobbling like a monster," Banks said. "People tell me he's really not that type of person. Maybe he had to do what he did because he might look like a punk if he didn't. Maybe he has to act out what he says on his records."

Wallace didn't deny being present, but he said he wasn't the one who beat Banks down. Without implicating the person who did do it, Don Pooh and Mark Pitts insisted that Wallace was not involved because they insisted that he stay in his car when the fracas took place. "Who knows who beat the shit out of duke?" Wallace said later. "That whole block was lined up with cars."

When Wallace and his people got in their cars to leave, they didn't realize that Camden police would soon issue a warrant for his arrest. The legal documents were sent to his mother's apartment as opposed to his new Fort Greene duplex.

Six weeks later, after finishing a show at Pulsations in Philly, a surprise was waiting for Wallace and his entourage. He noticed flares on the ground, and police giving directions.

"We were thinking it was a police escort, 'cause there were so many people outside that club," Wallace recalled. Police led their cars to a parking lot, where more officers were positioned around the car. Once the caravan stopped, the drama started.

"I swear on my mother, niggas rolled out on their stomachs and pointed rifles with infrared beams on my truck," Wallace said. "Meanwhile, I'm in the passenger seat, with a bottle of Dom Pérignon, pissy drunk, like 'Oh my God, what the fuck is going on?'"

Next thing Wallace knew, he was lying face down on the ground with rocks and bugs in his face while a police officer pointed a shotgun with a flashlight mounted on it right at his head. "They took me to the precinct and niggas was giving each other mad high fives and doing belly slaps," Wallace recalled. But some of the police also asked him for autographs.

"They were like, 'My daughter Meghan loves ya,'" Wallace recalled with a grin. "So I'm talking to Meghan on the phone, and she telling me she want to go to my concert. I'm like, 'Yo, Meghan . . . talk to ya pops.'"

Since the law considered him a fugitive, Wallace spent three days in jail after the arrest. Ms. Wallace was so angry with him that they went through a period of not speaking, just as in his crack-selling days.

"That shit made my moms think of the old Christopher," Wallace said, "like I was still on the same bullshit. I'm telling her I ain't touch him, I didn't rob him, and she looking at me like 'Whatever.' That's my ol' M.O., y'knowhatumsayin'?"

"I'd rather be dead than in jail," said Wallace, reflecting on his short stint in the pokey. "I was shaking, throwing up 'cause that shit was mad dirty. Rats and mice all over. That shit was the worst."

Tupac Shakur could agree with Wallace on that point. And by the fall of 1995, he decided to do something about it.

During the summer of 1995, Suge Knight and his lawyer David Kenner flew by private jet from Los Angeles to New York to visit Shakur at Dannemora Prison and make him an attractive offer: sign with Death Row, and all his problems would be solved. He'd be out of jail with money in his pocket, and the security that comes from knowing that no one would mess with him anymore.

It sounded too good to be true (and it probably was), but what else was Shakur going to do? He wasn't in any position to hold out for a different solution. Control was important to him, and as a prisoner he had none. Serving the four years was not an option.

"I want a house for my moms," Shakur told Knight as the first order of business. They discussed money and a few other points, but not with the usual protocol for negotiating a deal with a major record label. David Kenner represented both sides—both the label and the artist—a clear conflict of interest. He drew up a handwritten three-page contract. "It was only because he was in prison that he signed it," said Shakur's attorney Charles Ogletree. "Tupac was saying 'My freedom is everything. If you can't get me my freedom, you can have access to my art.'"

Normally the transfer of a contract from one company to another for an established artist could take months, even years. Shakur was signed to Interscope—but Death Row had its distribution deal through Interscope. Handshakes between Kenner and Knight and label co-owners Jimmy Iovine and Ted Fields were all that was needed to transfer Shakur's contract from one company to the other. All Shakur had to do was sign and it was a done deal.

Close relatives and friends urged Shakur not to sign with Knight, but they didn't have the money or the credit to get him out. Interscope had advanced all they were going to advance without any more money being guaranteed by Death Row.

Shakur's manager, Watani Tyehimba, a former Black Panther who had known Tupac since childhood, visited him in prison around that time. "I know I'm selling my soul to the devil," Tyehimba remembered Shakur telling him.

Shakur nonetheless signed Kenner's document. Within a week, the New York Court of Appeals granted bail.

And, just like that, Shakur was free on October 12, 1995. He got on a private plane and, within hours, he was in a Tarzana, California, recording studio. It didn't matter to him that Suge put up only $250,000 of the $1.4 million, with Interscope and MCA kicking in the rest. Suge made him a promise and kept his word. In the process, he won Tupac's enthusiastic loyalty. Suge said he would get him out, and he did. It was just as he had learned in his childhood: revolutionaries had rhetoric but gangsters made things happen. Good behavior, ironically, would have kept him in jail. Getting down with the Gs, however, would get him out, get his mama a house, and put him right back in the hot seat.

The Death Row crew that Shakur had joined was in disarray. Snoop was in court every day fighting a murder charge, and as far as Knight was concerned, Dr. Dre wasn't pulling his weight either—he was taking too long to perfect his beats. Death Row needed a superstar, someone who could step up immediately and start producing massive hits. Knight thought Shakur was that person.

From Knight's perspective, Dr. Dre was acting like Patrick Ewing. Sure, he was a great center—talented but temperamental. And he wasn't putting up the numbers like he used to. After a drunken night in 1994 where he raced the police down Wilshire Boulevard in his Ferrari, Dre was sentenced to 180 days in a Pasadena halfway house with work-release privileges during the day. Since then he'd been slowly fading away from the sound lab, spending more time in his Woodland Hills mansion than in the mix at Can-Am Studios where Suge made sure his team was pushing out hits 24 hours a day, seven days a week.

"He rides like I ride," said Shakur after signing with Suge Knight. In Tupac, Knight found someone who worked as hard as he did.

Knight hoped that bringing Shakur to Death Row would have the same impact on Death Row as Shaquille O'Neal's departure from the Orlando Magic had on the Lakers. Like Shaq, Pac was a tireless competitor who would put up big numbers every night of the week. And from Shakur's standpoint, he was joining a championship organization. He finally had the kind of backup that, in his mind, would help him through everything. "I'm gonna make Death Row the biggest company in the whole world," Shakur promised Knight. "I'm gonna make it bigger than Snoop ever made it."

"It's like a machine," Shakur said. "That's what Death Row is to me. The biggest, strongest superpower in the hip hop world. In order to do some of the things that I got to do, we gotta have that superpower."

In quick order, the machine he described went into overdrive. The first night after he got out of jail, Shakur recorded seven songs. In a matter of weeks, Shakur recorded enough material for a double album. Fueled by alcohol, weed, blistering talent, and raging emotions, Shakur poured out a musical avalanche.

Pac was a studio prodigy, more like a one-take jazz musician than a punch-me-in rapper. "I didn't realize a rapper could write the lyrics and deliver the vocals as fast as he could," marveled producer Johnny "J" Jackson, who had worked previously with Shakur on "Pour Out a Little Liquor," and later produced many of the best tracks on *All Eyez on Me*.

"After I'd been there laying down the tracks for an hour or two, he'd come in, sit right down, and write three verses in fifteen or twenty minutes," recalls Jackson. "Then he'd go into the booth and deliver the vocal—and it was on to the next track."

In Shakur, Knight had met his spiritual soul mate. Here was someone who worked even harder than Knight did, which was damn hard. Knight kept a bedroom at Can-Am Studios, and would often sleep there. Shakur treated the studio the way Knight once treated the football field—with focus and ferocity. Gone were the days of waiting week after week for Dr. Dre to finish a track. Shakur just banged the tunes out like clockwork. All that weed and Hennessy would slow most people down, and by the time they got to the booth, their vocals were mush. Shakur's words never slurred, and his mind never blurred.

And in Knight, Shakur had met someone who was even more hot-tempered than he was. As one of Shakur's friends put it, "That street shit had to be dealt with, and Suge had the power on the street."

"He rides like I ride," said Shakur. "With Suge as my manager, I have to do less. 'Cause before niggas wasn't scared of me. So I brought fear to them. Now I don't have to do that to do that. Muthafuckas is scared shitless of Suge."

Shakur's small jail cell had been replaced by a spacious suite at the Peninsula Hotel and an apartment on Wilshire Boulevard, among other places. Soon he had cars, all the luxury steel and rubber a black boy could dream of. Knight showered Shakur with more diamond-encrusted jewelry than he could wear, and gave him the keys to one of four Rolls-Royces to celebrate Snoop Dogg's February 20, 1996, acquittal in his murder case. There were trips to Mexico, Vegas, and Hawaii. And since Shakur had his marriage with longtime girlfriend Keisha Morris annulled within weeks of his release, life around Pac became the Motor Booty Affair, part two.

But it wasn't enough. It never was.

He still had the nightmares. He wore a bulletproof vest everywhere he went, and rolled with a team of bodyguards. He always made sure that wherever he sat he faced the door. Loud noises would trigger post-traumatic flashbacks. He

Randy "Stretch" Walker in a 1992 photo for his group the Live Squad. Friends said the rapper was the only person who could have reunited Wallace and Shakur.

told a writer who interviewed him soon after his release that, while driving to the recording studio, he heard a backfire that sounded like a gunshot, and tensed up while he was behind the wheel.

Death was not an abstract concept to Shakur. It was an ever-present reality—almost like a companion.

"Like Malcolm X knew he was going to die, I knew I was going to get shot," Shakur once said. "I know I'm not going to live forever. But I know I'm going to die in violence. All good niggas, all the niggas who change the world, die in violence. They don't die in regular ways. Muthafuckas come take their lives."

All through his 11 months with Death Row, it was work-play-work for Shakur. One minute it was the studio, the next it was an appearance at a late October *Soul Train* event, and the next he was in Westwood at Monty's Steakhouse, a popular U.C.L.A. hangout that became the unofficial Death Row commissary. A few scant weeks ago he was on lockdown with "three hots and a cot." Now he had a luxury suite at the Westwood Marquis, keys to a luxury high-rise, and a plate full of lobster tails. He had come a long way in a very short time.

"I can't eat all this," Shakur said. "It's too much."

Combs, meanwhile, made himself scarce. He was supposed to make an appearance at Miami's "How Can I Be Down?" conference in Miami on October 21, 1995, but skipped it when he heard that Knight was bringing an "army" to Collins Avenue. On November 30, 1995—exactly a year to the day he and Shakur were assaulted at Quad Studios—27-year-old Randy "Stretch" Walker was murdered while driving near his brother's house on a residential street in Queens. His SUV was being followed by a black Acura that began shooting at him with a high-powered rifle. While trying to escape, his SUV crashed and flipped over. Police said the killers fired shots into the wreckage before fleeing the scene. No suspects were ever arrested.

Wallace found out about Walker's death not by watching the news, but via his SkyPager's voicemail. He was friends with Walker, too—Big and Pac had made a record with Stretch that was supposed to appear on the first Thug Life album. He had been expecting Walker to arrive at the video shoot for "Get Money" by Junior M.A.F.I.A. "I was busy all night," Wallace said. "I checked my messages, and the first one was from Stretch, saying, 'Yo, how do I get to the shoot, dog?' By the time I got to the last message, it was Stretch's wife, screaming and crying, saying, 'Big, where the fuck are you? Somebody killed Stretch.'"

The date of the murder seemed like more than a coincidence. Word on the street speculated that Walker was murdered as revenge for the Quad Studios shooting of Shakur, even though he repeatedly denied being involved. Despite the fact that Walker and Shakur had been close since before the actor starred in *Juice* when they were both temporary label mates on Tommy Boy Records, they fell out after the shooting. Shakur was angry that Walker never came to visit him while he was being held at Rikers Island or at Dannemora. Walker felt wronged that Shakur had implicated him in the VIBE interview as being a part of the shooting. He was incensed that Shakur would question his manhood for doing as the armed bandits asked instead of rushing them. Walker felt that by standing up to them, Shakur had endangered all of their lives.

In his response to Shakur's comment in VIBE, Walker stated that he remembered only one gunshot, not five, raising the question of whether Shakur was really shot in the head—as he claimed. Walker suggested that Shakur's head injuries could have come from being pistol-whipped, and that Shakur's gunshot wound in the groin might have been self-inflicted. "He tried to go for his gun and made a mistake," Walker told Fab 5 Freddy. "But I'll let him tell the world that. I ain't even going to get into it all like that."

"Why would he go and do an interview like that?" Walker said. "He's supposed to be a street nigga, he should have kept it in the street . . . I want him to get a reality check. Recognize what the fuck he's doing. Niggas on the street live by rules. And that rule right there, that's a rule never to be broken."

Whoever had broken the code of silence, Walker was the one who ended up dead. And after his death, the conflict between Wallace and Shakur only escalated.

"I think he would have been the only one that could bring Big and Pac together," Cease reflected years later. "'Cause he knew the real on both ends. He used to be trying to tell Pac, 'Yo, nigga, you trippin'. You know Big ain't have nothing to do with that shit.' And Pac would tell Stretch, 'I ain't trippin.' What are you on the other side?' But I think at the end of the day Stretch woulda brought Big and Pac together. Just by being here, he woulda said, Someone put an end to this shit."

When asked by the British author William Shaw what he felt when he heard about Walker's murder, Shakur's response was uncharacteristically cold.

"I didn't feel," Shakur said. "I felt for his mother and his wife. I didn't feel anything for him. Honestly."

A statement he later made to *The Source* mirrored that sentiment (or

Lil' Cease, Wallace, and Combs didn't let a little East-West tension stop them from doing their thing in L.A.

lack thereof). "He didn't do what your dog is supposed to do when you get shot up," Shakur said. "When I was in jail, nigga never wrote me, never got at me. And he started hanging around Biggie right after this. I'm in jail, shot up, his main dog, and he hanging out, going to shows with Biggie. Both these niggas never came to see me. Ain't no words. The rules of the game are so self-explanatory."

Life on Death Row seemed to be changing Pac, much as life on the corner had changed young Chris Wallace. Though he was known for his harsh statements against his perceived enemies, Shakur was like Muhammad Ali—there was always an implied wink. Ali could call Frazier a gorilla or an Uncle Tom up and down the street, but no one (other than, perhaps, Frazier) thought he really meant it.

"I always called Pac the George Jefferson of the music business," said Luther Campbell, who knew Wallace and Shakur and tried to encourage them to iron out their differences. "He's a little guy running around, you know, he just be talkin'. He don't mean nothing. He ain't gonna hurt nobody. He just be talkin' talkin' talkin'. You know, little guy disease."

Former Tommy Boy publicist Laura Hines, who set up some of Shakur's first interviews when he was a member of Digital Underground, noted his "profound sense of victimhood." If he got it into his head that someone was his enemy, she said he would often brood over it to the point of obsession. "More than anything," she said, "he never wanted to feel vulnerable."

After moving to Death Row, Shakur's public pronouncements became more menacing, as if the shooting and the jail time had transformed him into something even he wouldn't recognize. Tupac the "Ridah"—West Coast slang for a gangsta at war, derived from drive-by shootings—was even more dangerous than Tupac the thug. And the "real" Tupac was no longer visible.

"Pac was like a chameleon," said Big Syke, a rapper who collaborated with Shakur. "Whatever he was around he turned into. And when he got around Death Row he tried to be that."

Never was this more apparent than at a 1995 Death Row Christmas party held at the opulent Chateau Le Blanc mansion in the Hollywood Hills. Independent record promoter Mark Anthony Bell, a high school friend of Combs's, was reportedly escorted to an upstairs room where he was interrogated about the shooting of Knight's friend Jake Robles, and asked to provide the home addresses of Combs and his mother. Bell told police that when he refused he was beaten. The questions kept coming, and Bell said Shakur was whispering instructions in Knight's ear. Knight then allegedly forced Bell to drink a champagne flute of his urine. He told police that he attempted to jump off a second-floor balcony to escape. Bell said Shakur was punching his hands, making him let go of the railing. Bell said he was pulled back into the room, and that Suge then offered him money for the information.

The next day, at a Valley hospital, Bell was treated for numerous bruises, a hemorrhaging left eye, and a deep laceration on his left elbow. Four days later he filed a robbery and assault claim against Knight, Shakur, and the other men he recognized there. The district attorney refused to press charges because Bell didn't report the assault at the time the police showed up—despite the fact that Knight was standing right there at the time.

Bell filed a civil suit against Knight and Death Row, settled out of court, then took his $600,000 and moved out of the country. But that wasn't an option for Biggie and Puff, who were still trying to conduct business as usual.

But it was at a party at the House of Blues, when Shakur ran into a familiar face, that the war between East and West truly got personal.

The familiar face belonged to Wallace's wife.

Lil' Kim would later tell VH1 that she was carrying Wallace's child but aborted the pregnancy at his request, a story that many people close to Wallace deny.

According to Lil' Cease, Kim took her relationship with Wallace more seriously than he did. "It wasn't nothing serious," Lil' Cease said of Kim. "Big had love for her 'cause she was part of the team," Cease continued. "She was from around the way. She came up with us. Of course there's love there. But all this crazy, like, 'We was in love.' And 'We was gonna do this.' I don't know about that. Unless he saying that shit to Fay. I'll be honest. Big was married, and then besides the marriage he was fucking with Charli. So what place did you stand?"

When Faith Evans and Christopher Wallace's marriage began to fall apart, it wasn't a huge blow-up but a gradual fade-out. Both were on the road constantly, and Evans never stopped wondering about whether or not Wallace was faithful.

There wasn't much to wonder about—he wasn't. On one hand, he was involved with his protégée Lil' Kim, who seemed to enjoy taking public digs at Evans. Wallace had also begun seeing Tiffany Lane, a tall beauty from Philadelphia who appeared as the Faith look-alike in Junior M.A.F.I.A.'s "Get Money" video. Lane would soon become known by her rap alias, Charli Baltimore. "He had done a show in Philly, and I asked if I could take his picture," Lane recalled. "But he snatched the camera from my hand and said, 'Let me take a picture of you instead.' We became mad cool friends after that."

Though Wallace told her of his plans to make her part of "The Commission"—a rap super group that would also include B.I.G. and Jay-Z—Lane understood that she was not the only woman in Wallace's life. Even so, things sometimes got a bit out of hand.

"There were so many girls," she said. "They didn't care who was standing next to him. If they wanted to flash their tits or pull up their skirts while wearing no underwear, that's exactly what happened. Sometimes he looked more scared of those girls than I was. It's impossible for any man to be around that much shit and not test the waters."

Faith still cared for him, even when their marriage was deteriorating. "I tried and tried, acting like this or that didn't happen," she said. "It's like I gave up hope. But I never stopped doing for Big. He was my husband."

Big might not have admitted it to Faith, but the marital tension bothered him, too. DJ Enuff remembered him playing her album—the one with sad songs like "You Used to Love Me"—over and over while riding on the tour bus. "When he was depressed, we were all depressed," Enuff said. "He would play all the slow jams. He didn't want to be talked to. No one could bother him. All he wanted to do was hear that damn Faith record. I love Faith, but, you know, Can you put something else on? But he was going through it. Then he would be, like, This is my baby. I love her. Faith did something to him that no other woman did to him. I don't know what it was, but he really did love his Faith."

Tiffany Lane met Wallace after a concert in Philadelphia and they began a relationship. He had big plans for her rap career as Charli Baltimore.

Evans figured that Wallace must be enjoying the life of a gigolo. But she didn't enjoy being married to one. "I knew that wasn't what I wanted for my marriage. I didn't want my husband to be doing that at all. And we just kind of separated." Aside from her personal life, Faith did not feel respected professionally. She had an almost platinum album with her solo debut *Faith*. But she thought people weren't really checking for her. Too many people were caught up in the fact that she was Wallace's wife, not that she had an incredible voice or could write songs, which she was doing long before she met her husband. She felt the need to prove that she could make a go on her own.

She came out to Los Angeles, stayed with a friend, and started working with a group called Tha Truth. She went out with friends one night, and ran into Treach from Naughty By Nature. Treach told her that Tupac wanted to say hi. "So I met him," she said. "And pretty much that was it. We took a couple of pictures in the club, and he told me, 'Yo, I want to work with you. I like your song. I heard your stuff when I was locked up.' I was basically like 'Cool, maybe we'll work together.'"

That she would be so friendly with a sworn enemy of her husband might seem

Faith told Biggie that she only laid down some vocals on a song with 2Pac. Shakur said there was more to it than that.

dubious to outside observers, but Evans insisted that the rivalry never crossed her mind. As far as she knew, Wallace didn't consider Shakur an enemy.

"Big still totally liked him," Evans said. "He never gave me the impression that he was not feeling [Shakur]. He always said that was his boy. Of course, once [Shakur] started dogging him out, [Wallace] said, 'Duke is wild,' like, 'I don't know what the fuck is going on,' but he always had good things to say about Pac. Biggie really wanted to understand why this guy was saying he had set him up when he knew he didn't. I wanted to be able to ask him myself."

She didn't try to hide the fact that she'd run into Shakur the next time she talked with her husband.

"I met Pac," she told him.

"Word? What did he say?" she remembered him asking. "I know for a fact that he still had hope that they would figure it all out,"

she said. She could tell that Wallace just wanted to talk to his old friend and ask him, "How could you even think I would do some shit like that?"

Then Faith ran into Shakur again, this time at the release party for the *Waiting to Exhale* soundtrack. They talked about the song he wanted her to sing on. That night, they went out to Can-Am Studios to record some rough vocals.

"I was definitely naive and hasty going to the studio without it being something that was officially cleared," Evans admitted after the fact. "I didn't know until I got to the studio and saw all these Death Row cats that this is where I am. You don't even know what I was feeling inside. I was petrified."

As she left, Shakur said that he would talk to Bad Boy about getting a song clearance. And as far as she was concerned, that was that. Evans didn't realize that anything was amiss until she started getting calls from Wallace.

"You don't be seeing Misa out there?" Wallace asked. Misa Hylton-Brim, Combs's former girlfriend and the mother of his eldest son, Justin, was alleged to be dating Suge Knight at the time. She later denied this. But the rumors served their purpose, ratcheting up the tension. There was a persistent story that Knight had posed for a photo holding Combs's son in his lap, and that he planned to turn the shot into a magazine ad with the caption: "Bad Boy Can't Take Care of Their Own." The ad never appeared, but the atmosphere of stress was getting thicker.

Evans assured Wallace that she hadn't seen Misa. She was hardly in touch with anybody from New York, and hadn't even met Suge. Evans wasn't worrying about any deeper implications. She hadn't done anything wrong. She had told Wallace the truth. But she had neglected to mention the song she recorded.

It wasn't until the January 14, 1996, issue of *The New York Times Magazine* hit the stands that all hell loose.

The cover photograph featured Knight in a red suit flanked by Snoop and Tupac, who was holding a few thousand dollars in cash. The article was written by Lynn Hirschberg, who had spent months around Knight, getting deep inside the Death Row camp. She went with them to a prizefight in Las Vegas and hung with Knight at his custom-car shop hours before he flew to New York with David Kenner to bail Shakur out of prison. But none of these details caused as much furor as a single exchange on page 50:

"The wife of a top rapper bought this for him," Knight said of Tupac's outfit.

"Who's that?" asked Hirschberg.

"Notorious B.I.G.'s wife, Faith Evans. She bought him this and a suit and some other stuff," Knight said, turning to Shakur. "And how did you thank her, Tupac?"

"I did enough," Shakur replied, his eyes gleaming with mischief.

In a subsequent VIBE interview, Powell asked Shakur directly about the rumors of his relationship with Faith. "You mean the rumor that I fucked her?" The rapper began laughing hysterically. "I ain't gonna answer that shit, man. You know

I don't kiss and tell." Shakur's response never ran in the magazine, but it didn't matter. The damage was already done.

This time it was Evans who received a loud knock on her hotel room door early one morning. She was back from Los Angeles, but had moved out of the Fort Greene duplex and was staying in a midtown Manhattan hotel.

"Biggie was banging on the door so loud that I wanted to call the cops," Evans recalled. "I couldn't do that. I had to finally let him in."

Wallace wasn't just upset; he was wrathful.

"He went bananas," said Evans. "He was screaming. He was cursing. He was grabbing me like this," she said, mimicking with both of her hands the way that Wallace grabbed her arms and shook her.

"I was crying, like 'No, no, no. You know that didn't happen. It's not like that.' I couldn't say anything but the same thing over and over again."

Wallace started tearing up the room. He pushed her against the wall.

"But I was so busy crying and upset and scared, none of that mattered," she said. "I was just waiting for the whole argument to be over or for him to leave, or for him to do whatever he was gonna do. Just do it."

She fled to the bathroom and Wallace left the hotel room.

Moments later she heard a quieter knock. It was D-Roc.

"You all right?" he asked.

"No," Evans said, still bawling. "You know that shit ain't true."

"I know, I know," D-Roc said. His deep, gravelly voice was calm. "Chris don't believe that. He don't believe that. The nigga is just mad. You know? He mad."

For the first time, Evans chuckled through her tears.

"I can see that."

A few weeks later, it was Faith's turn to be angry again. She and Wallace were picking up the pieces of what happened to them and how things went wrong. He had been questioning her about Shakur and she decided that she wanted to get in a question of her own: was he messing around with Lil' Kim?

"Yes," he replied, quietly.

"Her too?" she said, incredulous.

"You caught me," he said, sounding almost relieved. "I pulled it off all this time, but yeah, I've been fucking her."

"The way they played it, I would have never known," Evans said. "Never, ever, in a million years. I was totally shocked."

It made sense when Evans thought back on all the clues. The skit on *Ready to Die*, where Kim did the voice of the girl having sex with Biggie. The fact that Kim was the one who went on the radio reporting that Evans and Wallace were having problems—even before the whole Tupac debacle.

"It was just strange to me, like, 'Why is this little girl talking to my man like that?'" Evans said. "*She's* making the announcement that me and Biggie broke up?"

Faith made a subtle but lasting statement when she had the B.I.G. tattoo on her right breast altered to read "B.I.G. FAY." That got his attention. Wallace made one last attempt to patch things up by inviting Evans down to New Orleans for a show that he was doing with Junior M.A.F.I.A.

"You should come with me," he said. She knew by then he was seeing Tiffany Lane as well as Kim, so as far as she was concerned, their relationship was over. But she still loved him. She couldn't help it. And she wanted to see Kim. For real.

"I was determined to get her," Evans said with a laugh. "I knew she was going to be there. I remember being backstage. I was telling all of the guys, 'Don't let her come on this side, 'cause I'ma punch her out.'"

"I don't like to fight," she said, in retrospect. "I ain't no troublemaker. But when somebody does something to me and it makes me feel like I gotta get them, God, I won't rest."

Back at the hotel, Wallace worked his charm. After all, they were still married.

"That's the awkward thing about love," Evans said. "When it ain't right, you just can't walk away. You can't just leave it alone. You just gotta be like, oh, come back for one more time."

She got her revenge on Kim a few weeks later. In March, Faith found out she was pregnant. By the time Wallace found out that he had another child on the way, there were other issues that had to be dealt with.

As the year came to a close, East-West tensions were at an all-time high, and it wasn't just Wallace and Shakur's problem anymore. On December 16, 1995, after Wallace mentioned playfully on the radio how Snoop and the Dogg Pound were in town to film their video for "New York, New York," someone shot up the group's trailer on location in Red Hook, Brooklyn.

The video depicted Snoop, Daz, and Kurupt as Godzilla-like creatures, stomping through Manhattan, knocking over monuments. Snoop kicked over one of the World Trade Center towers. Although the lyrics to the song had nothing to do with dissing New York, people got offended by the video.

Capone and Noreaga responded in kind with "L.A., L.A." The song, which also featured Queensbridge all-stars Mobb Deep and Tragedy, specifically took Daz and Kurupt to task. In the video, the L.A. duo are thrown off the 59th Street Bridge, bound in rope from head to toe. Within a month, Ice Cube, Mack-10, and W.C. would jump into the fray, calling themselves the Westside Connection.

"It's getting to the point where people from the East Coast won't be safe out here," Dr. Dre observed. "And vice versa."

"It was horrible," said Audrey LeCatis, a former employee at Arista, Bad Boy's parent label. "Everybody was on edge. And you couldn't do what you needed to do. You couldn't get shows. You couldn't do your job. The whole industry was sick with that bullshit. And it was bullshit."

Despite all that happened, including the embarrassment of the Faith and Tupac controversy, Wallace never said anything publicly about what was happening. He didn't drop any response records, didn't make a call to radio gossip jock Wendy Williams, or indulge in any of the usual knee-jerk responses that so often result when rappers are embroiled in a public feud.

Instead, Wallace was calm about the whole thing. Methodical even. His few comments were conciliatory, never emotional. "If the muthafucka really did fuck Fay, that's foul how he just blowin' her like that," Wallace told VIBE in one of his few interviews during that time. "If honey was to give you the pussy, why would you disrespect her like that? If you had beef with me and you're like, 'Boom, I'ma fuck his wife.' Would you be so harsh on her? Like you got beef with *her*? That shit doesn't make sense. That's why I don't believe it."

Whatever he may or may not have believed, Wallace, Evans, Combs, and the rest of the Bad Boy Family flew to Los Angeles for the Soul Train Music Awards in March 1996. Faith was nominated for Best New Artist and Female Artist of the Year. Wallace's "One More Chance (Remix)" was nominated for Song of the

Biggie joined forces with a young Jay-Z for the 1996 classic "Brooklyn's Finest," on which Big answered Pac's anger with humor.

Year (pitting the Brooklyn rap don against pop stars like TLC and Whitney Houston). Bad Boy artists Total and Craig Mack also made appearances.

From the time they landed at LAX, there was static in the air. A *Details* writer working on a profile about Combs described one incident that occurred just days before the awards ceremony. Riding in the back of a rented Mercedes, Combs happened to pull up next to Knight and Shakur, who were waiting at a stoplight. The reporter witnessed Combs's driver pass a gun back to one of the bodyguards. Afterward, Combs emphasized to the writer that this was not an offensive gesture, but more like a "just in case any shit goes down get ready" gesture. While their cars idled at the light, Knight and Combs looked each other in the eye and exchanged nods. Shakur seemed to have missed the whole thing.

"We made eye contact, acknowledged each other, the car left," Combs told the writer immediately afterward. "I don't want you to be saying, 'We were driving by, the gats started coming from everywhere, they started taking aim, but the cops were there, so they can't do what they intended.' It don't be that type of vibe. Everybody around may want it to be—want the two powers against each other, almost like spiders in a jar. But Death Row are doing good, they paving the way for us to do good." Combs took great care to put a positive spin on things: "He ain't my friend, but everything's cool."

Nothing much was cool that night at the Shrine Auditorium, the site of the Soul Train Awards. A stylist didn't have Wallace's size 14EEE shoes. He almost pulled out of his performance out of frustration.

In their dressing room, Combs convinced Wallace to go on with the show. He borrowed shoes from a bodyguard, then took to the stage performing "One More Chance" with Combs and Faith Evans. But that was as close as he and Faith would get all night. Although she was three months pregnant with his son, their brief reconciliation was over. During the ceremony, they sat on opposite ends of the auditorium and left separately.

Death Row was very much in the house. Tupac's *Me Against the World* won the award for Best Rap Album. Biggie's remix of "One More Chance" won R&B/Soul or Rap Song of the Year, beating out Whitney Houston, but Wallace heard boos when, during his acceptance speech, he gave his obligatory shout out to Brooklyn. While Big stood on stage dressed in a white suit, Tupac was running around the aisles wearing camouflage from head to toe. The real drama didn't happen until after the Bad Boy contingent got ready to go back to their hotel.

"After Big won his award, we was leaving," Cease recalls. "Suge, Tupac, and two other niggas rolled up in a Hummer. Pac got stuck in the window trying to hop out and shit. I guess he was trying to surprise a nigga. He got stuck in the window, hat falling off, he's all dressed up in fatigues, looking real crazy. And he's just yelling, *Westside nigga! Da da da da.*"

"That was the first time I really looked in his face," Wallace said later. "I looked into his eyes and was like, Yo, this nigga is really bugging the fuck out."

Big didn't say nothing. Big just looked at him like, What's wrong with you Pac? You tripping.

That's when Knight approached Wallace. "He was like, 'Yo, I wanna talk to him,'" Cease said. "'I just wanna talk to the man.' Nobody wasn't really holding a nigga back. Security wasn't doing nothing. So my boys took the guns off they waist. It was like, Man, you better back up. Back up."

According to Cease, Knight started calling for police. "Suge was trying to send a nigga to jail," Cease said. "He was like, 'He has a strap, officer. He has a strap.'"

"His niggas start formulating and my niggas start formulating," said Wallace. "Muthafucka starts screaming, 'He's got a gun! He got a gun!' But we're in L.A. What the fuck are we supposed to do, shoot out? That's when I knew it was on."

"Big's boys back him up into the limo and told him to get us the fuck out of there," Lil' Cease said. "They had niggas on both sides of the Shrine—all Death Row. They had that shit surrounded. They had they little plan set up. Fuck that. Pac was doin' what he do best. He put on a show."

"It was a whole lot of word play," said producer Stevie J., who was also there. "They guys got guns, our guys got guns. Nobody's crazy. Nobody wants to be the one to get the camera on them when they shooting somebody."

"He was on some tough shit," Wallace told VIBE's Larry "Blackspot" Hester. "I can't knock them dudes for the way they go about their biz. They made everything seem so dramatic. I felt the darkness when he rolled up that night. Duke came out the window fatigued out, screaming, 'Westside! Outlaws!'"

The moment was so cinematic, it reminded Wallace of Shakur's haunting screen debut, when he portrayed Bishop, a rebellious teenager who becomes a homicidal maniac in Ernest Dickerson's 1992 film *Juice*.

"I was like, That's Bishop!" Wallace said. "Whatever he's doing right now, that's the role he's playing. He played that shit to a tee."

And with an audience of industry heads and reporters on hand, the incident set off a frenzy of nervous gossip. The next day's *Hollywood Reporter* said Tupac was the one with the pistol, an assertion Wallace denied. The article also said that someone in Wallace's crew was handcuffed by police, but that no arrests were made.

It was the last time Wallace and Shakur would ever lay eyes on each other. Cease said neither of them even tried to sit down with the other and talk.

Shakur moved the war to wax, presenting his case through rhyme. Plugging into the power of rap, which Public Enemy's Chuck D famously likened to a black CNN, Shakur took the beef straight to Wallace with a track that rocked both coasts. "Hit 'Em Up" was perhaps the most scathing battle rhyme ever committed to tape. Set to the melody of JM's "Players Anthem" (the song Big and company were working on the night Pac was robbed at Quad Studios), the lyrics made Ice Cube's virulent "No Vaseline" sound like a ballad.

Seething with anger, Shakur's voice could only be described as manic as he openly declared war on Wallace, Combs, and all their friends and affiliations. Tupac had something for everybody—Junior M.A.F.I.A., Combs, the entire Bad Boy Records staff, Wallace of course, and Faith, too. "You claim to be a player but I fucked your wife," Shakur boasted. He even dissed Mobb Deep, one of New York's most highly regarded rap duos, presumably because they said "thug life we still living it" on their record "Survival of the Fittest." The man who declared thug life (a "movement" that he started) to be dead did not appreciate anybody else reviving it. "Don't one of you niggas got sickle cell or something?" Shakur taunted. (In fact, Mobb Deep's Prodigy was born with the blood disorder.) "You gonna fuck around and have a seizure or a heart attack. You better back the fuck up before you get smacked the fuck up."

The first time Wallace heard the song, which was leaked to mix-tape DJs in the summer of '96—and would later be accompanied by a music video—his eyes glazed over in disbelief. A powerful battle rhymer in his own right, Wallace could have come back with a classic response. But he chose to hold his tongue.

"The whole reason I was being cool from day one was because of that nigga Puff," he later explained. "'Cause Puff don't get down like that." As BDP had observed on their song "Stop the Violence" back in 1988: "real bad boys move in silence." And so it was with Combs.

Not that Junior M.A.F.I.A. didn't consider a response. "We heard that shit," Cease said. "I was mad. I was like, Damn he put *my* name in this one." But he was even more stunned by his friend's reaction. "Big was just sitting there laughing. Shit was like a joke to him. 'Hush,' he said. '*Silence is golden.* I'm not trying to start no battle. I'm trying to get a check. Let people buy the album when it come out and find out what I have to say.'"

"We was about to go write about them niggas," said JM's Larceny, who considered himself a 2Pac fan before "Hit 'Em Up" dropped. "But Big was like, 'Leave that shit alone. You gotta learn how to be the bigger person in a situation.'"

But Shakur just continued as many public insults against Wallace as possible, hoping to get some sort of response.

"Biggie is a Brooklyn nigga's dream of being a West Coast nigga," said Shakur in yet another incendiary interview. "None of my lyrics do you hear about me putting a gun to a pregnant woman's belly." (He was referring to a line on "Gimme the Loot" that Puff deleted before the album's release.) "You can't be a player killing babies, nigga. Robbing pregnant women ain't no player shit."

Shakur assumed that Biggie's song "Who Shot Ya"—and LL Cool J's response, "I Shot Ya"—were meant as a comment on the Quad Studios robbery. In fact, Wallace's song was recorded long before Shakur was robbed, and its lyrics reportedly addressed a minor disagreement between Wallace and LL Cool J, who was in the studio the night "Who Shot Ya" was recorded. Not that it mattered anymore. Shakur was stuck in warrior mode. Even though he would eventually acknowledge—on the song "Against All Odds," released posthumously under the pseudonym Makavelli—that he believed others were responsible for setting him up, he kept coming after Wallace, spurning all calls for public reconciliation.

"That's corny," Shakur said when VIBE's Kevin Powell proposed a meeting. "That's just for everybody else to be calm. For everybody else to understand what's going on. They just want to hear what the conversation is about."

Yet Shakur seemed more than willing to air his side of the grievances in public: "How can I be peaceful and leave my door open and be calm and be relaxed when I know the niggas that broke in my house are right across the street? I'll forgive, but never forget. I would rather been shot straight up in cold blood. To be set up? By people who you trusted? That's bad. They know in their hearts—that's why they're in hell now. They can't sleep. They can't go nowhere. They can't look at themselves, 'cause they know the prodigal son has returned."

Predictably, Tupac's fans were beginning to take up the cause. Luther Campbell recalled a concert in St. Louis that included himself, Biggie, and Busta Rhymes. As the top-billed artist, Biggie was supposed to close the show, but because of the controversy, the promoters changed their minds. "They asked *me* to close the show at the last minute," Campbell said. "I was like, what the fuck? He's the fuckin' hot cat." But when Campbell watched Biggie's performance, he understood why the promoters had changed their plan. "I ain't never seen no shit like that in my life," he said. "You had one side of the crowd for Biggie and one side for Tupac. The Tupac fans were singing that Tupac song, the dis song, and then you had Biggie fans screaming *'Biggie, Biggie.'* I was like, yo, this shit is *fucked* up. It was a sold-out crowd and them people was out there saying 'TU-PAC!'"

Through it all, Campbell marveled at the fact that Biggie never retaliated against Pac's recorded attacks. "If I'da went onstage, and public opinion woulda been screaming obscenities about me? I'da went in that motherfucker and I'da made some kinda record," Luke said. "They coulda checked me into the nearest studio right next to the fucking arena. It woulda came out right then, Jack. I know he was hurt by that, 'cause he jetted right afterward. We ain't even talk, but I saw the look on his face." After a while, Wallace didn't care what people thought.

"Guys were like, 'Go at him, man. Don't let him disrespect you like that. You're

B.I.G. now. Fuck that,'" DJ Enuff remembered. "But he couldn't do it. It shows how much love he really did have for Pac." Not that Wallace was immune to the peer pressure. "I remember one time in Atlanta," said Enuff, "he's talking to the crowd about the whole situation that's going on between him and Pac. He wouldn't even say Pac's name. 'We were friends and he thought I took his style' and this and that, and he started breaking the whole thing down and he said he felt it was all because of this record . . ."

Enuff didn't even have to be told. He grabbed two copies of "Big Poppa" and flipped them over. When he scratched in the opening piano line of "Who Shot Ya," the place went crazy. "That night he gave me a hug," Enuff recalled. "There were a lot of good shows, but there's only a few selective shows that were magical." And as if by magic, the silence was broken. "He felt he couldn't change society's mind," Enuff said. "Like, 'You guys think ["Who Shot Ya"] is about Pac? Fuck it, I'm gonna just start saying it like it is about him.'"

Whenever the subject of his old friend came up, Wallace shook his head. "There's shit that muthafuckas don't know," Wallace said. "I saw the situations and how shit was going, and I tried to school the nigga. I was there when he bought his first Rolex, but I wasn't in a position to be rolling like that. I think that Tupac felt more comfortable with the dudes that he was hanging with because they had just as much money as him." He always seemed to come up with a reason to believe that Shakur might become a friend again.

"He can't front on me," Wallace said. "As much as he may come off as some Biggie hater, he knows. He knows when all that shit was going down, a nigga was schooling him to certain things. Me and Stretch—God bless the grave. But he chose to do the things he wanted to do. There was nothing I could do, but it wasn't like he wasn't my man."

Combs's response in the pages of VIBE was more aggressive.

"I never knew of my life being in danger," he said calmly. "I'm not saying that I'm ignorant to the rumors, but if you got a problem and somebody wants to get your ass, they don't talk about it. What it's been right now is a lot of movie-making and a lot of entertainment drama. Bad boys move in silence. If somebody wants to get your ass, you're going to wake up in heaven. There ain't gonna be no record made about it. It ain't gonna be no interviews. It's gonna be straight up, 'Oh shit, where am I? What are these wings on my back? Your name is Jesus Christ?' When you're involved in some real shit, it's going to be some real shit."

Just because Wallace didn't directly respond to "Hit 'Em Up" didn't mean that he was above addressing his personal issues in song. Once word got out that Faith was pregnant, people began wondering out loud whether it might be Shakur's baby. In 1996 Biggie hooked up with a rising Brooklyn rapper named

Jay-Z and recorded a duet on the rapper's debut album, *Reasonable Doubt*. The song was "Brooklyn's Finest," and it sought to neutralize all the speculation with a single line: "If Faith has twins, she'll probably have two Pacs. Get it? Tu . . . Pac's." Instead of lashing out in anger, Wallace chose to defuse his pain with humor. Those who caught the joke understood that Wallace knew he was the father of Faith's baby. How else could he be so comfortable acknowledging the absurdity of the whole situation?

Faith wasn't exactly amused when she heard the song. "I was like, You know where you were that night," she said. "Why don't you count back? How are you gonna explain to your son, who looks just like you, that you made a record that's gonna be around forever saying I was having someone else's baby?"

But humor was Wallace's way of dealing with hardship since he was in elementary school. His wit had brought him this far and he knew it would never desert him. "I got to make jokes about the shit," Wallace said. "I can't be the nigga running around all serious. The shit is so funny to me because no one will ever know the truth. They'll always believe what they want to believe. Pac says he fucked her. I asked Faith, 'You fucked him?' She said no. So am I gonna hate her for the rest of her life thinking she did something, or am I gonna be a man about the situation? I can't hate nobody. That's not my nature."

Tupac Shakur had homeboys who were both Crips and Bloods, never claiming either set, but after a while it seemed as if he was beginning to choose sides. The tracks from his forthcoming *Makaveli* record made even *2Pac* seem tame. There were songs like "Hail Mary," where he rapped, "Revenge is the sweetest thing, next to gettin' pussy." There was "Toss It Up," where he said, "arrivederci" to "Dre," who was "fruity as Alizé." One of the best songs on the album was also the most troubling, "Me and My Girlfriend." The girl in question was his "nina," street parlance for a 9mm. He rapped about the gun with romantic abandon, calling it "the only girl I adore" and "the reason that I stand tall."

Another subtle but telling stance were the shout-outs he gave on the single "To Live and Die in L.A." Among the locations featured in the video is Compton's Leuders Park—Leuders the home base of the Park Piru Bloods, near Knight's old neighborhood. The song's lyrics referred to "M.O.B." and to "Neckbone, Heron, and Buntry," some of Knight's closest Piru enforcers.

Rappers have had a long history of shouting out the names of real street cats in their songs. But in a place like Los Angeles, where gang territorial conflicts are every bit as complicated as those in the Middle East, shouting out members of an entire set would be like performing a song in a Tel Aviv nightclub and shouting out members of the P.L.O. and Hamas. You'd better have balls of steel, or the rock-solid street connections to hold you down.

Quiet as it was kept, not everyone in Los Angeles was scared of Death Row, particularly the Southside Crips. Southside occupied many of the Crip territories neighboring Compton Blood neighborhoods like Leuders Park and Fruittown, and they were becoming bolder about the fact that they didn't appreciate Suge Knight and his homies throwing their money and wealth in their faces all the time. Word was out that it could become quite lucrative to the man bold enough to embarrass Death Row in a way that everyone could see.

Travon "Tray" Lane was out at the Lakewood Mall with his fellow Piru homeboys Kevin "K.W." Woods and Maurice "Lil' Mo" Combs. Tray wore an expensive, diamond-encrusted Death Row Records pendant around his neck worth thousands of dollars—and it meant the world to him. It meant that he was one of the chosen ones. The pendant let everyone know he wasn't some "slob nigga," that he ran with the crew and the man that had Los Angeles on lock.

Lane certainly wasn't expecting to get rat-packed by a bunch of Southside guys when they walked out of the Foot Locker. The fight didn't last very long, but by the time it was over, Lane was missing his pendant. Somebody was gonna pay for that shit. Indeed. Somebody had a problem.

Fifty percent of business partnerships, like marriages, end badly. It's just the way things happen in the entertainment business. The creative guy wants to go in one direction; the money guy wants to go in the other. It's happened to all of the truly great record companies founded by two different people.

Jerry Wexler decided to leave Atlantic, the label he co-founded with Ahmet Ertegun, because he wanted to produce R&B and Ertegun wanted to pursue '70s arena rock. Their parting was bittersweet but respectful. Wexler got a nice settlement, credit, and royalties on all the records he produced.

When Rick Rubin decided to leave Def Jam, the label he founded in his NYU dorm room, he and Russell Simmons had a heart-to-heart in a Greenwich Village diner and settled the majority of their issues with a handshake.

But when Dr. Dre decided to leave Death Row in March of 1996, he left with only the clothes on his back, and his name as an artist. That's it. The masters and publishing rights to all his hits with Snoop, even his own songs, were all left behind. This split was more akin to Tina Turner's divorce from Ike Turner than it was the proper dissolution of a friendship and partnership.

It took some time in jail for Dr. Dre to realize that Death Row Records was run much the same way. "I got wrapped up in all that old Hollywood bullshit," Dr. Dre told Ronin Ro in a VIBE cover story. "You know what I'm saying: the clothes, the jewelry, the fly cars with the big sound systems pulling up in front of the clubs. But incarceration brought me down to earth and actually turned Dr. Dre back into Andre Young."

Things had been going sour for a while. With all the guns and the hangers-on in the studio, the atmosphere at Can-Am was more akin to a prison than to a creative environment where free experimentation could take place. The straw that broke the camel's back was the night Dre witnessed a studio engineer catch a beat down for rewinding a tape too far. After that, it was hard for him to stomach the work.

Death Row wasn't really his label anymore—if it ever was. In an early interview, Dre described his relationship with Knight in terms of a family: "Me and Suge, we like brothers and shit," he said. But as time passed, Dre realized he had no control over who was signed to the label anymore.

"It got to the point in the studio where brothers were sticking their hands out like, 'Yo, what's up? We just signed with the label,'" Dre recalled. "And I was like 'I don't even know you.'"

"You Can't See Me" and "California Love"—songs recorded for the *Helter Skelter* project with Ice Cube and for Dre's own follow-up to *The Chronic*—had the original vocals erased so Tupac could rap over them. Suge wanted Dre to do all the production on Hammer's comeback album—which was like asking Francis Ford Coppola to cast Jean-Claude Van Damme instead of Al Pacino to play Michael Corleone in a sequel to *The Godfather*.

Dre had seen his oldest friend, Eazy-E, die of AIDS, and yet, because of their business disagreements, he never got a chance to say a proper good-bye. As Danny Glover put it in *Lethal Weapon,* Dre was "getting too old for this shit." He had done his share of partying, bedded his share of girls, smoked his share of chronic, and was coming to realize what all mature adults realize after a while—there's more to life than partying.

As Dre faded himself out, Pac was moving up. "Suge is the boss of Death Row," Shakur said, "and I'm the capo. That's my job to do what's best for all of Death Row." Shakur criticized Dre for not being present at Snoop's trial. "He was owning the company and he chillin' in his house; I'm out here in the streets, whoopin' niggas' asses, startin' wars and shit, droppin' albums, doin' my shit, and this nigga takin' three years to do one song! I couldn't have that. But it was not my decision. Suge was coming to me. Death Row can never be weak, no matter what."

Knight eventually came by Dr. Dre's house to pick up the master tapes of his Death Row recordings. Suge claimed he came alone and Dre called the cops. Dre claimed that Suge rolled deep, with "eight or nine muthafuckas," and that he gave Knight everything he wanted after making copies for himself.

But quiet as it was kept, Dre was not the only one growing weary of life on Death Row. For the six months he spent there, Shakur seemed to be the label's staunchest supporter. "I'm a soldier," he said. "I don't give a fuck if I don't get along with anybody else on the label. This is for Death Row. When it comes to the point where I feel it can stand on its own, I will move on. But me and Suge will always do business together, forever."

In the opinion of one Harvard Law School professor, Tupac would have made a "damn fine lawyer." He'd clearly mastered the barrister's art of double-speak. On the surface, he had clearly stated his lifelong allegiance to Suge Knight and Death Row. But check the fine print: "When it comes to the point where I feel it can stand on its own," Shakur said, *"I will move on."*

According to court documents and sources close to Shakur, he was preparing to escape from Death Row. As a $300 million company, the label should have been able to stand on its own, with or without him. In the original contract Shakur signed in jail, all of his master recordings would belong to Death Row. Since he could finish at least one complete song every day, there were between 40 and 60 unreleased tracks just lying around. Even if he never recorded another song, Death Row would still have five albums' worth of material ready to go.

Tupac was playing a lawyer's game, hustling both sides against the middle. Even as he was loudly claiming lifelong allegiance to Knight, he was quietly pulling away on the sneak tip. He would have to step away gingerly, allowing Knight to save face, but on the other hand, to separate his business interests from Knight's.

The problem came when he opened a production company called Euphanasia. While Combs might not have been thrilled about Biggie's side projects—the cameos, the Untertainment venture, the Junior M.A.F.I.A. and Lil' Kim albums—he never tried to shut it down. But Shakur had to struggle to branch out under Suge's iron-fisted rule.

"We weren't getting copies of the financial accountings," said Shakur's family friend Yasmyn Fula. "We'd ask for them, and they'd send a present—like a car."

That's why Shakur wouldn't let his cousin Katari's group the Outlaws sign with the label—even though they appeared on "Hit 'Em Up" with him. "He didn't want them to live in bondage," said his mother, Afeni Shakur.

Shakur was represented by David Kenner on the West Coast and by Charles Ogletree for non-entertainment issues. When Ogletree attempted to settle some of the various lawsuits Shakur was facing, he'd reach a figure with the disgruntled parties, and then ask Kenner for money to close the deal. It never came.

"It was as if he had no life except that given to him by Death Row," Ogletree said. When the accounting finally did come in from Death Row, he learned that he owed the label $4.9 million. Although his quadruple-platinum album had earned the company $60 million, it was of no consequence. Everything from his cars to his bail to his jewelry had been billed back to him as recoupable assets. But when Shakur fired his lawyer David Kenner, even the most hardened gangsters on the Row were shocked. "Tupac was brilliant, but he wasn't smart," one insider told *The New Yorker*. "He didn't realize, or refused to accept, what any-one from the street would have known—that you can't fire David Kenner, that you can't leave Death Row."

After a tense appearance at the 1996 MTV Music Awards (during which host Chris Rock greeted Suge Knight in the crowd, then added, "Don't kill me"), Shakur decided he was ready to come home. On the morning of September 7, he told his girlfriend Kidada Jones that he was going to the Tyson fight in Las Vegas that night with Suge. He appeared listless and said that he didn't want to go, but he couldn't break his word. There was talk of him flying out to see his mother in Atlanta, but instead, they packed and drove to the Luxor Hotel.

"It looks so evil," Kidada said, looking at the black pyramid with the white cap. The security detail, normally so heavy, was in disarray. No one had proper weapons permits, so no one could carry guns. Normally there would be two body-guards assigned to Shakur—but on that night there was just one: Frank Alexander, and his attention was divided.

Shakur and Knight were late to the fight, as was customary, but their home-boy Tyson was still in his prime—it wasn't worth sitting down for anyway. In less than two minutes, Tyson disposed of Bruce Seldon. Shakur was ecstatic. "Did you see Tyson do it to him?" he told a camera crew. "Fifty punches! I counted. Fifty punches! I knew he was gonna take him out. We bad like that. Come out of prison and now we running shit."

Shakur made his way through the lobby of the MGM Grand, high on post-fight adrenaline, when he was stopped by a member of the Death Row entourage, the Mob Piru Blood Travon "Tray" Lane. Tray saw a face that he didn't like—it was Orlando "Baby Lane" Anderson, a Southside Crip who, Tray said, had jumped him with eight or nine other Southside guys at the Lakewood Mall and stolen his diamond-encrusted Death Row pendant.

Shakur walked up to Anderson, and asked him a question.

"You from the South?"

Suddenly, Shakur and the Death Row crew were on top of Anderson, punch-ing and kicking. The fight was quickly broken up, Shakur and Knight left the Grand, as did Anderson, who declined to file a complaint against them.

Shakur went back to the hotel, pumped up from the second fight of the night. He was ready to go to Knight's club 662 (the name spells M.O.B. on a phone key-pad) for the after-party benefit. He refused to wear his bulletproof vest, saying it was too hot. Instead of taking his Humvee, he decided to ride with Suge Knight in his black BMW 750.

The caravan rode first to Knight's house just off the Las Vegas Strip, then back onto the Strip toward the Flamingo Hotel. Normally there would be a car behind them filled with armed guards—but tonight it was the Outlaws and a bodyguard, none of them armed. As they were waiting at a traffic light, a white Cadillac pulled up to the right of Knight's BMW. The driver's left hand came out, holding a .40-caliber semiautomatic pistol. Fourteen shots were fired into the passenger side door and then the Cadillac slipped off into the night.

Tupac was hit four times as he attempted to climb into the back seat.

When the police arrived Knight—with his hands the air—tried to explain that he and Shakur were the victims. Shakur was rushed to University Medical Center's intensive care unit. He lost a lot of blood, and then, two days later, his right lung. Four days later, doctors induced paralysis, so that Shakur wouldn't hurt himself by tossing and turning.

His eyes opened briefly when Kidada Jones played Don McLean's "Vincent" on the stereo next to his bed. The song was a favorite of Tupac's, one from his lean days with his mother and sister in Baltimore when it was the only record they owned. At the time another of his prized possessions was a book of paintings by Vincent van Gogh, given to him by a neighbor.

"Do you know I love you?" Kidada asked. Shakur responded to questions by moving his feet and squeezing her hand. "Do you know we all love you?"

Shakur slipped into a coma.

"I feel close to Vincent van Gogh," Shakur once told Kevin Powell on Rikers Island. "Nobody appreciated his work until he was dead. Now it's worth millions.

Shakur and Knight's last ride together down the Las Vegas strip, September 7, 1996.

I feel close to him, how tormented he was. Marvin [Gaye], too. That's how I was out there. I'm in jail now, but I'm free. My mind is free. The only times I have problems is when I sleep."

Tupac Amaru Shakur drifted into permanent sleep on Friday, September 13, 1996, just after 4 P.M. He was 25 years old.

Faith Evans's phone rang the Friday night that Shakur died. It was Wallace and he was crying. "He was in shock," Evans said, "and I believe it's fair to say he was probably afraid."

"I know so many niggas like him," Wallace said. "So many rough, tough muthafuckas. When I heard he got shot, I was like, 'He'll be out in the morning, smoking some weed, drinking Hennessy or whatever.' You ain't thinking he going to die." But after six days of fighting for his life, Shakur surrendered. "When he died, that shit fucked me up."

"When you're around muthafuckas," Biggie continued, "you just keep thinking a nigga making so much money, their lifestyle should be more protected. You know what I'm saying? Their lives should be more protected where things like a drive-by shooting ain't supposed to happen. You know what I'm saying? I was thinking that that shouldn't have happened, man. He's supposed to have lots of security. He ain't even supposed to be sitting by no window."

Wallace had little time to mourn his friend. He was having problems of his own. Because of the records that Shakur had made, Wallace and other New York rappers like Mobb Deep and Capone and Noreaga suddenly found themselves on the suspect list. Every time MTV News mentioned Tupac's death, they flashed pictures of Wallace and of Randy "Stretch" Walker, amid sound bites about the East Coast–West Coast rap war.

Wallace felt horrible about Shakur's death—and he was upset about how his name had gotten tangled up in the mix. The Saturday after Shakur died, his old friend dream hampton asked Wallace if he was going to the funeral.

"Naw, man," he told her. "This nigga—he made my life miserable. Ever since he came home. He told lies, fucked with my marriage, turned fans against me. For what?" Even if he wanted to attend, he knew that his presence would be a distraction for the family. Wallace would do his grieving in private.

Wallace often wondered how things had gotten so serious. But when asked about it, he said it never occurred to him to pick up the phone and put an end to all the beef.

"He ain't no phone nigga and I ain't no phone nigga," Wallace said. Lil' Cease was even more candid about it.

"I don't think it was too much pride. I think it was too serious," Lil Cease said.

"Everybody was scared of Suge. And then we was just more like, not even sweating it. They tripping on some tantrum shit. We didn't wanna indulge it and make it worse than what it is. They was trying to destroy Big's career. Like they was really investing a lot of time into trying to destroy my man's shit."

Tupac Shakur loved the spotlight. And Suge Knight should have done any and everything to stay out of it.

But it was too late. All Eyez were now on Knight. And it wasn't a good thing.

In the week that followed Tupac's fatal shooting, a gang war broke out in Compton. According to a Compton police affidavit based on the information of confidential reliable informants close to both sides, members of the Death Row Records Piru faction who were in Shakur's motorcade said that Tupac's shooter was the same guy whom they beat down at the MGM Grand: Keefee D's nephew, Orlando "Baby Lane" Anderson. "It's on when we get back to Compton," one of them said. And it was.

From the 9th to the 13th, bullets flew across Compton. Some shooters were members of the Southside Crips and others were Leuders Park, Fruittown, and Elm Lane Pirus. Lines divided right along red and blue. Neighborhood Crips, Kelly Park Crips, and Atlantic Drive Crips backed Southside. The Mob, Leuders Park, Fruittown, and Elm Lane Pirus backed Death Row. In the end, Southside Crip Bobby Ray Finch, Fruittown Piru Marcus Childs, and Elm Lane Piru Timothy Flanagan were slain in the attacks.

Houses were raided, heads busted, and Orlando Anderson ended up in custody. He was also a suspect in an April 12, 1996, gang-related murder, but was released for lack of evidence.

The authorities, however, had all the evidence they needed to put Suge Knight behind bars.

When Shakur died, suddenly it was open season on Knight. The first thing that happened was the media, being so hungry to find out what happened to Shakur, got a copy of the surveillance tape showing Knight and Shakur stomping Anderson.

The kick, which constituted assault, was a violation of the parole plea bargain that Knight agreed to when he pleaded no contest to two counts of assault against George and Lynwood Stanley at S.O.L.A.R. Records and received a suspended prison sentence of nine years and five years house probation, thirty days in a halfway house, and five months of house arrest. One of the conditions of that plea was that he not get into any more fights or associate with known gang members.

Ooops.

The kick, essentially, closed the door on an era of Death Row because of everything else it revealed.

In January 1996, Suge signed a young singer to Death Row and rented his Malibu Colony beach house from her father. There was no law against that, and that kind of favoritism is a part of how Hollywood works.

Not the Hollywood legal system, however.

Gina Longo, the young woman he signed, was the daughter of D. A. Lawrence Longo—the same Longo who negotiated with David Kenner for Knight's plea bargain.

It got worse.

The reason Knight assaulted George and Lynwood Stanley in the first place at S.O.L.A.R. back in 1992 while *The Chronic* was being recorded was allegedly because they insisted on using a pay phone that Suge demanded always be free. The person calling him on that phone was calling from prison and could never predict exactly when he was going to call.

That person was former bounty hunter and Blood drug kingpin Michael "Harry-O" Harris, one of David Kenner's big-time drug-dealing clients, who now claimed that he was a silent partner in Death Row Records. Harris said he was the one who put up the $1.5 million to finish *The Chronic* before Knight and Dr. Dre shopped it to Interscope. Other than a shout-out in the liner notes, Harris claimed that he received nothing that was due to him. He said he was soon abandoned by Kenner, who moved on to work directly with Knight.

Harris had the documents to back up his claims. There was a May 1 business license filing with the Los Angeles County Clerk's office for GF Entertainment (short for God Father). There was a filing in Sacramento that same year listing GF's directors as David Kenner and Lydia Harris—Harry-O's wife.

Harris broke his silence on January 19, 1996. He was taken seriously enough that Interscope attempted to negotiate a settlement before Harris filed suit in Superior Court.

After Shakur's death, the rap photographer Ernie Paniciolli had a heart-to-heart conversation with Wallace. Paniciolli had been photographing hip hop culture since its inception, and Wallace, who used to see Ernie's work in magazines like *Word Up!* and *Fresh* when he was just a fan, respected him. The two men were at the same video shoot on a chilly September night and Paniciolli hopped in Biggie's Pathfinder SUV to keep warm.

"What's up?" said Ernie, slamming the door.

"You ain't come here to talk to me," Wallace said, smiling. "You just came to get in out of the cold."

"Yeah, whatever."

They sat in silence for a minute. Wallace was listening to a Tupac album on his CD player.

"Yo, man, what's the deal with all this?" Paniciolli asked. He didn't have to spell it out for Wallace. He was curious about all the talk of an East versus West rivalry. As an elder who had seen hip hop grow from the days of park jams to a multi-million-dollar business, it never made sense to him. "I'm not a writer or a reporter. I'm a photographer, man. I tell my story with pictures," Paniciolli said. "Talk to me."

Wallace paused, listening to the song for a minute.

"Let me tell you something," Wallace said in a low voice. "In five years me and Duke would have been doing things together. We would have been recording together and we would be taking all the money 'cause individually nobody can touch us, and together you *know* nobody can touch us."

He shook his head, thinking of all the good times they had shared together, and imagining all the lost opportunities. First Stretch got killed, and now Tupac. And to think they had all given up the street life to get into the music industry because it was supposed to be safer.

Faith Evans's phone rang again. "Kim's here," said the voice on the other line, "at the studio." It didn't matter that she was seven months pregnant. Evans had a bone to pick—and the little boy growing inside her would have to understand.

"Naturally I caught a cab to the studio," Evans said. She brought her cousin along with her.

"Here's what we're gonna do," Evans told her when they got to Daddy's House, the midtown Manhattan recording studio that had been built to Puff's exact specifications. "I want you to look in every room."

She waited for a few minutes, and her cousin came back.

"I ain't see her," her cousin reported. "Stevie J is in there and Puffy, and some light-skinned girl."

Evans walked up to the room in question. Sure enough, the "light-skinned" girl sitting at the table writing rhymes was Kim. Puffy and Stevie J were busy at the mixing board. Evans looked at her for a long time. This was her chance for a heart-to-heart conversation. They could talk about Christopher sister-to-sister. But instead she decided to kick her ass.

"I ran in there so fast and I just jumped on her," Evans said. "I might have gotten in two good hits. It was over like that, because by the time Puffy and Stevie saw me they turned around and got me off of her.

"I was so happy to be on her like that," Evans says with a cackle of delight. "I would never, ever do that again. But I was so mad. She must really be out of her mind to think that she could just be going around talking on the radio about me and my husband. Oh *no*. I was mad, mad, mad. And I felt like that was really all I could do."

Wallace didn't have to worry about Faith beating Tiffany down next. The New Jersey Turnpike would take care of that.

Biggie hadn't had a good week. Tupac was dead, and everyone thought he had something to do with it. The Nathaniel Banks assault case in Camden, New Jersey, was nearly resolved, but then, like a dummy, Wallace caught some more cases: On March 23, 1996, soon after coming back from L.A., Wallace and D-Roc were arrested outside the Palladium at 4:30 in the morning. They were coming out of a Faith concert when two fans started talking shit. When they jumped into a cab, Wallace and D-Roc followed them for two blocks. At the corner of Union Square and 16th Street, they smashed out all the cab's windows with a baseball bat. Police arrested them and charged them with assault.

"When Pac died, that shit bugged me out," said Wallace. Not a single news report about Shakur's murder failed to mention their feud.

Days later Wallace and Cease were busted again, this time for smoking weed on the street outside of Fulton Mall in Brooklyn.

Then, in July, police officers came to Wallace's crib in Teaneck after Mase dropped by and illegally parked his car in a fire zone outside Wallace's home. The cops came to the door, smelled weed burning inside, and returned with a search warrant. Inside the house they found a big bag of marijuana and four semiautomatic weapons with infrared sights, enlarged bullet clips, and filed-off serial numbers. Lil' Cease was arrested along with Wallace, and other members of Junior M.A.F.I.A. went in with him on charges of disorderly conduct.

On September 17, Wallace, Cease, and Tiffany went to the Lexus service department to pick up their car. It wasn't ready, so the dealership loaned them a Dodge Astrovan that they could drive home.

Cease was rolling too fast and the brakes weren't right. It was raining, and the road was slippery.

"I had just paid the toll, and we were on the turnpike going north," Cease said. "So I'm hitting this turn, and the shit just starts sliding on the water. We went over the curb on the over side. I'm lucky no car was coming the other way. My face was fucked up on the steering wheel. B.I.G. couldn't get out . . ." Tiffany flew up and hit the windshield. She woke up feeling something wet on her head and hearing Wallace's voice.

"Wake up, Ma!" he said. "Wake up!"

"I'm thinking it was rain," Tiffany recalled. "It was actually blood."

Her ankle was fractured. She would need a neck brace and numerous stitches for the gash on her forehead. Lil' Cease lost his top row of teeth on the steering wheel. Wallace, meanwhile, couldn't move. He was trapped between the seat and the dashboard, and had to be cut out of the van. As the saw blade sliced through the metal-and-fiberglass van, Biggie lay in the rain unable to move. It would be a while before he could move around again.

No, it had not been a good week. But the worst was yet to come.

ONE MORE CHANCE
(THE REMIX)

CHAPTER 7

66 I'm the rapper with clout everybody yap about
Check it out—guns I bust 'em
Problems with my wife don't discuss 'em . . . 99

There he was, flat on his back in his room at the Kessler Institute for Rehabilitation, with the answer to all of his problems ringing in his ears.

Slow down, B.I.G.!

Slow down. That's what he should have told Lil' Cease as they drove home through the rain. Slow down. What he should have told himself before he and D-Roc ran after that cab and smashed out the back windows on account of those dudes talking trash. Slow down. What he should have thought before he, Cease, and Money L got popped for smoking blunts at the Fulton Mall—stupid. Smoking in public when he already had fresh possession and gun charges from that embarrassing arrest in Teaneck.

And now here he was in West Orange, New Jersey, in the same room Christopher Reeve had occupied after he was paralyzed in a horseback riding accident. Damn. If something like that could happen to Superman, what about the Black Frank White, Mayor of Bed-Stuy, and King of New York? Was Reeve thinking about the same sort of thing when he was there trapped in this room, unable to move without assistance?

If Wallace turned his head to one side, he could look at the wheelchair, waiting there for him. He could look down at his shattered femur—the thick bone running through his thigh—and think about all the work that lay ahead of him. Those damn parallel bars! Because of his weight, he'd be lucky to get out of the wheelchair on his own. He'd probably have to use a cane for the rest of his life. But at least he was alive.

Slow down.

It wasn't as though he had much of a choice. He couldn't do much with a shattered leg. No parties. No studio sessions. No shows. No planes to catch. Nothing. But all that seemed less important now.

He was supposed to be working on his next album. He could still work on lyrics. "I'll make your mouthpiece obese like Della Reese. / When I release, you'll lose teeth like Lil' Cease. / I used to be strong as Ripple be, until Lil' Cease crippled me."

It didn't matter what he went through in his life, he could always find something funny to say about it. That was the way he dealt with uncomfortable situations—he made fun of himself. "Black and ugly as ever . . . The chicken gristle eatin' Slim-Fast blending fat greasy mother fucker." Being a rap star made it easier to laugh at self-deprecating jokes.

He didn't even need to read the papers or listen to Wendy Williams to know what people were saying about the accident. *Big felt so guilty and sad about Tupac's death, the nigga flipped out, got pissy drunk, and rolled his car.* Anyone who knew him knew that he didn't know how to drive, but that didn't matter. People always ran with the speculation first. He could always break his silence and try to explain his side of the story, but then again why should he? Anyway, he didn't want anyone seeing him like this. It was too embarrassing.

He used to make records bragging about rolling around in a Lexus. Now he had a new phat ride: the wheelchair by the side of his bed. It wasn't just a question of his leg healing before he could walk again unassisted—he'd have to go through weeks of rehabilitation to earn that right again. He couldn't even sleep on his stomach or his side because of the pain. The only thing he could do was lie there on his back. He hadn't been this limited in his movements since his mother wouldn't let him walk past the stoop at 226 St. James.

Wallace reflected on a conversation that he'd had a few days ago with his therapist, the guy they sent in to help patients deal with the latent mental and emotional effects that result from having a crippling accident. An older white man, soft-spoken, who on the surface had absolutely nothing in common with a young black thug from Brooklyn. And yet this man sat and talked with him, not at all intimidated by him or who he was supposed to be.

"You're probably the only person in here who doesn't have too much to say," the man said to him.

Wallace nodded, grunted, and kept listening.

"When you're on your feet," the man continued, "you're always looking straight ahead. But when you're crippled, and you're on your back, you're looking at the sky. You're looking at God. Why don't you talk to him?"

Wallace laughed. This guy was buggin'. Biggie, the "Hail Mary full of grace, smack the bitch in the face" nigga talking to God? He wouldn't know where to begin.

But as he lay there, alone in the dark, completely sober for the first time since he stopped being Christopher Wallace and became the Biggie Smalls, he stopped laughing. And before long, he did find himself talking to God. What surprised him even more was how quickly God responded.

So he started talking to Him. About where he was. And where he was going.

"God was like, you moving too fast, BAM! Slow down. Lay in this bed for two months and think about what you're going to do," Wallace said to himself. "Think, Big. Focus your mind."

It was the first time in nearly three years that he'd had the chance to think about anything. He was a creature of impulse—and his life was driven by passionate bursts of activity. As soon as he got money he spent it. Sometimes on himself, but mostly on his family and friends, just as he did when he was in the game. Back then he never thought about the future. Like when he met Faith and married her without really thinking about it. The women who threw themselves at him at the studio, backstage, the hotel lobby, whatever. Most of them got a chance. But now he had what those girls in the video used to beg for, "one more chance."

Faith Evans with Christopher Jordan "C.J." Wallace, born October 30, 1996.

The party was about to stop. Friends had become enemies, some had even ended up dead. There was much to regret and lots of time to think about it: the weed charges. The gun charges. The assault charges. The lawsuits that could have easily been avoided. Losing Faith, both figuratively and literally. Tupac's accusations, musical threats, and now his murder.

On top of everything else, his fan base was beginning to shift. The same people who once called him the savior of East Coast hip hop were now calling him the cause of its ills. All the Gucci, glam, and gun talk was now beginning to lose its luster. People were saying that a nigga had gone Hollywood. That success had made him soft. His head was swelling.

And in the midst of all this turmoil, another Wallace was about to make his debut. The little boy he always wanted. On October 30, a new Christopher Wallace made his debut: Christopher Jordan Wallace. When Wallace saw his son being born, he made up his mind: From now on, it was all about building a foundation. A future. Time to get his priorities straight and, as his mom would say, get a life. The situation was still tense between him and Faith, but they both agreed that it was important for their child to have two parents, and that they'd work things out for him. They couldn't always agree with each other, but they both agreed that they adored their new son.

Holding another little life in his hands reminded him of something that he hadn't really thought about since T'Yanna was born—here was someone who didn't care about the Notorious B.I.G.—only Christopher Wallace.

He would sit in his wheelchair, holding the boy, so vulnerable, so innocent, in his hands. Looking at the new life, and playing with his daughter, who would come visit him at Kessler, gave him new perspective on his own life, and what he had to do. Seeing his daughter and son gave him a reason to work hard at healing himself so he could get on with living his life.

When he first had T'Yanna, he was young, dumb, and didn't really care whether he lived or died. When she woke up and said, "I want my daddy," and he wasn't around, it wouldn't faze him. But now, staring down at Christopher Jordan Wallace Jr., it was different. He had the maturity to know that he was needed. "When I'm looking at my daughter or my son," Wallace said, "it's something to live for. When I finally realized it, at least it wasn't too late."

"Your life is not a stage," his mother would often remind him during their frequent phone conversations. "You don't have to be a performer."

Yet that was precisely what he was—a performer. And he had to get back on his feet. And back in the studio. Not just because he was losing his fan base. Not just for the sake of his ego. He needed a hit record to secure his future. A tour to keep money coming in so he could realize his other dreams, like a house for his mother, a new life for himself away from the hustle and bustle of New Jersey and New York. The means and location to establish a legacy for his children, a financial seed that could flourish long after his departure from earth.

He had talked to God from his bed, and God answered him back, clear as day.

Wallace needed a plan. A life after death.

Sean "Puffy" Combs, meanwhile, had never stopped planning. He had a master plan for his company that went into effect way before Wallace suffered his car accident. Combs knew the only thing that would guarantee Bad Boy's survival in the rap game was hits.

In the lobby of his office, on a white placard with blown-up black block letters, was a reminder of Combs's credo. These were the principles that people who wanted to stay in his presence needed to share: LIFE IS NOT A GAME. ONLY THE FITTEST AND MOST AGGRESSIVE WILL SURVIVE. SLEEPING IS FORBIDDEN. A SECOND CANNOT BE WASTED. ONCE SECONDS ARE LOST YOU LOSE. AND LOSING IS FOR LOSERS.

As B.I.G. had grown larger over the years, so had the infrastructure of Bad Boy Records. The fledgling days of the company, being run from Combs's childhood Mount Vernon home, were long gone: They had Manhattan offices now, bright, shiny, and futuristic, a vision of glass and steel. And a custom-designed recording studio, Daddy's House, nestled in Times Square, his very own Cape Canaveral from which countless rap rockets would blast off into the uppermost reaches of the pop atmosphere. The success of B.I.G, Craig Mack, Faith Evans, and the Bad Boy vocal group Total and 112 had not only outshone Uptown Records, it established Combs as a true pioneer, a force to be reckoned with, and a person who hated to be second-guessed. It didn't matter what record he wanted to sample, what clothes he wanted to design, or even pursuing the seemingly absurd notion that he could one day become a rap artist himself, Puff wanted to do it his way— no questions asked. You doubted him at your own risk.

"We call him the Lord—that's the joke," said Evans to a reporter. "The Lord said. And if it's not like the Lord said, then it has to be changed."

When Puff wasn't in the studio, he was in a dance club, watching the floor, observing firsthand what was getting the crowd pumping. When he wasn't in a club, there were frequent stops at Hot 97, which had transformed itself from a Latin dance-music station to the nation's first genuine 24-hour hip hop station, pumping Bad Boy releases from day one.

It wasn't just about being the best rap label in the world for Combs—it was about being the most exciting company in the world, breaking all the rules, selling Harlem to the Hamptons and vice versa. While his old mentor Andre Harrell was taking over Motown Records in a bid to recapture the magic of Berry Gordy, Puffy looked to the future. He wanted Bad Boy to be the hip hop Bill Gates, with Bad Boy as the genre's dominant operating system. Every magazine, music video channel, and radio station would feature one of his artists. The best way to win the so-called East vs. West musical argument was to flood the market with sheer volume. He said as much on a song with Lil' Kim: "I got no time for fake niggas / Just sip some Cristal with these real niggas / From East to West Coast spread love niggas / And while you niggas talk shit we count bank figures."

As usual it was all there in the lyrics. "Thought I told you that we won't stop" was more than a cute slogan sprinkled all over 112's first smash hit, "Only You." For Combs it was a way of life, and summarized his 24-7-365 lifestyle. Nothing ever got in the way of progress. Not City College, not getting dropped by Uptown, not the war of words and threats between his camp and Death Row, nothing. But all the stress of the threats, the bad press, the eyes of the street began to weigh heavily on Combs. It was no longer fun to be at Bad Boy. One constantly had to look over one's shoulder. And business was beginning to suffer.

"We needed focus," recalls Ron Lawrence. "Puffy knew that we couldn't do it in New York because of all of the bullshit that was going down. We needed to just get away from all that stuff."

So after the Soul Train Awards incident and the showdown between Big and Tupac on March 29, 1996, Puff decided it was time to get out of town—in characteristically dramatic fashion. Within days after the event, Puffy escaped to the relative quiet of Maraval, Trinidad, with his core group of record producers, Stevie J, Deric "D-Dot" Angelettie, Nashiem Myrick, and Ron "Amen-Ra" Lawrence, engineers Axel Niehaus and Tony Maserati, a slew of drum machines and samplers, discs and DATs, several crates of records, and a mission.

"Puffy had a master plan," remembered Lawrence. The producer recalled a meeting at Daddy's House between the Bad Boy heads and the stable of "Hitmen" just prior to their departure.

"For the next two years, I wanna have radio on lock," Puffy said. "Call the girlfriend, wifey, or whatever, and let 'em know that you're not gonna be around for a few weeks. We're gonna get away from all this drama, put our heads together, and when we come back, we're coming back with hits."

Teddy Riley had been one of the first hip hop producers to discover the Caribbean Sound Basin on the island of Trinidad. It offered the best of both worlds—an island paradise with pristine beaches, sunshine, and sand, coupled with a recording studio modern enough to handle the demanding sonic needs of a major rap producer spoiled by the 48-track behemoth studios scattered around Los Angeles, Atlanta, and New York City. Combs hoped that the waters of Trinidad would do for his sound what the waters of Miami Beach did for young Cassius Clay.

"If I'm trying to be the heavyweight champ in 1996," Puff told a reporter, "I gotta go away for a little training camp."

Combs wasn't kidding. With his Hitmen production squad in full effect, he took over the entire studio. As long as an engineer was at the board someone was at work 24 hours a day. The first week alone

T'Yanna Wallace, age four. "When I'm looking at my daughter or son," said Christopher Wallace, "it's something to live for."

was responsible for 35 complete tracks—some of them destined to be multi-platinum hits for Wallace, others for Combs's own forthcoming solo album *Hell Up in Harlem*.

"It was like a training camp," said Lawrence, agreeing with Combs's analogy. "We woke up and we went straight to the studio. We got on the drum machines and, um, till late, till early in the morning. It was just, just a working cycle. Got up, ate breakfast, you know, at times we played some ball or jumped in the pool, but it was just constant work."

Every day produced potent songs. They were bankable hits that would more than finance the expense of putting up so many people in an island paradise for a month.

Before they flew down to Trinidad, Angelettie brought a "whole bunch of records" by Lawrence's apartment and started throwing them on the Technics 1200 turntables in his home studio. He put on Herb Alpert's "Rise." The second Lawrence heard the break, he liked it: not the trumpet part of the popular '80s instrumental jam record—a staple of roller rinks from coast to coast—but the bass break in the beginning. "I was like, yo, this is what we got to do when we get down there."

And that was how they did it. Someone would come up with the beat, some-

Puffy and his hand-picked production squad, the Hitmen, poured all their energies into making B.I.G.'s album *Life After Death* a classic.

one else, like Stevie J or Chucky Thompson, who could play numerous instruments, would come in and sweeten the track. To "Hypnotize," J added a bass line, played on a keyboard. On another track, it might be live drums. Almost all of the Hitmen produced records that were collaborations. Invariably, Stevie J or Lawrence or Angelettie would end up with a credit on a record produced by Nashiem Myrick or Carlos "Six July" Broady, or vice versa.

"That's why there's so many names on the records," said Angelettie.

"We would have an assembly line," explained Lawrence. "Somebody would bring a sample, and then somebody else would put drums to it. And then someone else would add some additional production to it. And at the end of the day, once the sample goes down the line, it's created into a masterpiece. So everybody played a different role."

"No one got an ego or wanted to get a big head about 'Man, I don't want . . .'" said Stevie J about a collaborative spirit that was reminiscent of what the Funk Brothers did for Motown, or what the MGs did for Stax. "Whatever its gonna take to make this a number one classic, not a hit, but a classic, let's do it. We want to be remembered as a group of people who make classic material, not just hot beats for today."

Nashiem Myrick took specific moments from the Dramatics's "In the Rain" and expanded it into the dramatic "Somebody's Gotta Die." What started off as a simple piano loop and some atmospheric echo effects from the old record became a full-blown symphonic blockbuster by the time the crew was finished.

Even before Wallace had the chance to add his vocals, the track exuded ambiance. Dark alleyways, gunshots, and mystery. The sound was cavernous bounced over 48 full tracks, the same amount that film composers use for major motion picture soundtracks.

"Every song is a movie," said Angelettie, co-producer of such hits as "Been Around the World," "It's All About the Benjamins," and "Mo Money, Mo Problems." "If we don't have a story, we don't do it."

The visual element was one of the most important elements of the new sound Puffy was urging his Hitmen to go for. The idea was to provide drama—to expand the realm of the sound, to provide backing tracks that would make the sonic movie that was *Ready to Die* feel like a low-budget film.

If a Dr. Dre–produced gangsta rap album evoked the gritty, visceral feel of an early Martin Scorsese flick à la *Taxi Driver*, Combs was going for epics of Michael Bay proportions—think *Armageddon*. Strings, sound effects such as gunshots, slamming doors, footsteps, voices murmuring in the background.

Another thing Puffy was known for was his blatantly pop records. They were homages to the point of being remakes. The unspoken rule among producers was that if you could recognize it, it wasn't a good sample. To the Pete Rocks and

RZAs of the world—guys who would paste together sonic collages one drum hit at a time—songs like MC Hammer's "U Can't Touch This" were sacrilege. Not just because of the wack rhyme—but because the Rick James "Superfreak" loop was so obvious and unimaginative. Puffy didn't care.

"Yes, I'm a beat jacker," he told Jeannine Amber. "That's my shit! But you can't say you ain't gonna dance to my shit. When that muthafucka comes on, your ass is jigglin'."

If it was a hit in his ear, it was a hit. Old or new. His approach was to take records from the late '70s and early '80s that people would easily recognize—and sample them anyway. Not only did he want his records to sound orchestral and huge—he wanted to capture the pop sound of the '80s, and use that as his sonic base to rock a party and move major units. No one else had the balls to do it.

"People never really gave us the credit for that," Lawrence said. "They look at it as, well, you know, you just took David Bowie's 'Let's Dance.' But they never really understand or gave us the credit for the artistry that actually went into it."

Puffy reasoned that if the white-bread radio programmers in their early forties who still controlled the airwaves could identify the sample, they'd be more prone to play a given record. In order to pass muster with "The Lord," every record needed to have a *big* sound. And if it was already based on a hit song, it made it even easier to be a hit song. It could be a bad investment to write new songs. Why take the chance?

Wallace had worked his way back to normalcy, and by the time he was ready to begin recording *Life After Death* in earnest during the fall of 1996, he was itching to go. Recording was not only an escape from his condition, it was an escape from the Kessler Institute of Rehabilitation.

At first he thought the people there, like most white folks, were going to be afraid of him. That they would look at his appearance, the fact that he had guys like D-Roc and Cease around him, and give him problems. "I was, really, was thinking they was gonna give us bullshit 'cause I'm like a young rapper," he said. "I got a thug nigga sleeping in there making sure nobody don't come in there fucking with me. Every morning these niggas is wheeling me to muthafucking therapy. I got two big-ass niggas. Junk jewelry, diamonds, you know what I'm saying? I'm rolling up in therapy and nothing but old people. And I'm running in there with some real Brooklyn shit. They was feeling me, though. They gave me my love. When they asked they kids who I was, they were like, 'You got *who* up there!?' Then they start saying, 'My daughter likes your new video.'"

He would sit there in his wheelchair, or in bed, thinking of rhymes, ready to get back to work. Combs would come by to visit him, bringing tracks, some of them from the Trinidad sessions, others hot off the boards of an outside producer. A fellow patient alerted Wallace to the fact that, with a doctor's promissory note, he could get a weekend pass to go to the recording studio.

"I was locked up, thinking of escape," Wallace joked. "I got into the studio and started knocking out joints."

And the joints started piling up. Fast. Wallace recorded at a breakneck pace, his idle time making his brain work overtime. The records poured out of him.

"He was a late afternoon, evening dude," remembered Deric Angelettie. Part of his responsibility as the A&R executive responsible for the record was to organize all of Wallace's recording sessions, help clear samples, hire and organize the producers of the various tracks, and keep Wallace in the recording booth, happy, on the job.

After his accident, Wallace recorded at a breakneck pace, all that idle time making his brain work overtime. He'd get wheeled into Daddy's House and sit around, smoking and listening to tracks real loud.

"I'd usually tell Big, 'Be at the studio around six.' Which meant eight, eight-thirty," said Angelettie with a laugh. "And he'd be there until two or three or five, depending. And we'd just be in there writing and bullshitting."

Wallace would show up with either D-Roc, Lil' Cease, G, or another member of Junior M.A.F.I.A. driving him, either get wheeled in his wheelchair, or, as he got a little more mobility, walk in with a cane, sit around and listen to tracks. Everything would be laid out for him to make the environment as conducive to his creativity as possible.

"Every day, the same shit," Angelettie said, chuckling. "You walked into Studio A or B, there's ice and glasses, and cups, liquors, and chasers. Alizé, Moët, Cristal, whatever he was feeling like. Bacardi. They was really on Bacardi Limon for a minute, 'cause that's when it first came out. Plenty of Dutch Masters and Backwoods. Lil' Cease had the weed out, rolling L after L for Big and the rest of the crew. A little bit of chocolate thai. Might be one or two chicks sitting on the couch, or in the lounge. There'd be empty bags of food, or they just ordered food. His cronies making phone calls,'" Angelettie said with a laugh, lost in the memory. "Bitches, phone calls, and the beat real loud."

Because it was 100 percent dedicated to Bad Boy projects, Daddy's House offered a level of comfort and flexibility that wasn't possible anywhere else. Located just off of Times Square, it had a club-like atmosphere. There was a private lounge. Huge color monitors with PlayStations and VCRs connected for movie and video-game binges. All the latest samplers and effects, a mixing board to die for, and speakers powerful enough to rival Madison Square Garden's.

"It was home," said Angelettie. "You can take your shoes off, you can work as many amount of hours you want. You could keep going even if the engineer is tired. You know what I mean? We can stop the session if we need to continue something else. We could do whatever we wanted to do in there. And it was family in there so like, you know, whatever we did in there stayed in there. Bitches coming there to freak out, y'knowhatumsayin'? If somebody was in there doing something a little extra besides weed, then that's what happened."

D-Dot Angelettie's job was to keep the volume high, the atmosphere chill, but to make sure that, no matter what, records were getting made. On the surface, it may have looked as if Wallace was wasting time and money. But when he finally recorded his vocals, he was as regular as clockwork. Twenty to 45 minutes later and you had a hit song, like a "Mo Money, Mo Problems." A complex album cut like "Niggas Bleed" might take an hour or so. If things got too relaxed, Angelettie was always the one who cracked the whip.

"When it got beyond regular bullshit, and we starting to like toss money away," Angelettie said, "then I'd step in and be like, 'Come on, son, clear the room. Give Big an hour.'"

Wallace would sit there just as if he was in his old bedroom on St. James Place, listening and murmuring lyrics to himself, over and over.

"A lot of times we be sitting on the floor a half an hour, just me and him," Angelettie recalled. "And I'd be like, 'What you got?' When he did 'Hypnotize,' he just leaned over to me and whispered 'Biggie Biggie Biggie, can't you see? Sometimes your words just hypnotize me.' He just hummed it to me. Went back to nodding. Passed me the L, and he'd just keep nodding."

Once the rhyme reached critical mass in Wallace's head, it was important to track the vocal immediately and try to get it right the first time. "Once he's ready to lay, he want to lay it and go," remembered Angelettie. "He don't want to lay it and sit around for an hour. That's his final task. He'll lay it, put it on cassette, give us a pound, and they cleaning up they shit and they out. He ain't sitting around chilling after that."

There was only one other condition that was crucial to Wallace's process: Puffy couldn't be there when he laid his vocals. They would spend hours talking about the albums, line for line, but if he could help it, he recorded alone.

"He would try not to go into the vocal booth if Puffy was around," recording engineer Lynn Montrose confirmed. Montrose, one of the few female engineers in the industry, recorded numerous vocals for Wallace's album, and always found the rapper charming and polite. "You don't want to go into the vocal booth and as soon as you go in Puffy is like, 'No, I don't like your tone,' or whatever. That would be a large part of his waiting; waiting for Puffy to leave."

Most songs could be recorded in a day. Others took longer. It depended on

Celebration time at Daddy's House after the completion of *Life After Death*. Puffy's sweatshirt is by Brooklyn Mint, the clothing company Wallace was trying to start before he died.

his general mood, and what was happening in his life. "He might have been too busy, or he might have gotten too high, he might have had a stressful day," remembered Angelettie. "The Faith shit, still got the Tupac shit, still got baby-mother drama, and you still got to pay bills. Your normal life still goes on, so he's dealing with a lot of shit. Every day is not happy and peppy and bursting with love."

But time wasn't the biggest factor. Quality was.

"Big is the true MC—he doesn't have a certain style, per se. He fits every song," said Myrick. "He writes like a songwriter would write. He writes in melody. That's why he has these different styles on each track and it fits so perfectly, it fits like a glove. A lot of MCs are just lazy, you know, they just have they set rhythm and how they rap, and they go at that in every song. Big comes different in every song. Every flow is different."

At times he called himself "the black rhinoceros of rap" or "the praying mantis," but the animal Wallace resembled most was a chameleon. For a song like "Warning" or "Gimme the Loot," Biggie was a master narrator, switching perspective, voices, and flows two or three times in one song. And then there were the freestyle showcases, the songs that would take him back to his basement days of rhyming over breakbeats while 50 Grand worked the decks, way before he ever dreamed of becoming a superstar. Those were the kinds of tracks that DJ Premier specialized in producing.

Both Premier tracks on *Life After Death,* like "Unbelievable" before them, were instant classics—stripped down, intricate lyrical workouts tailor-made for a Jeet Kune Do MC like Wallace. Nothing cute to hide behind, just naked, raw rhythms, the kind of stuff that Puffy, with his pop sensibilities, hated.

"Puff didn't like 'Kick In the Door,'" Premier recalled. The song was more avant garde than anything Premier had ever done. The beat was a loop of a horn line from a classic Screaming Jay Hawkins song, "I Put a Spell on You," matched to a funky drum pattern that was deliberately offbeat. It was a sink-or-swim track that had the potential to be either the dopest thing ever or something locked away and forgotten about. Everything depended on the vocalist.

"We were arguing in the elevator," remembered Premier, who made a special trip up to Daddy's House to preview the track for Combs.

"This joint ain't hot," Combs told Premier. "Pre, you ain't giving me that Tunnel banger," Puff said, referring to the N.Y.C. nightclub that Funkmaster Flex turned into the compulsory testing ground for rap hotness. "You ain't hitting like you did last time with 'Unbelievable.' I need something hotter."

"Has Big heard it?" asked Premier, unfazed.

"Nah. He ain't heard it yet."

"Why don't you give it to him? If he don't like it, I'll change it," Premier replied.

"But I ain't feeling this," Puff said.

Hours later, Wallace heard the track at Daddy's House. "Man, are you crazy!?" he said, dialing Premier on his cell phone. "Yo, come back tonight. Let's track it tonight."

Premier came to the studio to upload the sample and tune up the track. "There was a lot of Bacardi Limon in the house," Premier remembered. The beat was playing loud, and Wallace, as usual, sat there nodding to the beat. There were people all over the place, and, like clockwork, a few cops showed up, and the Lysol scramble was on.

"I was like, damn, what the hell is going on," remembers Premier, "and everyone else was like, 'The police is here again.' They said it happened all the time. So we put our trees out, waited. I told [Big], 'Damn, you just in here working, doing your thing. Why they giving you a hard time?'"

> **"This joint ain't hot," Combs told DJ Premier after listening to the "Kick in the Door" demo. "Has Big heard it?" Premier asked, unfazed. "Nah," Puff said. "Why don't you give it to him?" said Primo. "If he don't like it, I'll change it."**

But nothing stopped the lyrical bum rush. After the cops cleared out, Big got back to work. Premier was surprised by how upbeat Wallace was despite hobbling everywhere he went.

"It was two, three in the morning, and you're sitting there, tired of waiting. And them boom, he's finally like, 'Yo, I'm ready,'" Premier recalls of the session for "Kick In the Door." In typical fashion, Wallace finished the first two verses in less than half an hour. "Your reign on the top was short like leprechauns / As I crush so-called thugs, fake willies and rapper dons," is how he began, one of the hottest rap records ever. He spent a few days thinking about the third verse, then finished it later.

Between the studio, his court dates, and physical therapy, Wallace was too busy to be depressed about breaking his leg. He was making progress. He knew that the record was good, he was having fun, and once the Camden case was settled for $40,000, one of his biggest legal hassles was out of his head. With his healthier diet, he was even losing weight now that he could move around a little more. His sleep apnea was getting better too, giving him more restful nights.

"He lost about thirty pounds," remembered his mother. "He said, 'Ma, I'm gonna be out there wearing my Calvins,'" suggesting that he intended to follow in Mark Wahlberg's footsteps as an underwear model. "You watch."

That was the ultimate goal of *Life After Death:* to cut through all the distractions and get all eyes on B.I.G. Wallace wanted his fans to know that—despite his riches and stardom—all was not gravy. He'd been through the murder of Tupac, people being jealous of his success, the love triangles, all of it was weighing on him. The album was a fictional outlet for Wallace to deal with all of it, and make some great music in the process.

"I call this album *Life After Death,* because when I was writing stuff like 'Fuck the world, fuck my mom, and my girl,' I was dead, man," Wallace said. "There was nothing but anger coming out about everything: about having to go out to sell crack, to hustle for a living. Nothing but anger. But now I can't do that anymore.

"People know that Biggie ain't on the corner selling drugs no more. Why would anyone want to hear about that? I got other problems now, like people in Brooklyn. It's these goddamn haters, man. It just isn't good enough for them to say, 'Damn, he's from Brooklyn, he was selling drugs and robbin' muthafuckas and he took a talent that he had and he built it into something so strong that we're proud of him.' Instead, they're like, 'Fuck Biggie.'"

The album was a way for Wallace to get things off his chest, yet at the same time keep all his different audiences on their toes. A song like "Somebody's Gotta Die," "Niggas Bleed," or "I Got a Story to Tell" would remind people that hip hop has never had a better storyteller. A rhyme like his verse on "Kick In the Door" or "What's Beef" would demonstrate that he was a rapper's rapper whose skills went way beyond dropping designer brand names. On "Notorious Thugs" and "Playa Hatas," he would prove that nobody could freak as many different styles as B.I.G. And with "Hypnotize" and "Mo Money, Mo Problems," he proved that even his more mainstream joints could rock a hardcore crowd. And just in case you forgot, he could still smack you with a grimy classic like "Ten Crack Commandments."

The goal with *Life After Death* was to make an album that wouldn't as much improve upon its predecessor as dwarf it. *Ready to Die* was a slice of Brooklyn life, a street record that aspired for higher things, *The Terminator* of rap records. But *Life After Death* was supposed to be *T2:* twice as long, three times the budget, more special effects, but losing none of the character and personality.

As his friend and BK heir apparent Jay-Z observed, B.I.G.'s first album was "told from the outside looking in" whereas *Life After Death* was "told from the inside looking out." Or, put another way: "*Ready to Die* wanted to achieve that success and then in *Life After Death* it was coping with that success and dealing with that success."

Yet despite his newfound maturity as a lyricist and as a person, Wallace still wanted to be acknowledged for what he was: the baddest rapper alive.

"Who's your favorite MC?" Wallace asked Chairman Mao during one of the *Life After Death* sessions. When the esteemed rap scribe didn't answer quickly enough, Wallace jumped in—"See, I want you to say 'Big.' Without hesitation. He's the best."

"I mean some MCs that I see I kinda assumed in the beginning had genuine love for me, they look at me now like, 'Oh, that's that nigga right there, he crossed over. He used to be hard.' Nigga, I'm the hardest nigga in hip hop. My shit comes off so strong and my hardness is sincere because I lived all that shit.

"I used to do a whole lot of fucked-up shit," he said. "And it was really expressed on *Ready to Die* and you couldn't really expect me to still be doing fucked-up shit on *Life After Death* because it would be kinda phony. [This time] I was just more focused on making records. Certain feelings, certain emotions I just wanted to express in my music. I got a newborn son. My peoples just had kids. I'm just trying to blossom more into being a father and a man. More than just that buck-wild teenage nigga that was just out there wildin'. I don't want muthafuckas to just look at Big and say, 'Oh shit, there go Big the dope MC.' I want people to look at Big like, 'Look at Big. He grew. He's a businessman now. He's a father now. He's taking control of his destiny. He's movin' up.'"

The sound of *Ready to Die* was largely shaped by one producer, Easy Mo Bee. This time around, with a real staff of Bad Boy hit makers on retainer, the process was more of a team effort. Even outside producers like Mo Bee, RZA, Havoc, Buck Wild, Kay Gee, and Clark Kent would have their records altered by Puff and the Hitmen so that, as a cohesive whole, every track on the album would fit into the story being woven through Wallace's lyrics.

Easy Mo Bee, for one, felt frozen out by the new process. For many of the producers, besides the beat itself, there was less interaction on the content of the song. Bee was at the "I Love the Dough" sessions while Jay-Z and Wallace were pacing around the room, mumbling to themselves as they both wrote their verses in their heads, but they both left before they recorded their verses. He wasn't around when they actually laid them, despite leaving word to call him when they got back. "Goin' Back to Cali," another Mo Bee beat, had no title when he left the demo behind—it was a chopped up variation of Zapp's "Mo Bounce to the Ounce," no vocoder effects or nothing.

"I wanted L.A.'s attention," Mo Bee told *XXL.* "That was always the L.A. anthem. You got this East Coast/West Coast bullshit, and I felt that maybe through music or a beat, anything that gets everybody in harmony."

"At first he was going to be in heaven with all white and doves, then the concept changed to a grave-yard," said Michael Lavine, who shot Wallace for the *Life After Death* album cover at Cypress Hills Cemetery, Brooklyn, New York, in February 1997.

But there was a controversy over the song's title. "If I was there, that song wouldn't have been titled no 'Going Back to Cali,'" Mo Bee said adamantly. "I would have disapproved the title because once again, the climate at that time. I was traveling back and forth in California. And every time I got off the plane, it was like my eyes were looking left and right like, yo, yo, yo. I'm set up to go some-where just looking left and right, checking everybody out, trying to make sure I say the right thing to everybody.

"I know for a fact, even if Big wasn't thinking nothing like that, Puff knew that I was uncomfortable with that and he knew that I probably would have tried to argue against it. I loved it though. Beautiful song. But the title? 'Going Back to Cali'? Oh, I was not cool with that.

"When the song got made and it was final I couldn't even get a copy. When I found out the title my heart dropped, man. I was like, Yo, why'd they name that shit that, man?"

The simple answer was because they could. Not that it was necessarily a good idea. But *Life After Death* was being assembled the way a movie is. Mo Bee got a taste of the Hollywood pecking order firsthand: Actor (Big), Director (Hitmen), Producer (Puff), and then somewhere way down at the end of the line, the screenwriter.

"The producers are like the screenwriters," Angelettie explained. "They come with the ideas. And we take that screenplay. And we're producing that. And we're directing that. And you get your credits, like you supposed to. Producers would give us tracks that were eight tracks and we may finish them with thirty-eight tracks. 'Cause we added strings, vocals, extra choruses, people singing in the background. We were known for sound effects."

But there was no question about which track mattered the most: whichever one contained B.I.G.'s vocal. When he was sizing up the premier track that became "Ten Crack Commandments," Wallace remembered a sidebar to Khary Kimani Turner's article in the July 1994 issue of *The Source*, "The House That Crack Built," about drug dealing in Detroit. The sidebar offered practical insights on the finer points of drug dealing. And Big decided that the Primo track offered the perfect way to adapt it as a song. The result was a masterpiece that everybody was feeling. (Well, almost everybody: Public Enemy's Chuck D, whose voice was sampled for the song's opening countdown, was offended by the song's drug theme and filed suit for the unauthorized usage.)

The double album was all but complete when Big and Primo got down to work. "I didn't know it was going to be called 'Ten Crack Commandments,'" remembered Premier. "He just told me, 'I want it exactly the way you laid it out on the promo, don't change anything.' And I was like, no problem."

Someone wheeled Wallace into the booth, and he sat there, head up, ready to rip shit. Primo's track began to play, and Big burned through the whole song in a few short takes from his wheel chair, as he did most of that second record. It still hurt too much to stand without a cane or a walker. But Big didn't seem to mind. Like everything else life handed him, he found a way to make it fun.

He told Premier, "When I do my first video, I'm gonna dance in my video." Premier said, "I was like, 'Word, Big? You think you gonna be able to dance?' And he said, 'Watch.'" Then Wallace raised himself slowly out of the wheelchair, almost able to support himself without assistance. He did a little wiggle and bounce with his shoulders, then plopped back into the chair with a smile.

"Ten Crack Commandments" was the last song recorded for *Life After Death*. As soon as he finished the verse, Wallace was elated. He knew, right off the bat, that the song was something special: Biggie talking about the crack game like an old grandfather schooling the youth who are still caught up in the grind. He didn't tell them not to do it, but his advice was so real, he might have prompted a few to have second thoughts.

"As soon as we finished that record, Biggie yelled on the mike and said, 'Preme, it's over! It's over! I'm the greatest. I did it!'"

That memory has stayed with the veteran rap producer ever since. "Those are exactly the last words I ever heard that man say."

While Big concerned himself with being the greatest MC ever, Combs was focused on making the biggest rap record ever. Clocking in at over twenty songs, *Life After Death* was a double-barreled blast calculated to slay the competition and scare the mainstream into submission without compromising Wallace's artistic vision.

On songs like "My Downfall" and "You're Nobody Till Somebody Kills You," Wallace was already playing with macabre imagery, much the way he had done with *Ready to Die.* There were no direct references to Tupac on the album (except the ones deeply embedded in the lyrics to "Long Kiss Goodnight"). Nor were there any tearful tributes. But death and enemies were lurking behind every other track. If you listened carefully to songs like "Long Kiss Goodnight" you could convince yourself that he was speaking about Shakur's murder. It was as if Wallace and Puffy were throwing it in the face of the whole morbidly fascinated audience. Like, you thought they were gonna kill me? *What?* I'm still here.

Puffy decided to do the photo shoot in a graveyard. After rejecting the idea of posing amid clouds with angel wings. The album cover, with Biggie posing by the hearse, was almost a taunt, the kind of bodacious move that Muhammad Ali would make, like daring people to doubt him and then proving them wrong. Wallace wasn't as much taunting death as he was asserting that I'm here to stay. Even if my album cover and title appear morbid my career is nowhere near death. *Life After Death* was meant to be a resurrection of sorts.

"I never did nothing wrong to nobody," Wallace told Chairman Mao while recording the album. "I ain't never did anything wrong to Tupac. I ain't never do anything wrong to Faith, nothing wrong to Kim, nothing wrong to nobody. And I kept quiet. I kept my mouth shut. I figure if I had been sitting here riffin' it'd seem like I had a point to prove. I know I ain't do nothin', so it don't make sense for me to say nothin'. I just let everybody do they thing. On March 25, all answers gonna come out. You gonna hear what Big got to say. And on top of hearing what I got to say, you gonna spend thirty dollar to hear it. Fuck it."

The album was finished in late January of 1997 to meet a March 25 release date. The hype machine was in full gear; Wallace had cover stories lined up with all the rap magazines and a major feature in *Spin.* There was a national radio promotional tour lined up, along with television interviews, and plenty of concert spots. There were plans to do two big video shoots. It would be the largest promotion ever for a Bad Boy artist. Puffy was drawing on all of Arista's clout to ensure a number-one slot when the album debuted.

But in order to make the plan work certain things had to happen. First of all, Wallace had to go back to Cali.

YOU'RE NOBODY TILL SOMEBODY KILLS YOU

CHAPTER 8

❝ Yea though I walk through the valley
of the shadow of death
I will fear no evil—for You are with me.
Your rod and your staff, they comfort me.
You prepare a table for me
in the presence of my enemies. ❞

Christopher Wallace couldn't stop smiling.

The King of New York was in high spirits as he sat by the pool at the Four Seasons Hotel in Los Angeles. The sun was bright, there were women by the pool, and he was just sitting back, loving his life. And who could blame him? It was Valentine's Day, February 14, and here he was, posted up by the pool at the Four Seasons Hotel with a Frosty glass in his left hand and a blunt in his right. A Brooklyn thug basking in the sun like a sea lion. It was a scene worthy of his first single, "Juicy," in which he fantasized of "Living life without fear. / Putting five carats in my baby girl's ear. / Lunches. Brunches. Interviews by the pool. / Considered a fool 'cause I dropped out of high school."

He had accomplished everything he had ever set out to accomplish. It was a beautiful thing. But was also kinda scary.

I couldn't think of a single rapper who didn't lose a step after they blew up. Big Daddy Kane. Ice Cube. Chuck D. Even at times, the God of all Gods, Rakim. More than anything, I was wondering how someone who was as successful as he was could avoid falling off.

"What keeps you motivated?"

Wallace smiled.

"Knowing that I got a three-month-old son that has to survive," he said. "And making sure my daughter's straight." He had already accomplished most of what he said he'd do on "Juicy" less than three years before. But he was far from finished. "I still ain't there," he said. "I still got a lot more things to do."

Like what?

"I wanna master this rapping shit, so I can kind of be confident in what I put out. You know what I'm saying? Like if TLC or Boyz II Men drops an album, they know they're gonna sell five million. I wanna kind of be comfortable in my status as an MC. And at the same time, I wanna open up a few businesses. Name it Big Poppa's Chicken and Waffles. Everything in the restaurant is real big. Like, the tables are big, the chairs are big, it's a big clock, a big jukebox, the forks is extra big. Food, the chicken is big, the waffles are big, everything is just real big. You know, I'm trying to get with Heavy D today, and I want to talk to him about opening up a 'Big and Heavy' big man's clothing store. You know, try to get me some of these labels that I mention ever so much in my raps, that their sales is boosted up so much in the urban areas, you know, saying all these kids wanting to get $300 glasses, and $700 sweaters . . ."

The more Puffy was talking about being a rapper, it seemed that the Notorious B.I.G. had his sights set on being a full time C.E.O.

"I'm around a nigga like Puffy who's learned from niggas like Russell and Andre and Clive, you know? Even when he on the phone. I'm in his conversations. I'm not supposed to be. I hear that money talking and I'm like, Okay. What you going to do? How much you gave for this? I'm always asking questions. And he's not that nigga that's gonna lie. He tells me."

Meeting of the minds: When Nas stopped by this 1995 Notorious B.I.G. recording session, the rap giants were on good terms. But competition over who was the true "King of New York" would strain their relationship.

Wallace definitely wasn't the mad rapper anymore. But his old fears weren't unfounded. The sharp change in his surroundings, the way his music changed after the success of "Player's Anthem," the fact that he never once responded to Tupac Shakur's disrespectful antics—or anyone else's for that matter—all could lead one to believe that the thrill was gone, and the champ had gotten punchy. The disses weren't just coming from the West Coast anymore, but from the East. Groups like the Roots, whose video "What They Do" was a parody of champagne-popping clichés—many of which started with Biggie. The digs were subtle, but obvious if you knew what you were looking at. Raekwon's *Only Built 4 Cuban Linx* album contained a scathing skit that attempted to draw Nas into Rae's conflict with Biggie.

On Nas's 2002 song "Last Real Nigga Alive," he traces the roots of the competitive friction among the three brilliant young MCs. "Big told me Rae was stealing my slang," he raps. "And Rae told me out in Shaolin Big would do the same thing." Nas kept his cool, even when Biggie subtly dissed him on "Kick In the Door." Six years later, he's still big enough to admit that "I borrowed from both them niggas." Brooklyn's own OGC took things even further, with a video featuring one of the rappers in the group, at a New York concert, knocking an overweight rapper with a leather jacket, Coogi sweater, and Kangol off the stage.

Wallace shrugged the whole thing off. He didn't care if the audience wanted "Ready to Die Again." His life had changed and so had his music. The important thing was for him to be happy.

"I remember when I was in high school," he recalled, "and an English teacher once went around the class asking, 'What would you hate to lose more than anything in the world?' Everyone else was like 'my moms,' or 'my gold chain.' The teacher finally got around to me. I said, 'My temper.'" It was a funny story, but he was very serious. "If I lose my temper, something's gonna go down," he said. "My temper be fuckin' up sometimes. I say grow from your mistakes and hopefully you can stand the repercussions.

"I often have to say to myself, watch what you're doing, Big, 'cause you're not on Fulton Street anymore. If a nigga say, 'Fuck you,' you can't shoot at him. You just can't do it, Big."

Wallace's eyes glimmered as his hearty chuckle filled the air. "Okay, fine, I'll be the cool dude. I have security, and they can handle that. I'm just the cool dude. Write the raps, do the shows, all that. It's not like I'm biting my fingers, like, *Damn, I wanna shoot somebody,*" he said, bugging his eyes and munching on his fingertips, mocking the image of a trigger-happy psycho.

The beef between coasts didn't make any sense, either socially or financially. Never did. Imagine if, during the heyday of the '60s soul movement, there was friction between Motown and Stax, with all of Detroit pitted against Memphis, with the Four Tops and Sam and Dave coming to blows, and Marvin Gaye bragging that he slept with Wilson Pickett's wife. Sure, Motown competed with Stax for radio play, market share, and record sales, but it was understood that each label broke new ground for the other. People who grew up on Stevie Wonder eventually discovered Isaac Hayes. Everybody made money—and the music that resulted was unforgettable. With hip hop, egos seem so fragile and success seems so fleeting that both must be carefully guarded and jealously defended.

"This shit is beautiful, man," Wallace said again "It feels like a few million miles from Brooklyn. You got palm trees and all types of shit right here. I wouldn't want to lose it for nothing in the *world.*"

"Being out in Cali was a major vacation for him," said DJ Enuff, who declined an invitation to join Big and crew on that trip. "I think he escaped so far that he forgot about reality. You're in the wolf's den, you're in California, you're in the home of Tupac, who was just killed a half a year earlier. What are you doing out there? So who's to say, when you go out to Cali, you know, Pac's peoples or Suge's peoples or whoever's peoples won't say, Yo, let's get this nigger Big. You know. Pac's dead, why he ain't dead?"

But Biggie was not thinking those negative thoughts. He was sitting on top of an album that he knew was going to put him back on top, silence all the naysayers, and slaughter whatever competition remained. There was confidence in his voice, ease in his demeanor, and a sense of purpose in his eyes. This wasn't the same kid I met three years ago on St. James standing on his stoop, wondering whether or not his album was going to go gold, and fearing that if he did blow up, plush surroundings would deaden his ability to make compelling music.

The purpose of the California trip wasn't just to ball out: There was business to do. Besides making videos for his own album, Wallace was writing the lion's share of the lyrics for Combs's album, tentatively titled *Hell Up in Harlem.* "Big was trying to get in a different zone," said Lil' Cease. "You doing shit for another nigga, you don't want to get their stuff in your mode. Los Angeles was where Puff was at, so Big was like, 'All right—that's where you wanna do it? All right, fuck it.'" Wallace had no fear about being in California. "Big never tripped about nothing," said Cease. "Especially with that chronic out there. We could get away from everything, really focus on this music shit and knock it out. That's why we was out there."

Combs's move to Los Angeles was a way to test the waters, to see how much resistance Bad Boy would face breaking the very expensive *Life After Death* album to the second-largest radio market in the country.

A full year before the California trip, Sean "Puffy" Combs revealed one of the promotional secrets behind Wallace's and Craig Mack's initial success: "[We] donated three months outta their life to go on a major tour," he said. "That's the way you bug radio, believe me. Be nice to everybody, work overtime, do two shows a day, make everyone like you. Give up three months, then your records will last two years."

Those two years were up. Now Combs had to figure out a way to get people to fall in love with Wallace all over again, this time with at least some of the audience potentially hostile.

The grass roots were on Combs's mind when he came out to Los Angeles with Wallace. It was easier for people on the West Coast to resent Combs, and to hate Biggie when they were figures on MTV, always lounging in expensive cars, sipping champagne, living the high life. The best way to break through that was for people to see them out in the clubs—hanging out, partying, making stops at the mix shows, being seen out and about. The more they were seen, the more approachable they were, the more Los Angelenos would realize that they had love for the West Coast—and love for them.

"Big thought, 'While I'm out here, maybe I can try to clear some of this shit up,'" Lil 'Cease explained. "He used to call Puff, like 'Yo, Puff, call somebody at the radio station. Tell 'em I wanna come up and talk about some shit.' Like fuck it, I'm out here. I might as well get something done. Instead of just me sitting around waiting for this nigga to make a move. I could be out here doing something."

Cease said that Puff was happy to help. "He was like, 'Oh, you wanna work while you out here? I'll set you up an itinerary.' That's when Puff started setting up shit for Big to do. Interviews. Record stores. All the magazines. Big was doing it. He was like fuck it. I got some shit coming out. Let me get my shit together. He out there hustling. Scrambling. Like end of the day, nigga ain't thinking about none of that East-West shit. It's time to work, it's time to work. You can't stop him from his business."

Not even a federal investigation was enough to slow his roll. Biggie was aware that his movements were being monitored while he was in Los Angeles. They were out to prove that rap labels like Bad Boy and Death Row were just fronts for criminal activity. And the undercover agents weren't very subtle about it. Who else could these white men taking pictures be? Rap photographers always introduced themselves.

When Combs and Snoop appeared together on *The Steve Harvey Show*, hopes were high for some sort of reconciliation between Bad Boy and Death Row.

"One time Big was in front of the hotel," Cease recalled. "I came downstairs, and he was waiting for the limo to pull up. So the nigga's just sitting out there with the cane in front of the hotel, and I'm like, Hold up. I see a man in front of him taking a picture. Then the dude jumped in his car, made a U-turn and drove away. I said, 'Did you do a photo shoot?' He's like, 'Nah, it's the feds.' He said it real nonchalant. And I'm like, *Word?* Big said, 'Yeah, I'll pose for a picture. At least I got some protection.'"

"There was some nervousness about them being out there," remembered Wallace's manager and close friend Mark Pitts. "But once he got out there, Big had a way of putting people at ease." Pitts recalled how Wallace and his entourage went out to a club and met some resistance from people there—some of them bitter about Tupac's recent murder and suspicious that Wallace must have had something to do with the shooting, as revenge for Tupac's "Hit 'Em Up" and the whole Faith debacle.

Wallace, unfazed, stared them straight in the eyes and smiled. "You know you love me, stop playing." From that moment on, tensions at the club were eased and a good time was had by all.

There wasn't any overt tension coming from Death Row. Since Tupac's murder, the company was in a tailspin. Despite having recently renamed itself the "New and Untouchable," Death Row Records was anything but impregnable.

Dr. Dre, the musical heart and soul of the label, the most powerful producer in the industry, let alone the West Coast, had left. Snoop Doggy Dogg was quietly preparing to break out. Creditors from limo companies to American Express were filing suits. There were reports that the FBI, ATF, and DEA were investigating everything from drugs to money laundering and the label's alleged ties to the Mob Piru Bloods and jailed drug dealer Michael "Harry-O" Harris, who supposedly supplied the seed money to get the thing started in the first place.

Steve Cantrock, the Coopers & Lybrand accountant who did the label's books, was in hiding and was supposedly blabbing to the FBI (and the *Los Angeles Times*) about being beaten and coerced into signing a $4 million IOU for overdrafts on the Death Row Records expense accounts. And now Suge, because of his role in the fight at the MGM Grand scant hours before Tupac's fatal shooting, was facing a parole violation. A surveillance camera captured Knight, Shakur, and several associates kicking Orlando Anderson as he lay on the floor. The arrest violated his probation stemming from a 1992 incident in which he reportedly pistol-whipped two aspiring rap producers for using a phone that was specifically reserved for him.

Despite numerous character witnesses, and a bizarre recantation of the assault charges from Orlando Anderson, it all came down to this—Suge Knight, in a blue jail jumpsuit, pleading with the judge for a break.

Knight's own probation officer recommended he be sent back to jail. There were no bargains to be struck because of the way his last deal with Lawrence Longo had blown up in everybody's face. Now that Death Row was openly under federal investigation, those who could began slowly pulling away from Knight. He would finally get to see how people really felt about him, and whether it was better to be loved or to be feared.

"I am a man, your honor," Knight said in his defense. "I have a family, and I would like them to know the truth." It was the morning of Friday, February 28, but there was nothing good about it.

"I've been through a lot this year," he continued. "I lost my best friend. A lot of people don't realize how it is to lose a best friend. I always wanted a little brother, and now he's not here. Besides all that, I'm not mad, but I'm disappointed at Tupac's mother.

"While I'm incarcerated, people tell her that the songs I paid for and marketed is her songs. And she made statements saying that she never got any money.

I got signed documents where he received over $2.5 million, even before she was supposed to receive money. And beyond all that, when he was incarcerated, I gave his mother $3 million. But when the media gets it, it turns around that I left him for dead, I left him with zero, and that I'm this monster.

"And if I look like Frankenstein, even though Frankenstein could be the nicest creature on earth, when he failed or when he died, everybody applauded. They clapped instead of cried."

Knight continued with his rambling, stream-of-consciousness statement. But as he talked, he eventually found his way to the point. Referring to Anderson's beat-down at the MGM Grand, he said, "It's not a nine-year kick. This guy wasn't harmed, wasn't anything broke on him. If you ask anybody that seen me fight, your honor, the first they'd tell you is, 'That guy wouldn't be standing there giving statements.' When I fights, sir, I fights. But I've changed my life to get away from fighting," Knight added. "And it might be the last time I speak to my family, I could go to jail and anything can happen. But I'm not here for the judge to feel pity for me, I'm just speaking from my heart."

Judge Stephen Czleger looked unmoved.

"You really had everything going for you," he said. "You blew it."

He slammed his gavel and handed out the sentence. Nine years.

With Tupac dead and Suge Knight off the streets, Bad Boy was making its presence known—in Los Angeles recording studios, in the clubs on Sunset Boulevard, and on local radio stations. The message being sent wasn't subtle—while our enemies fall, we stand tall.

Snoop Dogg and Puffy Combs made a joint appearance on *The Steve Harvey Show* a few weeks before Knight was sentenced, both publicly declaring an end to the East Coast–West Coast beef.

The feeling was that, with Suge behind bars, the streets were open again. When the cat's away, the mice will play. Puffy showed up at the House of Blues one night for a concert that featured Warren G. and Nas. Heads turned as he laughed it up with fellow rap industry notables, enjoying the show from the V.I.P. balcony.

The locals didn't take this open presence kindly. The feeling around town was that Bad Boy was getting a little too comfortable.

One security guard who worked the door at many of the hot nightclubs that Combs and Wallace frequented warned that the Bad Boy Family was being much too visible in Los Angeles. The streets were watching. It was all well and good to ball out, and have your fun, but better to do it privately.

"You need to tell your boys to get the fuck out of here," the guard said one night. "This is still Suge's fuckin' town."

Combs didn't show any signs of slowing down, and neither did Wallace.

"L.A. fucked Big's head up," said Klept of Junior M.A.F.I.A. "Just by being out there, and seeing how much love you getting and all the gazillion bitches on some extra, extra shit. So that's why he got relaxed, not being on point."

While Wallace enjoyed his time by the pool, his Valentine's Day bliss didn't last.

Charli Baltimore had gotten suspicious. Any woman in Wallace's life eventually did. She looked all over the room searching for proof. She found it in Lil' Cease's discarded jeans: photos of Wallace with another woman.

Cease was asleep in his room when all hell broke loose. The phone woke him up. It was Biggie.

"Muthafucka, I told you to move the pictures, nigga! I'm not fuckin' with you no more. Why the fuck you don't listen?"

"What?" Cease asked, perplexed.

He took the elevator upstairs. D-Roc met him near the elevator.

"The police is here." D-Roc said.

"What happened?" Cease asked. Then he thought about it. He had changed when he was in Wallace's room and left his pants behind.

"Oh, shit."

The room was a mess. Wallace and Baltimore had had a blow-out. She threw jewelry of his out the window, including one of his rings. They had to check out.

When they got to another hotel Wallace answered the door. His shirt was off. And it was the first time he ever remembered Wallace ever really being mad at him.

"Yo, I'm not fuckin' with you, don't even come near me, nigga." He gave him the keys to another room, telling him to leave.

"It wasn't my fault," Cease said. "She went through my pockets. She violated."

Wallace's anger would pass. But as he once said, the last thing he ever wanted to lose was his temper.

Whatever his mood, he was up bright and early the next morning, Saturday, February 15. There was plenty of work to be done. His primary reason for coming out west two weeks before the Soul Train Music Awards was to shoot a video for his album's first single, "Hypnotize." The clip, which would take three days and $700,000 to shoot, was more than just a promotional spot to help sell records. It was a loud, expensive statement that let the world know, "I'm back and bigger than ever."

In 1996, Death Row had upped the ante for hip hop videos with Hype Williams's breathtaking "California Love," a post-apocalyptic vision of Dr. Dre, Tupac, and a band of freakazoids roaring through a desert wasteland as hip hop road warriors. The clip pushed hip hop visuals even further than Hype had taken things with his earlier videos like Wu-Tang Clan's "Can It Be All So Simple" and Biggie's "Big Poppa." It was more than just using wide lenses, slow dissolves, dramatic lighting, and an expensive wardrobe. Hype realized that rap videos could aspire to the level of Michael Jackson's groundbreaking "Thriller" video. They could be mini-movies in their own right with their own narratives and moods. His video for R. Kelly's "Down Low," based on Tony Scott's *Revenge,* was a massive hit on MTV. Rappers were already making audio movies—having visual narratives that were as compelling as their songs was the next logical step.

Though he wasn't as famous as Williams, Paul Hunter was moving music videos in a similarly cinematic direction. Hunter was a young video director who had just started making a name for himself. His clip for Aaliyah's "One in a Million" caught Combs's attention and he hired Hunter to direct "Can't Nobody Hold Me Down." With its underwater photography, unique lighting, and dazzling group performance shots, the video helped the audience get used to a concept that, at first, seemed rather far-fetched: Combs as a credible rapper.

With "Hypnotize," Hunter had twice the budget and an even bigger agenda: to make one of the most exciting rap videos of all time. The idea hit him as he was walking through JFK Airport's '60s-style TWA terminal. His cell phone rang.

"'Sup, Paul. It's Puff. You got any ideas, 'cause we ready to go."

Hunter paused. He didn't have a clue. But he had to come up with something quick. He looked around the terminal and saw people walking through a tunnel.

"Yeah," Hunter said. "I see you and Big driving down a tunnel. Backwards."

"Sounds hot," said Combs. "What else?"

"Hypnotize," as Hunter and Combs conceived it, was to be a mini-adventure movie, full of intrigue and high-speed pursuits worthy of James Bond. Biggie and Puffy dodging bad guys on foot, being followed by cars with tinted windows, black helicopters chasing their speedboat. The two would elude danger until they finally reached a players' hideout, featuring beautiful women of all shapes and shades—even a few mermaids swimming in a fish tank behind the couch. Throw in some dancers, a live panther, and Biggie doing the shake and shimmy—somehow it would all make sense.

One month and three quarters of a million dollars after that cell-phone call, Hunter, with a Steadicam on his shoulder, filmed Puff, Big, and some women on a speedboat just off Santa Monica. The opening scene of the video called for Wallace and Combs to be lamping Big Willie–style with a couple of beautiful females, sharing a champagne toast, the last quiet moment in the video before black helicopters thunder down from above and ruin the mood. Everything had to be perfect, from the currents of the waves and the cloud cover, to the timing of the shots, or else hundreds of thousands of dollars in rentals and personnel would go to waste.

There was trouble from the start.

Earlier that afternoon, when Wallace had shown up at the set with D-Roc and

**The Notorious
B.I.G. brandishing
some hardware in
a promotional
shoot at Conart
design studios in
Los Angeles.**

the rest of his peoples, they scared the shit out of the boat's captain. He took one look at the tall and (in his mind) ominous black men smoking weed and exchanging profanities, and suddenly he didn't want to rent out the boat anymore.

"He changed his mind," recalled Hunter. "He saw a lot of rappers, it was loud, and it wasn't as organized as he wanted it to be. He started talking about safety rules and stuff like that."

A tall, lanky presence with long dreadlocks and a calm demeanor, Hunter handled the situation with the captain the best he could.

"We just kind of Bogarted him," Hunter said. "We said, 'We're not going to let you out of this deal,' and we got on the boat."

Soon the boat was on the open water. Moving fast, skipping across the waves like a flat stone. Slapping the bottom of the boat against the water so hard, Hunter could barely keep the camera focused while Biggie rapped along to the playback. Biggie was driving the boat, just after finishing off a huge blunt. "I was praying to God that we didn't run into a rock or another boat."

But at least a trained sailor was onboard. Sort of. Despite his misgivings about the whole adventure, the captain stood next to Wallace and Combs, protecting his boss's investment. But Combs didn't want to see him in the shot. "Puff put his hand on top of the guy's head, and he literally started strong-arming him to his knees," Hunter said. "He was down on his knees, driving the boat. You could see him pop his head over the steering wheel to see if we were gonna crash into somebody."

There was no crash. On Sunday, the production moved to dry land, but it was no less nerve-wracking. One shot involved Wallace and Combs in a convertible being pursued by men on black motorcycles who were shooting at them. While Wallace rapped, Puffy drove the car into the Spring Street tunnel in reverse. Hunter was excited by the fact that the same tunnel was one of the locations used by Ridley Scott in *Blade Runner*.

"I said we're gonna make this look like a movie," Hunter said. "We approached it like the big boys, but we had to do it in a lot less time."

Time was money, and Hunter ran a tight, highly organized production. Combs micromanaged everything from the clothing to the action. Meanwhile Wallace mostly chilled with his homeboys in his trailer, smoked weed, and looked for food to eat. Hunter remembers him as being very cooperative, questioning nothing about where the camera was or what was expected of him. "He just seemed like a funny guy," Hunter said. "The most intimidating presence was the people around him. One on one he was like a soft teddy bear. All he wanted was a bowl of cereal and some fruit and he was happy."

Production on "Hypnotize" wrapped early Tuesday, February 18, but not before filming all Monday evening on a Culver City soundstage teeming with female extras, sexy dancers, an animal trainer, and attractive swimmers wearing huge rubber fish tails.

Around 8:40 P.M., between camera setups, Hunter and his assistant directors kept things moving as quickly as they could on a rap video set. After all, call time had been four hours ago, and things were only just getting started.

The female extras stood on the sidelines trying their best to look pert and pretty, some of them complaining about standing around all day and how it wasn't fair that they weren't getting fed. The professional dancers worked on their routines. Choreographer Fatima Robinson gracefully put the girls through their paces, a seductive routine that fell somewhere between the Dance Theater of Harlem and Atlanta's famous strip club, Magic City. Cameramen, boom operators, gaffers, makeup artists, and other assorted crew members lined up to get some catered soul food (downwind from the extras who stood on the cold soundstage in cocktail dresses, looking hungrily at the spread). Combs huddled with Hunter, talking about the rest of the setups for the night, and asking for slight adjustments.

While all of this was happening, the real star of the show was wheeled onto the set.

"ALL RIGHT!" said a beefy white trainer, flanked by two assistants and carrying a walkie-talkie. "Nobody approach the cat!"

The cat in question was a huge black leopard that went by the name of Crystal. Hunter couldn't get the panther that Combs had requested, but any large jungle cat would suffice in a pinch. Crystal stared with confusion as everyone on the set looked toward her cage with shock, backing up. She sauntered around the cage, reacting subtly to the beat of "Hypnotize" as the song played in the background.

D-Roc stood next to G and Lil' Cease, watching the cat being wheeled on the set. D-Roc chuckled, turning toward Cease.

"Whose idea was it for this shit?"

"Puff's," said a nonchalant voice behind them.

The three of them turned around and saw Wallace, sitting in a director's chair near the monitors where Hunter and Combs were looking at some footage. The tiny monitor showed Wallace, leaning on his cane, rhyming, and an identically dressed Combs, making rhythmic hand gestures, dancing in front of the Panaflex camera moving up and down on a SuperTechnocrane with a telescopic lens.

Wallace soaked in the scene, his chair parked directly in front of the cage. The two baddest black cats in the room stared at each other.

"The cat just adds ambiance, that's all," Wallace said.

"That's some ill shit," said Lil' Cease, his reddened, heavy-lidded eyes widening slightly with admiration.

Wallace turned toward Cease with a smile on his face. "You got to show the cat who's boss. That's all." He made eye contact with Crystal, still sauntering in her cage. "Lookit. This is my shit! They better let that cat know who's running this video."

Everyone within earshot laughed.

"I'm about to call my barber and have him cut my initials into his fur," said Wallace. "I'm trying to sell five million albums this time out, nigga. If I need to, I'll ride that cat like a horse."

One of the animal trainers nailed an O-ring into the ground and attached a long, heavy cable to it, pulling, making sure that the connection wouldn't give. The main trainer began talking to Hunter, who was trying to take it all in.

"You've got to keep the music playing," the trainer said. "Let her get used to it so she doesn't jump when you turn the sound up. I want to let her walk around a little bit, to settle down, to get comfortable."

Each assistant held one door to the cage open as the trainer walked in and attached the chain to Crystal's collar, leading her out.

"Quiet," he barked. "No sudden movements."

Wallace looked directly at the cat. He started twitching, making nothing but sudden movements, bugging his eyes to look crazy. He barked at the cat, taunting her. D-Roc and Lil' Cease laughed.

Once the trainer connected the cat to the O-ring, Combs and Wallace stood about five feet away. The dancers began moving in the background, and Hunter conferred with his cinematographer, getting their camera angles together. The trainer walked up to Wallace, handing him the chain that controlled the cat.

"The cable is actually holding on to the cat," the trainer explained. "She's stronger than you or I could imagine."

"I'm telling you, I can handle that," Wallace replied with schoolyard bravado. "That chain is for the safety of the cat. 'Cause I'm a wild nigga."

"What if it breaks loose?" the trainer asked.

"I ain't gonna run," Wallace replied. "I'm in no condition to run." He pointed to his leg and the cane for emphasis. "If you see me and the cat in the jungle and I run into the cat, help the cat."

While Wallace talked shit, the trainer threw the cat her favorite teddy bear. Quick as a flash, the cat snatched the bear in her powerful jaws, wagging her head from side to side.

"That's Puff," Wallace said, grinning and nodding toward D-Roc and Cease, who were cracking up. "That's how it's gonna snatch up Puff if he gets too close."

Combs, who was standing closer to the cat than Wallace, had a slightly different expression.

"Playback!" yelled Hunter.

The music kicked in, and Wallace started rapping. He delivered his lines with even more ferocity and energy than he'd shown before the cat's arrival, as if inspired by the big jungle creature. Puff, who had been dancing in his charismatic camera-hogging fashion before, became noticeably more subdued in the cat's presence. He danced behind Wallace, close to him, but was careful not to step on the cat's tail.

As soon as the take was over, and Combs moved away from the cat, laughter erupted on the sidelines from both friends and crew.

"Puff's shook," Wallace said, laughing. "I told you the cat ain't like you!"

Wallace strolled onto the stage, flanked by Combs and the Bad Boy quartet 112. They were greeted with a loud unpleasant sound—boos coming from the cheap seats. "What up, Cali?" Wallace said, smiling.

With the video in the can, there wasn't much for Wallace to do out west but hang out, make a few radio appearances, both in Los Angeles and up north in the San Francisco Bay area, and make promotional plans for the next few months.

When they came back to Los Angeles, Wallace and D-Roc went by the tattoo parlor on Sunset Boulevard, near the House of Blues, where they got tattoos of the Twenty-third Psalm etched into their forearms. It was Big's first and only tattoo, and "a whole lotta work" for the tattoo artist Mark Mahoney, who had just finished with Shaquille O'Neal. Big had recorded a song with Shaq for the ball player's album. O'Neal invited Wallace to his record release party. They talked briefly about B.I.G. even being in Los Angeles, and the tension in the air.

"Yo, man," O'Neal said, "be careful."

Don Pooh could have used that advice himself. On Friday March 7, the night of the 11th Annual Soul Train Awards, Don Pooh, who now worked for Violator Management, overseeing the career of the female rapper Foxy Brown, had his mind on a million other things besides watching the L.A. traffic.

While he talked on his cell phone leaving the Fatburger on La Cienega across from his hotel, the Nikko (now Le Meridien), Pooh ran past one car without seeing another one coming from the opposite direction. His body crashed against the windshield and he rolled over the hood of the car onto the concrete, a broken bone sticking out of his leg.

"I swear to God, there was this lady all in white, staring down on me while I was flat on my back, holding my hand, telling me that it's gonna be all right. It's gonna be all right. I turned and she was gone," remembered Pooh.

Pooh was admitted to Cedars-Sinai Hospital, located within walking distance of the hotel. Violator Management head Chris Lighty paid for Pooh's admission by putting the bill on his platinum corporate American Express Card, and Pooh was rushed into surgery, where pins were inserted into his shattered leg. Hours later, while he lay in his hospital bed, the phone rang in Pooh's room. It was Wallace.

"What the fuck? You trying to break yourself up, man?" Wallace joked over the phone. "I just broke my legs too, man. What, you want to have a cane just like I do?"

The two friends reminisced about good times and caught up with each other's recent movements. Wallace told Pooh how excited he was about the new album.

"I'm trying to focus this time around," Wallace told him. "I'm really trying to do it. World tour, the whole nine. I'm just trying to be real humble, man, and just give it my all." He told Pooh to get better, and promised him, "we're gonna get out there and we're gonna do this, y'knowhatumsayin'?"

Wallace started his reelection campaign as the "playa president" of hip hop that night, using his *Soul Train* appearance the way a politician does a convention. Wallace was there to present an award to Toni Braxton for Best R&B/Soul Album. With no Tupac and no Suge, no one anticipated anything like the drama that had happened the previous year.

Wallace's name was called and he strolled onto the stage, flanked by Combs and the Bad Boy R&B quartet 112. They were greeted with a loud unpleasant sound. Through the magic of television, the murmur sounded like applause to the home audience. But inside the Shrine Auditorium, there was no doubt—those were boos coming from the cheap seats. That's where the general public sits, the people who had to pay to come to the show. Some of them threw up hand signs, their fingers intertwined to form a *W*, representing "Westside."

"What up, Cali?" Wallace said.

He was showered with more boos, but ignored them. He smiled at the audience, not looking at all as if he anticipated anything bad. His eyes glimmered with that same confident, sarcastic expression that was his trademark, especially when he was in situations like that, outnumbered by playa haters. It was the same face that all politicians, from Richard Nixon to Bill Clinton, have used in front of hostile crowds, never letting them know that their disapproval bothered the candidate in any way whatsoever.

Stop playing, Wallace's expression said. *You know you love me.*

A few hours later, in his suite at the Westwood Marquis, Wallace was still in a playful mood. He sat with his driver Gregory "G" Young, who ordered food for both of them. D-Roc popped his head in for a minute, but G was hanging the tightest tonight. He and Wallace watched the time-delayed telecast, waiting to see how the tense appearance looked on TV.

As usual Big had jokes. About himself. The other presenters. Everybody.

"Maxwell is such a smooth muthafucka, boy, you know he got to be from Brooklyn," Wallace said as G laughed. "I bet you he be getting all them exotic bitches, too."

Wallace looked beat, but of course their work was not finished. Room service had delivered a sausage pizza, which was resting on top of his bowling ball paunch as he leaned back in an easy chair.

"I'm supposed to be in the studio at ten tonight," he said. "But I'm kinda tired and want to relax and shit."

Wallace was to go record his vocals for the Bad Boy CEO's forthcoming album *Hell Up in Harlem*. One song, set to a sample of the theme from *Rocky*, was called "Victory." The other, built around a Barry White break, was an ode to hundred-dollar bills titled "It's All About the Benjamins." Wallace was supposed to write both his and Puff's verses for "Victory," putting down a reference vocal for Puff to record over later. Then he would lay his verse for "Benjamins" and be out. The plan was for him to come back to the hotel, grab a quick nap, then go to the airport in time for an 11 A.M. flight to London to kick off the international press tour. That was the plan anyway. None of the bigwigs from Arista, who had set the whole thing up, knew that he wasn't going.

"I canceled that shit," Wallace said. "I just ain't fucking with it," he offered as an explanation. "I don't want to go to Europe right now. The food is horrible. I know I'm supposed to be mature and want to try different things and sample different lifestyles, but I just ain't in the mood for that shit right now. I just finished my album. It's about to drop in two weeks. I'm loving Cali and I've been out here a month, and I don't want to go nowhere."

Even if he wanted to, some of his road dogs didn't have passports with them. There was no way he was going out there without his full team. He smiled, took a bite from his pizza and a swig of Sprite. His eyes remained locked on the TV.

"The weather is positive, the women is positive, and the weed is positive." G and some of the other guys in the room chuckled. "That's why I came out here, to kick back and relax. Too much snow at home."

Keith Sweat came on the television screen, and Wallace smiled. "That nigga is dope," he says. "I love that nigga Keith Sweat. Wendy Williams on Hot 97 said that nigga is 41 years old. For real, Keith is the smoothest 41-year-old nigga I ever seen in my life."

Wallace was getting older himself. He was now the father of two children.

"What's being a father like?" I asked.

"Cool," he said, "but I can't really do it the way I want to do it, 'cause I'm mad busy and shit. But I want to wake up with my kids, get 'em ready for school and take 'em to school. I want to participate in all that shit."

He sat back, munched on his pizza, and cracked a few more jokes, waiting to see himself on the screen. Did he ever get sick of seeing himself on TV?

"Hell no!" Wallace said. "I'm like damn, am I big enough on screen? I need more shine. I want to do a little sitcom or something. I got a little personality. I think I could do something like that." He'd already appeared on a couple of TV shows and read for a film, but he was sure there would be time for that later.

"What's the biggest misconception you think people have of you?" I asked.

"Probably thinking I had anything to do with that Tupac shit," Wallace said. "Fuck it. If the muthafuckas want to hate me because they think I did something, they probably ain't the right people to be fucking with anyway. You know what I'm saying?"

"Could you have imagined, a year ago, that Tupac would be dead and Suge would be in jail?"

"I wouldn't, but I wouldn't have been surprised," Wallace said.

"There's certain ways you supposed to go about shit, you know what I'm saying? When you start making a whole bunch of money, you kind of got to, like, slow down. When your lifestyle is moving too fast, it's got to be on you to slow that shit down. You know what I'm saying?

"You just can't keep being pissy drunk, drinking liters of Hennessy and smoking two, three ounces of weed. You partyin', you fuckin'. And as soon as niggas say something slick, you beatin' they ass. Something's bound to happen, you know? You got to be big enough to say, fuck it.

"See, I was kind of flowing down that river, too, for a second," he explained. "But when I had that car accident I was in the hospital for, like, two, three months. And it kind of made me able to sit down and be like, 'Big, you're moving too fast. When you get on your feet, it's time for shit to change.'"

A few moments later, Wallace saw himself on the screen. He was expecting the boos, but the television broadcast polite applause. Anyway, the people in the room were more focused on the gold-plated diamond-encrusted likeness of Jesus hanging around Biggie's neck. It glimmered in the stage lights. "The Jesus piece is banging," Wallace said happily.

G laughed. "It's crazy, son!" he yelled. "It's off the hook!"

I asked Wallace if the piece was meaningful to him or just a cool accessory.

"I think that if there were more people that were into the Lord, there would be a lot less shit going on in the world," he said.

"I think people need to realize that these are tests and obstacles that everyone has to go through. A lot of niggas want to give up and do wrong, but they don't even think God is in their corner. What I respect about God is that he always steers you in the right direction."

He rolled up his sleeve to show me the fresh tattoo on his inside right forearm; in the form of a weathered parchment, were the verses of Psalm 23:

The Lord is my light and my salvation, whom shall I fear?
The Lord is the truth of my Life, of whom shall I be afraid?
When the wicked, even my enemies and foes, came upon me to bite my flesh
They stumbled and fell.

"This is how I feel sometimes," he said. "I want to feel like this all the time. That's why I went and got it, to reassure myself that no matter what goes wrong, no matter how bad shit is looking, God is right here. He's not behind you, He's right here. As long as you believe in Him and in His strength, all these jealous people, all these sharks, all these bitches that's out here to get niggas and expect you to fuck them and get on some real ghetto grimy shit and these haters—He'll stop all of that. He's gonna find you the road to take to avoid them."

Pushing his sleeve back down, Wallace continued. "What I'm doing right now is right. I'm taking care of my mother, my kids, and my peers. It's legal and I'm using a talent that I have to express myself and get paid, so it's only right that I follow the road without having to be involved in all of that extra shit."

It wasn't that Wallace was born again, or that he was about to join his mother at the Kingdom Hall any time soon. But he had matured. Now he didn't need anyone else's approval for the way he decided to live his life: not his record labels, not his boys—nobody's approval but God's. He had taken the time to evaluate his relationships and decide who was in his corner and who wasn't. Wallace felt that Puff was one of the people who had joined his true circle of trust.

"You know, I used to think Puff was just one of them happy-go-lucky niggas, man. I knew so many niggas like that in the drug game, get-rich bitch niggas. Mostly that's what I always thought he was. Like, one of them, niggas in the hustling game that just knew a bunch of people, was mad cool, and that used to happen to be in a neighborhood where there were a lot of crack heads. He had a little bit of money, put it into the drug game, and quickly he made a whole bunch of money. But he never went to war with no niggas. He never had problems with no niggas trying to take money from him, because he just was a cool nigga. That's how I always looked at Puff, like there's a cool nigga who just happened to be in the right position at the right time. Not really a fake nigga, but I knew he wasn't no street nigga. And at that time, when I first met him, street niggas meant everything to me."

Wallace paused for a moment as if he was reminiscing. "But after getting to know him, and know his views and his feelings about certain things, I know he was a real nigga. He's just an all-around cool dude, you know. He ain't no problem nigga. He just want to have fun. He was telling me today that he didn't even get to enjoy the success of Bad Boy, because when he first got everything, he was more on some 'People ain't think I could do it because I got fired from Uptown' shit, and he worked hard to prove himself. And then when we started blowing up, that's when the East Coast–West Coast stuff started jumping off. And now after all that shit is over with, he has to deal with all these rumors about him," Wallace said, making an allusion to the "Puff Daddy is gay" rumor that Wendy Williams spread on Hot 97 (a rumor that eventually cost her that job).

"It's too much," said Wallace, shaking his head in disbelief. Then he switched into manager mode. When Combs became an artist, Wallace agreed to steer his career. This role reversal was the ultimate expression of trust. "It's just an obstacle, that's what I told him. If you were to fold now, it would be a waste of time. Just hurdle over that shit."

Lil' Kim?

"Let Kim do her thing," he said. "She's cool when she wants to be, but she moves too fast, and she don't understand shit," he said. "I would hate for her career to be so hot in the beginning, but she hurt so many people and got so many people mad with her ways and actions on her way to the top that when it's time for her to do something else, everybody turn they back on her. She don't understand humbleness. I never had to deal with that with niggas. I tell niggas what to do and they do it. Kim's always like 'Why can't I do it this way?' So many headaches. I'm not asking your opinion, I'm telling you to do shit. 'Well, I don't want to do it that way,' and we argue and we bitch and she does it the way I want it, and the shit's a hit. And now she's on some new kick and I'm through with it. The album is out, let's move on."

Wallace exhaled. "I just wish I could be with someone like Cease. Not 'cause Cease does whatever a nigga tell him to do, but he respects my judgment. I would never tell you to do something that would have you fucked up. I only do it the right way, 'cause that's the only way I know how to do it. My track record is looking pretty good. She make it seem like I want to sabotage her shit."

Faith?

Wallace laughed. "We still ain't speaking, but it's all good. I can't chase her. She wants certain things that I can't do. But she brought a beautiful son into this world, so I'm happy about that. I can treasure that forever, even if your relationship doesn't work out. I always wanted a son and I got one, and that's all that matters to me."

Are you satisfied yet?

"Nah, I ain't have that yet," Wallace said. "I feel there are a few more dues to be paid on my part. I think there are a lot more lessons I need to learn, a lot more things I need to experience, a lot more places I need to go before I can finally say, okay, I've had my days." Wallace's voice grew more forceful. "A lot more shit has to go down. 'Cause I want a lot more."

"Niggas ain't the same young buck, 40-drinkin' niggas that don't give a fuck if they live or die. I want to see my kids get old. I want to go to my daughter's wedding. I want to go to their son's wedding. And you ain't gonna be able to see it wildin'."

Later that night, G, Wallace, Cease, and D-Roc went to see *Donnie Brasco* at a theater around the corner from the hotel. Wallace liked the movie, and by the time they drove over to the studio it was still in his head. It flowed right into his verse for "It's All About the Benjamins." One of the greatest rhymes of his career, it just leapt from his tongue: "I been had skills, Cristal spills / Hide bills in Brazil, about a mill' to ice grill / Make it hard to figure me, liquor be, kickin' me / In my asshole, undercover, 'Donnie Brasco.'"

By the time Wallace burned through the tracks he recorded that night, they didn't even have time to eat the Italian food they had ordered. They had a busy day coming up.

The last full day of Wallace's life, Saturday, March 8, was not unlike any other Saturday in his life. He called his mom and both his babies' mamas to ask about his kids, listened to the music he made in the studio the night before, and asked his peoples, "Where the party at?"

Voletta Wallace was surprised to learn that her son was still in Los Angeles, that he hadn't left for London yet. She told him that she was helping her sister Melva with her wedding rehearsal. They had to go buy champagne for the wedding. She inquired about his safety in the way mothers do, but Wallace assured her that he was fine, that they had plenty of security, both off-duty police officers as well as some guards they hired from a private firm. She would only later learn about the phone calls from New York warning her son that he wasn't safe.

One person who was pissed at Wallace for missing the London flight was his manager, Mark Pitts. Pitts and "D-Dot" Angelettie went by Wallace's room to pay him a visit.

"Big argument," Pitts recalled with a laugh. "Big, big argument. My argument was, dog, we gotta do this, man. We got to do this, dog. You're messing up. We gotta do this. And his thing was just, like, 'Yo, I'm tired. I need a break. I just finished my album. I don't really feel like getting on no plane right now to go overseas.'"

All wasn't lost. Wallace played them the rough mixes of the vocals he recorded the night before to "Victory" and "It's All About the Benjamins." Angelettie was completely blown away by Wallace's verse on "Victory," not just the way he slayed the intricate rhythm, but his lyrics as well. They were blazing from the opening line: "Hey yo, the sun don't shine forever / But as long as it's here baby girl then we can shine together."

"Oh my God," Angelettie said.

Later on, when Wallace talked with Lance "Un" Rivera, who was in New York, it was about how excited he was for March 25, the day that his album would come out, shock the world, unite the coasts, and make the radio stations play all Biggie, all the time.

When he was alone, he called Jan to ask about T'Yanna. They laughed and joked for a long time.

"I was looking sexy up there, right?" Wallace said of his appearance at the Soul Train Awards the night before.

"You know you looked good," said Jan. "You know you were looking sexy." Out of all the women in his life, she had never lost her love for Christopher. Never let herself become poisoned by the jealousy of competing with other women.

"He was telling me that he really missed T'Yanna a lot," Jan remembered. "He really wanted to see her. And that was kind of the first time I ever heard in his voice that he really missed her like that. I told him to call me when he touched down someplace steady where we could make arrangements. Someone could bring her out to see him."

When he talked with Faith, the conversation quickly deteriorated and they hung up on each other. Wallace finished his pizza, got dressed, and got ready to go out to party instead of going to the studio to lay more vocals.

"Biggie was supposed to go to the studio that day. He didn't want to go to the studio. He was like, 'I finished my album. I just want to celebrate with you,'" Combs remembered. "'I just want to have a good time. Let's go to this VIBE joint. Hopefully I can meet some people, let them know I want to do some acting.' That made me proud; he was thinking like a businessman."

G rounded up the troops and they hopped in the Suburban and drove to Andre Harrell's house, where Puff was staying. They didn't even get out of the car. They just sat there for a long time, blasting "Life After Death" at high volume, ready to go. It was about to be on.

The party, sponsored by VIBE magazine and Qwest Records, was at the Petersen Automotive Museum, located on the corner of Fairfax and Wilshire, a huge postmodern building with a car protruding from its side. It was billed as an official after-party for the Soul Train Awards—a post-awards weekend celebration. Because of the number of New York–based record industry heads in town and the fact that Bad Boy was out in force, it was also seen as an informal record release party for *Life After Death*. Every major celebrity, music executive, baller, and attractive female in town, it seemed, had an invitation.

VIBE's fashion editor (and eventual editor in chief) Emil Wilbekin had a bad feeling the moment he walked into the party. The son of Cincinnati's Commissioner of Buildings and Inspections, Wilbekin had been trained, from the time he was a kid, to always look for exits, to assess the safety of any building he entered. There were too many people inside this spot, and too many crowded out front.

"Escalators, up and down, glass railings, and no elevators," Wilbekin said. "The place was basically a death trap. I felt weird from the moment I walked in there."

Wilbekin peeped the room, nodded his head a few times, and decided to leave.

"I said, I'm not having this, and my friends were like, 'You can't leave, you work for the magazine, it's their party,' but I was like, 'I'm leaving,'" Wilbekin said. "I don't know why, but when my mind told me to leave, I left."

He missed a hell of a party.

Music was blowing, gin was flowing, ladies were dancing, and the fellas were just sitting on the sidelines saying wow. From the accounts of many who were there, it was one of the best parties they had ever seen.

"That party was sick," remembered Angelettie. "We must have popped eight hundred bottles of Cristal. Smoked about fifteen pounds of chronic. It was crazy. Women all over the place."

It was an especially sweet occasion for Angelettie, not only because he was hanging out with college buddies like Combs and Pitts at the pinnacle of their success, but also because of the way people were reacting to the songs that he produced. "The Theme" by Tracey Lee had the crowd moving. Then the DJ mixed in Big's new single "Hypnotize" and the place went bananas. The song played no less than eight times in a row. It was the first time Big had ever heard it in a club. He smiled brightly, his eyes hidden behind dark glasses.

Combs sucked in the atmosphere with a smile on his face. It was his kind of scene: model chicks and wall-to-wall celebrities from Wesley Snipes and Chris Tucker to Whitney Houston and Bobby Brown. It was the sort of party he dreamed about throwing when he and Angelettie were promoting at Howard, and now he was a guest of honor, the man profiting from every fifth record the DJ threw on the turntables. Combs was a good dancer, and normally he would have been out there on the floor showing off some moves, but he stayed next to Wallace the whole night by request.

"Big was like, 'Yo, Puff, tonight could you just sit here with me all night?'" Combs recalled later. "And I thought, cool, we're gonna sit here and kick it. We was drinking and listening to records, sitting at the table the whole night." Cane in hand, Wallace surveyed the room, his mood chipper. "He's proud of himself," Combs recalled, as if reliving the moment. "Talking about how stuff's gonna be better when his record comes out."

Hours before his death, Wallace was surrounded by admirers, drinking champagne toasts as his music rocked the party.

"I'm gonna make them love me," Wallace told Combs. "I can't wait till they hear that track 'Goin' Back to Cali' so they know I got nothing but love for them."

Faith Evans was at the party, too. She and Wallace made eye contact and barely nodded toward each other. Neither one said a word.

Def Jam founder Russell Simmons sat near Combs and Wallace.

"I was throwing paper at him, telling him how much I liked his record," remembered Simmons. "These girls were dancing for him, and he was just sittin' there, not even moving his cane. I wanted to be like him. He was so cool, so funny and calm."

As with many Los Angeles music industry parties, there were gang members from both the Crips and the Bloods in attendance. Among the guests were Dwayne "Keefee D" Davis and his nephew Orlando Anderson. The two men, reputed members of the Southside Crips, had been implicated in Tupac Shakur's shooting. DJ Quik was also there with a posse of Mob Piru Bloods from his Compton stomping grounds. Because no one was throwing up signs, who-riding, or otherwise attracting attention, few people thought anything strange was going on. The party was blazing, but from all accounts, drama-free.

But like all good things, the party came to an end. With almost 2,000 people overcrowding the place, and 200 more clamoring to get in downstairs, fire marshals shut it down at 12:35 A.M. The word was already out: those in the know were supposed to head over to the house that Interscope executive Steve Stoute had rented in the Hollywood Hills. This would be a "real" party, a low-key event where everyone could chill without all the hangers-on and autograph seekers.

As people filed out by escalator and elevator, Combs and Wallace hung back momentarily, slowed by Wallace's bum leg. They posed for a few quick photos, and, five minutes later, made it downstairs to the GMC Chevy Suburbans that they had been renting all month from Budget Rent-A-Car of Beverly Hills. A few weeks earlier he had stopped by Beverly Hills Motoring to check out their customized bullet-proof car armor, but did not buy it.

Puffy climbed into a white Suburban with three of his bodyguards at the head of the motorcade. Behind him was a forest-green Suburban with G driving, Wallace riding shotgun, and D-Roc and Cease sitting in the back. Puffy's other bodyguard and close associate, Paul Offord, drove behind Wallace's vehicle in a black Chevy Blazer, flanked by an off-duty LAPD officer.

A few cars back, Deric "D-Dot" Angelettie, Mark Pitts, and rapper Tracey Lee shared a white limousine.

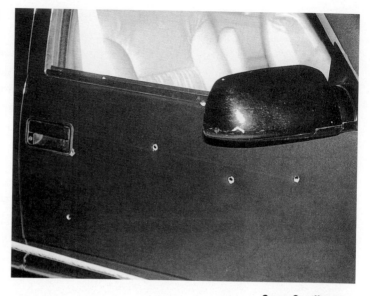

Seven 9-millimeter slugs ripped through the GMC Suburban's door and window, striking Wallace in the chest and abdomen.

"It just happened that the limo that me and Mark were in was facing the opposite direction of where the Suburbans was, and we couldn't make a U-turn," Angelettie remembered. "We had to go out the driveway of the museum, and the police had the blocks blocked off, so we had to drive the long way around and catch up with them and meet the cars going this way."

Inside Wallace's car, G turned on the CD player as they pulled out. "Goin' Back to Cali" started booming, and everyone in the Suburban smiled. The song sounded good. "Y'all niggas is a mess thinkin' I'm gon' stop / Giving L.A. props," Biggie rhymed. "All I got is beef with those that violate me / I shall annihilate thee."

Puffy's Suburban, still in the lead as the group made their way to Fairfax, crossed Wilshire Boulevard to make a left, passing through the yellow light just in the nick of time. Wallace's car, heading north on Fairfax, was stopped at the light in the left turn lane.

Soon after Wallace's green Suburban stopped at the light, a black Impala pulled up to the right side of the dark green Suburban Wallace was sitting in.

Wallace turned his head, expecting to see some fans or somebody he knew, asking where he was rolling to; better yet, it could be some fly females wanting to join the caravan.

From his vantage point behind Wallace in the backseat, Lil' Cease could see the man who was driving the car. A black man with a receding hairline wearing a bow tie and crisp shirt. Cease focused on the man's hands. His left hand on the steering wheel, and his right hand holding something else. He couldn't quite tell what it was until he stuck it out the window.

It was a .40-caliber automatic.

BOOM!

People standing outside the Petersen Automotive Museum, many of them black and Latino, knew the drill the second the first shot rang out. Anyone who'd ever gone to a few hip hop parties knew the drill. It wasn't the Fourth of July, so no one had firecrackers. Only one thing could make that crisp, sharp sound. Everyone ducked down.

BOOM!

Lil' Cease and D-Roc ducked in the backseat, seeing the muzzle flash, trying to pull Wallace down in his seat.

BOOM!

Combs's white Suburban screeched to a halt and everyone inside ducked down.

BOOM!

Mark Pitts, D-Dot Angelettie, and Tracey Lee were chilling in the back of their limo as it took the long way around Wilshire behind the museum to the back of Fairfax. They ducked down instinctively when they heard the shots.

BOOM!

Offord and the off-duty cop, blocked by the white Toyota Land Cruiser, could hear the shots but couldn't exactly see what happened. Offord slammed on the brakes.

BOOM!

The dark Impala moved north, toward Wilshire, making a right on Ogden.

BOOM!

Cease and G scrambled out of the car and started pointing in different directions. "I was right behind Big," said Cease. "I jumped out of the car, searching myself to see if I'm shot. But the only one they hit was Big."

D-Roc remained in the car. Frozen. Looking into Christopher Wallace's eyes.

His friend looked back at him without saying a word. He couldn't. He was breathing hard. Trembling like a leaf. His tongue sticking out as he fought for air. Slumping toward the steering wheel.

"Biggie was just looking at me with this real shocked expression," D-Roc said, "like he couldn't believe it."

D-Roc looked up. Puffy had made it back across the intersection and was at the passenger side door, which was now riddled with bullet holes.

"Big!" he said frantically, pulling open the door. "BIG!"

"Where's the hospital!" Combs screamed. "WHERE'S THE HOSPITAL!" It was impossible to tell how badly Wallace was hurt, but they knew not to wait for an ambulance.

Puffy's driver Kenneth Story replaced G in the driver's seat, Puff hopped in the back, and the car roared off toward Cedars-Sinai Medical Center, which was less than five minutes away. They ran lights and honked horns, turning the Suburban into an ambulance.

By the time D-Dot and Mark Pitts's limo made it around the block, car horns were honking. D-Dot rolled down the window.

"Someone shot your man, Puff. And Big, too," Angelettie remembered somebody saying. Already the misinformation was spreading.

The limo peeled out as Pitts and Angelettie made an educated guess that their friends must have gone to Cedars-Sinai.

Their limo reached the hospital a few minutes later, and pandemonium had broken out. People from the party stood out in front of the ER entrance crying.

Stevie J asked everyone in the room to hold hands with him and get down on their knees and pray.

Los Angeles Times

MONDAY, MARCH 10, 1997
COPYRIGHT 1997 / THE TIMES MIRROR COMPANY / CCI / 88 PAGES

Notorious B.I.G., left, leaves a party with producer Sean Combs shortly before being shot to death.
Associated Press

Gangsta Rap Performer Notorious B.I.G. Slain

■ **Crime:** Star is shot to death in vehicle after leaving music industry party in the Mid-Wilshire district.

By ERIC LICHTBLAU, CHUCK PHILIPS, and CHEO HODARI COKER
TIMES STAFF WRITERS

Rap music star Notorious B.I.G. was shot to death along Museum Row in Los Angeles' Mid-Wilshire district early Sunday as he left a music industry party, a brazen attack that marked the second drive-by murder of a gangsta rap celebrity in the last six months.

B.I.G., born Christopher Wallace, was leaving the party at the Petersen Automotive Mu-

seum about 12:30 a.m. when police believe someone in a dark car pulled up alongside the passenger side of the GMC Suburban in which he was riding and fired several shots inside.

The 24-year-old rapper, who had earned rave reviews and big sales in giving voice to the violent edge of the streets, was declared dead at Cedars-Sinai Medical Center at 1:15 a.m. His body was identified Sunday afternoon at the Los Angeles coroner's office by his ex-wife, singer Faith Evans, and his

Please see RAPPER, A16

LORI SHEPLER / Los Angeles Times

■ The rap artist sat for an interview last Friday, above, and said he was changing his ways. He died early Sunday morning. **F1**
■ Robert Hilburn writes that the consensus is that it's time to take the *gangsta* out of rap-if only it were that simple. **A16**

Clinton [...] of China [...] Plan, Ai[...]

■ **Campaign finance:** GO[...] possible funneling of illegal [...] U.S. lawmakers. Feinstein s[...]

By DAVID G. SAVAGE and RICH[...]

WASHINGTON—Past and pre[...] Sunday that the White House's up[...] of a possible Chinese governme[...] congressional members, but Repu[...] knew about it widens the fund-rais[...]

"I certainly wasn't advised o[...] that. And the president wasn'[...] advised of that," said former Chie[...] of Staff Leon E. Panetta, who lef[...] office in January. Current Chief o[...] Staff Erskine Bowles said the FB[...] did tell some "mid-level staffers'[...] at the National Security Counci[...] about the intelligence warnings[...] but they did not pass the informa[...] tion to higher-ups.

The question of when the Whit[...] House first heard of the allege[...] attempt by China to influence th[...] U.S. political system could prov[...] crucial, Republicans said. Th[...] Democratic National Committe[...] has already been obliged to return[...] thousands in questionable cam[...] paign contributions because the[...] came from fund-raisers wit[...] business links to China, such a[...] former Commerce Department o[...] ficial John Huang; Johnny Chie[...] Chuen Chung, a Torranc[...] businessman; and Yah Lin "Char[...] lie" Trie, a former Arkansas res[...] taurateur.

Last year, the FBI briefed a[...] least six members of Congress[...] including Sen. Dianne Feinstein[...] (D-Calif.), after receiving evi[...] dence that Beijing had targeted[...] them to receive laundered cam[...]

Coming just six months after Shakur's death, Wallace's murder was front-page news.

Combs was on his knees praying. Faith was there. A doctor in a white coat walked toward them, slowly.

Pitts went inside, while D-Dot stood off to the side, comforting a female friend.
"NOOOOOOOOOOOOOO!"

D-Dot rushed through the doors of the ER. It was Lil' Cease, rolling around on the floor. Screaming. Holding his head in anguish.

Seven 9-millimeter slugs had ripped into Wallace's chest and abdomen, causing massive injuries and internal bleeding. Doctors tried to resuscitate him for twenty minutes, but he never regained consciousness.

Christopher George Letore Wallace was dead. It was 1:15 A.M. He was 24 years old.

Outside the hospital, the police had cordoned off the green Suburban. The press was already there, with television cameras. Flashbulbs were going off.

The cops on the scene, aware that the Bad Boy entourage included off-duty officers, started asking questions. Why didn't anyone call an ambulance? Why didn't anyone get, at the very least, a partial license plate number? Why didn't anyone pursue either the shooter or the white Land Cruiser? Were the moonlighting officers trying to avoid embarrassing revelations about their after-hours gig?

Combs, Pitts, and D-Roc sat there, passing around a cell phone. Which one of them was going to make the call, the hardest phone call that any one of them ever had to make? Mark Pitts passed the phone to D-Roc.

"How am I gonna call this man's mom?" he asked in despair. "I grew up with this kid."

But D-Roc knew he had no choice.

The phone rang, reverberating loudly through 226 St. James. Voletta Wallace reached up, clicked on the lamp by the nightstand next to her bed, and looked at the clock. It was 5:21 A.M.

Something was wrong.

"Hello?" she said.

"Ms. Wallace?" It was Damien. She heard screams and cries in the background. "Ms. Wallace?" She knew Damien was a hard rock. The kind of Brooklyn-bred ruffian her son looked up to because he was hard and loyal. The silent type who wasn't prone to outbursts of emotion. And she could hear him on the other line. Sobbing.

"Ms. Wallace?"

Voletta Wallace dropped the phone. She didn't need to hear anything else.

THE LONG KISS GOODNIGHT

CHAPTER 9

> **“**Laugh now cry later,
> I rhyme greater than the average playa hater,
> and spectators buy my CD twice.
> They be like, Damn he's nice . . .**”**

Don Pooh never got that early morning phone call on March 9.

Though he was in the same Los Angeles hospital as Wallace, his friends didn't want him to hear such startling news from just anyone, especially given his delicate condition. They wanted to break it to him gently, for him to hear the news from "family." So while Pooh slept, someone called downstairs and requested that they suspend phone service to Pooh's room for the night, thinking that they were doing him a favor.

They forgot about the television in his room.

"I wake up, and the television news is on," remembered Pooh, "and I hear this voice say 'Brooklyn rapper slain. Details after we come back.' I'm figuring it's an up-and-coming rapper that lived in L.A., who moved from New York and got in a fight with someone at a club and got killed. The last thing I'm thinking is that it's a big star."

But when the news came back, he saw a picture of Christopher Wallace. Then they flashed the roped-off crime scene at the Petersen Automotive Museum, then the bullet-ridden green Suburban, then images of people crying outside of the emergency room of Cedars-Sinai Medical Center.

"Nurse! NURSE!"

Pooh picked up the receiver. The line was dead. He threw the phone at the wall. Then the bottle of water on the table near his bed. Then the utensils. He had a full-blown temper tantrum.

"Come here! Come here!"

The nurse walked in.

"They just killed my friend! Turn on my fucking phone! They killed my friend!"

The nurse looked at him with a mournful expression. Tears rolled down his cheeks. It didn't really matter who he called. It wasn't going to change what had happened.

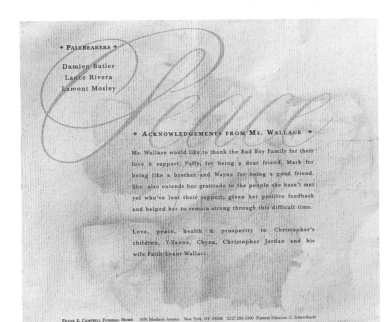

+ PALLBEARERS +

Damien Butler
Lance Rivera
Lamont Mosley

+ ACKNOWLEDGEMENTS FROM MS. WALLACE +

Ms. Wallace would like to thank the Bad Boy Family for their love & support, Puffy, for being a dear friend, Mark for being like a brother and Wayne for being a good friend. She also extends her gratitude to the people she hasn't met yet who've lent their support, given her positive feedback and helped her to remain strong through this difficult time.

Love, peace, health & prosperity to Christopher's children, T'Yanna, Chyna, Christopher Jordan and his wife Faith Evans-Wallace.

FRANK E. CAMPBELL FUNERAL HOME   1076 Madison Avenue   New York, NY 10028   (212) 288-3500   Funeral Director: C. Schweikardt

Wallace's friends and family gathered to pay their final respects in a spirit of peace.

"I was supposed to meet up with him that night," Luke recalled. "Me and Snoop was in the studio in L.A. doing a song. That was the first time we ever really linked up after our little controversy. So we're in the studio doing our song and Biggie was at the party and we kept in contact with each other. I was gonna take Snoop and them over there with me after we finished recording." They expected it to be a quick session, but they never did complete the song.

"Snoop had a police guy as his security," said Campbell. "That's who told us what happened. The police guy heard over his radio that Big had gotten shot at this party. And we was like, Naw, man. And that's when the phones started ringing. Everybody's phone started ringing at the same time: the studio phone, Snoop's phone, my phone, every damn phone in the place. All I remember is a bunch of goddamn phones ringing. And people saying, 'Big got shot.' It shut that whole session down. We was all in shock."

By the time Voletta Wallace and Jan's plane landed at LAX, the rest of the country had been talking about Wallace's death all morning and afternoon. The mood that carried the day was numb, mournful shock.

Los Angeles's Power 106 and New York City's Hot 97, America's two biggest urban radio stations, both owned by Emmis Communications, did a live, nationwide simulcast. It was both a tribute to the Notorious B.I.G. and a discussion of the previous night's events. The radio stations were inundated with phone calls—everyone from artists to local fans. Some crying, some talking about the good times, all of them decrying the violence and senseless nature of it all.

"We need to talk intelligently and tell people there is no rivalry," said Dr. Dre, calling in from L.A.

"I'm sick of this shit," said a mournful Q-Tip from New York. "We need to wake up. If we say we're ready to die, we're going to die."

By the next morning, candles and flowers marked the spot where Wallace was shot in front of the automotive museum. People in his Brooklyn neighborhood were holding vigils on Fulton and St. James. A graffiti artist in the Bronx was already working on a mural in Wallace's honor. Some record stores started moving copies of *Ready to Die* to the front of their record stores, and called BMG record distributors to order additional copies of *Life After Death,* anticipating even higher sales of what was already supposed to be the hottest album of the quarter. Tempo Records, located across the street from USC on Hoover Street, planned to double its initial order of the album.

"We did the same thing when Miles Davis and Tupac died," said the store's manager, Raymond Comeaux. "Whenever an artist dies, we pack the shelves."

At the downtown offices of the *Los Angeles Times,* where I was working as a staff writer, the Metro and Calendar sections had an early morning meeting, dividing up the coverage. As quickly as the various stories came together for Monday's paper, the more people we talked to, the more we realized how little we actually knew. There were conflicting stories on everything from the number of shots fired, to the make, color, and type of vehicle reported fleeing the scene, to the direction they traveled in. The code of the streets was in effect: Those who knew wouldn't tell, and those who told didn't know.

Despite the attendance of over two thousand guests, hundreds of whom were standing outside of the venue networking, macking, or waiting for their cars at the time of shooting, no one saw "anything." As LAPD Detective Raymond Futami told the *L.A. Times,* "I think that there's a lot of people who are not coming forward. I'm sure there's a little bit of an intimidation factor . . . because of the reputation of some of the people who are involved in this case." The same thing that happened with the Tupac Shakur case was about to happen with Wallace's murder investigation, lots of speculation but little cooperation.

As we got off the phones with our various sources, the different water-cooler theories abounded: It was a drive-by performed by a crazed fan who blamed Big for Tupac's murder in Las Vegas. It was a professional hit, orchestrated by Suge Knight, the telltale sign being that it came six months to the day after Tupac was shot—surely that couldn't be a coincidence. Then there were reports of Combs hiring gang members as part of his security detail, most likely Crips, since many Bloods were already aligned with Suge Knight. The theory—which Puff vehemently denied—was that these members killed Wallace over money that either he or Combs owed to the gang. The hit was actually meant for Combs, who had enemies on both coasts who, as he would later rap famously on "Mo Money, Mo Problems," would "rather see me die than to see me fly."

The problem was that none of the theories, however plausible or implausible, could be proven. The only thing that was certain was that two of the best and most popular rappers in history were dead, and both of them, Geminis born within weeks of each other, were murdered in nearly identical fashion. There have been other tragic moments in music, like the 1959 plane crash that claimed the lives of the Big Bopper, Buddy Holly, and Richie Valens; or in 1970 when

Janis Joplin, Jim Morrison, and Jimi Hendrix died within months of each other; and, more recently, John Lennon's 1980 assassination in front of the Dakota in Manhattan. Even the 1994 suicide of Kurt Cobain, whom Biggie once called "that crack head who killed himself." But this was different. These guys were from the street. They had been shot at before, and in Tupac's case, shot numerous times. And even though both swore that they had mellowed out and were heading for new frontiers—Tupac, with his engagement to Kidada Jones and his quiet moves toward leaving Death Row, and Wallace with his children, new album, and new mature perspective—they were now both dead.

Who was responsible? And why? Were the motives as nakedly obvious as revenge? Or was something much more sinister afoot? Both of these rappers were franchise players, big moneymakers for their respective labels—both of which were under investigation by federal agents. Who would possibly benefit from two such deaths?

The scuttlebutt in the street was that Death Row must have been involved somehow, no matter how tangentially. There were whispers about how Suge

Busta Rhymes arrives at Wallace's memorial service on March 18, 1997.

Knight and his associates blamed Combs for Jake Robles's death in Atlanta in 1995. People said the Bad Boy family was living it up too publicly in Los Angeles, almost reveling in the fact that Shakur was gone and that Knight was incarcerated. No one had any proof, but anyone with a chair in a barbershop had an opinion on the matter.

Norris Anderson, who was running Death Row while Suge Knight began serving his sentence, quickly deflected blame for the situation when questioned over the phone by Philips and Williams. His statement appeared in the initial *L.A. Times* coverage of the event on March 10.

"It's ludicrous for anyone to blame Death Row," claimed Anderson. "Snoop and Biggie and Puffy have been in the press recently trying to squash all the media madness. This is a terrible tragedy. Death Row knows how bad something like this can feel. It happened in our own backyard with Tupac just a few months ago. My condolences go out to Biggie's family. I feel horrible for them. This killing has got to stop."

Ms. Wallace, flanked by Jan and Faith, stood in the Los Angeles county morgue and officially identified the body of Christopher Wallace, signing off on the death certificate. None of them had gotten any sleep. Jan was in such shock that by the time she unpacked her bag, she realized that everything she packed was useless—she had been on automatic pilot. Faith cried silent, bitter tears, realizing how frivolous their last arguments were, and guilty about the fact that they saw each other at the party but didn't even speak.

Ms. Wallace was staring at her little boy. His mouth was slightly open. That mouth would never smile again, never tell another joke, never say, "Come on, Ma." She wanted to cry but she couldn't. She was too angry.

Who did this to Christopher? And why?

She had lots of questions but there was much work to be done. There was a funeral to arrange. There were grandchildren who would need to have the concept of death explained. She had to get out of Los Angeles. She had to go home.

First, Wallace's body had to be transferred from Los Angeles back home to New York. Clive Davis selected the prestigious Frank E. Campbell funeral home on the Upper East Side of Manhattan to handle the arrangements (which were paid for by Arista Records). As the place where last rites were held for Rudolph Valentino, Judy Garland, John Lennon, and Jacqueline Kennedy Onassis, Campbell's knew how to offer privacy for very public people.

Ms. Wallace kept up a strong, stoic face through the whole ordeal, even as everyone else around her began to crumble with grief.

Journalist, filmmaker, and friend dream hampton was with D-Roc and Cease within hours of Wallace's passing. They sat in Wallace's hotel room, surrounded by reminders of a man who had planned on living, his custom-made Versace shirts and pants strewn around the room. D-Roc sat in shock talking to himself. Cease was inconsolable. The three of them had seen so much over the last four

Mary J. Blige and Lil' Kim gave each other support in their grief after Wallace's funeral service.

years, from the corner of Fulton, when all they could do was dream about living the high life, to flying first class and living that dream. And now the biggest dreamer of all was gone.

"This nigga who ain't never hurt nobody . . ." D-Roc said, the words tapering off in silence. "I could see if it was one of us . . . I been shot mad times, niggas get shot . . ." He kept reasoning out loud, stoically trying to make sense out of nonsense, then slowly melting into tears.

Within hours of Wallace's death, many of the New York–based music industry people who had planned to take the Sunday night red-eye pushed up their flights, trying to get home on the first thing smoking.

"I just wanted to get out of there," said Emil Wilbekin. "I felt scared." He ran into some of his colleagues at the airport, all of them with listless expressions. "I remember that no one would even talk to each other. Everyone just wanted to get home and feel safe."

Flying back to Miami, Luke thought about the friend he'd been speaking to on the phone until just before he was shot. "I mean, I'm on the plane, and the thought of him just goin' out there with the intentions of goin' to the awards, having a good time, and now he has to come back in a box up under the plane? That just stayed in my mind. Yo—he's coming back in a box up under the fucking plane."

Combs's people also wanted him to leave Los Angeles, pleading for his safety. But the mogul was paralyzed by grief and guilt. For the first time in his life he didn't know what he really wanted to do anymore, or where he wanted to go. He barricaded himself in a hotel room. Again, just like he did after the City College tragedy, his mentor Andre Harrell was there to help pick up the pieces. "Andre called me up and said, 'Yo, I need for you to go get him out,'" said Alonzo Brown. "We called the chief of police and orchestrated the whole move out of Los Angeles."

"I was stuck," Combs said. "I did not want to leave him. I still didn't really cry yet, 'cause I really didn't want to accept it. So then I'm about to get on a plane. And as I'm seeing the plane pull up, that's when I break down. I'm about to leave L.A. without my man, you know what I'm sayin'? He's at the morgue, just lying there. That shit was just so fucked up to me. I wanted him to be with me, sitting right there with me, going back to New York. I would just sleep a lot. I wanted to wake up. I just knew it was a dream."

That was how Christopher Wallace looked in his casket: as though he was sleeping. Lying in a velvet-lined coffin made of beautifully polished mahogany, Wallace was dressed in a white suit with a matching derby—an outfit worthy of his status as a man of respect. His face looked peaceful, but none of the people there felt peace at his passing. Everyone felt the same thing: This was a light that was snuffed out much too soon.

"They had him dressed up like Big Poppa," said DJ Premier. "They dressed him up nice, but it was hard to look at him like that."

The revered rap producer paused momentarily at the memory.

"I've seen many young brothers in a casket before, but the one with Biggie in it was really, really hard to swallow just because it was like, 'Damn, I just saw you when we finished the album.'"

Many of those in attendance were surprised that the casket was open. On one hand, it gave them a chance to see his face one last time, to touch it, to say good-bye. On the other, it was a poignant reminder of the fragility of life, of the fact that someone they all knew, loved, and shared jokes with was now dead. Both Combs and Lance "Un" Rivera broke down when Christopher Jr., held up to the casket by Rivera, smiled and touched his father's face. There were very few people who weren't overwhelmed with intense waves of grief.

"I'm not good with funerals at all," admitted Easy Mo Bee. "I didn't even go to my cousin's own funeral, man. I went to Biggie's funeral."

Seeing the body also had a sobering effect on Wallace's first producer.

"I went past the casket and I seen him laying there," Mo Bee continued. "They had to tell me to keep moving. I was just standing there, staring at him, man. Shit broke me up. I just wanted to go, since I didn't get to go to the studio and see him do his vocals for the last time, and since I wasn't there to tell him, please don't call that song 'Goin' Back to Cali,' please don't do that. Because I didn't get to be there for none of them last moments, I had to go to his funeral."

Over 350 family members and friends packed in to the elegantly appointed viewing room, consoling one another, many with visible masks of grief. Besides obvious people like the members of Junior M.A.F.I.A. and close friends who toured and worked with him, other guests included Busta Rhymes, Jay-Z, D.M.C. of Run-D.M.C., Mary J. Blige, Heavy D, Foxy Brown, DJ Kool Herc, Flavor Flav, and Queen Latifah. Former Mayor David Dinkins, although he'd never met Wallace, attended at the behest of Clive Davis.

Ms. Wallace read from the Book of Job. The Bad Boy quartet 112 sang their song "Cry On." Sean Combs said a few words of remembrance. Faith sang a beautiful rendition of "Walk With Me, Jesus" that made women and tough guys alike openly weep with grief.

As D-Roc and the other pallbearers carried the casket to the hearse, fans and members of the media watched as other people came out from under the funeral home's red awning onto Madison Avenue. Lil' Kim crumpled like a rag doll into Mary J. Blige's waiting arms. Pepa walked out with tears in her eyes, as did Bad Boy recording artist Mase. The rest of the family quietly filed into the waiting limos and SUVs to make the trip to Fresh Ponds Crematory in Middle Village, Queens. The driver led the procession of 20 cars south toward the Brooklyn Bridge.

The whole crew was heading for Fulton Street. One last time. A lot of us who had gotten to know Big as journalists but didn't get to go to the funeral were out there. Rob Marriott was out there. Karen Good. Abbie Kearse of MTV News. And so was I.

Roughly 800 people crowded both sides of the block on St. James between Fulton and Washington, waiting for Wallace to come home. They had been waiting, in the freezing cold, since 10:00 that morning. And now it was after 1:30.

There were so many people out, it was impossible to walk on the sidewalk. People sat on top of cars, stood on stoops, hung out of windows. Looking. Waiting. Anticipating. Curious. Nervous. Wallace's entire demographic was represented: the fifteen-year-old mothers with their baby strollers, snapping gum, looking out at the crowd, the kind of girls whom Big rhymed about robbing on the train for their "#1 Mom pendant" on his verse on "Gimme the Loot." Eight- and nine-year-old boys who had hung up posters of him on their walls from *Word Up!* and *Fresh* magazine, just as he had years before for his rap heros. Teenage boys and young men, many of whom knew him, who were caught up in the everyday struggle of the illegal paper chase that Big wrote about in many of his rhymes. His music was dedicated to them, and became the soundtrack of their lives, much the way Marvin Gaye's *What's Going On* or Stevie Wonder's *Songs in the Key of Life* was to their parents.

Old women held candles, saddened to hear about the death of another young black man, one who had done good with his life and had seemingly put the illegality and negativity behind him. Others cried about his tragic death, crying for his mother Voletta, who was known around the community for more than two decades, but also crying for their own sons and nephews, some who had already died, and some who were well on their way to the funeral parlor.

Some of the same women to whom Wallace had defiantly dedicated his song "Juicy"—the ones who used to call the cops on him when he was on the corner selling drugs "trying to feed my daughter"—were out here crying, defending his legacy. Some stared angrily at the cops lying in wait in riot gear, who seemed so sure that something was going to jump off, and at the numerous members of the television and print media, the kind of people who care about black talent only after it's tragically taken away.

One woman, looking down from a stoop, let the visitors know how she felt about their presence as Rob Marriott watched. "Fuck these white muthafuckas! Get off my block! Y'all ain't allowed."

A woman with flowers and a Biggie T-shirt hanging over the front of a baby carriage strolled the streets, a wool cap over her head. Her name was Shirley Wright, and she had traveled all the way from Los Angeles. "I am here representing peace," she said.

Others in the crowd weren't feeling the California love.

"We East Coast ridaz now, fuck them West Coast niggas!" one tall black kid said, his eyes brimming with anger. "That was my man right there," said a shorter kid about Wallace. "He never forgot us."

On the stoop in front of 226 St. James, well-wishers created a shrine of cards, pictures of Big, and candles. Audwin Sookra burned the edges of dollar bills and blew them out, placing them on the ground next to a picture of Wallace. "Biggie always wanted money to burn," he said. He raised his head and nodded at a couple of guys standing nearby. "I don't want anyone to steal this," he said, looking down at the partially burnt dollar. "No one should profit from this."

When Wallace's funeral procession reached Brooklyn, a crowd was waiting on the streets. The scene resembled a memorial for a deceased head of state.

As he spoke, a few brothers walked the sidelines, carrying a box of T-shirts for sale. The message on the front said "In memory of the Notorious B.I.G." with a likeness of his latest magazine cover silkscreened on the front. Wallace's body was not yet in the ground and people were already trying to make a buck. Judging from the number of T-shirts visible in the crowd, business was booming.

The temperature had dropped despite the presence of the sun. People stomped their feet and blew into their hands to keep warm. Anguish turned into tension. Pathos to humor.

Ten more minutes passed. It was five minutes to two.

"Nigga delinquent," one man near Marriott said.

"He better get his ass on," said a woman, "or he ain't gonna see Tasha today. Too cold out here—shit!"

An old man opened his front door and stepped out onto the stoop. He saw a crowd forming around his car, all trying to get the best vantage point for the coming procession. People were sitting on the hood and the trunk of his old Cadillac.

"Get off my car!" he yelled. "Some people have to go to work."

A few people moved, but most just ignored the old man. Everyone was standing on top of whatever they could find, anything that would give them a better view of the motorcade. Along with the TV camera trucks doing live remotes, there were cars parked up and down both sides of the street. Many drivers didn't anticipate a gathering of this size and didn't make the proper arrangements.

Heads turned as car horns blared in the distance. The sounds of applause and screaming could be heard coming down the block.

Biggie was home.

The shiny black hearse rounded the corner and turned onto St. James, heading toward Fulton, moving very slowly. In front of the motorcade rode a black man on a bicycle, holding up a handmade cardboard sign: CHRISTOPHER WALLACE, THE GREATEST OF ALL TIME. He wasn't a Bad Boy affiliate, just a Brooklynite expressing what everyone was feeling. Eight more stretch limos and 20 other cars followed behind the hearse, and through the windows people saw Ms. Wallace, Faith Evans, and the whole Bad Boy family and waved at them. Some waved their fists in a final triumphant gesture, saluting rather than celebrating. Tears flowed from the eyes of hardrocks and babymommas. No one could feel the cold anymore.

Flowered cars moved by, one with the letters B.I.G. spelled out in red carnations. Another arrangement in yellow said, "For Daddy."

In another limo Lil' Cease, D-Roc, and other members of Junior M.A.F.I.A. raised their hands and funeral programs through the open sunroof. Bigging up Brooklyn, sending the love right back, smiling through their tears. It was almost as if they were saying, "Look at all these people out here—our nigga made it." They took a long look so the memory would last. At least nobody could take that away.

And then, just as suddenly as it arrived, the cavalcade was gone. After hours of waiting, the whole thing had lasted ten minutes.

People stood in hushed, stunned silence. Then a great wave of sadness rushed over the collective. Women's breasts heaved with sobs. Men's shoulders shrugged, some of the men embracing total strangers.

Then it happened. The beat to "Hypnotize" erupted from a speaker outside the Underground nightclub at 977 Fulton.

"Uh! Uh! Uh! *Hot!* / Sicker than your average, Poppa twist cabbage off instinct / Niggas don't think shit stink / Pink gators for my Detroit players / Tims for my hooligans from Brooklyn . . ."

Biggie was alive. Right there. Right then. Yes, everyone went crazy. Euphoria rippled through the crowd. It was just like the moment in a New Orleans jazz funeral when the dirge becomes a party.

Some kids along Fulton jumped on top of a Dumpster and started waving their hands and shaking their hips to the music. Other people started dancing on top of the cars. The old man looking out for his Cadillac suddenly lost his temper. "Get off my car!" Nobody could hear him. They were too busy dancing.

Everyone was having a good time except for New York's finest. The cops didn't like the sudden shift in energy. Fearing that the situation was getting out of hand, they moved forward trying to disperse the crowd. They pulled some of the kids off the cars and arrested them.

The crowd wasn't trying to hear it—not that the cops cared.

A SWAT team appeared on a rooftop. Cops in full riot gear—helmets, Plexiglas shields, and billy clubs—started moving through the crowd randomly handcuffing anyone who didn't get out of the way. People ran, ducking, and diving. A paddy wagon pulled up. Some young men got into shoving matches with the police. News cameras captured the melee.

"He wouldn't have wanted it like this!" a middle-aged brown-skinned woman named Vanessa Edwards yelled frantically, her eyes wet with frustration. The cops kept pulling people off the cars.

One cop wrestled a young man to the ground and began to pummel his head with a can of pepper spray. Julia Campbell, a thirtyish white woman with a cherubic face and a press pass, stepped forward.

"Why are you doing that? Why are you using pepper spray?"

"Move out of the way, lady," he said.

"I'm with the *New York Times*," she protested. "You can't tell me where to go!"

The cop didn't hesitate. He sprayed pepper in her face, and her glasses offered no protection from the stinging, choking cloud.

As she screamed, another cop stepped in behind her and put on handcuffs. A black teenager who saw the whole thing walked right up to Campbell.

"Now you see how they treat us! Now you know how it feels. Fucked up, ain't it? You all right?"

Within ten minutes, the whole block was cleared of people. The old man stood in front of his Cadillac with a dismayed look on his face. The windows were broken, the hood and the roof dented by heavy boot prints.

"Hypnotize" kept playing somewhere in the background.

"That Brooklyn bullshit," Biggie said. "We on it."

And the beat never stopped.

Sean Combs rode a motorcycle along an isolated country road, surrounded by a bucolic landscape and a pristine blue sky. After so much pain, so much darkness, so much gloom, it was the first beautiful day he could enjoy. He rode tall, the wind blowing on his face, and for a brief moment, all was right in his world.

He didn't see the bump in the road until he ran right into it. His body hit the pavement at the same time as his bike. And as usual, he couldn't have this painful, private, embarrassing moment to himself—never that. Privacy had no place in the world of Puff Daddy.

Of course, there was a camera around to capture the whole thing. Puff wouldn't have it any other way.

"He wiped out," said Hype Williams, the director of "I'll Be Missing You," a tribute song for Christopher Wallace. "It just so happened that we got it on film, so we used it in the video. Luckily we didn't have to take him to the hospital and we were able to keep filming."

Combs's wipe-out suddenly became visual metaphor, and, in a manner that can only be described as Combsian, he managed to flip a negative situation into something that greatly benefited him. His serene motorcycle ride suddenly represented the good times he and Wallace shared in Los Angeles, the bump in the road the Los Angeles beefs they were oblivious to, and the wipe-out the aftermath to Wallace's being murdered right in front of him. All of it captured, and documented for the world to see, not unlike the numerous photos taken right after the shooting, the public outpouring of grief, and now, like Williams's cameras, the whole event recorded for posterity.

Combs's reaction to the accident, despite his injuries, was similar to the way that he handled misfortune so many times before. He picked himself up, dusted himself off, and got right back to work. The process of getting back on his feet started with the recording of "I'll Be Missing You."

After Wallace was killed, Combs had contemplated getting out of the business altogether. He didn't necessarily contemplate suicide, but he thought about death a lot, almost as if he wished it had happened to him. For days at a time, he would lie in bed, unable to sleep, eat, or even move. "Sometimes I wanna pull it, end it all with a bullet," he rapped on the song "Pain," recorded after Wallace's murder. "Hard to live life to the fullest with all this bullshit."

Why not get out? He already had plenty of money—close to $100 million at this point. He could sell the company, take the cream, and whip up some of the other ideas that he had bubbling—fashion, films, restaurants, whatever he wanted. Few people would consider him a sucker for cashing in his chips.

And during the weeks he spent in inconsolable isolation, the people closest to him wondered—when they were out of earshot—if he might just slowly fade away. Do like Russell Simmons and find him a Lyor Cohen type to take over the day-to-day operations of Bad Boy while Puffy collected checks and sat on a white sand beach somewhere, contemplating his next move.

But Combs wasn't ready for his *Godfather II* Corleone-style moment by the lake, watching the sun set and the leaves blow around, remembering happier days. Nobody was better at kicking himself in the ass. Just looking at how other people were reacting was enough to get him jump-started.

"I saw the strength of Biggie's mother," he told *Rolling Stone*. "If she ain't going to give up, if she ain't jumping off no bridges—she's having to get up and go to work, still take care of the kids—I've got to get myself together."

He also saw a music video.

While he was lying in bed early one morning, MTV played the 1983 Police hit "Every Breath You Take." Listening to the song, which is actually about a disgruntled lover stalking his ex-girlfriend, Combs felt comfort. The "every step you take" aspect of the lyrics made him feel as if he was being watched and protected from above by his new guardian angel—Wallace.

So like the Lox before him—whose "We'll Always Love Big Poppa" was the first song dedicated to Wallace's memory—and like KRS-One before them (who dedicated several of his Boogie Down Production albums to his dear departed DJ Scott La Rock, shot down in the streets of New York), Combs decided to move forward in the name of his man—and write a song about it.

He gathered those closest around him to work on the song, figuring that it would be a beneficial place to work out his grief, but at the same time create a lasting tribute. The Bad Boy family immediately got to work on "I'll Be Missing You." It was decided that the proceeds from the single would go into a trust fund for T'Yanna and Christopher Jr. But of course the song was about more than that—it was a way for Wallace's friends and fellow artists to express their feelings in song.

This mural on Ward Avenue in the Bronx was painted within 24 hours of Wallace's death. It was the first of many tributes to the fallen giant.

The recording session was tense. There were times when Combs and Evans, overwhelmed with grief, would leave the studio in tears.

There was Faith, crying as she lay down her vocals, her voice emoting the strange mixture of emotions that almost always follows the reaction to someone's death. Combs would sometimes have to leave the room, overwhelmed by all the emotion. But of course none of this pain was private. Not only was it being recorded for public consumption, but a reporter was there witnessing the whole thing.

"You can have all the success and money in the world, but at the end of the day it doesn't really mean a thing," Combs told Chuck Philips, who was in the studio watching Combs and Evans record the song. "I can't be happy right now because my best friend is dead. I know God doesn't give you anything you can't handle, but I'm really struggling with it, man. I'm having a tough time here."

"Me, Stevie J, Faith, and 112 sat in a studio four days in a row," remembered Deric "D-Dot" Angelettie. "No sleep. We made two versions before that one, but I came into the studio with that Police sample, and I think that was it."

Another version of the song sampled the Harold Melvin and the Blue Notes' classic "I Miss You," but that choice was considered too maudlin. The goal—for the first time in a Bad Boy single release—wasn't to make a song that would rock a dance floor. It was to make a song that could express the conflicted emotions one always feels at a wake—the sadness of someone's passing, and the joy that comes from people getting together to remember someone they all loved. All set to something that rhymed and had a backbeat. The song was supposed to make you cry and nod your head.

"It wasn't always the Police remake," said Faith, "but we kind of knew once we heard it. I was like, yeah, that's definitely going to be it. It was just a more popular song to cover. And then lyrically, I don't think I really strayed too far away from the original lyrics, it's just that the original song was more about a love interest other than the loss of somebody. So I just had to change a few words, write a few phrases. It's not like I had the big idea. But it just came together well, it worked."

"We're party animals," said Angelettie. "And we just had to say, 'We miss you, but we miss you in a happy way.' We wanted to rejoice and not be sad, because the Lox song was already sad. We had to find a way to pick it up, because at the end of the day, Big was why we were here, so we had to let him know."

If the song was poignant, the video was a celebration.

The most memorable shot in the video isn't Combs grooving on a people mover, Faith Evans singing movingly into the camera, or even Combs leading a group of children (including three-and-a-half-year-old T'Yanna Wallace) up a hillside dressed in their Sunday best. It's a shot of Combs himself. He's alone, dancing in the rain, spinning in a black designer silk suit as the water pours down from above.

It's shamelessly self-centered, and made more than one person question aloud how much did Combs really care about Wallace if he's dancing like that in his video, some even going so far as to liken the act to dancing on Wallace's grave. But the failure to understand the beauty of the moment would also be a failure to understand the beauty and genius of Sean "Puffy" Combs.

Before Wallace's death, "Can't Nobody Hold Me Down" sounded like a study in arrogance, the words of a man taunting G-men, God, and gangsters, bragging about how much money he had and a "Benz that he ain't even drove yet." The beat of one of hip hop's most enduring social commentaries, "The Message" had been co-opted and reworked as a party anthem for a man who seemingly cared more about his cars, caviar, and carats then he did about his people.

After Wallace's death, the same song, and the very same lyrics, became a study in perseverance. Now Combs was a man who refused to be stopped—no matter how high the stakes, no matter what the score. It didn't matter how many people hated him, how many people wished him ill, or even, more seriously, how many people wanted to kill him; in the end it didn't matter. He was going to do his thing his way. As he danced, one realized how now the chorus of a throwaway pop song like Matthew Wilder's 1983 "Break My Stride" could become a mantra of resilience, a mission statement: "Can't nobody break my stride. Can't nobody hold me down. *Oh no.* I got to keep on moving."

Lots of other things had changed, too. When Puff first decided to make the transition to artist, Big—who was eager to explore the business side of show biz—was going to be his manager. But in death, Big did more for Puff than any manager could ever do.

Puff also changed the name of his album. Instead of *Hell Up in Harlem,* Puff's solo debut was now called *No Way Out.* "We changed it because it didn't apply no more," Angelettie said. "And [Combs] felt boxed in."

But he wasn't. Instead, the record that was supposed to be his swan song ended up rising from the flames like a phoenix.

Just as *No Way Out* transformed the life of Combs from well-known executive to pop superstar, *Life After Death* transformed Wallace from pop superstar into a figure of iconic status. Perhaps the most surprising thing was that Biggie's death wasn't what made him an icon—it only prevented Wallace from enjoying it. Had he not been murdered, *Life After Death* would have helped Wallace attain the status of KRS-One or Rakim—artists who are damn near worshiped by the rap community like living gods.

The title *Life After Death* was, as no reviewer failed to note, prophetic. Some of the same people who, before his death, whispered about how the money had gone to Wallace's head, were now some of the same people praising his genius—a genius on ample display. It was an amazing last statement—all the more sad, because it proved that the rapper was reaching a level of talent with his gift that was truly joyous to behold.

Life After Death was nothing short of a gangsta rap *Songs in the Key of Life,* the stylistically diverse Stevie Wonder double album that made listeners wonder if there was anything Stevie couldn't do. It was the same with Biggie's second album—there was so much variety (beats, flows, styles, subjects), all springing fully formed from a skull shaped like a colossal Olmec head.

Songs like "Somebody's Gotta Die" and "Niggas Bleed" showcased Wallace's eye for detail—with narratives so vivid and indelible that a music video would have actually diminished them. "I'm Fuckin' You Tonight," on the surface, was a raunchy sex rhyme that was almost pornographic in detail—but technically it was a tour de force. Instead of simple rhyming couplets, Big buried rhymes in the beginning and middle and end of his lines—an amazing display of poetic skill that was not meant for the page but the ear. "Some say the Ex makes the sex / Spec-TAC-ular, make me lick you from your neck to your BACK then ya / SHIV-erin', tongue de-LIV-erin' / Chills up that spine, that ass is mine."

"Kick In the Door" showed that even in the most off-kilter environment, Wallace could stutter step and fake out the beat with all the dexterity of Allen Iverson's crossover dribble. With "Notorious Thugs," rapping alongside Bone—his emulation of their style wasn't parody but the deepest form of respect. Songs like "Hypnotize" and "Mo Money, Mo Problems" proved Wallace to be the master of the pop rhyme—he could still freak a radio edit, and then turn around and drop a "Ten Crack Commandments," which, like its older brother, proved that *nobody* could rip some Premier gutter beat better than the master. Never has an artist attempted to please so many different audiences simultaneously and done it so brilliantly.

Life After Death was quickly certified quadruple platinum. It became the biggest-selling release of the year, tying *Please Hammer Don't Hurt 'Em* as the top-selling rap album of all time (though it had the numerical advantage of being a double album, multiplying its SoundScan numbers by two), and by January 2000 it had sold 10 million copies.

Meanwhile Combs was exploding as a solo artist. Wallace and others had encouraged Combs to make a rap album as a way to enjoy his success. And from his appearances in their videos and the way he told them how to attack their vocals, it was clear that he wanted to be a performer, too. This was the very thing Suge had taunted him about at the Source Music Awards. And now it was reality.

But nobody expected it to work this well. "Can't Nobody Hold Me Down," a one-off experiment, had shot up the pop charts. "I'll Be Missing You" became a smash, going triple platinum within weeks of release and occupying the No. 1 spot on the pop charts for most of the year. It remains the biggest-selling single in the whole Bad Boy catalog, raising funds for the Christopher Wallace Foundation.

Lil' Kim posed with a box containing Biggie's ashes for a *People* magazine profile that appeared four months after Wallace's death, when she was still living in his New Jersey condo.

Combs was right—his authenticity was his marketing. It wasn't as if he was proclaiming himself a gangster—that was more the world of his father and his friends—but he was selling himself as someone who knew enough about the underworld to rise above it, even if he was, by association, a part of it. The more he defended himself, the more he sounded more deeply involved. He sounded like John F. Kennedy denying his father's bootlegging past, or Frank Sinatra insisting that his connections to various crime families was nothing more than him being polite to the guys he grew up with in Hoboken.

"I wish people would judge me by my actions, not by these ridiculous rumors," Combs said. "I'm not some evil underworld mobster from the 'hood. I'm a young, educated, hardworking black man trying to perfect my craft and earn an honest living. I'm building a legacy here. I'm not going to go down in history for some stupid gangsta B.S. No way, man. History is going to remember me as one of the greatest entrepreneurs and entertainers the world has ever encountered."

No Way Out was released on July 29, 1997, selling 2 million copies in less than two months. *No Way Out* and *Life After Death* traded places on the pop chart as Bad Boy cornered the market on both record sales and coolness.

Combs was joined by Faith, Sting, and a gospel choir for a stirring rendition of the year's top-selling single, "I'll Be Missing You," at the 1997 MTV Awards.

Wallace and the Lox gave him the street cred, but now Combs was the public face of not only the company but of New York hip hop. Grit was no longer the shit. Combs was playing gangsta glam on a whole new level.

"I've always been like a walking billboard for my company," Combs said. "The way I dress. The way I move. The way I dance. It all became a part of the Bad Boy lifestyle."

By the time that the Paul Hunter–directed videos for "Been Around the World" and "It's All About the Benjamins" were in heavy rotation on MTV, Combs not only seemed comfortable in the star role; he seemed born to it. One minute, as in the "World" video, he was a secret agent jumping out of planes—next he was dancing with Jennifer Lopez to War's "Galaxy" in a sensual mambo that got tongues wagging and gossip columnists typing (she was married to waiter turned restaurateur Ojani Noa at the time). Then with the kinetic "Benjamins" video, Combs tap-danced with Savion Glover. The two had a hoofing contest, trading staccato steps like two MCs in a battle. Amazingly, though Combs was dancing against one of the world's most respected tap dancers, he kept up.

It seemed as if there was nothing he couldn't do.

The September 1997 MTV Video Music Awards, the engineer of so many dramatic hip hop moments, set the stage for the most dramatic of all. With a 50-person choir dressed in white, Combs danced and bopped to the beat of "I'll Be Missing You." From a riser emerging near the front of the stage, Sting appeared, singing his original version of his Police hit "Every Breath You Take." From stage left, Faith appeared, singing the chorus about her slain husband. Above everyone, there was a huge monitor, playing footage from Biggie videos "Hypnotize," "One More Chance," and "Juicy," among others.

Four male dancers came out, spinning and dancing with Combs as he stood at the center of the stage, whipping the audience into a frenzy.

"Clap your hands for Big! Clap your hands for Tupac Shakur! Clap your hands for everybody we lost!" he said, his arms stretched out as sparks rained down from the ceiling, icing the finale.

For a few fleeting moments, Combs was the king of the rap game. Even his detractors, a group growing by the minute, had to admit that Combs had the genre on lock; either with hits he produced, hits on his label, or, damn, himself at the center.

"He's passed all these hurdles," said one music executive who preferred to remain nameless. "Those kids dying at CCNY, getting fired from Uptown, Biggie's death, the whole Suge Knight and Tupac shit. It's almost like he's a little superhero. I hate to sound like I'm on his dick, 'cause I'm not, but he's a very smart man."

But even Achilles had his heel, Superman his Kryptonite, and Samson his shorn locks. The one thing that did hold Combs down, even at the height of his success, was the specter of death.

He couldn't even escape it during the video shoot for the Hype Williams–directed "Mo Money, Mo Problems," another posthumous platinum smash off *Life After Death*. The clip, with its faux golf tournament, its dancers, and its scenes of him and Mase doing the wop in a zero-gravity parachute chamber, were calculated to make up for the fact that Wallace's only appearance in the video was from an old interview filmed in 1994. That's the incovenient thing about being dead. There could be no new pictures of Big Poppa. No more verses committed to tape. Though to be sure, every last scrap got resurrected and put to use.

But what could be obscured in a video was harder to gloss over in real life.

"How do you spell 'kill'?" T'Yanna asked her grandmother, Voletta Wallace. T'Yanna and Voletta were passing time at the golf course on Long Island where Combs and Mase were filming their faux golf tournament.

"K-I-L-L," her grandmother replied. The little girl drew a childlike likeness of Puffy, with big oversized tear drops. She held up her picture, which had a caption scrawled beneath her drawing: "Come Kill Us. Kill us please. Daddy dead, killed by gun."

Spin editor-in-chief Sia Michel, who covered the video shoot for the magazine, witnessed the entire exchange.

"For the rest of our interview, Puffy is visibly deflated," she wrote.

Despite the success of the album, Combs had a bittersweet feeling about the entire affair.

"I don't give a fuck if when this shit drops, I sell four million copies, I will not be happy," Combs said. "Give me Biggie back and you can take all the records you want. Take every record off the radio. That's just not the bottom line. I'm not happy. I want my muthafuckin' man."

WHO SHOT YA?

CHAPTER 10

> "I can hear sweat trickling down your cheek
> Your heartbeat sound like Sasquatch feet
> Thundering, shaking the concrete
> Then the shit stop when I foil the plot..."

Voletta Wallace still didn't have her man: the one who killed her son.

While Christopher Wallace's friends grieved, and the Bad Boy staff figured out how to respectfully market his album, his mother's primary concerns—after trying to pull herself together emotionally—were to figure out who would want to kill her only child, and to make sure that the Los Angeles Police Department didn't just sweep the investigation under the rug.

She didn't want to believe that police would ignore the death of a young black man who also happened to be a gangsta rapper. But she had seen Tupac Shakur's murder go unsolved for months. Even more people witnessed her son's shooting than saw Shakur get shot on that street in Las Vegas. Christopher was shot shortly after the party he was attending got shut down, forcing all the guests out onto Wilshire Boulevard at once. Somebody had to have seen something.

Yet besides the testimony of Damien "D-Roc" Butler, James "Lil' Cease" Lloyd, Paul Offord, Gregory "G" Young, and Combs—who would answer questions only when accompanied by his legal team—none of the other people in their cars, none of the people standing outside of the Petersen Automotive Museum, nobody who didn't have to talk stepped forward to help the police.

Detectives pulled together a composite sketch of the shooter—an African-American in his late thirties with a receding hairline and a bowtie—and a description of the getaway car—a black Chevy Impala SS—but little else.

The code of the streets was in effect.

"When it's a situation like that, you can't just spill," said one man who attended the party. "You always gotta alter shit. You puttin' niggas' business out there. It's not no little kiddie shit. That shit is real. What you say can have your ass killed the next day. That's what people gotta understand. When it's serious business like that, the best person is the silent person that shuts the fuck up. Let the shit play itself out, man. Truth'll get out there one day."

Not the way the Los Angeles Police Department was handling things. When the elite Robbery Homicide Division came to the murder scene and decided not to accept the case, a clear message was being sent—this was a "gangbanger" murder, not something worthy of the full resources of the department.

Ms. Wallace wasn't having it.

"I'm sick to my stomach over the way this case has been handled," she would say later. "There is a murderer out there laughing at my family and laughing at the cops. I've held my tongue for months now, but I'm fed up with the police just pussy-footing around."

"We are trying to do everything in our power to solve this murder," Detective Russell Poole, the newly installed lead investigator on the case, told the *Los Angeles Times*. "I understand that Ms. Wallace is upset, but I've tried to explain to her that you can't just throw a case like this together. You need witnesses—and we have none. We've interviewed hundreds of witnesses and the majority of them are not being totally candid with us. It's very frustrating."

Poole had no idea just how frustrating the case would become, nor that uncooperative witnesses would be the least of his problems. Two years after taking over the investigation he resigned from the LAPD, saying that he believed the department did not want the case solved. And now, in the seventh year since Wallace's murder, there has been lots of speculation, but no arrests, and no sign of real progress in the police investigation.

Tuesday, March 18, 1997, proved to be a pivotal date in the search for Wallace's murderer. On the same day that Christopher Wallace's remains were being taken on that last ride down St. James, the two dominant theories about who might have killed him were first revealed to the public. As these theories unfolded, they would transform a police department, divide a newspaper staff, and rock the hip hop nation to its very core.

The day started off with a *Los Angeles Times* headline on page one of the Metro section: PERSONAL DISPUTE IS FOCUS OF RAP PROBE. The story, written by Chuck Philips and Matt Lait, was the first to explore the possibility that Wallace was murdered over a financial dispute with members of the Southside Crips.

"Ironically the rapper . . . was apparently killed by a member of the same Compton Crips set he had hired to protect him on trips to Los Angeles during the last year," the report read. "An alleged member of the same set is the key suspect in last September's Las Vegas slaying of rapper Tupac Shakur, police said."

Bad Boy's association with the Crips reportedly stemmed all the way back to 1995, when Wallace was on tour promoting *Ready to Die*. Combs and others at Bad Boy were worried about Wallace's ability to perform on the West Coast—

particularly after the shooting death of Knight's friend Jake Robles in September 1995. One of Combs's right-hand men, Anthony "Wolf" Jones, was considered a suspect in the shooting, and Knight held Combs personally responsible. Going West, for any reason, was a dangerous proposition.

"Suge's beef wasn't with Big. Suge's thing was with Puff," Lil' Cease explained years later. "For what reason? Don't know. The nigga just wasn't fucking with Puff. And then he got down with Pac and Pac wasn't feeling Big."

Wallace didn't hire bodyguards—that fell under his label's purview. And beyond the off-duty police officers whom Bad Boy would routinely hire, additional security came from a close friend of Combs's father, Vaughn "Zip" Williams.

Williams was an old-school Harlem hustler once described as "the Yoda to Puffy's Luke." Combs has never denied knowing Williams and neither did Wallace. He was thanked in the liner notes to both *Ready to Die* and *Life After Death* as "Uncle Zip—The Spiritual advisor."

"The nigga that's a major figure that's a Crip is named Zip," said one New York–based source who spoke with VIBE in 1997. "That's like Puff's right-hand man. But he would never go out and expose that shit."

Williams was reportedly close friends with Orlando Anderson's uncle, Dwayne "Keefee D" Davis. In an interview with the LAPD following Wallace's murder, Davis told investigators about a meeting he had with Combs and Wallace in Anaheim, accompanied by about two dozen of his Southside brethren—including Anderson. According to Davis, "Zip" introduced the Southside crew to the Bad Boy camp, suggesting that they could provide protection whenever Combs and company were on the West Coast.

"I was in a room full of Crip killers," said a source who accompanied the Bad Boy entourage to Anaheim. "Puff said they're going to be doing security for us."

Some insiders believe that a dispute over how much money the Crips deserved for that security work might have gotten Wallace killed. "Puffy hired Southside Crips, and the Southside Crips started extorting them for more money," Reggie Wright told VIBE. "Southside wanted $100,000 for security services and [Combs] offered them $10,000. That's why Biggie Smalls is dead today."

The circumstantial evidence seemed compelling: Davis owned a black SS Impala matching the description of the car seen leaving Wallace's murder scene. Police confiscated the vehicle and hauled in Davis for questioning. Soon after both Davis and his car were released, and the police later declared that he was not a suspect. But the streets kept talking.

"We've never hired Crips or any other gang faction to do security for us," Combs told MTV after the theories were made public. "I would never put my artists in jeopardy, and I'm insulted to be asked that question."

Insulted or not, Combs couldn't deny that the Death Row crew had a tendency to hit below the belt. While Combs and Wallace seemed to ignore the

This Death Row chain was worn by a Compton gang member arrested as part of the Shakur murder investigation. But if a chain-snatching did lead to Tupac's murder, why was Wallace killed?

threats and taunts, publicly calling for peace, there were other voices calling for them to defend their pride.

Sources who spoke with VIBE asserted that a $10,000 bounty was offered on a gold-and-diamond Death Row Records pendant. The sponsor was never revealed, but it was widely assumed that persons affiliated with Bad Boy Records had something to do with it.

In July 1996—two months before Shakur's death—one of Knight's associates, Travon Lane, had his pendant stolen outside a Foot Locker at the Lakewood Mall. The chain-snatching led to Orlando Anderson's beat-down when Lane saw Anderson in Vegas. In theory, the beat-down led to Shakur's shooting hours later. Following this line of reasoning, Wallace's murder could have been a retaliation from Shakur's camp, or the Crips' way of collecting on an unpaid debt.

Combs steadfastly denied knowing any gang members. "Myself and all my crew, we know Zip as an acquaintance," he told VIBE. "Being a young black celebrity you have thousands of acquaintances. But as far as him introducing me to Crips, I can't say that happened. But I can't say that didn't happen neither. I can't say who I've met. It's not like all gang people wear rags on their heads."

Just after 4 P.M. on the same March day Wallace was laid to rest in New York, a random act of L.A. road rage blew the slain rapper's murder investigation wide open with a new, even more outrageous theory.

At the corner of Lankershim and Ventura, near the border of North Hollywood and Studio City, a green Mitsubishi Montero pulled up to the right of a '91 Buick Regal. The souped-up Montero was driven by a black man with a shaved head, flossing at the stoplight like a hustler, music booming.

The man behind the wheel of the weather-beaten Buick looked like a redneck—wife beater, long shaggy salt-and-pepper hair, a handlebar moustache, and a black marijuana leaf hat just like the one Dr. Dre wore on the cover of *The Chronic*. He turned his head toward the music, then back at the road, then back to the black man, who was now staring him down.

"Could I help you?" asked the white man, rolling down his window.

"Nah," the black man, said. "Nobody ain't looking at you, punk muthafucka."

"Do you have a problem?"

"I'm your problem."

The argument escalated into a chase through busy traffic. The black man eventually pulled a gun, but the white man shot first. When the smoke cleared, the black man at the wheel of the Montero was dead, and the white man in the Buick had a major problem. His name was Frank Lyga, a veteran undercover narcotics officer. And the body in the SUV would be identified as Kevin Gaines, a six-year veteran of the Pacific Division—another of the LAPD's own.

The press had a field day with the story: a black cop killed by a white cop who claimed that he acted in self-defense. The "crazy nigga" defense was controversial anywhere, but in a place as racially divided as Los Angeles, it did not go over well at all. Within weeks Johnnie Cochran filed a $25 million wrongful death suit against the department and the city. "The history of the LAPD—Rodney King. '92 riots. O. J. Simpson trial. Mark Fuhrman issue. Johnnie Cochran," Lyga said. "Now me."

At the eye of the storm was Detective Poole, a recent transfer to the Robbery Homicide Division who was assigned to the case. The son of a county sheriff, Poole loved his job. His small-town demeanor belied a sharp, meticulous mind, one that helped him rise to the crème de la crème of murder investigators, RHD.

As far as Poole could tell, Lyga's story checked out. A security camera confirmed that he was being pursued by Gaines's Montero. He called for backup three times. More important, it caught the pattern of the shots, two controlled bursts, strictly by the book, just as Lyga had described. Dispatchers heard Lyga's frantic pleas for backup before the shooting. And the gun found near Gaines's body was registered to him—eliminating the possibility that it was planted after the shooting.

Gaines, however, proved more troubling. This wasn't his first road rage incident—he'd pulled his gun on plainclothes officers twice. The officer's Versace wardrobe didn't fit his $55,000 base salary—nor did his collection of luxury automobiles: a Mercedes-Benz, a BMW, and an Explorer SUV. The license plate on his Benz—ITSOKIA—seemed to be a taunt directed at Internal Affairs.

And then there was the question of the Montero itself, fully tricked out with a built-in TV and VCR. How could a cop with a family of four afford such a fancy car? Actually, he couldn't. Gaines did not own the customized SUV he was killed in. That car was registered to Death Row Records. As it turned out, the patrolman had been having an affair with Sharitha Knight, Suge Knight's ex-wife and Snoop Dogg's ex-manager. Gaines was also one of several cops who moonlighted as security guards for Death Row.

Gaines's fellow officers told Poole that Gaines recruited them on occasion to work well-paying, off-duty security gigs for Death Row Records. His locker contained photos of Death Row artists. One officer, who worked undercover as part of a federal task force investigating the label, claimed Gaines and other officers "acted as lookouts and advisors" during drug deals. A narcotics dog detected the faint scent of cocaine in the Montero.

Poole never found any concrete reasons for Gaines to come after Lyga, but he did find a dirty secret—a group of LAPD cops working security for a rap label with ties to the gang underworld. When Poole asked for permission to fully investigate Gaines's background, he said he was instructed to back off and let Internal Affairs handle it. Poole's superiors decided that his discoveries didn't merit a search warrant. By keeping the investigation internal, public scrutiny of crooked cops could be avoided.

"They said Gaines is dead, we're not investigating any further," Poole recalls. "But we had dozens of officers who worked for Suge Knight and that's a no-no."

Then on April 9, 1997, Poole received a call from the Wilshire Division's Detective Paul Inabu requesting a photo of Gaines. His office was chasing down a tip that implicated Gaines in Christopher Wallace's murder. Poole used it as an excuse to take over the murder investigation that no one else really wanted.

When Poole and his partner Fred Miller first took over the Wallace murder investigation, they believed that the gang angle had some merit.

"No matter how many times Puffy denied it, we knew the Crips had worked as bodyguards for Biggie when he came to LA," Poole said.

But the more he learned about Gaines, Death Row Records, the events in Las Vegas surrounding Tupac Shakur's shooting, and what happened that night, Poole soon abandoned that angle.

The Wallace murder had all of the makings of a professional hit—it wasn't the kind of haphazard affair where someone just dumped lead in your car. The shooter had to know where Wallace was sitting (through tinted windows no less), shoot him and only him, and make a clean getaway in plain sight of almost a hundred witnesses, a carful of off-duty cops that was following Wallace's Suburban, and a team of undercover ATF and FBI agents. There was also the report that police-style radios were used—another sign of a well-planned hit.

Poole received a tip from an incarcerated confidential informant that Knight had hired a contract killer with an Arabic name—"Amir" or "Ashmir"—to carry out a hit on Wallace. That clue also seemed to match bodyguard Eugene Deal's statement that a "Nation of Islam guy" shadowed Combs and Lil' Cease's memory that the shooter wore a suit and bow tie, standard Fruit of Islam attire.

Poole narrowed his focus toward the off-duty cops that were working for Death Row. All roads led to Wrightway Security.

Former Compton cop Reggie Wright Jr. was one of Knight's childhood friends and came from the same north Compton neighborhood. His father, for many years, was the head of the Compton police department's Gang Homicide Unit. Despite the plethora of gang-related incidents that have been rumored over the years at Death Row—perpetual smack-downs, pistol-whippings, and the occasional busting of shots—Knight didn't keep his buddy with police connections at arm's length. Instead he used it to his advantage. Death Row became one of Wrightway Security's biggest clients. Having cops around the label offered unique advantages.

"The more police officers [Knight] had in his pocket, the more power he had," Poole said. "It was a very smart thing for him to do. He was able to beat felony raps because police officers were present. I got reports where [David] Kenner was interviewed in the Mark Anthony Bell thing where he says 'nothing happened there because the LAPD was present.' And that's one reason why it didn't get filed, 'cause when the DA read that, he didn't file charges."

No matter what Poole uncovered, he complained, "the brass" blocked any moves that might blow up in the face of the department—like a cadre of dirty black cops. It would soon be out of their hands.

Errolyn Romero was a nervous wreck when the FBI and LAPD hauled in the 24-year-old Bank of America assistant manager for questioning less than a month after her South Los Angeles branch was robbed.

"She thought we already knew who the suspect was," Robbery Homicide Detective Brian Tyndall said.

Tyndall had good reason to think the attractive young Belizean was in on the November 6, 1997, heist at the bank where she worked. After all, she was the one who ordered $300,000 in extra cash to be on hand—$722,000, shrink-wrapped and ready to go for the two armed men who arrived ten minutes after the cash had been delivered.

When Tyndall and his fellow officers informed her that she had failed her lie detector test, Romero began stuttering so badly she could hardly get a word out.

In 1999, Harry Billups, a.k.a. Amir Muhammad, was named as a possible suspect in Wallace's murder. He told the press he was a mortgage broker, not an assassin. He has never been questioned by police.

So she simply reached into her purse and slid a business card across the table. It had an LAPD logo on it and belonged to officer David Mack.

"It literally took our breath away," Tyndall said.

A nine-year veteran of the force, Mack was a former track star for the world-class University of Oregon team. He was a family man who would moonlight as a security guard in a movie theater to make some extra cash. But there was a dark side. It was at that same South Central theatre that he first met—and seduced—19-year-old ticket-taker Romero.

A search of Mack's house turned up $5,600 in fifty-dollar bills, a $7,000 deposit slip, $20,000 worth of receipts, and various pistols. Poole was most interested in the 9-millimeter ammunition, the same caliber slugs used to kill Wallace, and the black SS Impala with chrome wheels—an exact match for the shooter's car.

Poole became convinced that Mack was tied to Wallace's murder. For one, he was a Compton native with ties to the same Blood set that Knight favored. From the moment he was arrested, Mack reportedly renounced his police loyalties and claimed to be a Mob Piru. Other sources who talked with Poole confirmed Mack's presence at a number of Death Row Records functions and video shoots, some of them reportedly with Kevin Gaines and another friend, Rafael Perez.

Mack's first visitor at the Montebello City Jail the day after Christmas was his college friend Harry Billups, a.k.a. Amir Muhammad. ("Amir" was one of the possible names for Wallace's assassin provided by a jailhouse informant.) Curiously, Muhammad signed in to see Mack with a false social security number and false address, which upped the intrigue in Poole's mind. When Poole had his DMV photo pulled up, his angular face matched the descriptions of the shooter given by Lil' Cease and others.

Poole interviewed Damien "D-Roc" Butler and showed him a picture of David Mack. D-Roc said he had seen Mack standing near the exit of the Petersen Automotive Museum. Mack also took personal days prior to Wallace's shooting—similar to the way he took to the Bank of America robbery. Another similarity was the use of police radios for the bank robbery—and the memory of several witnesses of hearing radios prior to Wallace's shooting.

These and other clues made Poole want to investigate Mack as a suspect in Wallace's murder. At the very least he wanted the car and the ammo tested. But Poole says the LAPD brass barred him from taking his inquiry any further: "They told me, 'We're not going to get involved in that.' Their attitude was, 'Mack had already gone down for bank robbery. Let's not get involved in more controversy.'"

Poole felt so discouraged about the Wallace case that he wanted to move out of Robbery Homicide altogether. When David Mack's friend and former partner, Rafael Perez, became the primary suspect behind the theft of six pounds of cocaine from a downtown police evidence locker, Poole got his wish.

The cocaine, worth roughly $800,000 on the street, led to Chief Parks's forming the then top-secret Robbery/Homicide Division Task Force. Because they knew the culprit was a cop, handpicked members of the Robbery Homicide division, Internal Affairs, and Narcotics were pulled together into one unit. Tyndall and Poole soon joined.

The Task Force's primary target, the serious, quiet, unassuming Rafael Antonia Perez, became another person when he carried his gun and badge. In 1993, Perez joined the West Bureau Buy Team, an elite undercover narcotics unit. David Mack was the veteran on the team—and Perez became his right hand. On October 26, 1993, Mack shot a suspect who was about to shoot Perez, saving his life. The event bonded the men—by Perez's own admission—*de por vida*.

The following year Perez transferred to the Rampart Division. And when a spot opened up in Rampart's elite Community Resources Against Street Hoodlums team (CRASH), another friend of Mack's, Sammy Martin, sponsored Perez.

Rampart CRASH cops held their ground with gangsta swagger. They wore their own street clothes, had their own headquarters, and made their own rules. Their motto: We Intimidate Those Who Intimidate Others.

"These guys don't play by the rules; we don't have to play by the rules," Perez explained. "They're out there committing murders and then they intimidate the witnesses, so the witnesses don't show up in court. So they're getting away with murder every day."

Framing gang members for shootings, planting evidence, falsifying drug buys, beating down suspects and lying about it in court were standard CRASH procedures. As long as their arrest numbers were high, no one asked questions.

Perez began selling the cocaine he took from gang members. After one bust in 1997, when the suspected dealer's pager beeped, Perez and his partner returned the page and sold the drugs. Soon Perez has several dealers under his thumb. One attractive seller, Veronica Quesada, also became his mistress. Perez got her and her brother, Carlos Romero, suspended sentences and used them as informants when they got in trouble.

Weekend blowouts to Vegas and balling with Mack were the norm. They joined a cigar-smoking club and went on Caribbean cruises. Two days after Mack's bank robbery, they were in a ballers' suite at Caesar's Palace in Las Vegas, blowing through $20,000 as if it were no big deal.

It seemed like the party would never stop.

A month later, however, Mack was behind bars for the bank job, and three months after that, Perez was arrested on August 25, 1998.

After searching his house and finding guns, stolen police radios, and badges that had been reported missing, Poole became convinced that the evidence was pointing to a pattern of corruption that was larger than one or two bad cops.

Three former LAPD officers steeped in controversy: Kevin Gaines, left, lived with Suge Knight's ex-wife and worked as a part-time security guard for Death Row until he was shot by an undercover cop in a road-rage incident. David Mack, center, was convicted of bank robbery and suspected of having ties to Death Row and to Wallace's murder. Mack's friend, Officer Rafael Perez, right, was caught stealing pounds of cocaine from a police evidence room. He became the star witness in the LAPD's ignominious Rampart Scandal.

"Chief, it's more than this case," Poole recalled telling Chief Bernard Parks at a Task Force briefing about yet another member of the CRASH team, officer Brian Hewitt, who was accused of beating gang member Ismael Jimenez during an interrogation at Rampart. "You've got a group of vigilante cops at Rampart Division," said Poole. Officer Bryan Tyndall spoke up, adding that Poole still believed Mack was involved in the Christopher Wallace murder. Parks was incensed.

"Limit your investigation to the Jimenez case," Poole remembers Parks saying. Poole says he was warned by his supervisor not to bring up Mack, Perez, or the Wallace murder again.

Matt Lait and Scott Glover of the *Los Angeles Times* spoke to other officers who attended that meeting in the Parker Center. None of the officers who were present remembered things happening the way Poole described.

Whether it was the words of a "disgruntled cop," or fellow officers trying to cover their ass—there was no adequate explanation why Poole's forty-page report about all things Rampart, Mack, Wallace, and Death Row Records—complete with diagrams and illustrations—was reduced to two pages before it reached the district attorney's office. Poole said that his supervisors, Lieutenant Emmanuel Hernandez and Detective Supervisor Ron Ito, edited out anything that didn't have to do with Hewitt and Jimenez.

By September 1999 Mack was sentenced to fourteen years for the bank robbery. Right before jury selection began for the second Perez trial, Lait and Glover ran their first story connecting Mack and Gaines—highlighting their baller lifestyle, the fact that investigators were looking into their connections to Death Row Records—all the stuff Chief Parks never wanted the public to know. Investigators had also discovered Perez's technique of replacing evidence locker cocaine with Bisquik, and had linked him to eleven pieces of questionable evidence. Within days of the story, Perez turned into a state witness.

"We didn't know if he was going to talk about Biggie Smalls's murder, the bank robbery involving David Mack, home-invasion robberies, other additional narcotics," Detective Brian Tyndall told *Frontline*. "We just weren't sure."

Fifty hours and thousands of pages of transcript later, Perez implicated 70 fellow police officers of planting false evidence, ripping off drug dealers, and brutalizing suspects, among other things. More than 100 convictions were overturned as a result of what came to be known as the Rampart Scandal. The city was forced to pay the victims more than $40 million dollars to settle their claims.

Perez failed all five polygraph tests he was given—which independent experts from both his legal team and the district attorney's office found were flawed. But soon it wasn't about just his word anymore. By June 2000, the LAPD's corruption task force confirmed 80 percent of Perez's anecdotes—attributing those he was wrong about not to deception but to faults in memory separated from the time of the events.

Some details Perez never cleared up were his relationship with David Mack, the Bank of America robbery, or possible links to Wallace's murder.

"I considered him a very good friend who saved my life," Perez told investigators. "Was I involved in the bank robbery? No. Was it a big coincidence that we both ended up in this kind of trouble? It's a very big coincidence."

Chief Parks, when asked how all of this could happen under his watch, took the high road. "Most people are not aware that the Los Angeles Police Department found the misconduct and immediately took action," he said. Some cited the fact that Parks formed the Robbery/Homicide Task Force—later renamed the Rampart Task Force—demonstrated his commitment to rooting out corruption.

Not everyone was as impressed.

"We still don't know the extent of the scandal," said U.S.C. law professor Erwin Chemerinsky. "We don't know how many officers in Rampart Crash were involved; we don't know how many were complicit by their silence or how high it went. Every attempt to have a better investigation, Parks thwarted."

Detective Russell Poole resigned on October 25, 1999, a month after the scandal reached a fever pitch. He went public soon after, talking first with *Los Angeles Times* reporters Matt Lait and Scott Glover about his blocked leads.

Lait and Glover's first airing of Poole's theories about Mack, "Ex-LAPD Officer Is Suspect in Rapper's Slaying, Records Show," was so controversial that it divided the *Los Angeles Times* newsroom. The article was the first to fully reveal David Mack's connections to Death Row, the murder, and the Bloods. The article also revealed Amir Muhammad's name to the general public as a possible suspect, and stated that no one could locate him.

The problem was that it only took Chuck Philips three days to find Muhammad. In three weeks he negotiated an interview through Muhammad's lawyer, Bryant Calloway. And after the internal firestorm at the newspaper, it took five months to get the article published.

"I'm not a murderer, I'm a mortgage broker," Muhammad told Philips. "The story made it sound like I was some mystery assassin who committed this heinous crime and then just dropped off the face of the earth, which is the furthest thing from the truth." Muhammad said he worked out at the same fitness center almost every day. "I'm not that difficult to find," Muhammad insisted. He didn't address why he left a false social security number and address when visiting Mack, and Philips didn't ask.

Their conflicting stories about the Wallace murder put Philips and Lait on opposite sides of a major rift at the *Times*. The biggest source of strife came from something that the new lead detective, Dave Martin, told Philips: Muhammad was not a suspect in Wallace's shooting, and hadn't been one for a long time.

The back and forth about this matter between the *Times*'s Metro and Business sections got ugly. *Brill's Content* ran a story about the in-fighting three weeks after Philips's May 3, 2000, interview with Muhammad ran. The *New Times LA* and *LA Weekly* both reveled in the in-fighting, taking potshots at Lait and Glover.

In exclusive conversations for *Unbelievable,* Lait and Glover insisted that the Muhammad theory was alive and well when they wrote their article—and not just based on Poole's word. The duo said they had numerous documents, notes from other investigators, and well-placed sources that were already helping them with their comprehensive Rampart coverage.

"I can assure you that Scott and I were dealing with the highest levels of the department," Lait said. "If it were wrong, considering what we'd been doing, sure as shit they would have come out and said something."

Both sets of reporters might have been correct. The LAPD confirmed the veracity of the Lait/Glover story with the *Washington Post* on December 10, 1999, only to change its mind. And while Muhammad's attorney was assured by the LAPD that his client wasn't a suspect (directly contradicting what the *Washington Post* was told), they said they still wanted to talk to Muhammad—neither side tried very hard to make it happen.

On September 26, 2000, Russell Poole sued Chief Parks and the department, claiming his First Amendment rights were violated when they prevented him from blowing the whistle.

A year later, despite repeated dismissals of Poole and his credibility, Chief Parks would confirm the central points of Poole's argument.

"Perez is a good friend of David Mack's, who both were good friends of Gaines," Parks told Peter Boyer for an episode of *Frontline* that aired on PBS May 15, 2001, a year after the *Los Angeles Times* debacle and two years after the Rampart scandal broke. "And I think the picture reflected that we had some people in this department that were, in a coordinated effort, involved in some very serious criminal misconduct."

On April 9, 2002, Voletta Wallace and Faith Evans filed a civil suit against the LAPD, former police chief Bernard Parks, and two other chiefs, citing "deliberate indifference" to Christopher Wallace's murder and the subsequent investigation.

Captain Jim Tatreau, head of the LAPD's Robbery Homicide division, dismissed the lawsuit's allegations as ridiculous.

"I'd be so happy to be able to develop any information to solve that case," Tatreau said. "If they were LAPD cops, so be it. Like we haven't taken hits before?"

Steven Katz, the current lead detective on the Wallace murder investigation, said the Mack/Muhammad connection had been "looked into and documented" but wasn't hot. He gave the *Washington Post* the same excuse he gave the *New Times* two years earlier: "We've attempted to locate him. At the time we went to look for him, we could not find him." Mack's Impala wasn't tested, he said, because "there were other mitigating factors that led us to look into other directions."

Weeks later, Chuck Philips added another mitigating factor to the public's interest about the Wallace and Shakur murders.

When Philips's front-page piece "Who Killed Tupac Shakur?" appeared in the *Los Angeles Times* on the eve of the sixth anniversary of the rapper's shooting—September 6, 2002—it set off a firestorm that hadn't been seen in years.

Philips's assertions that the Southside Crips—specifically Orlando Anderson—were responsible for Tupac's murder weren't unfamiliar to anyone who had followed his *Times* coverage from the very beginning, or read Rob Marriott's "All That Glitters" in the May 1997 issue of VIBE (the same issue where my own final interview with Wallace ran). The cornerstone of both Marriott's and Philips's accounts was Tim Brennan's Compton Police Department affidavit, which Anderson's attorney Rene L. Campbell described as being "full of lies."

No less a gang authority than former Eight-Trey Gangsta Crip Sanyika "Monster Kody" Shakur had already written a VIBE article based on conversations he had with Suge Knight when both men were inmates at the California Institute for Men in Chino. Suge told Sanyika that "Baby Lane" pulled the trigger on Tupac Shakur. "I really don't know why Suge would say something like that," Anderson told Sanyika Shakur in another VIBE interview. "I wish they would find who did it so I can prove my innocence," he said. Just months later, on May 28, 1998, the 23-year-old was killed in a gang-related shootout at a Compton car wash.

What set off the frenzy was Philips's assertion that Christopher Wallace had personally provided the .40-caliber pistol used to kill Shakur. Until this time, nobody had even suggested that Wallace was in Las Vegas the night of the murder.

Philips wrote that the Crips "sent an emissary to a penthouse suite at the MGM, where Wallace was booked under a false name. In Vegas to party . . . [Wallace] had quickly learned about Shakur's scuffle with Anderson. Wallace gathered a handful of thugs and East Coast rap associates to hear what the Crips had to say."

Philips said he based his dramatic account on anonymous sources who were present at the meeting. "The Crips envoy explained that the gang was prepared to kill Shakur but expected to collect $1 million for its efforts," he wrote. "Wallace agreed, with one condition, a witness said. He pulled out a loaded .40-caliber Glock pistol and placed it on the table in front of him. He didn't just want Shakur dead. He wanted the satisfaction of knowing the fatal bullet came from his gun."

After the shooting, Wallace supposedly returned to New York to begin work on *Life After Death*—paying only $50,000 of the $1 million he was alleged to have promised. This part of Philips's story fit with the previously reported theories that Wallace had paid the ultimate price because he or members of his team had welched on a million-dollar debt.

Wallace's family and friends were livid.

"Place me in Vegas that night!" said Lil' Cease when I called him at 5 A.M. on the morning the story ran.

"I mean, people really got to start showing if they smart or dumb!" Lil' Cease continued. "People gotta start thinking. You done heard every theory from Suge on down to the East Coast/West Coast shit, on down to the Crips shit. But the last thing—you never heard a tiptoe of Big being nowhere near that murder."

Lil' Cease claimed he and Wallace watched the fight from Big's home in Teaneck, New Jersey—and heard about Shakur's shooting on the news like everyone else.

"And then why would you pay some niggas a million dollars? That's bullshit. Pac just had a fight with these Crips . . . They already got their plan set on what they gonna do, and so Big just gon' say, 'I'ma pay you to do this?' Y'all are gonna do it *anyway*. Like Big got a million dollars to be throwing away.

"And then how can a nigga in his prime sneak into Vegas?

Shakur's Death Row entourage attacked Orlando Anderson in a hotel lobby hours before Shakur was shot. Anderson was also present at the party on the night Wallace was killed. He maintained his innocence until he, too, was killed by gunfire.

You got athletes, celebrities, actors, people from all over the world. You gonna tell me six-foot-two 300-pound Biggie? Kangol? One of the hottest niggas on TV at the moment? Snuck into the hotel under a false name? And nobody came to that room? No housekeeping? Not one picture?"

When I contacted Chuck Philips at the *Los Angeles Times* on September 7, the day his story broke, Philips sounded harried, offering terse "no comments" to my questions. When asked why he broke the story now—before he could get his key sources to go on the record—Philips would only say "'Cause it's true." In the year that's followed, he has maintained that stance.

What bothered most people who read the report was the lack of specific sources. In the piece, Philips wrote that he based his reports on "police affidavits and court documents as well as interviews with investigators, witnesses to the crime, and members of the Southside Crips who had never before discussed the killing outside the gang. Fearing retribution, they agreed to be interviewed only if their names were not revealed."

Because no names were ever attributed to the information, no one could judge how believable it was. Which Crips talked? Did Zip break his silence? Keefee D? Was it an OG who said this or some new jack who wanted to make a name for himself? Without knowing who talked, it was hard for many readers to believe. What proof is there that Wallace was in Vegas that night?

And with the timing of the news, coming right on the sixth anniversary of Tupac's murder, and the *Los Angeles Times* promotional machine in full gear—down to maps and diagrams of the shooting—it seemed like the paper wanted to sell some papers around the controversy, instead of holding the story until some of these sources could at least come on the record. The end result was that the paper—and Philips—were accused of having an opportunistic, racist agenda against hip hop and Wallace in particular.

I'm one of the few people who got to know both Chuck Philips and Christopher Wallace on a personal level. About Chuck, I can say this—he's no racist. And he is by far the most meticulous, responsible reporter I've ever met. And about Wallace, I can also say this—he's no murderer nor willing accomplice either.

Philips, whom I've shared bylines with when I was at the *Times*, struck me as someone who never approached a story with a specific agenda—which I can't say about every writer and editor I worked with at Calendar. He could write about the music—and business—with equal aplomb because he respected the people behind it, from the interns to the CEOs. He was one of the only people at the paper who seemed to take the up-and-coming hip-hop moguls seriously and—unlike Frank Williams or myself—was in a position to guarantee them coverage.

The morning of the Tupac shooting, as Frank Williams and I worked on the September 9, 1999, story, "Star Rapper Tupac Shakur Badly Wounded," I remember being dumbfounded at how quickly the hardened Metro reporters made up their mind that it was an East Coast vs. West Coast beef before we even wrote a single word. The sidebar on rap violence was snapped up, edited, and laid out before Frank even had a chance to file his report from Las Vegas.

Chuck was different, though. When Shakur and later Wallace died, he was one of the few people at the paper who didn't immediately claim it was East Coast vs. West Coast. He was also the first to follow up both the Shakur and Wallace murders, chiding both the Los Angeles Police Department and the Las Vegas Police Department for dropping the ball as the leads in both cases got colder and detectives seemed to become even more indifferent.

The Death Row Records story was part of Chuck Philips's turf as a music business reporter for the *Times*. Philips had covered the company from the very beginning, when no one else was paying attention. He enjoyed a fairly good rapport with Suge Knight. Yet despite his professional respect for Knight, Philips did not shy away from writing pieces that did great damage to Death Row.

It was Philips who reported on Knight's questionable dealings with District Attorney Lawrence M. Longo—renting his Malibu beach house and signing his daughter Gina to a recording contract—which got Longo fired and got Knight's plea bargain reexamined. Philips wrote about Knight's run-ins with Mark Anthony Bell and Steve Cantrock, articles that created the atmosphere of outrage that helped send Knight to prison on a parole violation. They also laid the foundation for Connie Bruck's famous Tupac profile in *The New Yorker* as well as Ronin Ro's seminal book, *Have Gun Will Travel*, and, though he would probably be loath to admit it, Randall Sullivan's *LAbyrinth*.

I was as surprised as everybody else when the front-page story implicating Wallace was first published. But the fact that Chuck Philips wrote it made the allegations impossible for me to dismiss. Instead of allowing anger to blind my objectivity, I stepped back and re-read it numerous times for clarity.

When the smoke cleared, it all came down to whom I believed: gang members with their own questionable agendas and loyalties, or the friends and family of the accused. I chose the latter.

I personally don't believe that Christopher Wallace would pay to have Tupac Shakur killed. I believe this because I actually asked Wallace about the rumors, and he looked me in the eye when he answered calmly that, no, he didn't have anything to do with the murder. I think there was a part of him that was still down for Shakur, no matter how much shit his old friend talked.

Long before Philips's story broke, people around Wallace and Shakur were saying how, if they ever had a chance to sit down, they probably would have become friends again. Their beef just wasn't something that Wallace took seriously—which is why he could joke about it in songs.

The Chris Wallace I got to know was no saint, and he'd be the first to admit that he did have a violent side—but he was also smart. During our last conversations, he said he knew that people would suspect he had something to do with Tupac's murder no matter what. Just as it was with his song "Who Shot Ya"—everyone assumed it was written about Tupac despite the fact that he recorded it long before Shakur was shot in New York.

Speaking hypothetically, if Wallace ever did contemplate coming after Shakur—and I don't believe that he ever would—but if he did, he sure would have been a lot slicker about it than was depicted in the *Times*.

People who didn't get to know Wallace don't understand how paranoid he was about the people he met after he became a rap star. He was cool with many, but close with a few. If you weren't from around Fulton and St. James, with years in the game, he would never have handed a gun to you. And Wallace, with gun charges pending, a prior record, and federal agents trailing, had far too much to lose than to get caught up like this. If he did make a move against someone, it would have been with someone from Brooklyn he knew would "hold him down," not some cats whose loyalty he had to pay for. Wallace wouldn't even place himself in a scenario that stupid on one of his records, let alone in real life.

But let's be clear about this: Chuck Philips isn't the villain here. Focusing too much energy on him, it's easy to lose sight of the real problem—the Los Angeles Police Department. With the plethora of leads that have floated around over these seven years, why hasn't the LAPD done more to solve this case? Or, for that matter, why has the Las Vegas Police Department failed to solve Shakur's murder? Why is Chuck Philips still the only person to have talked with Amir Muhammad, or with the Crips in the car who rode on Tupac that night? Why have the police never questioned Chuck Philips about who his sources were? If they were in the car when Shakur was shot, they would be equal accomplices in the murder—and the statute of limitations on murder doesn't run out.

Why have so many leads gone nowhere? That's easy. The Los Angeles Police Department, in my opinion, doesn't give a damn about solving Christopher Wallace's murder. If it did, it would either disprove Poole's theories about David Mack or haul in the people listed in the affidavit, and start pressuring folks for names and details on both murders.

Since when does the Robbery Homicide Division have to wait on a lawyer to talk with Amir Muhammad, as Detective Katz told the *Washington Post*? They're cops—not journalists. When they care about solving a case, they will haul your ass in. That's the power of the badge.

And how hard could they have been looking if the suspect was running ads in local papers for his own mortgage lending business? Detective Poole never claimed he was absolutely right—he's claimed that he was prevented from fully exploring the evidence that he had in hand to remove all doubt that it wasn't gangs, the police, or both that got Christopher Wallace murdered.

"There were other people in the department working on [the Muhammad angle] and the documents show that," Lait says. "There were a number of detectives that were doing surveillance on locations that were linked to Mack and Mr. Muhammad," he says.

"Figure it out one way or the other, or rule it out if it's not valid. But they can't even rule it out," Lait says of the cops. "They're not talking to people."

Many of the people who could have answered essential questions about the Shakur case, like Alton "Buntry" McDonald, Aaron "Heron" Palmer, and Henry "Hen Dogg" Smith, on the Piru side and Jerry "Monk" Bonds and Orlando Anderson on the Southside Crip side have been murdered in the years since both Wallace and Shakur were killed. Time's running out.

When I called the LAPD's Detective Steven Katz to ask him whether or not anyone has talked with Chuck Philips about his Southside Crip sources, or with Amir Muhammad after three years of broken appointments, or if they had any hope of ever solving the case, our conversation was extremely brief.

"First of all, this case is in litigation, and I'm not making any comment on this case at all," Katz said.

"What about the new . . ."

"Let me stop you before you go on," Katz continued. "I'm not . . . making . . . any . . . comment . . . at . . . all. You can call our media relations department, I can give you the phone number: 213-485-3586."

"Okay. Is the case, at least, still open?"

"I'm not answering any questions on it."

"So the case is closed?"

"I'm not answering any questions," Katz said with flat, final determination.

This case remains on the shelf for one of two reasons: either because the powers that be don't care who killed Shakur and Wallace—or because they are afraid of where the evidence may lead.

So I'm urging anyone who reads this book and claims to have any love for Christopher Wallace to call the LAPD and tell the department how urgent it is to solve this case—or better yet, to come forward with any relevant information. That's the only way to make this a "redball" case—one that's a priority instead of an afterthought. That way, for better or for worse, Christopher Wallace's family, Tupac Shakur's family, and their millions of fans can have something that resembles a resolution.

SKY'S THE LIMIT

66 While we out here, say the hustlas prayer
If the game shakes me or breaks me
I hope it makes me a better man... 99

Dripping wet, the chubby little boy dressed in red, white, and blue swim trunks stares at the stranger standing in his grandmother's driveway with wide, curious eyes.

I stare back at him, just as curious. I'm smiling because he's gotten so big so quickly. He doesn't look anything like his baby pictures anymore. He's practically grown, with long thick limbs and a belly inherited from his dad. He's going to be a big kid—6'3", 225 at least. Even with his mother's fair skin, Christopher Wallace Jr. looks just like his father.

"Hey, C.J.," I say. I'm a little shaken, because, as I look at his face, I can't stop thinking about my last conversation with his father. What strikes me is how much he would have loved to see his son get this big.

"Is your grandmother here?"

"Yes," he replies, pointing toward the door. "She's inside." And without another word he scurries off toward the backyard to join his big sister T'Yanna and his little brother, Todd Jr., who are already splashing around in the pool.

Ms. Wallace appears in the door and invites me inside with a warm smile and a hug. We've only met a couple of times, but she welcomes me like family. "You just missed Faith," she says. Evans has dropped off her sons to stay with their grandmother while she performs a few concerts in the New York area. Ms. Wallace is all smiles today; the former elementary schoolteacher loves taking care of children—especially her grandchildren.

The house is bright and comfortable. Her son bought the land and started the construction before he was murdered. There's enough space in back for Ms. Wallace to do a bit of gardening, as she did when she was growing up in Jamaica. "I love flowers," she says. "If you call me in the summertime, I'm not in here; I'm out there in the garden." The air is filled with the smell of food cooking and the sound of kids laughing and playing. Right now Mrs. Wallace may be the happiest she's been since her only child was murdered.

When Ms. Wallace looks at her grandchildren T´Yanna and C.J. she sees her son. "There are steps that I've taken for both of them that my son asked me to do... I will die making sure of that."

The house's sitting room is like a small museum dedicated to Christopher Wallace. There's a huge oil painting of him over the fireplace, and framed photographs from various stages of his life stand on every flat surface. There are trophies from *The Source* and *Billboard* and MTV and various platinum sales plaques from Bad Boy. Over on the mantle is the first award he ever won, an artifact from the days before Christopher became Biggie. It's a tiny fireman with a hose in his hand, commemorating an outstanding elementary-school report on fire prevention.

For the first few years, Voletta couldn't talk about Christopher without crying. She still cries sometimes—but happier thoughts surface now as well.

We're sitting in the dining room, looking at pictures that bring memories flooding back—many of which appear in this book. She can still reenact entire conversations with her son. Like the day she walked into his first apartment, the Brooklyn duplex that he rented after *Ready to Die* started selling. She wasn't surprised to find it as much of a pig sty as his old room at 226 St. James.

"I looked around and said, 'My God! Is any human being supposed to be living like this?'" She plays up her disgust for comic effect.

"And he would look at me with his most loving smile and say, 'Tell me something, Ma. Whose house is this? Is this 2645 Eliot or 226 St. James? Yo, this is my house. I can do whatever I want.'"

Mrs. Wallace cracks herself up and the dialogue continues.

"'Did the cleaning lady even come into this room?'" I asked.

"'Yeah, but I told her don't touch my drawers. Ma, you wanna wash my drawers?'"

When Ms. Wallace does her Biggie impression, her shoulders hunch back and her voice drops a few registers. Her Jamaican accent and regal bearing disappear, and, for a few seconds, she speaks with a full on, corner-of-Fulton lilt. The tilt of her head, the way her eyes sparkle—it's clear where her son got his charisma.

She talks about cooking his favorite food: the red pea soup, the jerked turkey wings, the roast pork. Sea bass seasoned with scallions. She remembers how after he broke his leg the second time he adopted a healthier diet. She recalls his excitement over losing thirty pounds.

"Can you imagine me boy, getting' out of this hospital and losing a hundred pounds? I'm gonna be sporting those Calvin Klein drawers, Ma!"

She laughs when I ask about the women in Christopher's life.

"Everybody was his mistress," she says, "and they keep saying, Biggie loved me. And, He was gonna marry me." She rolls her eyes. "Please. Biggie loved that almighty dollar. That's what Biggie loved. That and his children."

What about Lil' Kim?

"Kim was my son's business partner. Do you hear me? Yes, they had an affair, but trust me, I did not hear him say [about her], 'Wife, love of my life.' And the same thing with Ms. Baltimore, Ms. Chicago, Ms. Maryland, and Ms. California. Everybody wants to say, 'Oh, I was his heart. I was his eyes. I was his nose.' How are you breathing then?" she says, laughing mirthlessly.

"Why couldn't you say you were a good friend or a groupie? Say I slept with him two or three times, but don't walk around saying he was gonna marry you. Hello—he wasn't divorced. Get a life!"

When she talks about Jan—who lives with T'Yanna in the house next door in this secluded Pennsylvania gated community—or about Faith—who calls her almost every day—her tone is totally different. Time, grandchildren, and tragedy have helped to heal any lingering misgivings. In some ways, she says, Faith has grown since her son's death.

As a solo artist, Lil' Kim has wrapped herself in the legend of Biggie Smalls. On one record, she refers to herself as "Miss White, the Queen of New York."

"If Christopher was alive today, Faith wouldn't be as happy," she says. Not that she thinks that Faith didn't love her son. She knows that she did. It's just that she knows how possessive her son could be, and how selfish. "I think Christopher would be calling her as if he still owned her," she says. Ms. Wallace is happy that Evans has found stability with her husband and manager Todd Russaw. She's glad Evans doesn't have to deal with Christopher's infidelity, and other problems that came from getting married too quickly. She's happy that Faith has finally found peace.

Ms. Wallace's life is peaceful for the most part. She divides her time between the Catskills and Brooklyn, where she oversees the Christopher Wallace Foundation, which provides money for schools under a program called B.I.G., which stands for "books instead of guns." The foundation is also making plans for a permanent community center in Biggie's old neighborhood.

"My goal is to have something strong in his name," she says. "If we have a community center, I can take a lot more kids off the street," she says. There is so much work to be done. The phone always seems to be ringing with one initiative or another. She is working on a book of her own with dream hampton, the story of a single mother's journey, raising a son, then losing him to the forces of darkness, and somehow carrying on.

The only time she gets really angry is when she talks about Los Angeles and the LAPD. That's her other main goal—bringing her son's assassins to justice.

What irks her the most isn't just that her son was under surveillance on the night he died. But that if they were on his case like that, why can't anyone solve his murder? She receives anonymous tips from time to time, and passes them on to her own private investigator. She's convinced that lots of people out there know more than they are telling.

"Where was this surveillance? Everybody is just hush hush! Why this great conspiracy? When my son died, they had twenty-one police officers working on the case. Then one day I called and it was ten. Then there were five. Then there were two. Then Russell Poole quit. Now everyone's resigning. Are you handing over information to those new people?"

It frustrates her that, with the exception of Faith and a few of Wallace's closest friends, no one else seems bothered by the fact that the case hasn't been solved.

"If they loved him so much," she asks bitterly, "how come they never ask about the investigation? Am I angry? Yes, I'm angry!" she says, exhaling loudly. Hell hath no fury like a mother who's been disrespected.

At that moment, C.J. and his half sister walk in the room, fresh from the pool, and ask "Mee-maw" for some food. Just like that, her mood brightens.

She has never claimed that her son was an angel, but she wants the world to remember the person she knew and loved. Not just the rap star who died in the so-called East Coast/West Coast war. She still doesn't care much for rap—but now it's for different reasons. When Christopher was alive she didn't like the music because of the profanity and the themes. Now, after listening to her son's records, she senses that the music lacks depth. She's beginning to realize just how much the music world lost when her son was killed.

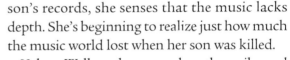

Voletta Wallace also remembers the smiles and the sarcasm, the talent her son displayed as a graphic artist as well as a recording artist. She still has the drawing he made on the night before he was killed: a picture of his heart breaking in two with T'Yanna's and C.J.'s names written inside.

She spends her time now working on the foundation and watching her grandchildren grow up. And sometimes, during quiet moments, she thinks about the little boy who was so special to her—and whom the rest of the world barely even knows.

"Things are smiling with me," she says as I begin to take my leave. "I'm doing good. My son took care of me. Social security will chip in." She pauses, looking out her window in the afternoon sun.

"Time will take care of them," she says. "Everyone that tried to get over on my son, time will take care of them."

Faith sings "Walk With Me, Jesus" at the 2003 B.I.G. Night Out benefit in New York. On her album *Faithfully*, she used the beats to "Juicy" and "Who Shot Ya" as a way of "paying homage to him without singing about him."

June 19, 2002. DJ Premier leans back in his chair behind the mixing board in Studio B at Manhattan's D&D studios. Behind him sits a well-worn MPC 60, the same one he's had for the last fourteen years. Looking down at the beat-up drum machine makes me feel as if I'm looking at the hip hop equivalent of B.B. King's legendary guitar Lucille. Primo's made magic with that thing, bent over in the corner of a loud, smoky room, pouring his soul in along with the soul records he's dug up over the years to make his classics.

Studio B is the smallest room in the building and has D&D's oldest board, but Primo wouldn't have it any other way. This is the room where all the history was made. And Premier wants nothing to do with the latest Pro-Tools software.

"When you record to tape, you get more of a raw, full sound because the tape can withstand a certain amount of pressure, decibel-wise," he says. "With digital, everything is compressed. It sounds good, and it's clear, but it cuts out all the beef that comes with it when you lay it down." He leans toward the dilapidated 24-track board and caresses it for a second, like an old lover. "Analog is straight raw," he says. "You get a better thickness."

Ever since he laced the Gang Starr sureshot "Dwyck" here, this is the only place Primo works. So many career-defining hits have been recorded here; the room just has a vibe. That's the thing about the real gems: You can't plan them. They just happen. From the time Premier finished chopping up "Impeach the President" to the time Biggie walked through the door, smoked a blunt, had his wick dipped by two honeys, and laced the track with his vocals, a classic was born. The whole thing took maybe four hours.

One of Primo's boys, a big cat from Brooklyn dressed in a sweatshirt and Timberlands, nods his head as Primo talks about the old days, smiling.

"Damn," he says, shaking his head and thinking about Biggie. "That nigga took three or four hours to make some shit that'll last three or four hundred years."

Premier laughs, then gets to talking about Nas rapping his way through the first verse of "New York State of Mind" off the dome, in one seamless take. It's the kind of stuff you can't just click a mouse and reproduce.

Eight months and three days later, on February 23, 2003, D&D Studios permanently closes its doors. The Pro-Tools revolution—and the fact that nobody records to two-inch tape anymore—finally put them out of business. No matter how important D&D once was to hip hop, it just didn't make sense financially. Because, increasingly, that's what music—even rap music—seems to be about nowadays: the bottom line. The soul of a record has little to do with it.

I am reminded about what Don Pooh said to me one night when we were rolling through the heart of Crown Heights in his truck, listening to "They Reminisce Over You" by Pete Rock & C.L. Smooth and talking about how much hip hop has changed since March 9, 1997—the day the music died. "Hip hop now is like this really fly girl with a big-ass scar across her face," Pooh said, wheeling his big truck toward the Brooklyn Bridge. "She still fly, but you can always see that scar. She didn't die. She's not dead. She's just not as pretty."

Premier claims he doesn't even listen to hip hop much anymore. The world's finest hip hop producer says something happened to the music he loves since the death of Biggie and Tupac. The thrill is gone. Everyone is more concerned with selling records than just making dope beats and rhymes. "Now it's about watering it down to where it's not even pure anymore," he says. "It's definitely rap—not hip hop." He insists that if Run-D.M.C. were an unknown group trying to shop a song like "Rock-Box" right now, they couldn't get a record deal. And he's probably right.

"People be like 'Oh, it's too hardcore," Premier says with a look of disgust. "Back then you have to be hardcore to even think about selling a record."

And now? When Terrell Owens, the braggadocious San Francisco 49ers wide receiver, appeared on *ESPN SportsCenter*'s Budweiser Hot Seat last summer, he blew through each question thrown at him. He said he feared no one on the football field, and compared his basketball game to Tracy McGrady's, saying that he could play in the NBA right now and be an all-star.

Quizmaster Scott Van Pelt only stumped him once: "Biggie or Tupac?"

"Wow!" he said, eyes widening. He paused. "I can't say both?"

Nowadays, whenever anyone talks about hip hop, those are the two standards of quality that are mentioned: Biggie and Tupac. Rakim, KRS-One, LL, Big Daddy Kane, Melle Mel, Run, Ice Cube, and Slick Rick could all make legitimate claims as the greatest of all time, but when it comes down to it, these two men have come to define the art form, much as Charlie Parker and John Coltrane have come to define jazz saxophone.

"Those two muthafuckas were bigger than life," says Nas, who was dissed on record by both artists—and has outlived them both. "There's gonna be all kinds of shit said about them. Forever. They were bigger than life. Bigger than Elvis."

Tupac's image itself has become a symbol of cult revolution—sandwiched on the T-shirt racks between Bob Marley and Che Guevara from St. Mark's Place in Greenwich Village to the tourist shops in Paris's Montmartre.

Biggie's legacy is different. Wallace's lasting imprint on hip hop is more musical than iconographic. He is a master of flow, of lyrical rhythm and technique—the Jordan to Rakim's Magic. While his catalogue of unreleased records isn't as large as Tupac's, the quality of many of the surviving freestyles is unsurpassed.

A closer reexamination of the albums *Ready to Die* and *Life After Death* reveals that the records work on two levels. The first level is the stories that Wallace tells, but the second is the sheer display of technique—the alternating fast and slow styles, the stutter steps, the double and triple rhyme schemes, and a structural integrity so complex that even a pop hit like "Hypnotize" is a seminar on MC skills.

Donald Harrison, the former Art Blakey Jazz Messenger who mentored Wallace about music from a young age, readily compares Wallace to another famous Chris: Charles Christopher Parker.

"He had a vast knowledge of the inner workings of music," says Harrison. "You can hear that when he's rhyming. I taught Chris what triplets were and eighth notes were and how to accent triplets like—DAH buh dah / AH buh dah—and how to accent eighth notes. That's basically a Charlie Parker thing. Bird would accent his triplets and his eighth notes."

Always a fan at heart, Wallace was thrilled to meet Kool Herc, the Jamaican DJ who moved to the Bronx and started hip hop.

Harrison also notes that as with jazz, hip hop's heroes are generational. It's not about Bird versus Cannonball Adderley or John Coltrane versus Sonny Rollins. Each one takes something from those who went before and interprets it in their own style, furthering the legacy.

"The main thing that's similar to be-bop is good MCs can improvise—freestyle," Harrison observes. "You hear guys paying homage to Biggie," he says. "They check out his style and they start building their style based on his style even though they may flip it but they still were influenced by him. And Biggie was influenced by Run-D.M.C. and even Tupac."

Unfortunately, because of their conflict, the lasting memory of Wallace and Shakur is as much about controversy and premature violent death as it is about two completely different approaches to rhyming. Yet each one set a standard by which others are measured: 2Pac was the master of profound, raw emotion—menace, rage, and love. Biggie was the master of style, narrative, and cynical reflection. Of course their conflict itself also affected the rappers left in their wake.

"That wasn't a battle," says Nas about the strife between the two rap giants. "It was beef. Tupac was on some straight war shit. Big was on some Mafia shit with class without saying names. Like, If we got beef I ain't gonna say your name. You know, I'ma just see you in the street. But take these subliminal words, maw-fucker, 'cause I ain't like you either. And Pac's shit was like, Fuck that. Let's blow the buildings down. Let's blow the city up. They're two different kinds of geniuses, like Malcolm and Martin."

"I thought he was smart to stay silent when Tupac started his war of words," Jay-Z stated in a VIBE cover story. "And on the real, I could tell the whole situa-

D.M.C. and Run look on as DJ Jam Master Jay shows young Biggie some love. Just a few years later, the two legends were gone.

tion made him depressed. We had worked hard to leave a certain kind of life behind, and from the beginning that thing felt like more than a rap battle."

When Wallace was killed, the King of New York's throne was suddenly vacated, and both Nas and Jay-Z felt entitled. Jay, who was closer to Big, dedicated his second album to his fallen friend. The song "The City Is Mine" essentially proclaimed that the rap game was his for the taking. Nas—who was the young don before Biggie even got on—didn't take the challenge lightly. His response on "We Will Survive" was thinly veiled but pointed: "It used to be fun, making records to see your response," Nas rhymed, addressing Wallace. "But now competition is none, now that you're gone. / And these niggas is wrong. Using your name in vain. / And they claim to be New York's king?"

As Jay-Z's star rose and Nas's fell, the competition became even fiercer. As Jay-Z became the pop idol, crossing over with Broadway show samples like "Hard Knock Life," Nas reemerged, blowing up with the underground classic "Stillmatic" in which he called Jay "the rap version of Sisqo."

Jay-Z responded with "Takeover," then Nas dropped "Ether" and Jay came back with "Superugly"—in which he was a lot less subtle about his relationship with Nas's baby mama. But before the battle got violent, it ended. It was all about lyrical skill—nothing more, nothing less. And both men, who had seen the two greatest pushed to war by forces beyond their control, refused to let it get out of hand.

Some people believe that if Wallace had actually responded to "Hit 'Em Up" with a true, name-calling response, things might not have escalated in real life.

"Everybody wanted to see the skill battle," says Wiz of Nas's Braveheart crew. "Believe me, that would have calmed the tension down if they woulda gone at it. Just like Nas and Jay-Z. The fact that Nas responded to Jay makes the people around him feel like, 'At least he said something.' We're not gonna be walking around with the grudge forever, like we got to get him back. Son got him back lyrically."

"Even if I woulda lost, I would have been happy to be a part of it," Nas said about his Jay-Z feud. "It was a great moment for hip hop that rappers are trying to relive right now through other personal beefs with other rappers. But it's not the same. The Jay and Nas battle was, respectfully, the greatest battle in hip hop. You can't ruin that by going out and shooting somebody."

But some fear that things are heading that way again with the current war of words between 50 Cent and G-Unit on the one hand and Ja Rule and Murder Inc. on the other. Both 50 and Ja are two of the hottest MCs to bust out of Queens in years. Both are often compared to rap's greatest—Ja to Tupac and 50 to Biggie. Both are aligned with warring companies. Both are multimillionaires with massive crossover appeal. Both keep trading personal barbs on records. And both have cynical audiences chomping at the bit to see which one gets shot first.

On March 9, 2003, the sixth anniversary of Christopher Wallace's murder, I caught up with Stevie J at Daddy's House studios. The hit man had seen a lot—and shared the benefit of his experience with me.

"We been there," J said about Murder Inc. vs. G Unit. "Everybody's got twenty guns. Let's talk about something else. Glorifying the gangsta life, that's rap music. Fly bitches and ménages à trois is rap life, too. Million-dollar homes and $100,000 cars is rap life, too. Taking care of your family is rap life, too.

"That's why I understand why [Puff] ain't want to sign 50. He don't want that over his head. He got kids. This guy has been there already. How does it feel when you have to go to Cali and all you want to do is get up and play with your kids?"

Stevie J thought about it for a second, then offered 50 Cent some advice.

"If I could talk to 50, I'd tell him, You made your bread and you safe, man, just change it up a bit. 'Cause your walk is your walk. No matter how you look at it. It's real, man. If you talk about it in every song, there's always gonna be somebody listening who's gonna try you."

Lil' Cease is quiet right now. He's upstairs in the small house that he, D-Roc, Banger, and a few other members of Junior M.A.F.I.A. call home now. He's looking at the lit cigarette in his hand as smoke curls toward the ceiling.

"I never smoked a cigarette until Big died, and I'm a chain-smoker to this day," he says. "So I know some of that shit messed a brother up. I was stressed just to see it. Just to, like, watch it. Muthafuckas talk about it, but nobody can never really know that feeling, unless you really see your man get struck down by bullets in your face. I think that's the worst thing. It's . . . it's fucked up."

Cease pauses to take a drag.

"Just looking at a nigga's eyes. He didn't say a word. Just looking at him. He ain't saying nothing. I never wish that on no man. Not at all. For something like that to happen to somebody so good. A good nigga."

Lil' Cease says he's frustrated he didn't see more that could help solve the case. And he's even more disappointed that the cops haven't done more, that the shooter hasn't been captured yet.

"You had police coming there and shutting down the party down for a fire hazard," he reasons. "Y'all got cops. And I just don't understand. It never come clear to me—I never seen somebody get shot two minutes after a fire drill. Where it's nothing but police and fire department. And they got nothing on the case?"

Lil' Cease is also convinced that they were under surveillance the entire time they were in Los Angeles. Wallace himself alerted him to the fact on the night of the *Soul Train* award ceremony.

"Big was in front of the hotel, he had that black suit on, black cane," Cease recalls. "He was waiting for the limo to pull up. So I come downstairs, and I see a man in front of him take a picture. I was like, Hold up. I said to Big, 'Did you do a photo shoot?' He's like, 'Nah, it's the feds.' The nigga jumped back in the car, made a U-turn and drove away. He was just real cool about it. He said, 'At least I got some protection.' He said, 'Yeah, I'll pose for a picture.' He said it real nonchalant. And I'm like, '*Word*?'"

Wallace's lifelong friends, Mike Bynum and Hubert Sams, back on the stoop at 226 St. James, June 2003: "When it's all said and done," says Sams (right), "he would have wanted to be here alive."

After Wallace was murdered, Cease discovered just how many pictures were taken of them all. "Police was showing me pictures of us that they had from the *Soul Train* awards," he says. "Pictures of D-Roc, pictures of me, pictures of Big. Matter of fact, there's pictures police showed me from the night when Big got killed. They showed me pictures from that party, asking me, like, 'Who is Jermaine Dupri?' Then I had to think to myself, like, Them muthafuckas was there."

Cease pauses, holding his head as the cigarette burns. "So y'all was there? I just don't understand it," he adds finally. "I can't put it together."

His mood brightens up when we talk about the day Wallace's funeral procession rolled through the old neighborhood. As he speaks of that last ride, it's as if he can still feel the wave of joy that rushed through the crowd.

"There was so many people on top of light poles, hanging out of fuckin' windows," he says with pride. "There were so many people, you couldn't even see the cars. And it was going on for blocks. It wasn't just St. James, it was Nostrand Ave. Fulton Ave. Everything he put his foot on, everything he stepped on, it's like a landmark. That nigga had an impact on so many people."

"You miss him a lot," I say.

"Ain't no words for that," Lil' Cease replies. "You know what I'm saying? Just missing a good person. Just missing a good dude that was pure. They don't make people like that. Just a good nigga. A nigga that didn't argue about nothing. A nigga that didn't make nothing a problem. You ain't got to pester him to do nothing for you. He did things, 'cause he want to. That's how he lived. He said, Go do you. I'm doing this for you. Take care of your moms, take care of your family. Take care of some good people around you. Get some people off the street if you can. That's how Big was. I'm gonna use you as a stepping stone to take twenty more niggas off the street. And they can each take twenty others. Big used to have a bank card, and we used to rock it. He would say, 'That's why I gave it to you—so you ain't have to ask me for it.'"

He laughs and I point out that while talking like Wallace he's fallen into his distinctive lilt and deep voice.

"I got tendencies of acting like Big," he continues. "Some people say when I talk on the phone I scare them. I sound so much like this nigga sometimes. Certain things I picked up: how I sit in the car sometimes. Certain shit I do, and I don't do it purposely. I was around him constantly. So it's him, too. I'm living for him."

He waits a moment to let the thought sink in.

"He didn't even get a chance to mark his territory. He didn't have a chance to enjoy it. That's how quick it was. Big didn't get a chance to start like Pac started. Pac had a boatful of music that still come out to this day. He done been in movies. Big died before the second album came out. He touched a lot of people in a short time, but Big didn't get a chance to touch nothing. That just goes to show how special he was. He was blessed. People like that man, they get to do their job within a short stay. What he had to do, he came and did it."

I ask what Big would be doing right now if he were alive.

"Big would be resting now," says Lil' Cease. "'Cause Big ain't the one that gotta be in the limelight. He loved the music. He loved it more, 'cause he get paid for doing his job. You've gotta work for something. And people who love it more do it better. He just loved to fuck with the music. More than doing it, he loved to listen to it. So the music shit was kinda like in him.

"Right now he'd have five albums and then rest," he concludes. "He never saw himself as that rapper being thirty years old and still doing it. He was planning to do a couple albums, then, 'Let my niggas do it.' That was his plan. That's what Big would have been doing. I know for a fact, Big woulda been trying to make other niggas shine. My shit, Kim shit, M.A.F.I.A. shit."

Lil' Cease crushes out his cigarette, then adds a final thought:

"A lot of people is at they peak right now because of Big. And he's not here to see it but there's people that's living off what he started. You look at people like

Puff. You got your Kim, you got me, you got Mark and Wayne still doing music. Look at Big's mom. She didn't want nothing to do with this music, but now she sees her son was an inspiration to so many people."

"Do you pray to Biggie?"

Hubert Sams can't help but chuckle when he thinks of some of the things people ask him when they want to talk about his friend Chris, who's become a hip hop deity. He's proud that Wallace still has such a huge impact on people, that he went from ashy to classy, all of that. But at the same time, he doesn't know if people truly realize the jewel of a person who was lost on March 9, 1997.

"He transformed himself in front of millions," says Sams, who still lives in Brooklyn not far from where he and Wallace grew up. "Millions started to love him. Was it for the right reasons or the wrong reasons? Do we know? Was it the glitter, the glamour? Why do these people love him? Do they love him now because of who he really was? That's the main question: Did they ever get to know the man behind the music, so to speak?

"I think right now what's happening, it's a feel-good thing to try to remember Big. But the loss . . . I don't know if it's really sunk in. It's a senseless loss. People try to say they carrying on the torch and burning the flame. And every other person says Big woulda wanted him or her to get the crown or whatever. But when it's all said and done, he would've wanted to be here, alive. Making more music, raising his kids actually, 'cause that's where he was really going."

Sams thinks hard before he speaks again. "He really got robbed. Because he laid his talent on the line for everyone, and when it came time to reap the benefits of his success . . . I mean, he couldn't see his kids grow in comfort. He didn't get to see that they don't have to worry about the things he had to worry about—your next meal, or just your moms scraping up pennies."

Sams finds himself thinking a lot about his old friend. Not a day passes when he doesn't hear his voice coming out of a radio, or echoing down some Brooklyn street. Every time Sams thinks about his own daughter, he thinks about Wallace– she shares his birthday, May 21.

Sams even admits to dreaming about Wallace sometimes. But unlike with others who have written songs about nocturnal Biggie visitations, Christopher Wallace never gives out advice about a rap career.

"All of my dreams," Sams reveals, "he's not talking about he's dead. It's just regular. He's not even on yet. We're just chilling. And it's just when I wake up, that's when the cruel reality hits you, like 'Aw, man.' We think we got robbed, but he really got robbed."

He pauses.

"It wasn't his time, man," Sams says. "It just wasn't his time."

IF YOU DON'T KNOW . . . NOW YOU KNOW

DISCOGRAPHY

by Chairman Mao

DISCO-DISCLAIMER: Catalog numbers are for original vinyl releases wherever possible. There may be alternate catalog numbers for overseas releases, reissues, CD singles, and promotional versus commercial copies. Entries are grouped by year of release, and subdivided into one or more of the following categories:

SINGLE: a commercially available release by the Notorious B.I.G.

ALBUM: a commercially available full-length release by the Notorious B.I.G.

COLLABORATION: a release by another artist featuring the Notorious B.I.G.

REMIX: an alternate version of a release by or featuring the Notorious B.I.G.

PROMO SINGLE: a promotional release by or featuring the Notorious B.I.G. that is also commercially available.

PROMO ONLY: a promotional release by or featuring the Notorious B.I.G. that is not commercially available.

PRODUCTION: a release for which the Notorious B.I.G. is credited as the producer.

EXECUTIVE PRODUCTION: an album for which the Notorious B.I.G. is credited as the executive producer.

RECYCLED LYRICS: a posthumous release that uses previously released Notorious B.I.G. vocals in a new recording.

BOOTLEG: an unauthorized release on an unknown or unofficial label.

LIVE RECORDING: a live performance with a DJ, whether on stage or in studio.

MIX TAPE: a full-length DJ mix incorporating recorded and live performances.

DEMO: an unreleased recording used to shop for a record deal.

SPECIAL THANKS to DJ Mister Cee, Max Glazer, Jared Boxx @ The Sound Library, A-1 Records, Steve @ www.tapekingz.com, and Russell from K-Otix for their help.

1991

DEMO
"Blind Alley Freestyle"; "Guaranteed Raw"; "Don't Love No Ho"

Biggie's original demo—which was recorded in DJ 50 Grand's basement and later redone at DJ Mister Cee's Bed-Stuy apartment for submission to *The Source*'s "Unsigned Hype" column—reveals him to already be a vocalist of great presence and confidence. (At the outset of the three-song cassette he even announces, "A

whole lotta niggas want Big to make a demo"; he later advises listeners to "Recognize the pedigree, you bitch-ass niggas," and ad libs a radio drop for mix-show mainstay DJ Red Alert at one point.) With 50 Grand cutting up breaks from the Emotions' "Blind Alley" (best known as the sampled music bed of Big Daddy Kane's "Ain't No Half Steppin'") and 45 King's bootleg remix of Take 6's "Spread Love," Big flows effortlessly on the first two tracks, bawdily boasting his lyrical superiority, as one would expect, but also (in a foreshadowing of "Juicy") expressing wishes to succeed in life and make his mother proud. "Don't Love No Ho," however, shows signs of additional conceptual sophistication. It begins with a heartbroken Big, rhyming in an exaggeratedly soft, gentle tone (over the laid-back rim shots of Tom Scott's "Sneakin' in the Back") lamenting a failed romance with a girl who's left him. Though he wins her back, his sadness gradually turns to disdain when he realizes how easily she's consumed by petty jealousy. Winning the girl apparently ain't all it's cracked up to be. By song's end, he's bitterly proclaiming, "I got three rules in life: don't get played with, played on or played out . . . Bitch, I love no ho. Fuck ya."

1992

UNRELEASED TRACK
"Biggie Got the Hype Shit" (Uptown)

After signing Big to Uptown Records, Sean "Puffy" Combs wanted to monitor his new artist's poise in the studio, thus the session for "Biggie Got the Hype Shit." It starts with a snatch of movie dialog asking, "Who is Biggie Smalls?" (taken from the Blaxploitation–era comedy *Let's Do It Again*), before kicking into the Jesse West and DJ Mister Cee co-produced track, based around the kinetic, bass-driven (and oft-sampled) bridge from James Brown's funk bomb "I Got to Move." It's hard to imagine Puff not being pleased with his protégé's performance. Biggie's intense, high-pitched delivery robustly commands the track. And, as they will remain throughout his career, his lyrics are a supreme blend of the coarse and clever: "Biggie Smalls got bitches in Brazil / Use a rubber if that bitch ain't on the pill . . . I'm not the type to toot my own horn / But toot toot." One of the voices on the chorus is that of Big's friend O, who later passed away and was paid a tribute on "Missing You." Unfortunately, the master reels for "Biggie Got the Hype Shit" were destroyed in a fire at the Bronx studio where the song was recorded, dashing chances of any official release.

COLLABORATION
"A Buncha Niggas"—Heavy D, also featuring 3rd Eye, Guru, Rob-O & Busta Rhymes, from *Blue Funk* (Uptown, UPT-10734)

Biggie's earliest guest appearances run the gamut from odd to essential. "A Buncha Niggas" features tinny, somewhat dated production, a silly, shouted vocal hook ("Tell me who's on the microphone? / A buncha niggas!") and one of the stranger combinations of MCs ever to appear together on a posse cut. A young Big commences his verse with the line, "I bring drama like you spit on my mama," but this relatively giddy performance has him sounding closer to Mr. Funky of Lords of the Underground than the Notorious one he'd become.

COLLABORATION / REMIX
"Buddy X (Falcon & Fabian Remix)"—Neneh Cherry (Virgin , Y-12665)

One of Neneh Cherry's last hits, "Buddy X" is, of all things, a pointed Lenny Kravitz dis that maintains its melodic cool. The overlooked remix provides an extra (large) treat: Big chips in a tight (though non-Lenny-related) twelve-bar tale of relationship woes, a narrative vignette he would later perfect on records with R. Kelly and Junior M.A.F.I.A.

COLLABORATION / REMIX
"Real Love (Hip Hop Mix)"—Mary J. Blige (Uptown, UPT12-54456)

1992's other Big guest shot is a classic. Biggie devotes a good chunk of his rhyme to affectionately bigging up the then-emerging Queen of Hip Hop R&B, while proclaiming himself hip hop's "Teflon Don." Throw in an irrepressibly funky guitar sample (this one culled from Betty Wright's "Clean Up Woman"), and suddenly the song is a buoyant party anthem despite its wistful lyric.

1993

SINGLE / REMIX
"Party and Bullshit (Club Version)"; "Party and Bullshit (Lord's Remix)"; "Party and Bullshit (Puffy's Remix)" (Uptown, UPT12-5468); also appears on *Original Motion Picture Soundtrack: Who's the Man?* (Uptown, UPT-10794)

Biggie's debut on the *Who's the Man?* soundtrack established his persona with an immediacy his first batch of guest appearances could only suggest. A fine vehicle for his storytelling skills and playful yet commanding cadence, "Party and Bullshit" presents the vivid panorama of a Crooklyn hood's night in the life—capturing a scene that constantly threatens to veer from recreation to chaos (in no small measure due to Big's unabashed gun talk). But just as a soiree with a female appears to defuse tensions ("Bitches in the back looking righteous in a tight dress / I think I might just hit her with a little Biggie 101 / How to tote a gun / And have fun with Jamaican rum"), a fight breaks out and our antihero, the cat boasting the bulletproof vest and "two .22s in [his] shoes," is briefly forced to become peacemaker (pondering, "Can't we just all get along?") before heading off into the BK evening with his lady friend.

The additional remixes on Biggie's first solo single can't match Easy Mo Bee's original—a hypnotic mesh of organ and sampled strings from ESG's breakbeat staple "UFO." Still, you could do far worse than Lord Finesse's jazzy revision, which makes good use of a cymbal-heavy drum loop and some echoed horns, and injects a D.I.T.C. influence to the proceedings. Minus the brass, and with his own breathy interjections more noticeable, Puffy's "remix" sounds virtually identical to Finesse's.

COLLABORATION / REMIX
"Dolly My Baby (Bad Boy Extended Mix)"—Supercat,
also featuring Mary J. Blige, Jesse West & Puff Daddy (Columbia, 44 74855)

Anchored by crashing snares, an irresistible chicken scratch guitar loop (from Herbie Hancock's Headhunters-era "Watermelon Man") and Mary J. Blige's sultry crooning, the "Dolly My Baby" remix is one of the finer dancehall-meets-hip-hop experiments—this despite horribly abrasive rhyming from Jesse West and Puff, who sound as if they swallowed too many Onyx pills before hopping in the vocal booth. Thankfully, Biggie's short but sweet verse (which includes his famous line, "I love it when you call me Big Poppa") ends things on a strong note.

COLLABORATION / REMIX
"What's the 411? (Remix)"—Mary J. Blige,
from *What's the 411? Remix Album* (Uptown, UPT-10942)

Replacing Grand Puba as Mary J.'s sparring partner on the "What's the 411? (Remix)," Biggie kicks the first verse of what would become "Dreams" over the wah-wah loop from Johnny "Guitar" Watson's "Superman Lover." Puff again plays hype-man with a funked-up, George Clinton–style effect in his voice.

1994

SINGLE / REMIX / PROMO ONLY
"Juicy"; "Juicy (Remix)" b/w "Dreams"; "Unbelievable"
(Bad Boy promo, BBDP-9005)
SINGLE / REMIX
"Juicy"; "Juicy (Remix)" b/w "Unbelievable"
(Bad Boy, 78612-79006-1) Certified gold 11/8/94
SINGLE
"Big Poppa" b/w "Warning" (Bad Boy, 78612-79016-1) Certified platinum 5/23/95

The singles that represent Big's initial commercial breakthrough still sound as infectious as they did upon their original releases. Though even at the time Puff and company's strategy of pillaging obvious sample material was literally nothing new, no one could dispute the proficiency of Team Bad Boy's execution. With Total's vocals sweetening the hook, "Juicy"'s resuscitation of Mtume's "Juicy Fruit" perfectly complements the celebratory nature of Biggie's rags-to-riches rhymes. Pete Rock's remix adds beefier drums and some Spoonie Gee sound bites but is otherwise the same.

Producer Chucky Thompson applies his keyboard countermelody technique (so prevalent on Mary J. Blige's *My Life* LP) to the Isley Brothers' "Between the Sheets," giving that sample workhorse fresh legs (and giving the single bicoastal appeal thanks to the track's "G-Funk"-esque leanings). Big's game-tight performance on "Big Poppa" also accentuates his Westside friendliness, co-opting a bit of then-regional slang into the chorus as he exhorts with Snoop-like smoothness, "Throw your hands in the ai-yaaa / If you's a true playaaa." The superb "Unbelievable" and "Warning" bring a once-again grimy Big back to Brooklyn with two of the hardest beats he's rhymed over, courtesy of DJ Premier and Easy Mo Bee, respectively.

The club and mix tape favorite "Dreams" (a.k.a. "Dreams of Fucking an R&B Bitch," a.k.a. "I'm Just Playin'") appeared as a bonus song on the promotional advance vinyl of the "Juicy"/"Unbelievable" single. A bawdy, comic fantasy in which Biggie rates the sex-abilities of various R&B divas (e.g., "I put Chanté Moore pussy in stitches / I'd fuck RuPaul before I fuck them ugly-ass Xscape bitches") over a loop from James Brown's "Blues and Pants," it's still one of the funniest songs (hip hop or otherwise) of its generation, and would inspire two response records, Lil' Kim's "Dreams" (actually also probably composed by Biggie), and 50 Cent's infamous "How to Rob." Apparently, though, not everyone appreciated the joke. The outraged reaction of various record-company executives, along with James Brown's refusal to grant permission to sample his music on songs with cursing or explicit lyrics, likely ended dreams of "Dreams"' official release.

COLLABORATION / REMIX
"Flava in Ya Ear (Remix)"—Craig Mack,
also featuring Rampage, LL Cool J & Busta Rhymes (Bad Boy, 78612-7901-1)
COLLABORATION / PROMO SINGLE
"Da B-Side (Dirty B Side)"—Da Brat,
also featuring Jermaine Dupri (So So Def, OAS 6533); also appears on
Music from the Motion Picture Bad Boys (Work OK 67009) Released in 1995

COLLABORATION
"4 My Niggaz"—Red Hot Lover Tone, also featuring Prince Poetry and
M.O.P., from Get the Phuck Off the Block! EP (red vinyl, white label 025038)
COLLABORATION
"Jam Session"—Heavy D and Troo-Kula, from NBA Jam Session
(MCA, MCAD-10786)
COLLABORATION
"Who's the Man"—Doctor Dre and Ed Lover, also featuring King Just and
Todd One, from Back Up Off Me! (Relativity, 88561-1242)

A flurry of guest appearances in which Biggie often outshone his host artists both preceded and accompanied the release of his own solo material. His grand opening slot on the "Flava in Ya Ear" remix brought additional heat to that summer's hottest record. The charming "Da B-Side" exhibited ample chemistry between Big and Da Brat, and provided a refreshing early indication of his openness to working in hip hop's poppier, non–New York realm. The dismal "Jam Session" finds Big trying to make the best of an unfortunate fusion of basketball references, annoying faux-reggae chatting, and lackluster production. "Who's the Man" is similarly uninspired. Surrounded by inferior talent, Big asks himself, "Who's the man? I see him every morning in the mirror." Indeed, he's the only enjoyable part of the song. "4 My Niggaz" is an unheralded underground track featuring Big amid yet another peculiar combination of MCs. A wonderfully grimy BK pairing, Biggie and M.O.P. are perfectly fitted to the rugged beat's clanging snares, rumbling bass, and high horn squeals; Tone (of the Trackmasterz) and Organized Konfusion's Prince Poetry less so.

COLLABORATION / PROMO SINGLE
"Let's Get It On"—Eddie F. & the Untouchables, also featuring Heavy D, 2Pac & Grand
Puba, from Let's Get It On (Motown, 314530313-2/4); also appears on a vinyl EP
(Motown promo 374631271-1) and a radio vinyl EP (Motown promo 374631266-1)
"Let's Get It On" is the first official release to feature Big and 2Pac together on the same track. Moreover, once you get past Heavy D's herky-jerky lead vocal, the song also happens to be a decent, down-tempo number with an underlying air of sadness. Though Big's rhymes are slightly lighter than Pac's, both verses reflect their authors' longstanding preoccupation with their own mortality.

COLLABORATION / PROMO ONLY / BOOTLEG
"Cunt Renaissance"—Crustified Dibbs (white label, JSAMA-5-A 1)

Leaked out by Jive Records in order to fuel the buzz on Caucasian rap sensation Crustified Dibbs (a.k.a. R.A. the Rugged Man), "Cunt Renaissance" is a cult classic. Big starts things off by singing, "Ain't no dick like the one I've got" and then details his sexual prowess. R.A. goes on to discuss the finer points of anal penetration (among other subjects) over a noisy, EPMD-style funk track. This one is not recommended for the faint of heart—or representatives of N.O.W.

PROMO ONLY
Craig Mack / The Notorious B.I.G. Teaser (Bad Boy promo cassette, BBDC-9007)

Being Bad Boy Records' inaugural acts, Big and Craig Mack were sometimes promoted in tandem, a good example being the teaser cassette featuring a side apiece of selections from each artist's debut albums. Though most of the material on Biggie's side remains true to the versions released on *Ready to Die,* there are two exceptions. On the "Intro," the music accompanying Big's dramatized birth is Marvin Gaye's 1977 disco smash "Got to Give It Up." Curtis Mayfield's "Superfly" eventually replaced it, probably because its 1972 release matched the year of Biggie's actual birth. On the version of "Me and My Bitch" included here the music is entirely different (a case of a failed sample clearance). The story of a thorough chick who is ultimately lost to the streets, on *Ready* the song was a sweeping, almost cinematic production characterized by a grandiose string melody and dialogue exchanges between Puff and Lil' Kim. Here, in its original configuration, and with the dialog mixed down slightly, "Me and My Bitch" relies primarily on a lovely guitar sample from Minnie Riperton's Stevie Wonder–composed "Take a Little Trip." This melodious groove offsets Big's impassioned performance and gives the song an intimate, personal, and arguably more affecting tone.

ALBUM
Ready to Die (Bad Boy, 78612-73000-2) Certified 4X platinum 10/19/99;
also appears as a 9-track vinyl (Bad Boy, 78612-73000-1)
and an 18-track double vinyl (78612-73005-1) Released in 1995

Upon *Ready to Die*'s release in October 1994, the rest of the world could attest to what avid hip hop listeners had suspected for some time now—Biggie Smalls was indeed the illest. Neophytes seduced by the broadcast-friendly benevolence of "Juicy" and "Big Poppa" (two songs added to the album in an attempt to smooth out its tougher core, the deeper tone of Big's vocals betraying their late-stage creation) undoubtedly received a shock to the system (not unlike the blunt-induced wheeze that separates tracks 3 and 4) when greeted by the grim outlook and less poppy production of the rest of the LP.

Songs like "Things Done Changed," "Everyday Struggle," the bleak title track, and the even bleaker closer, "Suicidal Thoughts," express the futility of ghetto

life in terms explicit and real enough to speak to the streets, but human enough to avoid myopia. Not since the Ice Cube of *AmeriKKKa's Most Wanted* and *Death Certificate,* or the tortured antics of the Geto Boys circa "Mind Playing Tricks on Me" had a rap artist attempted such a merger of bravado and pathos. More than any other artist that preceded him, Big was able to balance the pessimism of a harsh worldview with a craftsmanship, writer's flair, and personable quality that established him as an utterly compelling (and ultimately sympathetic) voice—no matter how pathological the content of some of the material on *Ready to Die*.

The heist caper, "Gimme the Loot," may include a merciless threat to rob a pregnant woman for her "#1 Mom" pendant, but Big's performance, in which he rhymes both parts of a conversation between would-be crooks Slick Rick–style, is so theatrically impressive and full of humor, any memory of lyrical indiscretions goes right out the window. His crude sex jokes on the original "One More Chance" surely offended late-arriving fans of the radio remix. Yet his verses are performed with such panache and cruel wit that they reduce the best routines of Rudy Ray Moore to simple toast by comparison.

With its random collection of producers (Trackmasterz, the Bluez Brothers, Lord Finesse, et al.), *Ready to Die* did not boast the all-star production lineup of Nas's *Illmatic,* or the organic sonic templates of Wu-Tang Clan's *Enter the Wu-Tang: 36 Chambers* or Black Moon's *Enta Da Stage*—both of which were commandeered by in-house aural architects, the RZA and Da Beatminerz, respectively. But along with those seminal albums, *Ready* signaled the illustrious return to prominence of New York hip hop as a creative and commercial force after years of Westside domination.

Though all the album's producers make strong contributions (and there's just one stinker—the leaden, reggae-tinged "Respect"), Brooklyn's Easy Mo Bee is clearly the unsung hero. Along with his track for Craig Mack's "Flava in Ya Ear" from earlier that year, Mo's *Ready to Die* work is the best of his career. On "Gimme the Loot," "Machine Gun Funk," "Warning," and the splendid Method Man duet "The What," his beats inject just the right amounts of melody and menace in support of Big's performances.

1995

SINGLE / REMIX
"Big Poppa (So So Def Remix)" b/w "Who Shot Ya" (Bad Boy, 78612-79020-1)
BOOTLEG
"B.I.G."

Although the "Big Poppa" remix features an all-new vocal take from Biggie, it also includes irritating ad libs by Jermaine Dupri, trying his best to assume the Diddy role. Ostensibly, this version was intended to give "Big Poppa" some additional Dirty South appeal, but given the original's general excellence and widespread adoration, So So Def's revision is so-so-superfluous.

"Who Shot Ya" is anything but. Biggie returns to his Crooklyn roots with a song as fearsome as the best of *Ready to Die*. The mid-song skit in which he places a gun in the mouth of an anonymous foe can still cause nightmares; it was strategically faded out when "Who Shot Ya" was later included on the posthumous *Born Again*. The ominous beat, a clever reworking of Stax Records songwriter turned solo artist David Porter's "I'm Afraid the Masquerade Is Over," first appeared as a brief interlude featuring Keith Murray on Mary J. Blige's *My Life* album. A version (ID'ed simply as "B.I.G.") with Big rhyming the first verse made the bootleg and mix-tape circuit. Finally, a rerecorded, complete take was released in early '95 to the rejoicing of hardcore fans who'd grown weary of hearing his radio hits for the umpteenth time. Rumors that "Who Shot Ya" was a snide commentary on Tupac Shakur's near fatal shooting at a Times Square recording studio run rampant despite the fact that the song was recorded before that incident took place.

SINGLE / REMIX
"One More Chance / Stay with Me"; "One More Chance (Hip Hop Mix)" b/w "The What (radio edit)," featuring Method Man (Bad Boy, 78612-79032-1) Certified platinum 7/31/95

Released in spring of '95, the "One More Chance" remixes represented the apex of the first crest of Biggie-mania in New York City. While Bad Boy's previous strategy with singles featured one side for the radio and one for the streets, "One More Chance" covered all bases by including two somewhat different instrumentals to accompany Big's vocal track of entirely new (and somewhat sanitized) lyrics. Of the two versions, both officially "co-produced" with Puff by Rashad Smith, the lush "Stay with Me" mix is the fan favorite, in which Big's mack-daddy musings ride a luscious piano loop from DeBarge's "Stay with Me" and creamy backing vocals by Faith Evans. The "Hip Hop Mix" resuscitates the Lou Donaldson guitar sample made famous by Craig G's late '80s Juice Crew gem "Droppin' Science" and swaps Faith's crooning for Total's. Shrewd DJs still intercut both versions, bringing appreciative partiers to a frenzy that few other rap records can reliably induce.

COLLABORATION / REMIX / PROMO ONLY
"All Men Are Dogs (Nine Dog MCs Mix)"—Bandit, also featuring Pudgee Tha Phat Bastard, Snagglepuss, Positive K, Raggedy Man, Grand Daddy I.U. & Grand Puba (London promo, 6890-1WT)

Biggie's 1995 posse-cut appearances were again characterized by strange combinations of personnel. For a track featuring as many vocalists as it does, the "All Men Are Dogs" remix coasts along with surprisingly few snags—its participants are all in good form, clearly overjoyed at the opportunity to push the boundaries of good taste and drop as many sexist sex raps as they can muster. While I.U.'s claim of possessing "sperm that jingle, jangle, jingle" is priceless, Big uses the forum to spew some of the most outrageous lines of his career: "Brooklyn freaky nigga with the most stuff / I'm Jesus' pops; Mary just blamin' Joseph." He ends his blasphemous verse with an evaluation of the Blessed Mother's oral sex skills.

COLLABORATION
"4 My Peeps"—Red Hot Lover Tone,
also featuring Prince Poetry and M.O.P., from #1 Player (Select, 21649-1);
COLLABORATION / REMIX
"4 My Peeps (Remix)," Red Hot Lover Tone,
also featuring Prince Poetry and M.O.P., from #1 Player (Select, 21649-1)

"4 My Niggaz" re-appears as "4 My Peeps" on Red Hot Lover Tone's second LP with slight alterations: M.O.P.'s part is shortened to include a final verse from Tone; a Poke and Tone remix based on Grover Washington Jr.'s "Hydra" is included. Big's rhymes remain intact.

COLLABORATION / REMIX
"The Points (U-Neek's Points)"; "The Points (Easy's Points)" w/ Coolio, Redman, III & Al Skratch, Big Mike, Busta Rhymes, Buckshot & Bone Thugs-N-Harmony (Mercury, 856 937-1);
also appears on Panther: The Original Motion Picture Soundtrack (Mercury, 314 525 479-2)

Easy Mo Bee's brawny mix of this song "inspired" by the movie Panther noses out U-Neek's tinny West Coast take on the production end. Still, neither version can avoid the meandering mess that comes with too many MCs and no clear song concept. Fortunately, Biggie rhymes first, saving most casual listeners from having to sit through the entire nine-minute snoozefest.

COLLABORATION / PROMO SINGLE
"Runnin'" w/ 2Pac, Dramacydal, Radio & Stretch, from *One Million Strong: The Album* (Mergela, 72667-2); also appears on a vinyl radio EP (Mergela promo 4582-1)

Biggie and Pac's sole other legitimate collabo (besides "Let's Get It On" and their live appearance together at Madison Square Garden) is this posse cut reputedly slated for Thug Life's first album, but which wound up on the Million Man March compilation, *One Million Strong: The Album*. A meditative take on the everyday struggle facing black youth (over the intro guitar sample to Bootsy Collins's "Munchies for Your Love"), it predictably loses steam when the lesser lights hog the mike, picking up when the two featured stars briefly drop verbiage. Notable for one of Pac's more disturbingly prescient couplets: "Don't say you never heard of me / Till they murder me I'm a legend."

COLLABORATION / PROMO ONLY
"Think Big"—Pudgee Tha Phat Bastard, also featuring Lord Tariq (Perspective promo, 23456)

"Think Big" is an underground classic that never saw commercial release due to sample clearance problems (the sound bite of contention: Quincy Jones's "Vegetable Wagon" from the *Come Back Charleston Blue* soundtrack). Producer Minnesota's punchy, horn-driven track is a masterpiece of aggression and provides the optimum setting for the words of a particularly belligerent Big, who boasts, "Ask your friends who's the illest / Lickin' shots, niggas screamin' 'Biggie Smalls tried to kill us.'" The best quip, however, actually belongs to the histrionic Pudgee, whose punch line–heavy verse concludes with the promise, "I'll make your people forget you / Like R. Kelly did to Aaron Hall."

COLLABORATION
"Can't You See"—Total (Tommy Boy, TB 676) Certified gold 7/13/95; also appears on *New Jersey Drive Vol. 1 Soundtrack* (Tommy Boy, TB 1114) and *Total* (Bad Boy, 78612-73006-1)

Big not only helped break the female R&B trio Total with his appearance on "Can't You See," but permanently popularized the term "chickenhead" as a part of the rap vernacular with his opening line, "Give me all the chickenheads from Pasadena to Medina . . ." His appearance elevates a generic James Brown–sampled ("The Payback") radio record to something greater. DJs found themselves back-spinning his introductory verse ad infinitum.

COLLABORATION
**"How Many Ways (Bad Boy Remix)"—Toni Braxton,
also featuring Puff Daddy (LaFace, 73008-24080-1-SA)**

On "Dreams," Big jokingly rhymed of Toni Braxton, "If that bitch give me action, guaranteed satisfaction." But Bad Boy's "How Many Ways" remix allows him little wiggle room—just four uncredited lines of lyrics amidst seven minutes of not-so-fun funk—thus leaving listeners anything but fulfilled.

COLLABORATION
**"This Time Around"—Michael Jackson, from *HIStory: Past, Present and Future, Book 1*
(Epic, E2K 59000)**

Michael Jackson's attempt to sound semi-rugged resulted in Biggie's recruitment for this song, on which the King of Pop angrily addresses all haters over a mediocre Dallas Austin–helmed new jack swingish production. The *HIS*toric pairing would be bizarre enough on its own, what with Michael cursing on the record, but then, not to be outdone, Big concludes his verse with an affectionate shout to "my nigga Mike."

COLLABORATION
"(You to Be) Be Happy"—R. Kelly, from *R. Kelly* (Jive, 01241-41579-1)

Musically and thematically, Big's excellent first collaboration with R. Kelly bears a striking resemblance to Faith Evans's equally intoxicating "You Used to Love Me." This proved ironic in light of Biggie's rhymes—a mournful tale of a love soured by mistrust and materialism—and his eventual estranged relationship with Faith. For his part, Kelly delivers a suitably tasteful vocal until he uncorks the ringer, "So give me that ass back, baby / 'Cause your lovin' is so damn good."

COLLABORATION / CO-EXECUTIVE PRODUCTION
***Conspiracy*—Junior M.A.F.I.A.**
(Undeas / Big Beat, 7567-92614-1) Certified gold 12/6/95
COLLABORATION
"Get Money"—Junior M.A.F.I.A.
(Undeas / Big Beat, 0-95694)
COLLABORATION
"Player's Anthem" b/w "Player's Anthem (Remix)"—Junior M.A.F.I.A.
(Undeas / Big Beat, 0-95750) Certified gold 9/7/95
COLLABORATION / CO-PRODUCTION
**"Realms of Junior M.A.F.I.A."—Junior M.A.F.I.A.,
also featuring Jamal, from *Conspiracy* (Undeas / Big Beat, 7567-92614-1)**

COLLABORATION
"Oh My Lord"—Junior M.A.F.I.A., also featuring Special Ed, from *Conspiracy* (Undeas / Big Beat 7567-92614-1)

The spring release of the Junior M.A.F.I.A. album was perfectly timed, creating a synergy with the "One More Chance" remixes that kept Big in heavy rotation on the airwaves and in clubs through the rest of the year. Instantly likable, "Player's Anthem" and "Get Money" provide the prototypical soundtrack for ghetto fabulous aspirations; you can almost hear the Cristal bottles popping within their incessantly hooky productions (from Clark Kent—on both versions of "Player's Anthem"—and Ezee Elpee, respectively). Biggie's relaxed, confident cadence directs the action with ease—even on "Get Money," when his lyrics again tackle thorny relationship drama (later portrayed as real-life marriage issues in the song's video). Big is supported by memorable performances by newcomers Lil' Cease and star-in-the-making Lil' Kim, who excels with brash assurance in the coveted final spot on each song. Apart from these two singles, however, the album *Conspiracy* offers just two other notable Biggie moments. The sleeper "Realms of Junior M.A.F.I.A.," a song featuring Big rhyming over ESG's old school breakbeat staple, "UFO," and "Oh My Lord," a Big-Klepto duet on which the JM apprentice so closely follows his mentor's cadence that it might as well be a Biggie solo track. (Though Special Ed is given both performance and production credits, his vocals are nowhere to be heard.)

LIVE RECORDING
"Live from the Palladium, August 5, 1994 (B.I.G. Freestyle Mix)"—Funkmaster Flex (Wreck / Nervous, WR 20116B)

With its conspicuous lack of crowd noise and participation, "Live from the Palladium" doesn't really sound as if it's live from the defunct NYC nightclub. It sounds a lot like Big on Flex's Hot 97 show doing "Unbelievable" (with a jovial Puff singing off-key choruses) over the beat from Mad Lion's "Take It Easy."

LIVE RECORDING / SOUNDTRACK CUT
"Me and My Bitch (Live from Philly)," from *The Show: The Soundtrack* (Def Jam, 314 529 021-1)

On *The Show* soundtrack, as was customary with in-concert performances, Big and Puff perform "Me and My Bitch" not over the instrumental used on *Ready to Die,* but over a track based around the intro to Zapp's slow-jam mainstay, "Computer Love." Though the performance is energetic, the sound quality suffers thanks to the conspicuous, dull roar of canned applause.

LIVE RECORDING / PROMO ONLY
"Real Niggaz Do Real Things" (Bad Boy promo cassette)

Though its existence predates the nastiest stretch of the Bad Boy–Death Row rivalry, this heavily bootlegged promotional release was nonetheless rife with regional irony: The Big East's Big rhymes all-too-briefly over West Coast instrumentals like "Deep Cover," "Ain't Nuthin' But a G Thang," and "Gin and Juice," leaving listeners craving more. A party favorite still guaranteed to control crowds, it's also the closest we'll ever get to hearing Big collaborate with Dr. Dre.

LIVE RECORDING
"Biggie Smalls Is the Wickedest" b/w "Garden Freestyle"—DJ Mister Cee, from *That Mister Cee Freestyle Shit* (white label, CEE 151); also appears on *Mister Cee Presents Brooknam's Finest Freestyles* (Tape Kingz, CEE155)

Big's featured moments on *That Mister Cee Freestyle Shit* (a collection of Cee's mixtape exclusives from the previous year) are legendary. The first commences with a suave intro ("I want y'all to grab y'all Dutch Masters, and y'all White Owls, and y'all Phillies, get you a fat sack, a pint of Hennessy and lay back . . .") over Isaac Hayes's "Ellie's Love Theme" from *Shaft* before Big rips the stinging beat to Casual's "I Didn't Mean To," dispatching both ribald threats ("Niggas press they luck and they get a butt fuckin' / Straight up the ass raw dog with the rash") and self-deprecating good humor ("Gettin' back to the black rhinoceros of rap / Big took a loss—how preposterous is that?") in equal measure. The second is a live concert excerpt in which Big and 2Pac jubilantly share the mike during the October 1993 Budweiser Superfest at Madison Square Garden (along with an out-of-breath Kane, Big Scoob doing what amounts to an excruciating B Real impersonation, and a likable young Shyheim). Big's verse, like his scrapped *Ready to Die* duet with Sadat X "Come On Muthafuckas," begins with a gun inventory—"I got seven Mac-11s, about eight 38s . . ." The whole thing can be recited word for word by scores of young rap fans today although few probably grasp the cleverness behind era-specific references like, "You can't touch my riches / Even if you had MC Hammer and them 357 bitches." (Both recordings were later reissued on an EP with two early Jay-Z freestyles.)

MIX TAPE
Best of Biggie—DJ Mister Cee (Tape Kingz)

Released in the spring of '95, Mister Cee's *Best of Biggie* mix tape collected all of Big's guest appearances and important singles, as well as his then-exclusive freestyles for Cee, making it one of the biggest selling mix tapes of all time. Lovingly compiled (in near chronological order no less) with little intrusive or extraneous cutting by the man who gave Big his first significant break in the music business, it is an essential document of the first half of Biggie's career.

1996

COLLABORATION

"Brooklyn's Finest"—Jay-Z, from *Reasonable Doubt* (Roc-A-Fella, P1 50592);
also appears as Roc-A-Fella, P2 50040

COLLABORATION / PROMO SINGLE

"Still Can't Stop the Reign"—Shaquille O'Neal, from *You Can't Stop the Reign*
(T.W.IsM., INTD-90087); also appears on vinyl EP (T.W.IsM. promo INT8P 6064)

COLLABORATION

"Young G's Perspective"—Blackjack, also featuring DSP
and Snakes of Junior M.A.F.I.A., from *Addicted to Drama* (Penalty, PEN CD 3034)

COLLABORATION / PROMO SINGLE

"Bust a Nut"—Luke, from *Uncle Luke*
(Luther Campbell Music, 050 161 000-2);
also appears on vinyl EP (Luther Campbell Music promo, P212 7175-1WT1BS)

Despite increasing personal and professional turmoil, Big's time continued through 1996 with another series of club- and airwave-dominating appearances with protégés and on other artists' records. Naturally, for every "Brooklyn's Finest" (a brilliant pairing with Jay-Z over the looped vocal melisma of the Ohio Players' "Ecstasy") there are throwaways like the Shaq and Blackjack records. "Bust a Nut," on the other hand, is a great throwaway: Big drops hilariously offensive verbal sexcapades that fall somewhere between "Cunt Renaissance" and the original "One More Chance," while Luke chimes in with an adults-only rendition of the Almond Joy/Mounds commercial jingle.

COLLABORATION

"Only You"—112 (Bad Boy, 78612-79061-1); also appears on *112* (Bad Boy, B0000039Q7)

COLLABORATION / REMIX

"Only You (Remix)"—112, also featuring Mase
(Bad Boy, 78612-79070-1) Certified gold 7/30/96;
also appears on *112* (Bad Boy, B0000039Q7)

Big's appearance on 112's "Only You" adds some necessary vocal beef to the quartet's whiny-bordering-on-wimpy love man routine. The original's saccharine update of KC and the Sunshine Band's "I Get Lifted" is replaced on the much better remix by Nashiem Myrick's way funky "Bounce Rock Skate Roll"–inspired bass line and clap track, and tacks on a Mase vocal after the second chorus—which means Biggie's 16 bars get moved up to the song's intro. It's a worthy slot, considering that Big's playfully frivolous rhymes resurrect a dangerously played-out "Monie in the Middle" reference and still come off more than credible: "Big up in your middle like Monie / She don't know me but she settin' up to blow me."

COLLABORATION / REMIX / CO-PRODUCTION
"Gettin' Money (The Get Money Remix)"—Junior M.A.F.I.A.
(Undeas / Big Beat, 0-95668) Certified platinum 7/9/96

This remix of Junior M.A.F.I.A.'s "Get Money" adopts an entirely new track (based on Dennis Edwards's "Don't Look Any Further"), adds an opening verse from Lil' Cease, all-new lyrics from Lil' Kim and Biggie, and a chorus interpolation of Shabba Ranks and Deborahe Glasgow's 1990 dancehall reggae barnstormer "Don't Test Me." The original's thematic sexual tug of war is also gone, replaced by more general ruminations on the pursuit of paper. With all eyes on his marital woes, Big slyly issues a "no comment" on the subject with the lines, "Problems with my wife? / Don't discuss 'em."

COLLABORATION / CO-EXECUTIVE-PRODUCTION
Hard Core—Lil' Kim
(Undeas / Big Beat, 7567-92733-1) Certified 2X platinum 3/14/01

Not only did Biggie write and oversee production of the songs that positioned Kim as "a female MC who gets busy like a nigga" (there's even an unofficially circulated tape of his reference vocals), he also made fleeting appearances on several of her first album's cuts, including "Take It," "**** You," and "Drugs," on which Big's echo-ey, multitracked voice damn near sings the chorus.

COLLABORATION / REMIX
"Crush on You"—Lil' Kim, also featuring Lil' Cease (Undeas / Big Beat, 1996, DMD 2342)

Widespread speculation that Kim and Junior M.A.F.I.A. were little more than performance puppets for Big's rhyme writing only increased when a studio dub of Biggie himself performing the lyrics to Kim's breakout hit "No Time" was aired on Mayhem and Riz's WNYU underground hip hop radio show. However, the only single Biggie actually shows up on from Kim's *Hard Core* solo is the LP's remixed second smash "Crush on You" (Kim herself does not appear on the original version), on which he supplies the charming, mumbled chorus.

COLLABORATION
"No Time"—Lil' Kim, also featuring Puff Daddy (Undeas / Big Beat, 0-95631)
COLLABORATION / PROMO SINGLE
"No Time"—Lil' Kim, also featuring Puff Daddy, b/w "Queen B." (a.k.a. "Queen B@#$h")
(Undeas / Big Beat promo, DMD 2315); "Queen B@#$h" also appears on *High School*
***High: The Soundtrack* (Big Beat, 92709-1)**

Amidst the dirty talk of Lil' Kim's salacious first solo single, Big's voice is heard asking "How you figure that your team can affect my cream?" or eerily promising,

"I rely on Bed-Stuy to shut it down if I die." Based on a terse Roberta Flack piano loop, the fantastic "Queen B.," which first appeared on the B-side of the "No Time" promos, also features two Big lines ("You niggas got some audacity / You sold a million now you're a half of me—now kick it, bitch") on the second verse. This song replaced the original version of "Big Momma Thang"—in which Kim disses Pac—on the *High School High* soundtrack.

COLLABORATION / PROMO ONLY
"You'll See" w/the Lox (Bad Boy promo, BBDP-9077)

This song, which resurrects the beat from Faith's "You Used to Love Me (Remix)" (itself a reworking of EPMD's "You're a Customer"), is really a showcase for the Lox on which Big delivers the last verse. "What you gonna do when Poppa catch an attitude?" he asks, "Drop to your knees and show gratitude." Though intended for Puff's solo debut album, "You'll See" wound up making its only "official" appearances on the Stretch Armstrong edition of Bad Boy's mix-tape series, and as the B-side to the very rare original "All About the Benjamins" promo single.

LIVE RECORDING
"DJ Enuff Freestyle 1" b/w "DJ Enuff Freestyle 2"—DJ Enuff, also featuring Freshco, from *Freestyle Collection* (white label, EFC 001)

Two Biggie appearances on DJ Enuff mix tapes are anthologized on this collection. The first features him flowing over the beat to Black Moon's "I Got Cha Opin (Remix)," enthusiastically dropping both off-the-head rhymes ("This is for the chumps who don't know who I am / I had a song on the soundtrack *Who's The Man* / The single was dope but the movie didn't slam / MCs is like J.J. mom—damn, damn, damn!"), and those from the Garden Freestyle / "Come On Motherfuckers." The second posits him alongside late '80s freestyle champ Freshco, delivering lyrics that also appear on "Machine Gun Funk" from *Ready to Die*.

1997

ALBUM
Life After Death (Bad Boy, 78612-73011-2) Certified 10X platinum 1/6/00; also appears as 24-track vinyl (Bad Boy, 78612-73011-1)

While most hip hop purists will readily declare *Ready to Die* as Biggie's greatest achievement, it's *Life After Death* that has made the larger impact on rap music as a whole. Despite token (and usually unconvincing) attempts at broaching styles from other markets (a Miami bass song here, a reggae track there, etc.) rap albums by respected New York artists before *Life After Death* still generally adhered to the traditional sound of New York hip hop—sample-based beats with few if any key-

board embellishments. With *Life After Death,* however, all the rules changed. Though content-wise the album remained intrinsically linked to sobering subject matter—what with its chronicles of street justice ("Somebody's Gotta Die"), beef ("What's Beef" and the 'Pac-directed "Long Kiss Goodnight"), envy ("My Downfall"), and mortality ("You're Nobody [Till Somebody Kills You]")—sonically it was less a "hip hop" album in the classical sense than an urban pop album. Along with Dr. Dre's *The Chronic,* this record represents the crucial meeting point at which the two genres became nearly synonymous. Where its predecessor was a grimy New York work supplemented by a smattering of commercial singles accessible to East and West, *Life After Death* was the first album from the Mecca of hip hop that made no apologies for its attempts to please fans of all markets. A great example is "Notorious Thugs"—a sensational pairing with Bone Thugs-N-Harmony in which Big flips the Cleveland quartet's quick-tongued, triplet rhyme style syllable for syllable. Rap hasn't turned back since.

All of which means that upon first hearing *Life After Death* and its unequivocally universal sound, you either immediately loved it or were immediately alienated by it (only to later grow to love it, or at least grudgingly accept it as an inevitable development of rap as a commercial force). Given the number of R&B hits Big had appeared on in the preceding year, his thrust for the commercial jugular shouldn't actually have come as much of a surprise. Save for the two collaborations with DJ Premier (the fearsome, Screamin' Jay Hawkins–sampled "Kick In the Door" and the equally strong "Ten Crack Commandments"), Puff and his Bad Boy staff of producers (known collectively as the Hitmen) embossed nearly all the material with an aural sheen that took the sweetened approach of "Juicy" and "Big Poppa" to new levels of digital crispness. While this production style naturally sterilized some contributions from grittier producers (most glaringly Havoc of Mobb Deep's "Last Dayz," which is drained clean of any semblance of danger), it polished the work of others (like Easy Mo Bee's surprisingly slick "I Love the Dough") and maximized the impact of the euphoric, in-house-produced singles ("Hypnotize," "Mo Money, Mo Problems") to a point where the songs just sounded bigger (and, as it would follow, better) than anything else out there—especially in club land.

Big had said that thematically *Life After Death* was to symbolize an elevation beyond the nihilism and despair so pervasive on *Ready to Die.* Some of this artistic effervescence resulted in pure filler (the garish "Another"; the goofy "Player Hater"; the formulaic though club-friendly "Nasty Boy"). But elsewhere this compassion manages to overcome sentimentality (and borderline syrupy production) and proves moving ("Missing You") and even contagious ("Sky's the Limit"). Of course, the emotional impact of Big's actual death inescapably hovers ghostlike throughout. Heard in a vacuum, "Going Back to Cali" might be dismissed as a contrived and musically sluggish attempt to appease West Coast listeners peeved by the Bad Boy–Death Row squabble. Knowing the circumstances of Big's murder, the song becomes tragic and ironic, lamentable for entirely different reasons. (Second pressings of the double CD feature an 11-minute, 25-second interview with Biggie at the conclusion of the first disc in which he discusses Tupac Shakur's death, the end of East Coast–West Coast tensions, and his ambition to retire early from the grind of recording and performing.)

SINGLE / PROMO SINGLE
"Hypnotize" (Bad Boy promo, BBDP-9089) Certified platinum 6/11/97
PROMO SINGLE
"Kick In the Door" (Bad Boy promo, BBDP-9112)
PROMO SINGLE
"Long Kiss Goodnight";
"Ten Crack Commandments" (Bad Boy promo, BBDP-9143)
PROMO SINGLE
"Lovin' You Tonight" (Bad Boy promo, BBDP-9106)
SINGLE / REMIX
"Mo Money, Mo Problems," featuring Mase and Puff Daddy;
"#!@ You Tonight," featuring R. Kelly, b/w "Mo Money, Mo Problems (Razor-N-Go Club Mix)" (Bad Boy, 78612-79109-1) Certified platinum 9/3/97
SINGLE
"Sky's the Limit," featuring 112, b/w "Kick In the Door";
"Going Back to Cali" (Bad Boy, 78612-79120-2) Certified gold 12/16/97

Detractors could say what they wished about Bad Boy's musical aesthetic, but no one could dispute its promotional savvy. Attuned to what DJs crave, the label kept both its top tunes and buzz-generating album cuts available as 12″ commercial and promotional singles in a timely manner. Apart from radio edits and the occasional ill-advised dance-market mishap, such as the "Mo Money, Mo Problems (Razor-N-Go Club Mix)," most of the above titles don't differ at all from their album versions save for the one element crucial for turntable technicians on the air, in the club, or on the mix-tape circuit: the wider grooves and fuller sound inherent in the 12″ single format.

COLLABORATION / EXECUTIVE PRODUCTION
No Way Out—**Puff Daddy & the Family**
(Bad Boy, 78612-73012-1) Certified 7X platinum 9/7/00

Though they are brief and at times peculiar, Big's appearances are indispensable to the creative milieu of Puff's solo debut, *No Way Out*. Given his ubiquitous presence on rap recordings these days, it may be hard for today's dilettantes to fathom just how absurd the notion of a full-fledged Puff Daddy rhyming career was to the hip hop cognoscenti in 1997. Though he always looked and acted the part of the rap star (and was genuinely respected for his marketing and A&R expertise), Puff seemed to possess few of the actual vocal talents necessary to express himself convincingly on record. His flat voice and robotic cadence were nearly bereft of emotion and personality compared with a genuine article such as Biggie. But when Puff released his solo album after Biggie's untimely death there was a surprising turnabout: what some critics and hip hop purists decried as opportunism on Puff's part, the general record-buying public embraced as the next best thing to Big himself. Biggie-mania continued unabated through the release of *No Way Out*. And Puff—rather than suffering by comparison with Big on the skills-o-meter— was celebrated and championed for carrying on in Big's name. His song "Pain" says as much, conjuring the image of Biggie coming down from heaven to bestow his blessing on Puff: "I live through you / Make hits continuous / That's what we do." Combs has since improved as a rapper, and his saturation in nearly all facets of urban culture has essentially rendered all debates of his musical merit moot. Damn that Diddy!

COLLABORATION
"Victory"—Puff Daddy & the Family, also featuring Busta Rhymes,
from *No Way Out* (Bad Boy, 78612-73012-1);
also appears on vinyl single (Bad Boy, 78612-79164-1) Certified gold 4/6/98
COLLABORATION / REMIX / PROMO ONLY
"Victory (Hip Hop Remix)"—Puff Daddy & the Family,
also featuring Busta Rhymes (Bad Boy promo, BBDP-9172) Released in 1998
COLLABORATION / REMIX
"Victory (Nine Inch Nails Remix)"
b/w "Victory (Drama Mix)"—Puff Daddy & the Family,
also featuring Busta Rhymes (Bad Boy, 78612-79164-1) Released in 1998

The LP's lead track, "Victory," is bombast personified: Puff and Big issue stern threats to those willing to test as a sample from the *Rocky* soundtrack builds and Busta Rhymes shrieks, "Where my niggas is at?" like a deranged parrot. Fortunately, Big's free-flowing rhyme ("Long nights I perform like Mike / Any one—Tyson, Jordan, Jackson / Action, pack guns / Ridiculous . . .") keeps your ears on their toes. Puff's writers even provide him with a couple of good lines ("You ain't gotta like me / You just mad 'cause I tell it like it is, and you tell it how it might be"). The various unnecessary remixes pile on more extraneous musical elements ("Nautilus" samples, industrial arrangements, operatic vocals) until your ears feel ready to explode.

COLLABORATION / PROMO SINGLE
**"Been Around the World"—Puff Daddy & the Family,
also featuring Mase (Bad Boy promo, BBDP-9118)**
COLLABORATION
**"Been Around the World"—Puff Daddy & the Family,
also featuring Mase, b/w "It's All About the Benjamins (Remix)"—Puff
Daddy & the Family, also featuring the Lox and Lil' Kim (Bad Boy,
78612-79126-1)** Certified platinum 12/16/97
COLLABORATION / REMIX / PROMO ONLY
**"Been Around the World (Armand's Freakshow Mix)";
"Been Around the World (Armand's Unreleased Project)";
"It's All About the Benjamins (Armand's Gangsta Mental Mix)" b/w
"It's All About the Benjamins (DJ Ming & FS Drum N' Bass Mix)"
—Puff Daddy & the Family, also featuring Mase (Bad Boy promo, BBDP-9135)**
COLLABORATION / REMIX / PROMO SINGLE
**"It's All About the Benjamins (Remix)"—Puff Daddy & the Family,
also featuring the Lox and Lil' Kim (Bad Boy promo, BBDP-9103)**
COLLABORATION / REMIX
**"It's All About the Benjamins (Rock Remix 1)"—Puff Daddy & the Family,
also featuring the Lox and Lil' Kim, Dave Grohl, Perfect, Fuzzbubble & Rob Zombie;
"It's All About the Benjamins (Rock Remix 2)"—Puff Daddy and the Family,
also featuring the Lox and Lil' Kim, Dave Grohl, Perfect, Fuzzbubble, Rob Zombie & Size 14
(Bad Boy, 78612-79126-1)**

"Been Around the World" only features Biggie as singsongy dispenser of the Lisa
Stansfield–inspired chorus, but with its exuberant, David Bowie–lifted beat and
twin monotonic performances by Diddy and Mase, the song works as a prototypical hip pop hit. A vintage Bad Boy moment.

The "It's All About the Benjamins (Remix)" is maddening. The original version (actually a Lox single featuring Puff distributed at an industry convention and subsequently widely bootlegged on vinyl) was already a great single—a
mindless material statement propelled by one of the most sonically powerful
and mesmerizing guitar loops hip hop had ever heard. Add on new rhymes from
Kim and Big, and it's a guaranteed home run, right? Well, somewhere along the
way someone decided to abruptly switch up said mesmerizing guitar loop (and
replace it with the Jackson 5 breakbeat staple "It's Great to Be Here") for Biggie's
part, robbing the world of the chance to hear the most celebrated rapper of his
era rhyme over the consensus beat of the year. "Benjamins" in its revamped form
is still a winner, but elephant-memoried train spotters still contemplate what
might have been. The cacophonous rock remixes do an even greater disservice
by obscuring Big's voice in power chords.

COLLABORATION / PROMO SINGLE
"Young G's"—Puff Daddy & the Family, also featuring Jay-Z
(Bad Boy promo, BBDP-9129); also appears on *No Way Out* (Bad Boy 78612-73012-2)

Despite featuring one of Puff's more sluggish performances, "Young G's" is a treat; while Big's rhymes don't stray too far from your basic crime rhyme braggadocio, his voice melds nicely with Rashad Smith's moody vibraphone melody. For his part, Jay-Z turns in a verse worthy of his deceased cohort's memory, chock full of thought, artful arrogance, and wit: "Solemnly we mourn all the rappers that's gone / Niggas that got killed in the field and all the babies born / Know they ain't fully prepared for this new world order / So I keep it ghetto like sunflower seeds and quarter waters."

COLLABORATION
"Keeps Your Hands High"—Tracey Lee from *Many Facez*
(Universal, U-53036); also appears on vinyl EP "Put Your Hands High"
(Universal promo, UNIR-20064-1) Released in 2000

Big's sole 1997 guest appearance was not on a Bad Boy track, but given the personnel involved—Tracey "The Theme" Lee, with whom Big shared common management in the person of Bystorm Entertainment's Mark Pitts—this can nonetheless be considered a family affair. "Keep Your Hands High" is not, as the title may suggest, a call for partiers to raise the roof, but a warning that foes keep their hands where our hosts' eyes can see. The title completes the couplet, "If you don't wanna die . . ." (Big's vocal was later resurrected for "Rap Phenomenon" off *Born Again*.)

COLLABORATION / REMIX / PROMO SINGLE
"Stop the Gunfight"—Trapp, also featuring 2Pac (Intersound 9268B);
also appears on *Stop the Gunfight* (Intersound 9268); also appears as
"Stop the Gunfire" from 2Pac, *In His Own Words* (Mecca MR-8807-2)
COLLABORATION / REMIX / PROMO SINGLE
"Be the Realist"—Trapp, also featuring 2Pac (Intersound);
also appears on *Stop the Gunfight* (Intersound 9268);
also appears as 2Pac, "Be the Realist" (Mecca MR-PRO-987-1-A);
also appears on 2Pac, *In His Own Words* (Mecca MR-8807-2) Released in 1998

The Biggie / 2Pac "Runnin' " track was redone with Dramacydal and Stretch's parts replaced by a mysterious cowboy hat-wearing vocalist named Trapp. "Be the Realist" attempts a similar trick with "Let's Get It On." Heavy D and Grand Puba's parts are edited out, Big and Pac's verses are flip-flopped, someone who sounds vaguely like Pac recites the title a few times, and two rhymed verses from Trapp are tacked onto the end. Judging by the title and the size of Big and Pac's names on the cover, this was a tribute put together after their deaths.

LIVE RECORDING
"Freestyle" —Funkmaster Flex, also featuring the Lox, from *The Mix Tape Volume II, 60 Minutes of Funk* (Loud 07863-67472-1)

Despite an annoying sped-up playback speed (a distraction easily remedied by pitching one's turntable to play at –2), the Funkmaster Flex freestyle finds Big and the Lox comfortably spouting rapper don decrees over the beat from Wu Tang Clan's "C.R.E.A.M." Big's verse reiterates his ascent from ashy to classy: "Went from eating no-frill cereals with food stamps / To Armani materials, copping Rembrandts."

1998

PROMO SINGLE
"I Got a Story to Tell" b/w "Last Day" (Bad Boy promo, BBDP-9178)

Bad Boy continued to issue *Life After Death* promo singles through 1998—the marvelous Buck Wild–produced, acoustic guitar–driven (and lyrically degenerate) "I Got a Story to Tell" being a welcome addition.

SINGLE / REMIX / PROMO ONLY
"Nasty Boy (Remix)" (Bad Boy promo, BBDP-9159)

The "Nasty Boy (Remix)" grafts Big's vocals onto replayed and sampled portions of Liquid Liquid's "Cavern," reviving melodic elements of Grandmaster Flash and Melle Mel's "White Lines" (the first old school rap hit based on "Cavern") just for good measure. The calculated musical move is unfortunately a little too obvious, upping the cheese quotient on an already cheesy club hit beyond toleration for anyone but compulsive dancing fools.

COLLABORATION / REMIX
"Runnin' (Stone's Remix)" w/ 2Pac, also featuring Deetah (MBA / Blakjam 050-16815)

In another bizarre attempt to revive "Runnin,' " the Big and Pac duet reappears in this only mildly interesting remix minus some of the original auxiliary vocals, but with additional, smoothed-out keyboard textures, female crooning on the choruses, and generic rhymes from someone named Deetah.

1999

ALBUM / RECYCLED LYRICS
Born Again (Bad Boy, 78612-73023-2) Certified 2X platinum 1/14/00; also appears as 18-track vinyl (Bad Boy, 78612-73023-1)

The premise of this posthumous album—collecting unheard or old but forgotten Biggie vocals, and retooling them alongside new tracks and guests—was flawed from the jump. Where 2Pac's nonstop recording habits left album-loads of material behind

after his death, most of Biggie's studio work had already seen the light of day in some form, leaving scant offerings to pick and choose through. Ultimately, simply battling sample clearance obstacles and reissuing some of the "unreleased" material ("Dreams," for instance), and licensing the stronger guest appearances would have made more sense than dressing up these leftovers. Though never officially released, Biggie fanatics were undoubtedly well familiar with "Come On" (a.k.a. "Come On Muthafuckas"), a Lord Finesse–produced duet with Sadat X that was left off *Ready to Die*. While they would certainly have welcomed an official issue of the original version, they didn't necessarily want to hear the song revamped with a new, but inferior, Clark Kent beat behind it. Attempts to resuscitate Big's third verse off "Real Niggaz Do Real Things" (on the Duran Duran–sampled "Notorious"), his appearance on Luke's "Bust a Nut" (on "Big Booty Hoes") and, strangely enough, nearly the entire vocal of "Everyday Struggle" (on the Nas duet "I Really Want to Show You") fell similarly flat. Even when paired with decent production (DJ Premier's "Rap Phenomenon"; Deric Angelettie's "Can I Get Down"), the results sound fractured and disingenuous.

That which wasn't already a part of the existing Biggie canon ("Dead Wrong") was usually recovered from so early on in his career that his higher-pitched tone and excitable vocal style didn't necessarily connect with listeners weaned on the heftier delivery of his later years. The inundation of vocal guests (many of whom became famous after Big's passing) on nearly every song, while perhaps a good idea on paper, not only made for some incongruous groupings (Biggie and Eminem? Biggie and Cash Money? Biggie, Beanie Sigel, and Ice Cube?), but served to highlight how little Big there really was on *Born Again*.

PROMO SINGLE
"Warning" (Bad Boy promo, BBDP-9031)
PROMO SINGLE
"Dead Wrong" (Bad Boy promo, BBDP-9288)
PROMO SINGLE
"Notorious," featuring Lil' Kim and Puff Daddy (Bad Boy promo, BBDP-9295)
PROMO SINGLE
"Who Shot Ya" b/w "Ten Crack Commandments" (Bad Boy promo, BBDP-9298)
PROMO SINGLE
"Juicy" b/w "Niggas Bleed" (Bad Boy promo, BBDP-9299)
PROMO SINGLE
"One More Chance / Stay with Me (Remix)" b/w "Dreams" (Bad Boy promo, BBDP-9300)
PROMO SINGLE
"Biggie," featuring Junior M.A.F.I.A. (Bad Boy promo, BBDP-9313)

PROMO SINGLE
"Hope You Niggas Sleep," featuring the Hot Boys & Big Tymers,
b/w "Big Booty Hoes," featuring Too $hort (Bad Boy promo, BIG 12″ PRO #1)
PROMO SINGLE
"Dangerous MC's," featuring Mark Curry, Snoop Dogg & Busta Rhymes,
b/w "Who Shot Ya" (Bad Boy promo, BIG 12″ PRO #2)
PROMO SINGLE
"Dead Wrong," featuring Eminem (Bad Boy promo, BIG 12″ PRO #3)
PROMO SINGLE
"Notorious B.I.G.," featuring Lil' Kim and Puff Daddy
(Bad Boy promo, BIG 12″ PRO #4)
PROMO SINGLE / REMIX
"Notorious B.I.G. (Remix)," featuring Lil' Kim and Puff Daddy, b/w "Biggie,"
featuring Junior M.A.F.I.A., (Bad Boy promo, BIG 12″ PRO #5)
COLLABORATION / PROMO SINGLE
"Biggie," featuring Junior M.A.F.I.A., b/w "Would You Die for Me,"
featuring Lil' Kim and Puff Daddy (Bad Boy promo, BBDP-9325) Released in 2000
COLLABORATION / PROMO SINGLE
"Who Shot Ya," "Hypnotize," and "Dreams" b/w
"One More Chance / Stay with Me (Remix)," "Mo Money, Mo Problems," and
"Flava in Ya Ear (Remix)"—Craig Mack, also featuring Rampage, LL Cool J & Busta Rhymes
(Bad Boy promo EP, BBDP-9356) Released in 2000

In a shrewd attempt to keep Big's back catalog in the mix, Bad Boy reissued a number of classic singles (some, as with "Juicy" b/w "Niggas Bleed," featuring different album-cut B-sides) in conjunction with the release of singles from *Born Again*. Collectors and DJs rejoiced; it turned out to be a decent consolation prize given the mediocrity of the actual album. Note to Marshall Mathers–philes: of the three eventual "Dead Wrong" promo singles, only one includes the album version featuring Eminem.

COLLABORATION / CO-EXECUTIVE PRODUCTION
***Forever*—Puff Daddy (Bad Boy 78612-73033-1)**
COLLABORATION / PROMO SINGLE
"Real Niggas"—Puff Daddy, also featuring Lil' Kim, b/w "Dead Wrong"
(Bad Boy promo, BBDP-9307)
COLLABORATION
"Real Niggas"—Puff Daddy, also featuring Lil' Kim, from *Forever* (Bad Boy, 78612-73033-1)

Big's "guest appearance" on Puff's messy second solo album (for which he also shares executive producer credit) is indicative of Bad Boy's first big slump. Like

Born Again's "Notorious B.I.G.," it's a failed attempt to rehash past glory—specifically, the rhymes from the original "Real Niggaz Do Real Things" promo. Here, the first verse gets pillaged while Puff and company don't even bother to really change the title or the chorus. Furthermore, the beat is tepid, Puff and Kim turn in stilted performances, and the whole fiasco comes off as a half-assed sequel.

SINGLE / BOOTLEG
"The Bitch Remix"—DJ Chase (HOTSHT-004)

A bootleg blend of Big's "Nasty Boy" vocal over the instrumental to Missy Elliott's "She's a Bitch" that's been known to enjoy some popularity in da club.

LIVE RECORDING
"Biggie / Tupac Live Freestyle"—Funkmaster Flex and Big Kap,
also featuring DJ Mister Cee and 2Pac, from *The Tunnel*
(Def Jam, 314 538 258-1)

Thank goodness Biggie and Tupac rhymed consecutively on this iconic concert recording, because it saved DJs from having to possess two copies of the record and manually cut their parts together. Licensing the live recording from his Big Dawg Pitbull cohort Mister Cee for his and Big Kap's album project *The Tunnel*, Flex goes a step further and edits out everyone else who originally appeared on it so you don't have to.

2000

LIVE RECORDING
"Now or Never"—Easy Mo Bee
from *Now or Never: Odyssey 2000*
(Priority, P2 53521)
LIVE RECORDING
"16 Bars" from *Lyricist Lounge 2*
(Rawkus, RWK 1190)

Two mementos from more innocent times: About 20 seconds of Big's voice on an answering machine message appears at the conclusion of producer Easy Mo Bee's "Now or Never." Eerily, Big is heard asking Mo Bee for a ride to the studio because he is scheduled to record a song with 2Pac that day. "16 Bars" is a lo-fi live recording at famed New York MC battleground, the Lyricist Lounge, from 1993. Big dispatches his tough talk a cappella, eventually winning over the even tougher crowd with the lines, "I'm pressin' hard, I'm leavin' creases / Cuttin' up bodies and talkin' to the pieces."

COLLABORATION / REMIX
"Deadly Combination"—Big L, also featuring 2Pac
(Corleone Entertainment, COR 1974)

The excellent if morbidly titled "Deadly Combination" posthumously pulls together a potent verse apiece from Pac, Big, and Big L over a chorus-less piano-based track by Ron G. Once again, some of the words strike disturbingly resonant chords. Pac: "My firepower keep me warm / I'm trapped in a storm and fuck the world till I'm gone"; Biggie: "Niggas keep stressin' the same muthafuckin' question: how many shots does it take / To make my heart stop and my body start to shake?" This vocal originally appeared as one verse off a posse-cut freestyle—along with KRS-One, Raekwon, and others—from a 1994 Ron G mix tape, and is often referred to as "Stop the Break."

COLLABORATION
"Why You Tryin' to Play Me"—Aaron Hall (AV8, AV 165)

A true curiosity, this one-sided 12″ single billed as "Aaron Hall featuring Christopher Wallace" from an indie label best known for its cut-and-paste-style party instrumentals. Somewhat Dru Hill-esque with its flamboyant minor key musical flourishes, the song provides Big with two solid eight-bar showcases—one at its outset, and another midway through.

COLLABORATION / PROMO SINGLE / RECYCLED LYRICS
"Woke Up in the Morning (Remix)"—Carl Thomas, b/w "The World Is Filled"
(Bad Boy promo, BBDP-9330); also appears on *P. Diddy & Bad Boy Records Present . . .*
We Invented the Remix (Bad Boy, 78612-73062-2) Released in 2002

In its original incarnation, "Woke Up in the Morning" consisted of Carl Thomas crooning his trademark melancholia over the track to "My Downfall"—a brilliant Carlos Broady–Nashiem Myrick production that extended a tricky-rhythmed portion of Al Green's "For the Good Times" into one of the more powerful moments off *Life After Death*. The "Woke Up" remix fuses the two by sticking Big's first "Downfall" verse on the intro, but the paranoia and fatalism of his rhymes can't help but belittle Thomas's jilted-lover lyrics.

CO-EXECUTIVE PRODUCTION
The Notorious KIM—Lil' Kim (Queen Bee / Undeas, 92840-1) Certified platinum 8/2/00

Big receives posthumous co-executive producer credit for this album, although he does not actually appear anywhere on the record unless you count all the shout-outs and quoted lyrics.

2001

COLLABORATION / RECYCLED LYRICS
"Unbreakable"—Michael Jackson
from *Invincible* (Epic, EK 69400)

Michael-Meets-Biggie part deux revisits the defiance of "This Time Around." However, *this* time around, Michael borrows Big's vocal from Shaq's "Can't Stop the Reign" to fill in the guest rap. While Big's cadence proves surprisingly compatible with Rodney Jerkins's synth-heavy track, the specifics of his words (underworld boasts and threats to "spray up your Days Inn") seem an ill fit, even for one of MJ's more aggro compositions.

LIVE RECORDING
"Notorious Big"—Sway and King Tech,
from *Wake Up Show Freestyles Vol. 4* (Hi Def Media, 5965-77504-2)

This nearly ten-minute track is composed of excerpts from Biggie's appearance on the famed West Coast radio program just days before he was murdered. It begins with an interview segment in which Big refutes two of 2Pac's more infamous allegations from their public feud: 1) that he was responsible for Pac's shooting in New York, and 2) that Big stole his rhyme style from Pac. Big also rhymes in the studio, performing verses from "Long Kiss Goodnight" (over Sadat X's "Stages and Lights" instro), "You're Nobody Till Somebody Kills You" (over Mobb Deep's "Hell on Earth" instro), and "Kick In the Door" (over East Flatbush Project's "Tried by Six" instro). Halfway through he gives up trying to self-edit his curses with a studio mute button and lets the profanity fly.

2002

COLLABORATION / RECYCLED LYRICS
"Notorious B.I.G. (Remix)," from *P. Diddy & Bad Boy Records Present . . .*
We Invented the Remix (Bad Boy, 78612-73062-2)

Though rampant bootlegs like the "Bitch Remix" and the British "Lights, Camera, Biggie" (which combines a Big vocal with the track to Mr. Cheeks's "Lights, Camera, Action") had quelled much of the novelty of Big sightings on record, Bad Boy continued to ransack its tape vaults past the point of exhaustion. The uneventful "Notorious B.I.G. (Remix)" maintains the Duran Duran chorus of the version off *Born Again* and retools the rest of the track with digital lifts from an old Sugarhill Gang joint.

COLLABORATION / PROMO SINGLE / RECYCLED LYRICS
"Unfoolish"—Ashanti (Murder Inc. promo, 314 588 986-1);
also appears on _Ashanti_ (Murder Inc., 314 586 830-1) and on _P. Diddy & Bad Boy Records_
Present . . . We Invented the Remix (Bad Boy, 78612-73062-1)

"Unfoolish" is another exercise in shallowness. Ashanti's original "Foolish" mundanely regurgitated the DeBarge loop most commonly associated with Big's "One More Chance / Stay with Me," so naturally "Unfoolish" (a.k.a. the "Foolish" remix) pillages a Biggie vocal. Only problem is that it's his first verse from "#!*@ You Tonight," a biting, ironic composition that flipped romantic R&B–rap tune conventions on their heads by mocking the trite sentimentality of songs like "Foolish."

COLLABORATION / RECYCLED LYRICS
"Niggaz"—50 Cent, from _God's Plan_ (G-Unit)

In the summer and fall of 2002, 50 Cent generated a New York City–wide street buzz more notorious than any artist since Biggie himself. So it's only fitting that the controversial Queens MC would "duet" with Big for one of his now-legendary mixtape albums. Though it recycles Big's performance on "Niggas" from _Born Again_, "Niggaz" makes a whole lot better use of it. The production from Miami-based boardsman Red Spyda is punchier, G-Unit's faux Last Poets–style ad libs gleefully interact with Big, and 50 freely flaunts his outlaw-cum-favored-son status: "There's no place like home—New York, New York / I run this city and I don't dance around like Diddy."

LIVE RECORDING / ALBUM / BOOTLEG
Made in England: Big & Puffy Live in London (white label, LL-7003)

Biggie's 1995 tour of the UK is documented in this live bootleg, which runs through "Real Love," "Dolly My Baby," "Party and Bullshit," and many cuts off _Ready to Die_. The sound quality is high and the performances spirited (if sloppy), but there is one recurring annoyance—selected curse words are backwards edited, though the logic behind which ones were chosen is a mystery. Also worth hearing for Puff's introductory exhortation: "Do we have any black people in the house tonight?"

COLLABORATION / RECYCLED LYRICS
"A Dream"—Jay-Z, also featuring Faith Evans, from _Blueprint 2: The Gift and The Curse_
(Roc-A-Fella, 440 063 382-2); also appears on _Blueprint 2.1,_ (Roc-A-Fella B0000297-02)

Finally, a song that revives Biggie's voice for some greater conceptual ambition than merely cashing in on his name—and one appropriately enough from friend and fellow Brooklyn rap don Jay-Z. 'Hov recalls a dream in which Big warns him of the trappings of success while encouraging Jigga to stay on his chosen path. With producer Kanye West's somber guitar chords and Faith Evans's impassioned vocals supplying the dramatic backdrop, a scratched-in snatch of Big's lead line from "Juicy" perfectly sets up some lost stanza or reconstituted rhyme from the man himself. That these words wind up being the rest of the "Juicy" verse is a bit anticlimactic, but also strangely appropriate. Nearly seven years after his death, the very rhymes that introduced Biggie Smalls to much of the world are still being tapped for inspiration. If that's not being ahead of your time, what is?

CO-EXECUTIVE PRODUCTION
La Bella Mafia—Lil' Kim (Queen Bee / Big Entertainment, 83572-1) Certified gold 4/8/03

Once again, Big receives posthumous co-executive producer credit for a Lil' Kim album, although he doesn't actually appear on the record.

2003

COLLABORATION / RECYCLED LYRICS / BOOTLEG
"Gun Talk"—DJ Green Lantern, also featuring Cam'Ron (white label)

Making its initial appearance on Green Lantern's *Invasion Part 2: Conspiracy Theory*, "Gun Talk" is the vocal from "Come On Muthafuckas" effectively blended over the ominous Neptunes-produced track for Baby and the Clipse's "What Happened to That Boy."

ALBUM / BOOTLEG
Unreleased & Unleashed (Bad Boy BIGGELP01)

With its faux Bad Boy logo, pixilated cover artwork, and a peculiar "Made In England" sticker, *Unreleased & Unleashed* screams bootleg from the moment you see it. Generally poor sound quality may not be enough to dissuade those desperately seeking two lost mix-tape moments: Big and Craig Mack freestyling over Redman's "Rockafella (Remix)" (originally issued on Doo Wop's Bad Boy mix tape) and an excerpt from "Stop the Break."

MIX TAPE
Rap Phenomenon—DJ Vlad & Dirty Harry (Alleycat Promotions)

West Coast tape masters pay homage to Biggie with the most sophisticated retrospective of his music yet. Staying largely clear of the same ol' hits, Vlad and

Harry instead devote plenty of play to unreleased gems like the mysterious 2Pac duet "House of Pain," and the Bandit–borrowed "Cars & Sex." A freestyle section provides plenty of treats as well, but Vlad and Harry's stunning series of blends takes the cake, pairing Big's Garden freestyle with M.O.P.'s "Ante Up" and "Party and Bullshit" with Nas's "Made You Look." Hearing Big's voice within the context of these and other current hits gives one the strange sensation of feeling as though he never left us. Considering the enormous shadow Christopher Wallace still casts over rap music, such wishful thinking may be closer to the truth than anyone might imagine.

BROOKLYN'S
FINEST

VIDEOGRAPHY

by Ralph McDaniels

Like the Notorious B.I.G., Video Music Box was born in Brooklyn. When I started the show in 1984, broadcasting throughout the tri-state area, it was the first program to showcase hip hop music videos. Biggie's mother once told me that he was an avid viewer of the show. She said he would sometimes point to the TV screen and say, "That's gonna be me, Mom."

The broadcast premieres of the Notorious B.I.G.'s videos were always special—like when a new Michael Jackson video comes out. From the groundbreaking "Juicy" clip—where we saw B.I.G.'s journey from street hustler to recording artist—to his final video performance in "Hypnotize," and even until the present day, B.I.G. has always captured the street's attention.

Puffy was known for his remixes before starting Bad Boy, and he always used his hottest artists to enhance new projects. He first showcased B.I.G. in a hip hop remix of "Dolly My Baby" by the reggae artist Supercat. Not everybody knew who B.I.G. was, but he stood out image-wise because he looked like the guys on the streets of Brooklyn, complete with gold fronts and a black bandanna wrapped around his head.

Soon after that, a young Hype Williams directed the "Flava in Ya Ear (Remix)" video, which featured B.I.G. up close and—in his own words—"black and ugly as ever." Shot with black and white film on a simple white background, the video was like Biggie's rhymes—stylish but hardcore.

I remember the first time I showed "Juicy" on *Video Music Box* in 1994. There was an instant buzz from the hustlers, drug dealers, and ghetto girls that the video captured their dreams. He gave hope to many viewers with the story and images. B.I.G. had his mom in the video and all his crew from round-the-way. He made it and took his peoples with him—not many artists really did that. "Juicy" took B.I.G. from getting arrested to drinking Moët by the pool. The streets saw that and said, "Who needs Robin Leach when we got Biggie?"

In January 1995 Sean "Puffy" Combs sent me the uncut version of "Big Poppa"/ "Warning" and told me, "Nobody else has it." Puffy, Hype Williams, and B.I.G. had created a ten-minute-long, two-song epic that showed the ghetto-fabulous lifestyle of the true player. Private parties, Jacuzzis, and backroom meetings went down as Puff drove through N.Y.C. making late-night deals on the phone with B.I.G. In the "Warning" segment, Puff and B.I.G. take on intruders in their mansion, like in the last scene of the movie *Scarface*. We played it for a little while, then Puffy sent us a new edited version. (He'd cut out the part where he gets shot.) "Warning" was the video that showed B.I.G. with his shirt off in bed with two chicks, as we hear the famous lyrics, "Who the hell is this paging me at five forty-six in the morning?" That one scene made a lot of overweight men feel good about themselves. He let big guys feel like they could be sexy.

The video for the remix of "One More Chance" was a star-studded "Damn I wish I was there" old-school house party. From Kid Capri to Miami's own Luke, everybody was in this one. Mary J. Blige, Queen Latifah, Da Brat, the reggae artist Patra, and up-and-coming Bad Boy artists Total sang the hook "Oh, Biggie, give me one more chance." B.I.G. rapped while seated on the edge of his bed with Faith Evans laid out under silk sheets waiting for her man. It was all about money-making ghetto thugs and sexy women having a good time. "One More Chance" reminded me of a video by Da Brat, "Give It to Me," but with a Brooklyn brownstone twist.

B.I.G. made a guest appearance in the Total video "Can't You See" introducing the Bad Girls to America. He also showed up in "Only You" (the remix) from his label mates 112. Shot in Times Square in New York City, "Only You" was another epic event. Laced in urban gear, B.I.G. rocked Times Square as if it were New Year's Eve.

The video that best captured B.I.G.'s playful personality was when he appeared as the late-night radio DJ in "You Used to Love Me" by his wife, Faith. That one was directed by my partner Lionel Martin, through our company Classic Concept Productions. Lionel knew that Biggie had a sense of humor, and he wanted to get B.I.G. in a situation the viewers wouldn't expect. The concept definitely worked.

Notorious B.I.G. introduced his Junior M.A.F.I.A. crew featuring Lil' Kim and Lil' Cease in the "Player's Anthem" video. Flanked by two honeys, B.I.G. arrives on a private jet and is met by JM at the airport. Dressed in a red leather three-quarter-length jacket, B.I.G. is looking fly. The whole crew takes care of business even though they are under FBI surveillance. The streets loved this video because it was totally "Big Willie"-style. B.I.G. also appeared in the controversial Junior M.A.F.I.A. video "Gettin' Money," where his real-life side girl, Charli Baltimore, played his then-estranged wife, Faith Evans. The video came out while B.I.G., Faith, and Tupac were all in the midst of controversy. At the time, B.I.G. apparently believed that Faith had slept with Tupac. The video shows Charli as a Faith look-alike being thrown out of B.I.G.'s mansion. That was drama.

The last video that B.I.G. actually performed in was "Hypnotize." The chilling thing about this video is that it opens with B.I.G. and Puffy walking through a parking garage where they're attacked by would-be killers. Puffy does some stunt-driving to get them to safety as B.I.G. performs for the camera.

That may have been his last video shoot, but B.I.G. certainly didn't disappear from the video screen. After his passing, he was commemorated by two very different tribute songs. "I'll Be Missing You" had a more mainstream look, with Faith dressed in a white dress blowing in the wind as she performed on a beautiful hillside while Puffy performed surrounded by kids. The video opened up with Puff falling off the motorcycle. You could tell it was not staged, and it was very symbolic at the same time—Puff had to get up and keep going. "We'll Always Love Big Poppa" by the Lox had a more street-level look. It was shot in Brooklyn with various cameos from Jay-Z to Lil' Cease representing for B.I.G. from the 'hood. The video showed that young street-corner cats had heart, too.

Other videos popped up later, and they always came with a creative challenge: how do you represent an artist who is no longer alive but fans still want to see? In "Mo Money, Mo Problems," director Hype Williams stopped the music in the middle of Puffy and Mase's performance and then cut to an interview with Biggie saying, "The more money you make the more problems you have." Then the music came back to B.I.G.'s verse in the song, with images of B.I.G. performing blue-screened behind Puffy and Mase flying through the air. B.I.G.'s absence was accentuated by the interview, but it worked. This video was a huge hit.

In "Sky's the Limit," Spike Jonze came up with another creative solution: He hired cute child look-alikes to play the parts of B.I.G., Puffy, and Lil' Kim while the group 112 appeared as themselves. In the video for "It's All About the Benjamins," when B.I.G.'s verse began, a Bad Boy street team held up signs that said his name. In the videos for the "Benjamins" remix and "Victory" he did not appear at all.

In 1999 the *Born Again* album was released with three videos: "Would You Die For Me?," "Dead Wrong," and "Notorious." All three included existing video footage and photos of B.I.G. intercut with performances from Puff, Kim, and Junior M.A.F.I.A. But by this time, I think the viewing audience had had enough of videos without B.I.G.

One of my personal favorite moments with B.I.G. was the night he hosted my birthday party at a club called Mirage in N.Y.C. After the crowd sang "Happy Birthday," an up-and-coming Jay-Z stepped on the stage and the DJ threw on the beat to "Get Money," which was the hottest new record at the time. That's when B.I.G. turned to me and said, "I guess I'm supposed to rhyme now." Jay-Z said, "Go ahead," and B.I.G. did his verse from "Get Money." The crowd went wild and then Jay-Z did the hook. Of course, our video cameras were rolling and I still play it on *Video Music Box* till this day. It's a classic.

God bless B.I.G. and his contributions to music, video, and hip hop.

NOTORIOUS B.I.G. MUSIC VIDEOS

"Juicy," 1994, directed by Sean "Puffy" Combs

"Big Poppa," 1994, directed by Hype Williams

"Warning," 1994, directed by Hype Williams

"One More Chance," 1995, directed by Hype Williams

"One More Chance" (remix), 1995, directed by Sean "Puffy" Combs and Hype Williams

"Hypnotize," 1996, directed by Paul Hunter

"Mo Money, Mo Problems," (featuring Puff Daddy and Mase), 1997, directed by Sean "Puffy" Combs and Hype Williams

"Sky's the Limit" (featuring 112), 1997, directed by Spike Jonze

"It's All About the Benjamins," 1997, directed by Paul Hunter

"It's All About the Benjamins" (Remix), 1997, directed by Spike Jonze

"Victory," 1997, directed by Marcus Nispel

"Biggie / Would You Die For Me?" (featuring Junior M.A.F.I.A.), 1999, directed by Marcus Raboy

"Dead Wrong" (featuring Eminem), 1999, directed by Brian Kushner and Marion Alston

"Notorious" (featuring Puff Daddy and Lil' Kim), 1999, directed by Sean "Puffy" Combs and Matt X

OTHER APPEARANCES AND TRIBUTES

Super Cat, "Dolly My Baby" (remix), 1993, directed by Parris Mayhew

Craig Mack, "Flava in Ya Ear" (remix), 1994, directed by Hype Williams

"The Points" (featuring Coolio, Redman, III & Al Skratch, Big Mike, Busta Rhymes, Buckshot, and Bone Thugs-N-Harmony), 1994

Total, "Can't You See?," 1995, directed by Sean "Puffy" Combs

Faith, "You Used to Love Me," 1995, directed by Lionel C. Martin

Junior M.A.F.I.A., "Player's Anthem," 1995, directed by Lance "Un" Rivera

Junior M.A.F.I.A., "Gettin' Money," 1996, directed by Lance "Un" Rivera

112, "Only You" (remix) featuring Mase, 1996, directed by Sean "Puffy" Combs & Alan Ferguson

Puff Daddy and the Family, "I'll Be Missing You" (featuring Faith Evans and 112), 1997, directed by Hype Williams

The Lox, "We'll Always Love Big Poppa," 1997, directed by Sean "Puffy" Combs and Hype Williams

AUTHOR'S NOTE

"What were the old days like?"

I walked into the offices of VIBE magazine on a humid August afternoon in 1998, and associate editor Hyun Kim asked me the question that made time stand still. I was only 29, and his question made me feel like an old man. But I knew exactly what he was talking about.

Back in 1989, when I was a high school senior and serious hip hop fanatic, I used to dream about following my favorite rap artists around, talking to them, gaining insights to their music and their personalities, living through them.

Hip hop coverage at the time was scarce. You might see the occasional article posing the question "Will This Rap Fad Ever Fade?" or perhaps a nightly news segment about break dancing. If you were lucky enough to find a magazine, it was probably *Word Up, Fresh,* or *Yo!* There was usually a cut-out poster inside and a story about Big Daddy Kane's favorite food.

Certain articles, like James Bernard's *Village Voice* review of Brand Nubian's *All for One* and Frank Owens's pieces for *Spin* on N.W.A adorned the walls of my Stanford University dorm instead of posters.

The old days. The golden age of rap journalism: between 1988 and 1995, when we thought we could change the world. Before the big money, backstabbing, and bullshit came into play. We referred to ourselves as the "Hip Hop Nation," which now sounds like the most absurd and corny phrase imaginable. Back then it meant something that we took very seriously. We were united by a righteous cause: to turn the urban youth culture of hip hop into a movement for positive social and political change. The movement had songs, like "Self-Destruction" and "We're All in the Same Gang," that sparked debate about issues like drug abuse and black-on-black violence. We had magazines like *The Source* and per-

338

formers like Biggie, who had a strong sense of self and could poke fun at himself, make light of what people whispered about him behind his back, and laugh with them.

Who knows what kind of records Wallace—or Shakur—would have made had they lived longer lives. We do know is that they always took risks with their work, trying things that no one else had tried before. Make your money. Get your paper. 'Cause that's what Big would want you to do. But at the same time, never stop making records that make people think. Sometimes it feels as though what died with Wallace and Shakur was the potential for greatness in hip hop. The desire to write record songs that could change the way people think about life, instead of dumbing-down and pandering to the lowest common denominator.

Get it together.

ABOUT THE AUTHOR

Cheo Hodari Coker, 31, has published cover stories, major features, and reviews in VIBE, *The Bomb Hip-Hop Magazine, The Source, XXL, Rap Pages, Spin,* the *Los Angeles Times, Premiere, Essence, Details, The Face, Rolling Stone,* the *San Francisco Bay Guardian,* and the *Village Voice.* He began his writing career while still enrolled at Stanford University, where he completed his bachelor of arts degree in English in 1995. He became a pop music staff writer for the Calendar section of the *Los Angeles Times* by the fall of that year and stayed there for two years, contributing more than 200 articles for the section.

Coker wrote the May 1997 VIBE cover story "Chronicle of a Death Foretold," which was published shortly after the murder of Christopher Wallace, a.k.a. the Notorious B.I.G. The article contained excerpts from Wallace's last full-length interview. Coker left the *Times* in September 1997 to pursue a screenwriting career. He co-wrote the hip-hop thriller *Flow* with Richard (*Uptown Saturday Night*) Wesley, which was purchased by New Line Cinema for John (*Boyz 'N The Hood*) Singleton to produce and direct, and has worked on subsequent feature film scripts about Bob Marley, Tupac Shakur, and Marion Barry for Warner Bros., MTV Networks, and H.B.O. Coker also wrote, executive-produced and created the animated series "The Devil's Music" for www.urbanentertainment.com.

Unbelievable is Coker's first book. He also wrote the N.W.A chapter in the *The VIBE History of Hip Hop,* published by Three Rivers Press, and the liner notes for *N.W.A's Greatest Hits* on Ruthless/Priority Records.

Coker lives in Los Angeles with his wife, Dr. Tumaini Rucker Coker.

SOURCES

Interviews

Conducted by Cheo Hodari Coker: Christopher "The Notorious B.I.G" Wallace, Voletta Wallace, Faith Evans, Jan Jackson, Matteo Capoluongo, Chi Modu, DJ Mister Cee, Hubert Sams, James "Lil Cease" Lloyd, Banger, Mark "Gucci Don" Pitts, Donald Harrison, Melvin Blackmon, Mimi Valdés, Emil Wilbekin, Don Pooh, Deric "D Dot" Angelettie, Rob "Amen-Ra" Lawrence, DJ Premier, DJ Enuff, Harve "Joe Hooker" Pierre, Easy Mo Bee, Mario "Chocolate" Johnson, Lynn Montrose, Stevie J. Sway, John Singleton, Donald Hicken, Russell Simmons, Andre Harrell, Alonzo Brown, Paul Hunter, Audrey Lecatis, Matt Lait, Scott Glover, Touré, Hype Williams, Det. Russell Poole, Ice Cube.

Conducted by Rob Kenner: Robert "Zaquael" Cagle, Luther "Luke" Campbell, Craig Kallman, Nas, Wiz of Bravehearts, Laura Hines, Michael Warren.

Conducted by Harry Allen (from VIBE Archives for his March 1998 "Harry Allen's Hypertext"): Nashiem Myrick.

Conducted by Fred "Fab 5 Freddy" Braithwaite: (from VIBE Archives in response to Tupac Shakur's interview with Kevin Powell: "The Vibe Q: 2Pac Shakur—Ready to Live," in VIBE's August 1995 issue): Andre Harrell, Christopher Wallace, Randy "Stretch" Walker, Sean "Puff Daddy" Combs.

Conducted by Raqiyah Mays: Michael Lavine, Ernie Paniciolli.

Books

Blow, Bruce Porter. New York: HarperCollins, 1993. (St. Martin's Press published the 2001 movie tie-in paperback I read.)

Born Fi Dead, Laurie Gunst. New York: Henry Holt, 1995.

Brooklyn! An Illustrated History, Ellen M. Snyder-Grenier. Philadelphia: Temple University Press, 1996.

Dark Alliance, Gary Webb. New York: Seven Stories Press, 1999.

Dream City: Race, Power, and the Decline of Washington, D.C., Harry S. Jaffe and Tom Sherwood. New York: Simon & Schuster, 1994.

Hip Hop Divas, Rob Kenner, ed. A VIBE Book. New York: Three Rivers Press, 2001.

It's Not About a Salary . . . Rap, Race + Resistance in Los Angeles, Brian Cross. London: Verso, 1993.

Kings of Cocaine: Inside the Medellín Cartel—An Astonishing True Story of Murder, Money, and International Corruption, Guy Gugliotta and Jeff Leen. New York: Simon & Schuster, 1989.

LAbyrinth: A Detective Investigates the Murders of Tupac Shakur and Biggie Smalls, the Implication of Death Row Records' Suge Knight, and the Origins of the Los Angeles Police Scandal, Randall Sullivan. New York: Atlantic Monthly Press, 2002.

Native Son, Richard Wright. New York: Perennial, 1989.

Rhythm and the Blues, Jerry Wexler and David Ritz. New York: Alfred A. Knopf, 1993.

The Enforcer: Spilotro—The Chicago Mob's Man over Las Vegas, William F. Roemer. New York: Ivy Books, 1995.

The Murder of Biggie Smalls, Cathy Scott. New York: St. Martin's Press, 2000.

The VIBE History of Hip Hop, Alan Light, ed. A VIBE Book. New York: Three Rivers Press, 1999.

Yes, Yes Y'all. The Experience Music Project Oral History of Hip-Hop's First Decade, Jim Fricke and Charlie Ahern. Cambridge, Mass.: Da Capo Press, 2002.

Documentaries and Films

Above the Rim
Written by Barry Michael Cooper and Jeff Pollack
Directed by Jeff Pollack
New Line Cinema (1994)

Behind the Music: The Notorious B.I.G.
Produced and directed by Mark Ford.
Segment Producer: Wesley Jones
VH1 (2001)

Driven: The Notorious B.I.G.
Produced by Tara Jessop Wilson.
Co-produced by Karla Hidalgo.
Writer/Researcher: Stephen Tolito
VH1 (2002)

Frontline: LAPD Blues
Written by Michael Kirk and Peter J. Boyer
Produced and directed by Michael Kirk
PBS (2001)

Juice
Written by Gerard Brown III
Directed by Ernest Dickerson
Paramount Pictures (1992)

King of New York
Written by Nicholas St. John
Directed by Abel Ferrara
Seven Arts Entertainment (1990)

Let's Do It Again
Written by Richard Wesley
Directed by Sidney Poitier
Warner Bros. (1975)

MTV's Industry Insiders: Hip Hop A&R
Produced by Nate Hayden
MTV Networks (2003)

MTV's Ultrasound: Biggie: A Life Story
Written by Andréa Duncan
Produced and directed by Nina L. Diaz
MTV Networks (1998)

Rhyme & Reason
Produced and directed by Peter Spirer
Miramax (1997)

Scarface
Written by Oliver Stone
Directed by Brian DePalma
Universal (1983)

Street Dreams
Hosted by Tony DoFat
Edited by Russell Naftal
Blackout Entertainment/Urban World
Entertainment (2002)

The Show
Produced by Robert A. Johnson, Mike
Tollin, and Brian Robbins
Directed by Brian Robbins
Rysher Entertainment (1995)

Welcome to Death Row
Directed by S. Leigh Savidge and Jeff
Scheftel
Written by Jeff Scheftel
Produced by Jeff Scheftel and Stephen
A. Housden
Xenon Pictures (2001)

Documents

Search Warrant No. 6CM094 and
Affidavit and Statement of Probable
Cause, Officer Tim Brennan, Compton
Police Department, September 25,
1996.

*United States of America vs. Gerald Miller,
Ronald Tucker, Roy Hale, Waverly
Coleman, Harry Hunt, Shannon Jimenez,
Raymond Robinson a.k.a. "Ace," Wilfredo
Arroyo a.k.a. "C Justice" a.k.a. "C.J.,"
David Robinson a.k.a. "Bing."*

Articles

Abrahamson, Alan, and Chuck Philips,
"Prosecutor Probed on Rap Mogul's
Probation," *Los Angeles Times*, October
25, 1996.

_____, "'Suge' Knight Judge Puts
Heat on Both Sides," *Los Angeles Times*,
October 29, 1996.

_____, "Rap Mogul Denied Bail,
Sent Back to Jail," *Los Angeles Times*,
November 8, 1996.

_____, "I'm No Milli Vanilli,"
Los Angeles Times, November 12, 1996.

Aldrich Amy, "A Woman of Her
Convictions: U.S. Attorney Leslie
Caldwell Has Nailed Some of New
York's Most Vicious Criminals, "
GW *Law School Alumni Magazine*, April
2002.

Amber, Jeannine, "Sea of Dreams,"
The Source, September 1997.

Anson, Robert Sam, "To Die Like a
Gangsta," *Vanity Fair*, March 1997.

_____, "Clive Davis Fights Back"
Vanity Fair, February 2000.

Anson, Sam Gideon, "Did Drug
Money Fund Death Row Records?"
LA Weekly, February 7–13, 1997.

_____, "Death Row Sentence"
LA Weekly, March 7–13, 1997.

_____, "Incarcerated Scarfaces,"
VIBE, December1997/January 1998.

Baker, Bob, "Suspect Became Known
As a High Roller," *Los Angeles Times*,
November 30, 1988.

Barrs, Rick, "Kiss It Goodbye,"
New Times L.A., June 15, 2000.

Benza, A. J., and Michael Lewittes,
"Biggie's Got Bigger Woes," *Daily News*
(New York), September 23, 1996.

Boyer, Peter J., "Bad Cops," *The New
Yorker*, May 21, 2001.

Braxton, Charlie, "B.I.G. Talk," *YUSH
Publications*, 1997.

Bruck, Connie, "The Takedown of
Tupac," *The New Yorker*, July 7, 1997.

Bryant, Scott Poulson, "Puff Daddy:
This Is Not a Puff Piece," VIBE,
September 1993.

Cannon, Lou, "One Bad Cop," *New
York Times*, October 1, 2000.

Century, Douglas, "Hip-Hop's Bad
Rap," *Radar*, Summer 2003.

Chairman Mao, "The Once and Future
King," *The Source*, April 1997.

Chazanov, Mathis, and Chuck Philips,
"Rap Singer Faces Charge of Murder,"
Los Angeles Times, September 4, 1993.

Cheevers Jack, Chuck Philips, and
Frank B. Williams, "Column One:
Violence Tops the Charts," *Los Angeles
Times*, April 3, 1995.

Coker, Cheo Hodari, "Ready to Die,"
Rolling Stone, November 3, 1994.

_____, "Mr. New Jack Swings
Back," *Los Angeles Times*, November 24,
1996.

_____, (additional reporting by
Carter Harris), "Chronicle of a Death
Foretold," VIBE, May 1997.

_____, "'Doggfather' Turns Into a
Peacemaker," *Los Angeles Times*,
February 22, 1997.

Coleman, Chrisena, Mike Claffey, Tara
George, and Stephen McFarland,
"Biggie's Final Trip to B'Klyn:
Motorcade Brings Rapper Home,
Passes Thousands of Fans," *Daily News*
(New York), March 19, 1997.

Cook, John, "Notorious L.A.T.," *Brill's
Content*, May 23, 2000.

Crowe, Jerry, "Atop the Charts from
Behind Bars," *Los Angeles Times*, April 8,
1995.

Daly, Steven, "The Player King," *Vanity
Fair*, August 2000.

Diehl, Matt, "Gangsta Lovin'," *XXL*, October 2002.

Domanick, Joe, "Knight Falls," *LA Weekly*, December 27–January 2, 1997.

Farber, Jim, "Notorious 'LIFE' Scores B.I.G.: Huge Debut for Rapper's Posthumous Release," *Daily News* (New York), April 3, 1997.

Fisher, Ian, "On Rap Star's Final Ride, Homage Is Marred by a Scuffle," *New York Times*, March 19, 1997.

Ford, Andrea, and Hector Tobar, "Two Receive Life in Prison Without Parole in Drug Case Crime," *Los Angeles Times*, November 27, 1990.

Freedman, Alix M., and Laurie P. Cohen, "Gangsta Life: In Rap Music Saga, Was Elite Accountant Victim or Perpetrator?," *Wall Street Journal*, March 20, 1997.

Giles, Jeff, and Allison Samuels, "Straight Out of Compton," *Newsweek*, October 31, 1994.

Gilmore, Mikal, "Puff Daddy," *Rolling Stone*, August 7, 1997.

Glover, Scott, and Matt Lait, "Fall of Partners Feeds LAPD Probe," *Los Angeles Times*, September 13, 1999.

————, "Beatings Alleged to Be Routine at Rampart," *Los Angeles Times*, February 14, 2000.

————, "Police in Secret Group Broke Law Routinely, Transcripts Say," *Los Angeles Times*, February 10, 2000.

————, "Most of Perez's Allegations Are Confirmed, Panel Told," *Los Angeles Times*, June 20, 2000.

————, "Perez Errors Raise Questions on Credibility," *Los Angeles Times*, May 13, 2000.

Gold, Matea, and Beth Shuster (additional reporting by Alan Abrahamson, Matt Lait, and Jim Newton), "Officer Who Shot Colleague Reported Being Harassed," *Los Angeles Times*, March 20, 1997.

Goldsmith, Susan, "Containing Rampart," *New Times L.A.*, February 22, 2001.

Golub, Jan, "Burying the Evidence," *New Times L.A.*, March 2, 2000.

————, "L.A. Confidential," salon.com, September 27, 2000.

————, "Who Killed Biggie Smalls?," salon.com, October 16, 2000.

————, "B.I.G. Trouble at the *Los Angeles Times*," salon.com, October 16, 2000.

Gonzalez, Angel, "Who Shot Ya?," *VIBE*, March 1998.

Gonzales, John M., and Frank B. Williams (additional reporting by Carla Rivera), "Fans Lament Star's Death, Violence As 'Madness,'" *Los Angeles Times*, March 10, 1997.

Gonzales, Michael A., "No More Drama," *XXL*, April 2002.

Good, Karen R., "Faith. Fully," *VIBE*, May 1996.

hampton, dream, "Hellraiser," *The Source*, September 1994.

————, "B.I.G. Mama," *VIBE*, March 1998.

Handelman, David, "The Notorious V.I.P.," *Details*, July 1996.

Herszenhorn, David M., "Reporter Working for *Times* Arrested While Covering Clash," *New York Times*, March 19, 1997.

Hirschberg, Lynn, "Does a Sugar Bear Bite?," *The New York Times Magazine*, January 14, 1996.

Hunter, Karen, "He's Hittin' It B.I.G.," *Daily News* (New York), March 6, 1995.

Ivory, Steven, "Family Matters," *The Source*, September 1996.

Jacobson, Mark, "The Return of Superfly," *New York*, August 14, 2000.

Jenkins, Sacha, "Why Kids Go Koo-Koo for Cocoa-Puff," VIBE, December 1997/January 1998.

————, "Holler If Ya Hear Me," *XXL*, January/February 2003.

Johnson, Cory, "Sweatin' Bullets," VIBE, February 1995.

Johnson, Ross, "What I've Learned: Suge Knight," *Esquire*, May 2002.

Jones, Charisse, "Still Hanging in the Hood," *New York Times*, September 24, 1995.

Kamp, David, "Don't Hate Me Because I'm Ghetto Fabulous," *GQ*, August 1999.

Katz, Jesse, "Deposed King of Crack Now Free After 5 Years in Prison," *Los Angeles Times*, December 20, 1994.

————, "Tracking the Genesis of the Crack Trade," *Los Angeles Times*, October 20, 1996.

Kaylin, Lucy, "Moguls with Attitude," *GQ*, April 1993.

Kriegel, Mark, "Kid from B'Klyn Saw His Fame in New Name Game," *Daily News* (New York), March 10, 1997.

Lait, Matt, "3 Kilos of Cocaine Stolen at LAPD: Officer Suspected," *Los Angeles Times*, August 7, 1998.

————, "LAPD Officer Arrested in Drug-Evidence Theft," *Los Angeles Times*, August 26, 1998.

Lait, Matt, and Eric Lichtblau, "Robbery Suspect Called LAPD Leader," *Los Angeles Times*, December 19, 1997.

Lait, Matt, and Scott Glover, "Ex-LAPD Officer Is Suspect in Rapper's Slaying, Records Show," *Los Angeles Times,* December 9, 1999.

_____, "Insignia of Rampart Anti-Gang Unit Raises Concern," *Los Angeles Times,* February 8, 2000.

_____, "71 More Cases May Be Voided Due to Rampart," *Los Angeles Times,* April 18, 2000.

Levy, Rachael, "Former Coaches Portray Knight in Positive Light," *Las Vegas Sun,* September 10, 1996.

Lichtblau, Eric, Chuck Philips, and Cheo Hodari Coker, "Gangsta Rap Performer Notorious B.I.G. Slain," *Los Angeles Times,* March 10, 1997.

Lichtblau, Eric, and Matt Lait, "Officer Charged in Bank Heist That Netted $722,000," *Los Angeles Times,* December 18, 1997.

Malone, Ambassador "Bönz," "Young, Rich & Deadly," *The Source,* July 1995.

Marriott, Michel, "Long Before He Was B.I.G.," *New York Times,* March 17, 1997.

Marriott, Rob, "Last Testament," VIBE, November 1996.

_____, "Ready to Die" VIBE, November 1996.

_____, "All That Glitters," VIBE, May 1997.

_____, "Bigger," *ego trip,* Vol. 3, No. 1, 1997.

_____, "R(Un)ning Things," *XXL,* 1997 (issue 2).

_____, "The Other Woman," *XXL,* 1997 (issue 2).

Mason, Kiki, "Making Motown Matter," *New York,* October 23, 1995.

Matthews, Adam, "D-Day," *XXL,* May 2003.

Mays, Raqiyah, "Pain Is Love," *XXL,* April 2002.

McDermott, Terry, "Rafael Perez: The Road to Rampart," *Los Angeles Times,* December 31, 2000.

_____, "N.W.A: Straight Outta Compton," *Los Angeles Times,* April 14, 2002.

Michel, Sia, "Last Exit to Brooklyn," *Spin,* April 1997.

_____, "The Mourning After," *Spin,* January 1998.

Millner, Denene, and John Marzulli, "Rapper's Latest Hit Was on a Joint," *Daily News* (New York), September 19, 1996.

Nelson, Havelock, "Rap's Next Big Thing," *Interview,* November 1994.

Newton, Jim, Matt Lait, and Scott Glover, "The Rampart Scandal: LAPD Condemned by Its Own Inquiry into Rampart Scandal," *Los Angeles Times,* March 1, 2000.

"Bullets over Brooklyn," VIBE, March 1996.

_____, "Parks Denies He Tried to Block Rampart Probe," *Los Angeles Times,* October 4, 2000.

_____, "Rapper Notorious B.I.G. Held on Fugitive Warrant," *Daily News* (New York), June 20, 1995.

_____, "Rap Artist Arrested in Assault with Bat" (Associated Press), *Los Angeles Times,* March 24, 1996.

Olen, Helaine, "Rapper Shakur Gets Prison for Assault," *Los Angeles Times,* February 8, 1995.

Ortega, Tony, "Who Killed Biggie Smalls? A B.I.G. Mistake," *New Times L.A.,* June 1, 2000.

Overend, William, "Adventures in the Drug Trade," *Los Angeles Times,* May 7, 1989.

Owen, Frank, "The Voice of Experience: With 'Ready to Die' The Notorious B.I.G. Hustles His Harsh Reality up the Album Charts," *New York Newsday,* October 5, 1994.

Pendelton, Tonya, "Leap of Faith," *XXL,* Fall 1997 (No. 1).

Philips, Chuck, "The Big Mack," *Spin,* August 1994.

_____, "Coopers & Lybrand Accountant Axed in Death Row Debacle," *Los Angeles Times,* February 8, 1997.

_____, "2 Say They Saw Attackers of Slain Rapper," *Los Angeles Times,* February 28, 1997.

_____, "Bad Boy II Man," *Los Angeles Times,* May 25, 1997.

_____, "Alleged Ties Between Rap Label, Drug Dealer Probed," *Los Angeles Times,* May 31, 1997.

_____, "Grand Jury to Probe Origins of Rap Label," *Los Angeles Times,* July 24, 1997.

_____, "Probe of Rap Label Looks at Entrepreneur Behind Bars," *Los Angeles Times,* September 1, 1997.

_____, "Investigation of Rapper's Slaying Comes Up Empty," *Los Angeles Times,* December 16, 1997.

_____, "Man No Longer Under Scrutiny in Rapper's Death," *Los Angeles Times,* May 3, 2000.

_____, "Possible Link of 'Puffy' Combs to Fatal Shooting Being Probed," *Los Angeles Times,* January 17, 2001.

_____, "Who Killed Tupac Shakur?," *Los Angeles Times,* September 6, 2002.

_____, "How Vegas Police Probe Foundered," *Los Angeles Times,* September 7, 2002.

Philips, Chuck, and Alan Abrahamson, "Rapper Leaves Tangled Financial, Legal Legacy," *Los Angeles Times,* December 24, 1996.

————, "U.S. Probes Death Row Record Label's Money Trail," *Los Angeles Times,* December 29, 1996.

————, "Rap Mogul Probed in '95 Case," *Los Angeles Times,* January 21, 1997.

————, "Police, Shakur's Entourage at Odds over Investigation," *Los Angeles Times,* February 4, 1997.

————, "Longo to Be Dismissed by D.A.'s Office," *Los Angeles Times,* February 23, 1997.

————, "Rappers Raise New Questions in Knight Case," *Los Angeles Times,* March 4, 1997.

Philips, Chuck, and Matt Lait, "Personal Dispute Is Focus of Rap Probe," *Los Angeles Times,* March 18, 1997.

Posner, Gerald, "The Rap on Puffy," *Talk,* August 2001.

Powell, Kevin, "This Thug's Life," VIBE, February 1994.

————, "The VIBE Q: 2Pac Shakur Ready to Live," VIBE, April 1995.

————, "Live from Death Row," VIBE, February 1996.

————, "All Eyez on Him," VIBE, February 1996.

Pristin, Terry, "Rap Star Faces Charges," *New York Times,* August 1, 1996.

Raftery, Tom (News Wire Services), "Rap Star Finds B.I.G. Trouble," *Daily News* (New York), March 24, 1996.

Ro, Ronin, "Escape from Death Row," VIBE, October 1996.

Romain, Louis, "Hard Times, Hard Rhymes: In the Midst of Everyday Struggle, B.I.G Remains Larger Than Life," *RapPages,* August 1994.

Rosenzweig, David, "Suit Says Chief Blocked Early Rampart Probe," *Los Angeles Times,* September 27, 2000.

Sager, Mike, "Cube: The World According to Amerikkka's Most Wanted Rapper," *Rolling Stone,* October 4, 1990.

Samuels, Allison, "Hit Man," VIBE, September 1995.

Samuels, Anita M., "The Young Man of Bad Boy," *New York Times,* November 6, 1994.

Satten, Vanessa, "Second Childhood," *XXL,* April 2002.

Satten, Vanessa, and Leah Rose, "High Times: Cease Ain't the World's Best Driver," *XXL,* April 2003.

Saxon, Shani (with Jeannine Amber, Hyun Kim, Aliya King, Jacob Ogles, Minya Oh, Shaheem Reid, and Corey Takahashi), "Back to the Essence: Friends and Family Reminisce over Hip-Hop's Fallen Sons," VIBE, October 1999.

Shakur, Sanyika, "Welcome to the Terrorzone," VIBE, December1997/January 1998.

————, "Shook One," VIBE, December 1997/January 1998.

Shaw, Jessica, "News & Notes," *Entertainment Weekly,* December 15, 1995.

Shaw, William, "Rhyme and Punishment," *Details,* April 1996.

Smith, Danyel, "Tuff Love," VIBE, August 1995.

Snow, Shauna, "Morning Report: Rapper Makes Bail," *Los Angeles Times,* October 14, 1995.

Stancell, Stephen, "The Bigs: Biggie Smalls, Big Daddy Kane, Big Skoob-Artifacts," *New York Beacon,* September 9, 1994.

Strange, Adario, "Death Wish," *The Source,* March 1996.

Strong, Nolan, "Feds Focus Investigation on Former Crack Dealer in Queens," allhiphop.com, December 23, 2002.

The Blackspot, "Stakes Is High," VIBE, September 1996.

Thompson, Bonsu, "Savior-Z Day," *XXL,* December 2002.

Touré, "The Professional," *The Village Voice,* December 13, 1994.

————, "Biggie Smalls, Rap's Man of the Moment," *New York Times,* December 18, 1994.

————, "The Life of a Hunted Man," *Rolling Stone,* April 3, 2003.

Turner, Khary Kimani, "The House That Crack Built," *The Source,* July 1994.

Valdés, Mimi, "Things Done Changed," VIBE, October 1995.

Waxman, Sharon, "A Notorious B.I.G. Open Case," *Washington Post,* April 17, 2002.

Weinstein, Henry, "6 Cocaine Traffickers Admit Guilt, Drugs: International Ring Was a Major Supplier of Crack to L.A. Gangs. The Pleas May Make the Case Against Alleged Ringleaders Easier to Prove," *Los Angeles Times,* December 13, 1989.

————, "1990 Saw Several Blows Struck in Drug War Narcotics," *Los Angeles Times,* January 28, 1991.

————, "Attorneys in a Fierce Battle over Drug-Suspect Business," *Los Angeles Times,* February 11, 1992.

_____, "Lawyer for Rap Mogul Known for Aggressive Work," *Los Angeles Times,* October 29, 1996.

Williams, Frank, "Unsolved Mystery," *Spin,* January 1998.

Williams, Frank B., and Shawn Hubler (with additional reporting by Tim Kawakami in Las Vegas and Cheo Hodari Coker and Mayrav Saar in Los Angeles), "Star Rapper Tupac Shakur Badly Wounded," *Los Angeles Times,* September 9, 1996.

Wilson, Elliott, "Bed-Stuy, Brooklyn's Biggest Bad Boy . . . The Notorious B.I.G.," *URB,* November 1994.

CREDITS

Text

page ix: Courtesy of Cheo Hodari Coker
page x: Michael Lavine
page xii: Geoffroy De Boismenu/ Corbis Outline
page xvi: Dana Lixenberg
page 10: Courtesy of Ms. Voletta Wallace
page 15: Courtesy of Ms. Voletta Wallace
page 16: Courtesy of Ms. Voletta Wallace
page 19: Courtesy of Ms. Voletta Wallace
page 20: Courtesy of Ms. Voletta Wallace
page 22: Marlon Ajamu Myrie
page 24: Carl Posey
page 27: Courtesy of Ms. Voletta Wallace
page 28: Courtesy of Ms. Voletta Wallace
page 30: Marlon Ajamu Myrie
page 33: Carl Posey
page 39: George DuBose/LFI
page 42: Courtesy of Ms. Voletta Wallace
page 44: Koi Sojer/LFI
page 53: George DuBose/LFI
page 54: David Yellen
page 56: George DuBose/LFI
page 64: Chi Modu
page 69: Donald Harrison
page 72: Dana Lixenberg
page 76: Koi Sojer/LFI
page 82: Koi Sojer/LFI
page 86: Philip Greenberg
page 88: Ray Tamarra
page 97: Philip Greenberg
page 101: Daniel Hastings
page 105: Philip Greenberg
page 108: Chi Modu
page 116: Clarence Davis/*Daily News* (New York)
page 118: Matthew Pearson, Jr.

page 123: Koi Sojer/LFI
page 126: T. Eric Monroe
page 132: G. N. Miller
page 135: Al Pereira
page 140: Jayson Keeling
page 144: Philip Greenberg
page 148: Chi Modu
page 151: Koi Sojer/LFI
page 152: © 2000, Lauren Greenfield. All Rights Reserved.
page 155: Koi Sojer/LFI
page 159: Jonathan Mannion
page 160: Koi Sojer/LFI
page 166: AP/Wide World Photos
page 169: AP/Wide World Photos
page 170: Sue Kwon
page 172: Dana Lixenberg
page 175: Caroline Torem-Craig/LFI
page 176: Bill Jones
page 180: Lenny Santiago
page 191: Corjuni/Corbis Outline
page 196: Dana Lixenberg
page 198: Andrew MacPherson
page 202: Maurice McInnis
page 205: Courtesy of Ms. Voletta Wallace
page 206: Piotr Sikora
page 211: Sue Kwon
page 215: Michael Lavine
page 218: Michael Lavine
page 221: © 1995, Delphine A. Fawundi-Buford
page 224: © 1997, Genaro Molina/ *Los Angeles Times*
page 229: Courtesy of Conart
page 241: Courtesy of Ms. Voletta Wallace
page 242: AP/Wide World Photos
page 246: Barron Claiborne/Corbis Outline
page 249: Courtesy of Ms. Voletta Wallace
page 251: AP/Wide World Photos
page 252: AP/Wide World Photos
page 256: AP/Wide World Photos

page 260: David Corio
page 263: Robin Bowman
page 264: Frank Micelotta/Getty Images
page 266: Eric Johnson/Corbis Outline
page 271: AP/Wide World Photos
page 274: © 2000, Al Schaben/*Los Angeles Times*
page 281: © 1997, Gary Friedman/ *Los Angeles Times*
page 286: Michael Lavine
page 289: Koi Sojer/LFI
page 290: Robin Bowman
page 291: Caroline Torem-Craig/LFI
page 294: Koi Sojer/LFI
page 295: Koi Sojer/LFI
page 297: Marlon Ajamu Myrie
page 300: David Corio
page 332: Philip Greenberg

Insert

page 1: Geoffroy De Boismenu/Corbis Outline
page 2: Bill Jones
page 3: Courtesy of Ms. Voletta Wallace
page 4: Carl Posey
page 5: Carl Posey
page 6: Manuel Acevedo
page 7: Manuel Acevedo
page 8: T. Eric Monroe (*above*); Mark Lennihan/AP Wide World Photos (*below*)
page 9: Shawn Mortensen/Corbis Outline
page 10: Dana Lixenberg
page 11: Courtesy of Ms. Voletta Wallace
page 12: Eric Johnson/Corbis Outline
page 13: Cati Gonzales
page 14: Michael Lavine
page 15: Guy Aroch/Corbis Outline
page 16: Barron Claiborne/Corbis Outline

ACKNOWLEDGMENTS

First things first: Our deepest gratitude goes to Voletta Wallace, whose strength of spirit is an inspiration to all who are fortunate enough to know her. Thank you for raising such an unbelievable young man, and thank you for making this book possible. We could not have done it without you.

Unbelievable was more than two years in the making, but the book actually flows out of VIBE magazine's entire ten-year history. Biggie was a guest performer at VIBE's launch party in September 1993, jumping onstage to thrill the crowd with a rendition of "Party and Bullshit." He was first featured in the magazine's NEXT section in August 1994, in a piece written by Mimi Valdés. He appeared on the cover three times: in October 1995 with Faith, in September 1996 with Puffy, and then in May 1997 after he was killed while leaving a party co-sponsored by VIBE. I know I speak for everyone who worked on this book when I say that it was more than a labor of love. We viewed it as our solemn responsibility to get this one right.

Big respect to the VIBE Books splinter cell: Art Director Mark Shaw, Photo Editor Adrienne R. Williams, Research Editor Sun Singleton, and Reporter at Large Raqiyah Mays. Your steadfast devotion to this effort has made all the difference.

To our wise and wonderful editor, Kristin Kiser at Crown and Three Rivers Press, who patiently allowed this book to become all that it needed to be: thank you for your vision.

To the rest of the Three Rivers team, production editor extraordinaire Jim Walsh, design guru Lauren Dong, manufacturing wiz Leta Evanthes, and the indefatigable assistants Claudia Gabel and Ellen Rubinstein, and publisher Steve Ross: thanks for remembering that it's darkest before the dawn.

To all of Biggie's family, friends, and colleagues who spoke with the author or the research team: thanks for entrusting us with your memories and insights.

Peace to all the journalists whose works are listed in the end notes. Write on.

To VIBE veterans Emil Wilbekin and Mimi Valdés, thanks for your guidance.

Thanks to Kenard Gibbs for supporting VIBE Books from day one.

Thanks to our agent Sarah Lazin for finally believing the unbelievable.

Thanks to Jeff Miller, David Korzenik, and Katherine Trager for sound legal advice.

Special thanks to Carter Harris, Beverly Smith, Karla Radford, Hyun Kim, Serena Kim, Kim Ford, Ali Muhammad, Damien Lemon, and Jacquie Juceam.

Big up to B-zo, Mao, and Uncle Ralph for dropping gems as usual.

And, of course, to Cheo: thank you for rising to this major challenge.

And to Sue and Tumaini, thank you for believing in both of us. We did it.

And to A, I, and M . . . everlasting love.

ROB KENNER
Editorial Director, VIBE Books

Italicized page numbers indicate
 photographs

Agnant, Jacques "Haitian Jack,"
 123–126, 127, 128
Allen, Woody, 29
Amber, Jeannine, 208
Anderson, Norris, 251
Anderson, Orlando "Baby Lane," 190,
 193, 225, 226, 241, 270, 271, 280,
 281
Angelettie, Deric "D-Dot," 56–57,
 61–63, *88*, 205, 206, 207, 209,
 210, 211, 216, 238–239, 240–241,
 242, 243, 244, 260, 261, 262
Annie Hall (film), 29
Atwater, Lee, 56

Bad Boy Records, 71, 85, 87–89, 153,
 203–208, 264, 269, 270
Baltimore, Charli (Tiffany Lane), 174,
 175, 196, 227, 290
Bambaataa, Afrika, 46, 47
Banger, 107, 296
Banks, Nathaniel, Jr., 167
Baraka, Ras, 57
Barnes, Leroy "Nicky," 32–33
Bedford-Stuyvesant neighborhood,
 16–17
Bell, Mark Anthony, 173–174, 274, 283
Bennett, Michael "Waterhead Bo,"
 34–35
Bias, Len, 31
Biggie Smalls. *See* Wallace, Christopher
Big Syke, 173
Black Arts Movement, 80
Blackman, Melvin, 18
Black Panthers, 7, 150
Blake, 107
Blakey, Art, 49, 294
Blanchard, Terence, 49
Blige, Mary J., 67, 69–70, 76, 110, 115,
 153, *252*, 254
Bloods gang, 34, 150, 153, 241, 250,
 278
Brand Nubian, 71
Broady, Carlos "Six July," 207
Brown, Alonzo, 47, 85, 154–155, 253
Brown, Foxy, 254
Brown, Nino, 133
Bruck, Connie, 283
Buck Wild, 214
Burns, "Hawk," 148, 162

Burrowes, Kirk, 110
Bush, George H. W., 31
Bynum, Arty, 21
Bynum, Michael, 18–20, *19*, 48–50, *297*

Calloway, Bryant, 278
Campbell, Julia, 258
Campbell, Luther "Luke," 163, 173,
 184–185, 249
Cantrock, Steve, 225, 283
Capoluongo, Matteo "Matty C.,"
 55–56, 61, 89
Capone, 179
Caribbean Sound Basin studio, 205
Cheese, 31, 42
Chestnut, Cyrus, 49
Chocolate (Mario Johnson), 92, 93
Christopher Wallace Foundation, 290
Chronic, The (Dr. Dre), 89, 94, 99
Chuck D, 216
Cleaver, Eldridge, 9
Clinton Hill neighborhood, 16–18
Cocaine and crack, 29–41
Cochran, Johnnie, 272
Cohen, Lyor, 64
Combs, Janice, 57–58, *59*
Combs, Justin, 116
Combs, Keisha, 58
Combs, Maurice, 187
Combs, Melvin, 56–57, 58, 59
Combs, Sean "Puffy," 2, 4, *64, 76,* 82,
 86, 108, 114–116, 140, *144,* 145,
 152, 163, *172,* 183, *206, 224,* 244,
 264
 AIDS benefit riot, 68–69
 bad-boy behavior, 68, 85
 Bad Boy Records, founding of,
  70–71, 86–89
 Blige and, 69–70
 Crips and, 269–270
 early years, 57–60
 East Coast–West Coast rap war,
  157–160, 186
 Evans and, 109–110
 firing from Uptown Records, 84–86
 gun ownership, 134
 hits for Bad Boy, focus on, 203–208
 "Hypnotize" video, 227–232
 Knight and, 157–158, 181, 270
 Life After Death and, 211–212, 214,
  215, 217, 281
 marketing and promotion, learning
  about, 63

 motorcycle wipe-out, 258–259
 party promotion, 62–63, 68, 116
 performing career, 204, 206, 228,
  233, 259, 260–262, 263–265
 producing method, 100
 promotional secrets, 223
 rap music initiation, 60
 Ready to Die and, 96, 98–100, 105,
  122
 record industry education, 63,
  65–68
 Rivera and, 107
 self-assessment, 116
 Shakur beating incident, 130–133,
  134, 137–138
 student takeover at Howard, 57
 style of, 60–61
 tribute to Wallace, 260–261,
  264–265
 Trinidad sessions, 205–207
 Wallace murder investigation, 268,
  269–270
 Wallace's crossover strategy,
  143–144
 Wallace's drug dealing, 78–79
 Wallace's funeral, 254
 Wallace's murder, 242–245, 250, 253
 Wallace's rapping, first encounter
  with, 55–56, 71
 Wallace's recording sessions, exclu-
  sion from, 210
 Wallace's relationship with,
  143–144, 236–237
 Wallace's signing with Uptown
  Records, 74–77, 79
 West Coast trip in 1997, 223–224,
  226–232, 240, 241, 242, 243, 244,
  245
Comeaux, Raymond, 250
Cooper, Mabusha "Push," 50
Cowboy, 47
CRASH, 276
Crips gang, 34, 150, 187, 193, 241, 250,
 269–270, 273, 280, 282, 284, 285
Cypress Hill, 71
Czleger, Stephen, 226

Daddy-O, 54
Daddy's House studio, 197–198, 204,
 209–210, *211,* 296
Davis, Clive, 88, 89, 163, 252, 254
Davis, Dwayne Keith "Keefee D," 241,
 270, 282

Daz, 179
Death Row Records, 92–95, 153–154, 168–171, 188–190, 224–225, 271, 272, 277, 283
Def Jam Records, 63–64, 155
Delvec, Chico, 21, 31–32, 42, 50, 107
Dinkins, David, 254
D.O.C. (Tracy Curry), 90, 91–92, 93
Dr. Dre (Andre Young), 89, 90–91, 92–94, 143, 153, 154, 158, 169, 188–189, 225, 249
D-Roc (Damion Butler), 2, 36, 42, 52, 74, 79, 83, 127, 161, 178, 196, 209, 228, 231, 232, 234, 238, 242, 243, 245, 252–253, 254, 257, 268, 275, 296
Drug trade, 29–43, 50–51, 78–79

East Coast–West Coast rap war, 3–4, 138, 157–160, 171–175, 176–187, 193, 214–215, 222, 226–227, 282, 283
Easy Mo Bee, 80–82, 82, 96–100, 122, 129, 214–215, 254
    Wallace's relationship with, 80
Eazy-E (Eric Wright), 90–91, 93, 94, 188
Edwards, Vanessa, 258
E-40, 160, 161
Enuff, DJ, 143–144, 161–162, 163, 175, 185, 222
Eric B. & Rakim, 48
Evans, Faith, 89, 140, 146, 148, 158, 161, 176, 192, 202, 204, 239, 241, 244, 264, 288, 290, 291, 291
    early years, 109–110
    Lil' Kim and, 178–179, 195–196
    musical career, 109–110, 175–177
    Shakur and, 175–176
    tribute to Wallace, 260, 261, 264
    Wallace's child born to, 179, 195, 202–203
    Wallace's funeral, 254
    Wallace's murder, 252, 279
    Wallace's relationship with, 109–114, 164–166, 175–177, 178–179, 203, 237

Fab 5 Freddy, 138, 172
Father MC, 67
Federal Bureau of Investigation (FBI), 150
Fields, Ted, 95, 168
50 Grand, DJ, 39, 53, 52–54, 56
Finch, Bobby Ray, 193
Fitzgerald, Daniel P., 126

Flanagan, Timothy, 193
Flash, Grandmaster (Joseph Sadler), 47
Flavor Flav, 254
Fresh Prince, 64
Fula, Yasmyn, 190
Fuller, Charles "Man," 125, 126
Funky Enough Records, 92
Furious Five, 47
Futami, Raymond, 250

Gaines, Kevin, 272–273, 275, 277, 279
Geto Boys, 71
Glover, Savion, 264
Glover, Scott, 277, 278
Grand Puba, 122
Griffey, Dick, 92, 93
Grubman, Allen, 155
Gutter (Suif Jackson), 32, 38–39, 42, 107, 112
Guy, Jasmine, 136

hampton, dream, 87, 127, 252
Harrell, Andre, 47, 63–65, 64, 66, 68, 69, 70, 75–76, 84–86, 114–116, 128–129, 130–131, 134, 137–138, 153, 154, 155, 156, 204, 253
Harris, Michael "Harry-O," 35, 94, 194, 225
Harrison, Donald, 49–50, 294
Harvey, Steve, 224
Havoc, 214
Hawks crew, 19–20
Heavy D (Dwight Myers), 62, 63, 65, 67, 68, 74, 254
Heller, Jerry, 91
Herdell, Brook, 167
Hernandez, Emmanuel, 277
Hester, Larry "Blackspot," 182
Hewitt, Brian, 277
Hicken, Donald, 124
Hines, Laura, 173
Hip hop. See Rap music
Hip hop soul, 68, 70
Hirschberg, Lynn, 177
Hitmen, 205–207, 206, 214, 215
Howard, Chris, 158
Howard University, 56–57, 61
Hunter, Paul, 228–232
Hylton-Brim, Misa, 145, 177

Ice Cube (O'Shea Jackson), 82, 90–91, 93, 183, 293
"I'll Be Missing You" (Combs), 260–261, 263, 264, 264
Inabu, Paul, 273
Interscope Records, 95, 154, 168, 194

Iovine, Jimmy, 95, 168
Ito, Ron, 277

Jackson, Ayana, 124–125
Jackson, Jan, 42, 83–84, 112
    child with Wallace, 77–78, 84
    Wallace's murder, 249, 251
    Wallace's relationship with, 43, 239
Jackson, Johnny "J," 170
Jackson, Michael, 64, 142
Jam Master Jay, DJ, 295
Jay-Z (Shawn Carter), 28, 180, 186, 213–214, 254, 294–295
Jimenez, Ismael, 277
Jodeci, 66, 67, 70, 85, 115
Johnson, Manuel, 90
Jones, Anthony "Wolf," 59, 158, 270
Jones, Kidada, 191, 192
Jones, Quincy, 88, 99, 158
Junior M.A.F.I.A., 82, 99, 107, 130, 148, 148, 159, 161–163, 164, 196, 209, 257, 296
Justice, 107

Kallman, Craig, 163
Kane, Big Daddy (Antonio Hardy), 48, 52, 53, 96
Katz, Steven, 280, 284, 285
Kay Gee, 214
Kenner, David, 34–35, 94, 154, 168, 190, 274
Kenner, Rob, 3
Kent, Clark, 214
Kid Creole, 45
Klept, 107, 227
Knight, Marion, Jr. "Suge," 3, 152, 169, 177, 191, 225–226, 270, 280, 281
    Bell beating incident, 173–174, 274, 283
    childhood years, 90
    Combs and, 157–158, 181
    contract renegotiations, 115
    Death Row Records, founding of, 92–95
    Dr. Dre's departure from Death Row, 188–189
    East Coast–West Coast rap war, 157–160
    imprisonment of, 225–226
    intimidation tactics, 93–94, 115, 153
    loyalty to his artists, 153
    Philips and, 280, 283
    plea bargain and, 154
    record industry education, 92–93
    Shakur and, 152–153, 168–169, 170, 189–190

Shakur's murder, 191–192,
  193–194
sports participation, 90
Stanley brothers, 154, 193
Wallace's confrontation with, 182
Wallace's murder, 250, 251
Knight, Marion and Maxine, 90
Knight, Sharitha, 272
Kool G. Rap, 48
Kool Herc, DJ, 46, 48, 254, *294*
KRS-One, *82*
Kunstler, William, 69
Kurupt, 179

LAbyrinth (Sullivan), 283
Lait, Matt, 269, 277, 278, 279, 285
Lane, Travon "Tray," 187, 190, 271
Larceny, 42, 106, 107
Last Poets, 80, 81
Las Vegas Police Department, 284
Latifah, Queen, 155, 254
Lavine, Michael, *215*
Lawrence, Ron "Amen-Ra," 60–61, 62,
  63, 204–205, 206, 207, 208
LeCatis, Audrey, 179
Lee, McKinley, 153
Lee, Tracey, 242, 243
Letore, George, 14–15, *15*, 22–23
Let's Do It Again (film), *48*, 51
Levy, Stewart, 149
Lighty, Chris, 233
Lil' Cease (James Lloyd), 2, 42, 79, 82,
  98, 99, 103, 107, 109, 120,
  121–122, 123, 128, 130, 133,
  135, 137, 138, 146, 162, 163,
  164, 172, 182, 183, 193,
  196–197, 209, 224, 227, 231,
  232, 238, 242, 243, 244,
  252–253, 257, 268, 281, 296–299
Lil' Kim (Kimberly Jones), 107, 162,
  204, *252, 263*, 290, *290*
  Evans and, 178–179, 195–196
  Wallace's funeral, 254
  Wallace's relationship with, 162,
    178–179, 237, 290
Lil' Shawn, 129
LL Cool J, 48, 184
Lockhart, Calvin, *49*
Longo, Larry and Gina, 154, 194, *225,*
  283
Lopez, Jennifer, 264
Los Angeles Police Department
  (LAPD), 268–269, 275–276, 284,
  290
Lotwin, Dave, 101–102
Lox, 260, 261

Lucas, Frank, 32–33
Lyga, Frank, 272, 273

Mack, Craig, 86, 87, 89, *108*, 114, 116,
  148
Mack, David, 275, 276, *277*, 278, 279,
  280, 284, 285
Mack-10, 179
Macola Records, 91
Mahoney, Mark, 232
Main Source, 71
Malone, Bönz, 55, 142
Mao, Jeff "Chairman," 3, 214, 217
Marley, Bob, 143, 293
Marriott, Rob, 255, 280
Martin, Dave, 279
Mase, 254
Maserati, Tony, 205
Massenberg, Kedar, 107
Meiselas, Kenny, 87
Melle Mel, 47
Miller, Fred, 273
Mister Cee, DJ, *54*, 53–56, 70–72,
  74–76, 79
Mobb Deep, 55, 179, 183
Money B, 127
Money L, 42, 161
Montrose, Lynn, 210
Moore, Freddie, 130, 131, 133
Morris, Keisha, 170
Mourges, Melissa, 126
Muhammad, Amir (Harry Billups),
  274, 275, 278–279, 280, 284–285
Muhammad, Conrad, 158
Myrick, Nashiem, 87, 205, 207, 211

Nas, 71, 103, 221, *221*, 292–295
Nate Dogg, 94
Native Son (Wright), 103
New jack swing, 65
Newton, Huey P., 7, 56, 121
Niehaus, Axel, 205
Nino, 107
Noreaga, 179
Notorious B.I.G. *See* Wallace,
  Christopher
N.W.A, 91, 93

O, 38, 41
Offord, Paul "Big Paul," 59, 242, 243,
  268
OGC, 222
Ogletree, Charles, 168, 190
Old Gold Brothers, *39, 52*
O'Neal, Shaquille, 232
Ouderkirk, John, 154

Paniciolli, Ernie, 194–195
Parks, Bernard, 277, 278, 279
Parks, Gordon, Jr., 29
Patcher, Leon, 135
Pennix, Sybil, 67, 120
Pepa, 254
Perez, Rafael, 275, 276, *277*, 278, 279
Philips, Chuck, 251, 260, 269,
  278–279, 280, 282, 283, 284
Pierre, Harve, 62, 87, *88*
Pinkett, Jada, 121
Pitts, Mark "Gucci Don," 62, 87, 100,
  113, 130, 167, 224–225, 238, 242,
  243, 244, 245
  Wallace's relationship with, 86–87
Pooh, Don, 62, 161, 167, 232–233,
  248, 292–293
Poole, Russell, 269, 272, 273, 274, 275,
  276–277, 279, 284
Powell, Colin, 158
Powell, Kevin, 125, 137, 184, 192
Pratt, Geronimo, 149
Premier, DJ, *101*, 100–103, 211–212,
  216, 254, 292–293
Pryor, Richard, 30

Q-Tip, 249
Queen of All Saints high school, *30*
Quesada, Veronica, 276
Quik, DJ, 241

Raekwon, 221
Rampart Scandal, 276–278
Rap music, 46–48, 60, 71, 88–89, 283,
  292–296
Rather, Dan, 31
Ren, MC (Lorenzo Patterson), 90
Rhymes, Busta (Trevor Smith), 28, 70,
  251, 254
Riley, Teddy, 65, 205
Rivera, Lance "Un," 107–108, 148, 239,
  254
Ro, Ronin, 188, 283
Robinson, Fatima, 230
Robles, Jake, 158, 173, 270
Romaine, Louis "Atco," 109
Rome, Tony, 31, 42
Romero, Errolyn, 274
Ron G, 68, 129
Rooftop (club), 60
Roots, 221
Ross, "Freeway" Ricky, 30–31
Rubin, Rick, 64
Run-D.M.C., 48, 254, 293, *295*
Ruthless Records, 91, 93
RZA, 214

Sadat X, 99
Sams, Hubert, 6, 18–20, *19*, 27, 38–40, 48–50, *297*, 299
Shakur, Afeni, 120–121, 149, 190
Shakur, Mutulu, 149, 151
Shakur, Sanyika, 280
Shakur, Tupac "2Pac," 3, *118, 123, 126, 132, 135, 169, 176*, 189, 190, *191*, 217, 225, 226, 235, 283
    acting career, 82–83, 124, 126, 128–129
    Agnant's conflict with, 123–126, 127–128, 134–135, 136–137
    artistic legacy, 293, 294
    awards and honors, 181
    beaten, shot, and robbed at Quad Studios, 129–139, 172–173
    Bell beating incident, 173–174
    birth of, 6
    Death Row, association with, 169–171, 189–191
    early years, 120–121
    Evans and, 176–178, 192
    "gangsta at war" persona, 173, 184, 187
    Knight and, 152–153, 168–170, 189–190, 280
    murder of, 3, 5, 191–195, 250–251, 269, 273, 280–282
    paranoia of, 149–150, 171, 173
    as performance artist, 136–137
    prison life, 149–150, 151–153, 168–169
    rape arrest, 124–129, 135–136
    recording sessions, 170
    Walker and, 172–173
    Wallace's music, attitude toward, 82
    Wallace's relationship with, 5, 117, 120–124, 127–128, 138–139, 151–152, 173, 176–177, 179
    war on Wallace, 183–187
Shaw, William, 172
Shock G, 149
Siegel, Mark, 85
Simmons, Russell, 63–64, 65, 66, 115, 154, 155, 156, 241
Singleton, John, 82–83, 126
Slick Rick, 62, 97–98, 157, 293
Snoop Doggy Dogg, 4, 71, 94, 95, 143, 153, 157, 169, 170, 179, *224*, 226, 249
Sookra, Audwin, 256
Soul Train Awards ceremony of 1996, 181–182
Soul Train Awards ceremony of 1997, 233–234, 235

Source Awards ceremony of 1995, 155, 157–158
Stanley, George and Lynwood, 193
Stevie J, 182, 205, 207, 244, 296
Sting, 264, *264*
Story, Kenneth, 3, 243
Super Cat, 76, 83
Superfly (film), 29
Sweat, Keith, 235
Swing, Devante, 115

Tatreau, Jim, 280
Taylor, Susan, 58
Thompson, Chucky, 62, 207
Thug Life movement, 137, 183
Total, 87, 89
Touré, 108, 136
Treach, 176
Trife, 42, 106, 107
Tyehimba, Watani, 168
Tyndall, Brian, 274, 276, 277
Tyson, Mike, 127, 190

Undeas Entertainment, 148
Uptown Records, 63, 64–67, 70, 74–77, 78–79, 84–86, 154

Valdés, Mimi, 161, 165
Vanilla Ice, 93
Van Winkle, Robert, 92

Walker, Randy "Stretch," 122, 130, 131, 132, 133, 134, 137, *170*, 172–173
Wallace, Christopher "Biggie Smalls" "Notorious B.I.G.," xiv–xv, *xviii, 10, 15, 16, 19, 24, 27, 28, 33, 39, 42, 44, 53, 56, 69, 72, 76, 82, 86, 97, 105, 108, 116, 118, 123, 135, 140, 144, 151, 155, 159, 160, 166, 172, 180, 196, 198, 211, 215, 218, 221, 229, 241, 244, 246, 266, 286, 294, 295, 300, 332*
    acting career, interest in, 235
    artistic legacy, 293, 294
    auto accident and aftermath, 196–197, 200–203, 208–209
    awards and honors, 142, 148–149, 158, 181–182
    "Biggie Smalls" rap name, *49*, 51
    birth of, 6, 15
    business acumen, 148–149, 163
    business plans, 220–221
    charisma of, 75, 163–164
    childhood years, 15–16, 18–23, 26–27
    clothing preferences, 26, 145

    "cool dude" attitude, 222
    creative process, 79
    crew of. *See* Junior M.A.F.I.A.
    crossover strategy, 143–144
    double life, 22–23
    drug dealing, 29, 31–32, 35–43, 50–51, 78–79, 95–96, 148
    East MCs' conflicts with, 221–222
    family life, wish for, 7–8
    as father, 77–78, 83, 84, 202–203, 235, 239
    fatherlessness, attitude toward, 22
    federal surveillance of, 224
    "fresh" way of life, 27, 29
    funeral of, *249, 251*, 252–258, *252, 256*
    God and, 201–202, 203, 236
    gun ownership, 146, 280
    high school experiences, 27–28, 36–37
    humor of, 186, 201
    iconic status, 262
    Jamaican heritage, 20
    "keeping it real" concerns, 22, 108, 145–146
    last full day of life, 238–239
    love life, 43, 101–102, 163–166, 175–177, 178–179, 289–290
    marriage of. *See* Evans, Faith
    mature perspective, 200–203, 214, 235–237
    money, attitude toward, 4, 32
    money from rapping, 146–148
    murder of, 5, 6, 240–245, *242, 244*, 248–253. *See also* Wallace murder investigation
    "Notorious B.I.G." rap name, 102–103
    paranoia of, 108–109, 192–193, 284
    personalities of, 6–7
    police run-ins, 39–40, 41, 83, 167–168, 196
    publishing rights, sale of, 148
    rapping career, initiation of, 51–56, 71
    rapping talent, 43, 49–50, 75, 76
    record company, 147, 149, 163
    recording sessions, 3, 80–82, 95–100, 147, 209–212, 216
    road tours, 147–148, 160–162, 163–166
    Shakur beating incident, 130–133, 135, 137, 138, 139
    Shakur's murder, 191–192, 280–285
    signing with Uptown Records, 74–77, 78–79

success's impact on, 4–5
tattoo, 232, 236
tributes to, 7–8, 260–261, *260*, 264–265, *264*
video production, 228–232
Walker's murder, 172–173
weight situation, 27, 213
West Coast stars, admiration for, 143
West Coast trip in 1997, 2–5, 220–221, 222–225, 226–245
young people, concern for, 106
See also specific persons
Wallace, Christopher, music of (as Notorious B.I.G.):
"Bad Boy," 82
"Been Around the World," 207
"Big Poppa," 100, 143, 144, 145, 151, 185
Born Again, 8
"Brooklyn's Finest," 186
"A Buncha Niggas," 83
"Come On, Muthafuckas," 99
"Dead Wrong," 99
"Dolly My Baby," 76, 82, 83
"Dreams," 86
drug dealing experiences and, 95–96
"Everyday Struggle," 100, 104
"Get Money," 162
"Gimme the Loot," 98, 104, 143, 184, 211, 255
"Goin' Back to Cali," 214–215, 242
"Hypnotize," 207, 210, 213, 227–232, 240, 257, 262
"I Got a Story to Tell," 213
"I Love the Dough," 214
"If I Should Die Before I Wake," 98
"I'm Fuckin' You Tonight," 262
"It's All About the Benjamins," 207, 234, 238
"Juicy," 2, 4, 79, 100, 114, 143, 220, 255
"Junior M.A.F.I.A.," 82
"Kick In the Door," 211, 212, 213, 221, 262–263
"Let's Get It On," 122
Life After Death, 3, 208–217, *215*, 250, 262–263, 264, 281, 293

"The Long Kiss Goodnight," 217
"Machine Gun Funk," 99, 100, 104, 143
"Me and My Bitch," 104
"Mo Money, Mo Problems," 207, 210, 213, 262
"My Downfall," 217
"Niggas Bleed," 210, 213, 262
"Notorious Thugs," 213, 262
"One More Chance," 142, 143, 181
"Party and Bullshit," 80–82
"Playa Hatas," 213
"Player's Anthem," 161, 162, 221
"Ready to Die," 97
Ready to Die, 3, 89, 96–105, 106, 107, 114, 116, 122, 142, 146–147, 213–214, 250, 269, 289, 293
"Real Love," 76, 82
"Runnin'," 122
Shakur's attitude toward, 82–83
"Somebody's Gotta Die," 207, 213, 262
"Suicidal Thoughts," 96, 104, 106
"Ten Crack Commandments," 213, 216, 263
"Things Done Changed," 104, 134
"This Time Around," 142
"Unbelievable," 102, 103, 104, 114, 143, 144
"Victory," 234, 239
videos, 83, 143, 144–145, 151, 227–232
"Warning," 104, 115, 143, 144, 211
"The What," 104
"What's Beef," 213
"Who Shot Ya," 151, 184, 185, 284
"You're Nobody Till Somebody Kills You," 217
Wallace, Christopher Jordan "C.J.," 8, 202–203, *202*, 254, 260, 288, *289*, 291
Wallace, T'Yanna "Tee Tee," 8, 77–78, 84, 112, 203, *205*, 239, 260, 261, *265*, 288, *289*, 291
Wallace, Voletta, *15, 16*, 17–18, 27, 28, 29, 79–80, 168, 203, 213, 238, *246*, 265, *289*
arrival in America, 12–14

cancer experience, 83–84
childrearing by, 20–21, 22–23, 26
early years, 13
as grandmother, 77, 84, 288
house rules, 79–80
Letore and, 14–15, 22–23
memories of Wallace, 288–291
teaching career, 14, 18
Wallace murder investigation, 268–269, 279, 290–291
Wallace's birth, 15
Wallace's drug dealing, 35–36, 41–42
Wallace's funeral, 254
Wallace's marriage, 111–114
Wallace's murder, 245, 249, 252, 290
Wallace's relationship with, 2, 15–16
Wallace apartment on St. James Place, 15, *22*, 289
Wallace murder investigation, 250, 268–285, 290–291
Warren, Michael, 125–126
Warren G, 94
Whitewell, Mark and Scott, 150
Wilbekin, Emil, 240, 253
Williams, Frank, 282
Williams, Hype, 130, 144–145, *144*, 228–229, 258, 265
Williams, Wendy, 201, 234, 237
Williams, Willie, 264
Woldemariam, Phillip, 153
Woodley, Kurt, 66
Wright, Reggie, Jr., 270, 274
Wright, Richard, 103
Wrightway Security, 273, 274
Wu-Tang Clan, 71, 103

Yella, DJ (Antoine Carraby), 90
Young, Gregory "G," 209, 231, 234, 236, 238, 240, 242, 243, 268

Zane, 130, 131, 133, 134
Zauqael (Robert Cagle), 50–51, 78–79
Zip, 270, 282
Zulu Nation, 46

Also by the Editors of VIBE:

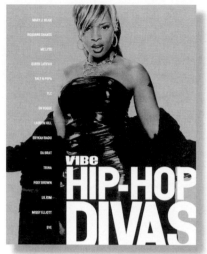

HIP HOP DIVAS
0-609-80836-2
$17.95 paperback (Canada: $26.95)

The first book to chronicle the dramatic rise of women to the top of the hip hop world. Includes Mary J. Blige, Lauryn Hill, TLC, Lil' Kim, Foxy Brown, Missy Elliott, Eve, and more.

TUPAC SHAKUR
0-609-80217-8
$17.00 paperback (Canada: $26.00)

There is nothing more tragic than a life cut short. This book may be the only lasting testament to the many faces of Tupac Shakur—of a life lived fast and hard, of a man cloaked in contradictions, of a young man who was just starting to come into his own.

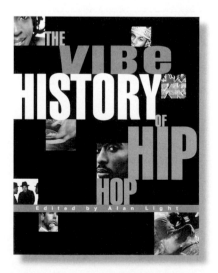

VIBE HISTORY OF HIP HOP
0-609-80503-7
$27.50 paperback (Canada: $41.50)

Music, fashion, dance, graffiti, movies, videos, and business: It's all in this brilliant history of the hip hop revolution, from its origins on the streets to its explosion as an international phenomenon.

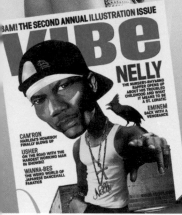
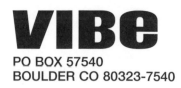